W9-ASF-258

D

Art and Creative Development for Young Children

ROBERT SCHIRRMACHER, Ph.D.
SAN JOSE CITY COLLEGE

DELMAR PUBLISHERS INC.®

Tennessee Tech. Library
Cookeville, Tenn.
379426

NOTICE TO THE READER

Publisher does not warrant or guarantee any of the products described herein or perform any independent analysis in connection with any of the product information contained herein. Publisher does not assume, and expressly disclaims, any obligation to obtain and include information other than that provided to it by the manufacturer.

The reader is expressly warned to consider and adopt all safety precautions that might be indicated by the activities described herein and to avoid all potential hazards. By following the instructions contained herein, the reader willingly assumes all risks in connection with such instructions.

The publisher makes no representations or warranties of any kind, including but not limited to, the warranties of fitness for particular purpose or merchantibility, nor are any such representations implied with respect to the material set forth herein, and the publisher takes no responsibility with respect to such material. The publisher shall not be liable for any special, consequential or exemplary damages resulting, in whole or in part, from the readers' use of, or reliance upon, this material.

Delmar Staff

Administrative Editor: Karen Lavroff-Hawkins
Managing Editor: Barbara A. Christie
Production Editor: Christine E. Worden

For information, address Delmar Publishers Inc.
2 Computer Drive West, Box 15-015
Albany, New York 12212

Copyright © 1988 by Delmar Publishers Inc.

All rights reserved. No part of this work covered by the copyright hereon may
be reproduced or used in any form or by any means—graphic, electronic, or mechanical,
including photocopying, recording, taping, or information storage and retrieval
systems—without written permission of the publisher.

Printed in the United States of America
Published simultaneously in Canada
by Nelson, Canada
A division of International Thomson Limited

10 9 8 7 6 5 4 3 2 1

Library of Congress Cataloging-in-Publication Data

Schirrmacher, Robert, 1946–
   Art and creative development for young children.

   Includes index.
   1. Art—Study and teaching (Primary)—United States.
I. Title.
N361.S39   1988   372.5′044   87-22141
   ISBN 0-8273-3033-2 (pbk.)

Delmar's Outstanding Series in Early Childhood

Home, School, and Community Relations: A Guide to Working with Parents, Gestwicki
Understanding Child Development—For Adults Who Work with Young Children, 2/E, Charlesworth
Infants and Toddlers: Curriculum and Teaching, Wilson
Health, Safety, and Nutrition for the Young Child, Marotz, Rush & Cross
Developing Safety Skills with the Young Child, Comer
Beginnings and Beyond: Foundations in Early Childhood Education, Gordon & Browne
Creative Activities for Young Children, 3/E, Mayesky, Neuman & Wlodkowski
Creative Activities for Children in the Early Primary Grades, Mayesky
Early Childhood Experiences in Language Arts, 3/E, Machado
Seeing Young Children: A Guide to Observing and Recording Behavior, Bentzen
A Practical Guide to Solving Preschool Behavior Problems, Essa
Early Childhood Practicum Guide, Machado & Meyer
Administration of Schools for Young Children, Click
Children In Your Life: A Guide to Child Care and Parenting, Radeloff & Zechman
Early Childhood: Development and Education, Gilley & Gilley
Mainstreaming in Early Childhood Education, Allen
Experiences in Math for Young Children, Charlesworth & Radeloff
Experiences in Music for Young Children, Pugmire
Experiences in Science for Young Children, Neuman

For more information, contact,

Delmar Publishers Inc.   1-(800)347-7707 WATS
Marketing Department   1-(518)459-1150
Two Computer Drive, West
Box 15015
Albany, New York 12212

Contents

Preface

This book is written for practicing early childhood educators and those preparing to work with young children, ages birth to eight, in public or private nursery, preschool, child care, and kindergarten settings. Teachers of infants, toddlers, and primary-grade children will also find this book useful. Sound principles and basic art media are appropriate regardless of the age of the artist.

The book is written from three different perspectives. It attempts to synthesize the author's training and experience as an artist, teacher of young children, and teacher educator. The book is neither a cookbook of activities nor a review of theory and research. It is readable and practical. There is a systematic attempt to merge theory with practice. Knowing what and how to provide for an art activity is as important as knowing why. The book, therefore is based on a developmental perspective. Knowing about child development, the nature of children's art, creativity, artistic elements, sensory stimulation, and aesthetics forms a backdrop for how one approaches the teaching and discovery of art. The teacher plays a key role as facilitator within a recommended art center approach, maximizing crea-

tive expression, responsible freedom, decision making, and discovery. The book closes with a resource of developmentally appropriate two- and three-dimensional art media and activities as well as extensive appendices.

FEATURES

Special features of the text include chapter objectives, summaries, and review questions. Abundant class-tested activities are included throughout the book. Age ranges are provided for many activities; however, these should be regarded as guidelines only. A teacher's knowledge of a child's developmental level must be the main guide in determining the appropriateness of any activity. A complete chapter on how to talk with young children about their art work is included.

SUPPLEMENTS

An Instructor's Guide containing answers to review questions is available free upon classroom adoption of the text.

Acknowledgments

To:

My wife, Carol, and daughters, Amanda Brooke and Lauren Taylor, with love. Thanks for your encouragement, support, and space. In answer to your question, "Yes, Daddy's book is finally done!"

David Black, professional photographer and advocate for children.

Faculty, staff, parents, and children at the Child Development Centers, San Jose City College and Evergreen Valley College.

Smithfield children and their parents, Mobile, Alabama.

Marie Lynch, former graduate student and kindergarten teacher. John Will Elementary School. Mobile, Alabama.

Anne Brandon, Directress. The Montessori Academy. Mobile, Alabama.

Leslie Welch, Director. L'Ecole School for the Gifted and Talented. Mobile, Alabama.

Preschool and Mothers' Day Out. Christ United Methodist Church. Mobile, Alabama.

Wendy McEarchern, owner and director of Green Fields School. Mobile, Alabama. Also, the members of Gulf Coast Day Care Association.

Margaret Mactavish, Director, First Congregational Early Childhood Center, and her teachers. Winter Park, Florida.

Teachers, children, and parents with whom I have worked in Michigan, Illinois, California, Florida, and Alabama who have helped me formulate my views on art.

Karen Lavroff-Hawkins, Administrative Editor, Delmar Publishers Inc. for your friendship, tolerance, and direction.

Staff at Delmar Publishers Inc. for your expertise in turning hundreds of double-spaced pages into a creative work of art.

The reviewers, whose advice and enthusiasm made this finished book a possibility, are Betty Spillers Beeson, Ball State University, Muncie, Indiana; Judith Peterson, Reading Area Community College, Reading, Pennsylvania; Arleen Prairie, Loop College, Chicago, Illinois; Holly Scrivner, Shasta College, Redding, California; and Raber R. Wharton, Cuyahoga Community College, Cleveland, Ohio.

About the Author

The writer is employed as a full-time Instructor with the San Jose Community College District. Currently, he teaches and supervises Early Childhood Education majors and parents at two on-campus laboratory child development centers (San Jose City College and Evergreen Valley College). His teaching responsibilities include early childhood education, child development, child guidance, and parenting courses. The author received his Ph.D. in Early Childhood Education from the University of Illinois. His experience includes teaching preschool, kindergarten, and first grade. He has also assisted in Montessori schools, directed programs for young children, and taught early childhood education at the undergraduate and graduate levels. He continues to serve as consultant to parent groups and public and private early childhood programs. As an advocate for developmentally appropriate education and quality care for young children, the writer is actively involved in professional organizations at the local, state, and national levels.

Unit 1

What Early Childhood Art Should Be

OBJECTIVES

After studying this unit, the student will be able to

- State the criteria or guidelines for early childhood art activities
- Apply the criteria or guidelines for early childhood art activities in critiquing ditto, photocopied, or mimeographed sheets; coloring books; crafts; holiday gifts
- Identify alternatives to activities masquerading as creative art

---

INTRODUCTION

Children's art fascinates adults. Although they may not understand it, parents are proud of their children's art. Early childhood educators also value children's art and allow ample time for it in the daily schedule. Although most young children are neither interested in nor ready for formal academics such as reading, all young children are interested in and ready for art.

Most of us recognize the importance of early childhood art, but not everyone would agree as to what it entails. Is scribbling art? Can coloring in a coloring book be considered art? This unit provides criteria or guidelines for determining the creative merits of an activity or approach to art. Traditional teacher-directed and product-oriented art activities will be critiqued. Activities masquerading as creative art will be identified, and alternatives suggested.

What is art? The great philosopher Susanne Langer believed that humans are born with an urgent biological need to create art. Art helps us put our life experiences into symbolic form. We are then able to stand back and clarify, critically examine, and share our experiences. But, how is this done? Actually, there are many ways to express one's experiences artistically. Some of these include

- literature
- drama
- music
- visual arts: plastic and graphic

For our present purpose we will focus on how young children use the visual arts to represent their life experiences. The plastic or three-dimensional arts include sculpture, ceramics, and architecture. The graphic or two-dimensional arts include painting, print making, and drawing.

HOW TO CHOOSE ART ACTIVITIES

What should be included in an early childhood art program? Mrs. Mills has baked cookies, and her toddlers will soon spread frosting on them for an art activity. Across the hall, kindergartners are neatly coloring in a butterfly ditto as part of their unit on spring. Their teacher reminds them that they have only a few minutes left for art. What can one say about these activities? Which have artistic merit? Do they represent the essence of what early childhood art should be? The author would respond negatively to these questions. Although spreading frosting may be an enjoyable tactile, perceptual-motor, and edible activity, it is not art. Simply coloring in a butterfly ditto strengthens eye-hand coordination and figure-ground relations, but offers little or no opportunity for creativity. A more creative version would be to let the children draw their own butterfly with little concern for realistic rendering.

WHAT EARLY CHILDHOOD ART SHOULD BE

Often it is easy to recognize negative examples or instances of uncreative art. Just what should one look for in planning an early childhood art activity? Early childhood art activities should

- allow children to be personally expressive
- subtly balance artistic process and product
- allow children to be creative
- allow for discovery and experimenting
- allow for active engagement and sustained involvement
- be intrinsically motivating
- be success-oriented
- be developmentally appropriate
- involve legitimate artistic media
- be available to all children

Allow Children to Be Personally Expressive

Young children need to express themselves personally with a variety of artistic media. The expression should be personal because individual children will approach art in their own unique ways. After visiting the zoo, a group of three-year-olds were encouraged to make or do something related to what they had just experienced. At the easel, Jean painted a caged black bear. Three children headed for the clay table. Jim squeezed a ball of clay and called it a seal. Tam rolled tiny clay snakes to make the hot shining sun. Kaley cut an outline of an elephant into a slab of clay using a Popsicle stick. Personal choice was reflected in the use of paint or clay. Further, the children at the clay table found three different ways to express what was personally meaningful to them.

Subtly Balance Artistic Process and Product

The art activities provided should subtly balance artistic processing and the making of art products. A good art program would understand and accept the fact that individual children can be oriented toward process, product, or both in their approach to art. Art processing includes the skills involved in a given art activity. For exam-

Figure 1-1 Processing with art media is as important as making a finished product.

The author observed a boy in a transitional kindergarten diligently working on a clay dinosaur. When the teacher announced, "Cleanup time; everybody clean up," he was devastated. He pleaded to take it home, or at least keep it out for display. He was near tears when he was directed to roll it back into a ball and return it to the clay tub. Clearly, he was product-oriented in his approach to art. Art is dependent on both process and product. Artistic processing is necessary to arrive at a finished product. Elaborating or refining a finished product involves processing.

Allow Children to Be Creative

Early childhood art programs should also encourage young children to be creative. Children can be encouraged to represent their world creatively by allowing them to choose

- what they want to make (content)

- how they want to go about making it (process)

- what it will end up looking like (product)

Generally, planned activities that are loosely structured set the stage for creative expression. For example, providing paints, brushes, and paper at the easel may be enough for some children. All they need is to invest time and pursue an idea. Others may need a teacher's subtle guidance. "Try to think of something that happened over the weekend, maybe someplace or someone special. This could give you something to paint." We rob children of the opportunity for creative artistic expression when we specify what the finished product should be or look like and exactly how to do it. For example, coloring, cutting out, and correctly pasting together a train does not involve much creativity.

Still, creative expression must abide by general rules, guidelines, and limits. Pretend-fighting with scissors is dangerous and not creative. Children need to be taught the proper way to handle

ple, paper work involves tearing, cutting, folding, pasting, stapling, braiding, and weaving. The product refers to the result. For example, processing with paper may result in a paper collage, paper weaving, or paper sculpture. Young children are process-oriented (see Figure 1-1). They enjoy art for the sake of doing and making, often with little concern for how it turns out. Perhaps this is why some children fail to claim their finished art products. They forget which one they did or merely toss it in the wastebasket as they depart. One carpool mother complained about how the back seat of her van was strewn with children's art. For these children the joy was in the actual doing or process rather than in what resulted, the finished product. Older children, however, become product-oriented. They are very concerned about size, shape, color, placement, detail, and realism. They are quick to put their name on their art and may become upset when papers tear or curl or when paint smears. It may be important for these children to take one or several art products home on a daily basis.

scissors and all other artistic media, equipment, and supplies. Rules need to be discussed and posted. "Chris, bring me your scissors. They are only for cutting paper."

Allow for Discovery and Experimenting

Children can arrive at artistic products through discovery and experimenting. For example, teaching sponge painting or printing directly may not be necessary. It is possible to provide paints and an array of sponges, cookie cutters, and Styrofoam shapes, and encourage children to see what they can do with these "painters" and the paint (see Figure 1-2). They may experiment by spreading paint with sponges or using the sponges in a stamping motion. Either way, they have discovered for themselves a new artistic technique through their own active experimenting. To plan each art activity with a predetermined product and step-by-step procedure robs children of the opportunity to personally explore, discover, invent, and creatively experiment on their own.

Allow for Active Engagement and Sustained Involvement

Art should actively engage your children. They are active physical beings, and their artistic expression should reflect this. They need upright easels to encourage sweeping whole-arm movements while standing. Clay needs to be torn, punched, pulled, rolled, flattened, pinched, and pounded. Recommended early childhood art activities will encourage and capitalize on the young child's need for sensory-motor exploration and movement. Ample blocks of time are needed to foster sustained involvement. Not all children are able to complete their art activity in a predetermined block of time. Some will want to continue working later, or even the following day. Other children will impulsively finish their art in a matter of minutes. "Look teacher, I'm done! What can I do now?" Teachers may want to encourage these children to continue their involvement. Obviously, few young children will work for hours at the same art activity. Still, they

Figure 1-2   Different brushes help Lauren discover and experiment.

can be encouraged to examine and extend their art. "Tara, I see you finished your painting. Is there anything else you want to add?" "Yes, I see. It is a turtle. Have you thought about where it lives or what it might like to eat? You have a lot of time and more paper, so keep working on your turtle." The teacher did not tell Tara her turtle was wrong or bad. She encouraged Tara to refine her art and continue her involvement. In this case, Tara chose to ignore the teacher's suggestions and announced that her turtle picture was finished. Over time, Tara may begin to see that additional time and effort spent working usually produce a more elaborate and detailed picture.

Be Intrinsically Motivating

Art—like music, movement, and play—is an intrinsically motivating activity. Children will engage in art for the sheer pleasure and reward inherent in painting, coloring, working with clay, or making a collage. The author believes that one of the major joys of being an early childhood educator is working with young children who are so intrinsically or internally motivated to learn and make sense out of their world. They manipulate, explore with all their senses, and ask endless questions. Although praise and rewards are effective, they are not always needed in art. The author observed a teacher rewarding a child's finished art product. "Oh, look how pretty Marla's painting of a house turned out!" Later, a small group of children were copying Marla's idea and style to the detail to win this teacher's praise. Their motivation for doing art had moved from internal to external. Instead, Marla's teacher could praise her efforts and involvement. "Marla, you are working so long and hard" or "I see a lot of action at the clay table. Sam will keep working until he gets it just the way he wants." Research by Lepper and Greene (1975) has shown that external motivation and techniques of behavior modification actually decrease a child's intrinsic motivation. Praising preschoolers' use of magic markers actually decreased their interest in using them. Anderson, Ma-noogian, and Reznick (1976) studied the effects of different rewards upon four- and five-year-olds' intrinsic interest in drawing. They found that monetary and symbolic rewards—e.g., money and stickers—decreased children's interest in drawing. A teacher's verbal praise, however, actually increased it. Still, it is recommended that the praise be aimed at the process and involvement rather than the outcome.

Be Success-Oriented

Early childhood art activities should be planned to be success-oriented. Choosing art activities that are developmentally appropriate and moderately challenging will ensure a child's success. In turn, feelings of success and mastery foster a child's positive self-concept. A major goal of early childhood education is to help children become competent and feel good about themselves. Activities that are too difficult or detailed may frustrate children and lead to failure. The danger is that young children may generalize their failure at a task to failure as a person. For example, a group of four-year-olds at summer day camp were given a group of cardboard insects to trace, cut, and paste. The objects were small, with many details, including thin legs and feelers. The cardboard was flimsy, and the scissors were dull. Papers were torn, and insect heads and tails were missing. Few, if any, of the children could match the teacher's standard, which was hanging overhead. The children became restless and frustrated. The camp counselor meant well but did not translate the developmental abilities of four-year-olds into a success-oriented art activity.

Be Developmentally Appropriate

What could be an alternative to the above? A good art activity can foster success by taking into account a child's developmental abilities. For example, the camp counselor, after reading a book on insects and taking a nature walk to collect specimens, could have encouraged the children to draw their favorite bug or create their own new one. What might a "butter-quito" or "spider-hopper" look like? There is no one right answer. There will be many possibilities, each one successfully rendered. Art activities that require excessive cutting, fine detailing, pasting of small pieces, or precise folding are not developmentally appropriate for young children with limited fine motor control and coordination. The author recalls a first attempt at origami, a precise Japanese paper-folding activity. Although the teacher produced an intricate, correctly folded swan, the author's looked like a lopsided beast. Feeling discouraged and unsuccessful makes it easy to empathize with young children who do not experience success through art.

Involve Legitimate Artistic Media

A recommended early childhood art program will involve legitimate artistic media. Children work with paint, watercolor, collage, paper, clay, prints, design, resist, and sculpture—the same media that adult artists use. Providing legitimate artistic media tells children, "You are creative artists, and you can be trusted with the appropriate tools and media." The materials, equipment, and supplies related to these media are basic, moderately expensive, and a good investment. Paint brushes, easels, or watercolor sets of good quality will last if given proper care. Generally, buying in advance and in bulk gets the major art expense for the year out of the way. Expense does not guarantee creative art. For example, one teacher distributed a precut doll shape to a small group of three-, four-, and five-year-olds. The children were instructed to glue on button eyes and precut fur for hair, sprinkle glitter, and attach a Popsicle-stick base. The activity was costly and short-lived, and involved little artistic processing. The doll puppets all looked identical. Creative input from the children was absent. Many parents and local businesses would be willing to donate extra fabric, trim, magazines, and papers to supplement the basic artistic media and hold down expenses. See Appendixes A and B for a list and sources of artistic junk.

Be Available to All Children

Art should be available to all children. Older infants who can hold a nontoxic marker or crayon can be subtly guided to make marks on paper. They can scribble seated in a highchair or sprawled atop a long roll of paper. Toddlers enjoy painting and using markers, crayons, and clay. The preschooler can be provided with an even wider array of legitimate artistic media. Since art is neither masculine nor feminine, both boys and girls should be encouraged to engage in art. If the easels or art center become monopolized by one sex, a teacher may need to do some social engineering. For example, girls in one kindergarten were drawing pictures of food to take to the housekeeping center. The boys avoided both of these centers and concentrated in the block area. After two days of this sex-segregated play, the teacher took action. She suggested that the boys work together with the girls in building a restaurant. One boy designed his own play money from scrap construction paper. Another painted a store sign.

All children should have access to art. Since art can foster a child's feelings of esteem and success, it is vital for children who have special needs, exceptionalities, or multicultural backgrounds. Art gives them the vehicle to validate themselves by making a personal statement: "I am unique, and my art proves it!"

Some teachers report that they use art as a reward for work completed. The good students get to visit the art center or engage in art. Others may be denied art. Although misbehavior and uncompleted work cannot be tolerated, the punishment does not fit the crime. The children in question may be those who need art the most. Academic deficiencies or behavior problems leave them with few routes for success in school. Success in art may generalize to success in academics. Art can also be used as a springboard to academics. For example, eight-year-old Dusty is a poor reader but draws detailed hot rods. Perhaps his hot rod drawings could be used as a way to help him talk, read, and write about his interests.

ACTIVITIES MASQUERADING AS CREATIVE ART

Merely labeling an activity "art" is no guarantee that the activity will have artistic merit. Likewise, uncreative activities are often mistakenly called "creative." There are too many activities that masquerade as creative art. Some of these include

- ditto, photocopied, or mimeographed sheets
- cut-and-paste activities
- tracing patterns
- coloring book pages
- dot-to-dot sheets
- crafts
- holiday gifts
- seatwork

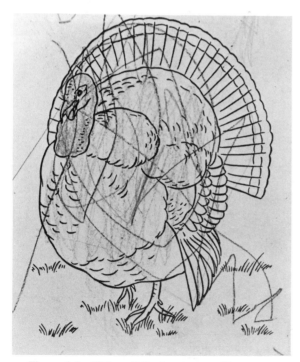

Figure 1-3   This activity is masquerading as art.

Although these activities may have some merit for developing fine motor control or eye-hand coordination, they lack artistic and creative merit. Activities that masquerade as creative art share the following criteria:

- an emphasis on teacher input and direction
- a high degree of structure
- a specified product

Lowenfeld and Brittain (1987) warn against the use of ditto sheets, coloring books, and patterns by citing the research of Russell and Waugamann (1952), who found that children who had originally been interested in spontaneously drawing birds lost their creativity when exposed to workbook drawings. They quickly changed their once creative pictures to resemble the common stereotype. Ditto sheets, cut-and-paste activities, and tracing patterns (Figure 1-3) have a high degree of teacher input and direction, with the responsibility for making art shifted from child to teacher. For example, Miss Sally drew a teddy bear and ran off copies for the children to color. They were encouraged to take their time, color neatly, and stay within the lines. The teacher imposed her concept of what a teddy bear should look like. A ditto sheet can easily become a cut-and-paste activity. Miss Sally could have asked the children to cut out their teddy bears along with a predrawn hat and cane and paste them on construction paper. Or, she could have provided cardboard patterns for the children to trace. These activities, however, lack artistic merit because the focus is on the teacher's concept of a teddy bear, not the child's. Instead, Miss Sally could have encouraged the children to represent their own personally meaningful symbol of a teddy bear without concern for a realistic use of color, shape, size, body parts, placement, or detail.

Teacher-directed art activities usually entail a high degree of structure, reflected in specific directions and step-by-step progression. The teddy bears in Miss Sally's room looked alike and appeared mass-produced.

Other examples of highly structured activities include coloring book pages and dot-to-dot sheets. Pages from coloring books reflect the artist's concept and representation of an object. A steady diet of coloring books frustrates young artists and leads them to question their own creative ability. Further, it denies them practice in making personally meaningful art. Instead, they merely complete someone else's art. This may be why some older children are at a loss when asked to draw anything they want. They have become too dependent upon coloring books and cannot create for themselves.

Dot-to-dot pages add an element of math to the coloring book page. Connecting the dots in proper numerical sequence results in closure by completing the picture.

Highly structured, teacher-directed art activi-

ties often focus on making a finished product, like Miss Sally's teddy bears. Sometimes teachers display their own finished product as a standard or model. Although well-intended, this practice will frustrate young artists who cannot trace, color, cut, and/or paste as well. Although a teacher quickly adds, "Do your best," children know that their product will never come close to looking like their teacher's.

Crafts and holiday gifts are examples of finished products that masquerade as creative art. Two small stones glued to a larger stone can be painted to resemble a frog. It looks like something, and it is useful in that it can be used as a paperweight. However, creative art may not look like anything and may not have any use beyond the initial joy of self-expression.

Crafts can be given as holiday gifts (see Figure

Figure 1-4 The perfect gift for a child to give

1-4). Most parents would be delighted to receive a paperweight or pencil holder constructed by their child. Although it is important to please parents, it is equally important to meet the creative needs of children. Providing for child input, planning, decision making, and creative processing guarantees that each finished product will be as unique and individual as the child who produced it. Gifts need not involve time or expense. A completed finger painting could also be ironed flat, framed, wrapped, and presented to parents as a gift. Taking the time to talk with parents about the nature of children's art will help them appreciate the finger painting for the unique gift it is.

Alternatives to activities that masquerade as art take a commitment of time and planning. Art should not be used merely to fill in extra time before lunch or dismissal. Merely coloring in the figures on a math, phonics, or reading readiness workbook sheet is not art. Generally, the figures are small, blurred, and drawn by someone other than the child. This is seatwork or busywork, not art. Art is more like turning your finished work over and drawing whatever you want.

SUMMARY

Sometimes activities that lack artistic or creative merit masquerade as art. Perhaps teachers merely forget to critically examine what they do with children. This unit provided some criteria or guidelines to help determine what early childhood art should be. Art activities that allow all children to be actively engaged, be personally expressive, be creative, experiment, and discover were recommended. Art should also be success-oriented, be intrinsically motivating, allow for both process and product, be developmentally appropriate, and involve legitimate artistic media. Not all those criteria will apply to any one activity. They can, however, be used as guidelines for planning appropriate art experiences.

SUGGESTED ACTIVITIES

1. Recall your earliest experiences with art. What did you do? Did you enjoy art? Why? How did your parents or teachers respond to your art? How do you feel at present about your artistic development? What, if anything, has happened since your childhood to influence your feelings and abilities in art? Write your impressions, feelings, and thoughts in a brief one-page diary.

2. Observe an experienced teacher conducting an art activity with a group of young children. Does the activity require the children to be creative or uncreative? List specific suggestions for making the activity more creative.

3. Visit an early childhood center during art time. Critique the ongoing art activity using our 10-point criteria or guidelines for recommended art activities. Does the activity masquerade as art?

4. Ms. Wilton, a kindergarten teacher, has made sturdy cardboard stencils of a cornucopia and harvest food as a tracing and coloring activity for her unit on fall. Critique this art activity. Suggest an alternative if necessary.

REVIEW

A. Place a T (True) or F (False) in front of the following:

_____ Art should allow children to be creative.

_____ Art should always result in something to take home.

_____ Children should be externally motivated to do art.

_____ Art activities should be planned according to a child's development.

_____ Discovering and experimenting through art are a waste of precious time.

_____ Art activities for young children should take no longer than 8 to 10 minutes to complete.

_____ Art activities should be planned to ensure a child's success.

_____ The finished art product is more important than the steps leading up to it.

_____ Art is best used as a reward for children who do their work or behave.

_____ It is important for children's art to very closely resemble what the teacher had in mind when developing the activity.

B. A teacher has run off a bunny pattern for Easter. Children will color, cut, and paste their bunny on an egg-shaped piece of purple construction paper. Critique the creative merits of this activity. Offer specific suggestions for making it more creative. How might you plan an Easter art activity without using any patterns?

C. Put an X in front of each activity that is masquerading as creative art.

_____ Staying within the lines and neatly coloring in the pages in a holiday coloring book.

_____ Cutting and pasting a picture of a seal carefully drawn by the teacher.

_____ Using watercolors to paint a picture that shows what each child liked best about a recent field trip.

_____ Coloring in a rocket ship picture, using red for all the areas marked 1, yellow for 2, and blue for 3.

D. Circle the correct term within each statement. Recommended early childhood art activities should have
1. an emphasis on (teacher/child) input and direction.
2. a (high/low) degree of structure.
3. a(n) (specified/unspecified) product.

Unit 2

The Complete Art Program

OBJECTIVES

After studying this unit, the student will be able to

- Describe and give an example of each of the four components of a complete early childhood art program
- List and explain the three major divisions for categorizing artistic styles or movements
- Use the art critique to discuss a work of art

INTRODUCTION

Although making art is a first priority, it is only one of the four major components of a complete early childhood art program. It is also important for young children to engage in sensory experiences; learn about art, artists, and their styles; and pursue beauty through aesthetics. This unit will focus on constructing a total or complete early childhood art program.

WHAT TO INCLUDE IN AN EARLY CHILDHOOD ART PROGRAM

It is important that children have ample opportunities to make art. However, although it is ba-

sic, processing with the media to make art is only one of four key components of any complete early childhood art program. They include

- Sensing and experiencing
- Making art
- Learning about art, artists, and their styles
- Aesthetics

The first two components should be emphasized during the early years, with the third and fourth components gradually introduced. Actually, the four components are interrelated, and the separation exists only for the present analysis. For example, making art is dependent upon sensing and experiencing.

Sensing and Experiencing

Children do not magically create out of a vacuum or in isolation. Art has an origin. It originates from something personally experienced, an idea, object of importance, event, feeling, or person. A child's daily experiences within the environment provide a potential bank of things to include in art. For example, Joshua's idea for painting a farm did not just automatically happen. It was related to spending the weekend at his grandparents' farm. Field trips are crucial because they extend a child's personal range of experiences to the wider community. For example,

taking a trip to the fire station provides new content for art.

Sometimes the term *disadvantaged* is used to refer to children who lack these basic environmental experiences. They may be uncomfortable discussing and being tested on things they have never directly experienced. It is dangerous to assume that all children have experienced and know about libraries, hospitals, airports, stadiums, skyscrapers, elevators, cathedrals, post offices, seashores, or museums. Encourage parents to take their children places and discuss what they have experienced (see Figure 2-1). This will help the children form concepts and serve as a backdrop for future learning. For example, an informal trip to the hardware store can

Figure 2-1   Young children can experience a variety of art forms.

be a simple but sensory-rich experience filled with the sound, smell, and touch of cut wood or tools classified according to form and function.

Young children are sensory gluttons. Infants and toddlers are fascinated by pattern and detail. They will follow a bug crawling across the floor or marvel at water dripping from a melted icicle. Unfortunately, adults may take these experiences for granted and need to recapture some of this childlike wonder and awareness. Young children will need practice in keeping it alive.

According to Piaget, children come to know their world through their senses and actions. Our role is to help children note details and use all their senses to build rich object concepts. For example, smelling and tasting are appropriate when visiting a bakery, while looking and listening are warranted during story time in the library. Objects such as nature specimens can be brought in for focused sensory exploration. "Let's look at the empty hornet's nest. Carefully touch the sides. How does it feel? Do you hear anything when you put your ear to the opening? Let's

wrap papier-mâché around a balloon and see if we can make our own hornet's nest."

Making Art

Young children need to be personally expressive and creative, and to experience success through art. Teachers can help children see the relationship between art and experience. For example, a child may ask, "Teacher, what should I draw?" or "I don't know what to make." A teacher can help a child refer to significant people, places, and things: "What did you watch on TV?" or "How did you celebrate this past holiday?" or "What do you remember about our story today?" Teachers can encourage children to give artistic form and substance to their ideas, urges, wishes, dreams, fears, or interests. The bulk of this book continues our discussion of making art.

Learning About Art, Artists, and Their Styles

Children may wonder: What is art? Who are artists? Why do they make art? Art is a basic

Figure 2-2 Young children can be introduced to the different artistic styles.

human need. People make art to reflect and symbolize their existence. Children's interest in and study of community helpers can extend to artists. Children can learn that while some artists make art for a hobby, others do it as a career. Some work at home, outdoors, or in a studio. Some artists exhibit and sell their works in a gallery. Famous artists have their works exhibited in a museum.

Children can also learn that artists work in different media. Although not all artists paint, all do have a pressing need to communicate. They use brush strokes, color, content, form, and the artistic elements to get their point across. Helping children to accept and value their own artwork will enable them to appreciate and value the artwork of others. Our intent is to expose children to their rich artistic heritage rather than teach art history. Children can learn that people everywhere and from the beginning of time have made art. It is part of a culture and tells us something about people: who they were, what they looked like, how they lived, what they wore, where they lived, and what they liked to do. See Appendix C for a discussion of the major artistic styles and movements.

Different artists use different styles. The same artist may use different styles at different times or periods. Children also have their own artistic styles. There is no one right or best way. Different styles are appropriate depending on the artist and what he or she is trying to say through art. Exposing children to the major artistic styles or movements serves two purposes (see Figure 2-2). First, it shows children that there are many possible ways to make art. Second, it shows the similarities between how they create and the styles that artists have used in the past and continue to use today. For example, children's art resembles both prehistoric art and modern abstract art.

A very simplistic breakdown of the major artistic movements includes

• Realistic or naturalistic
• Abstract
• Nonobjective

Realistic or naturalistic art attempts to represent people, places, and objects exactly as they appear. There is an emphasis on objectivity, detail, and photographic realism. Children who aim for photographic realism in their art will be disappointed because developmentally they lack the necessary perceptual, physical, and cognitive ability. Realism or naturalism is merely one of many styles. Many adult artists are successful and satisfied in spite of their inability to produce realistic or naturalistic art.

Abstract art bears only a partial resemblance to the object being represented. The object is somehow streamlined or distorted. An example would be a child who draws a box on two wheels and calls it a race car.

Nonobjective art involves a creative play with color, shape, line, and design. It is abstract art pushed to the limits. What is produced bears no resemblance to any actual object. For example, a child could paint racing swirls of paint to represent the speed and exhaust fumes associated with a race car rather than abstractly capturing its overall shape.

Art Critique Even young children can be taught to critique a work of art. First, a teacher provides some background information about the particular piece: who made it, what was the artist like, what was the world like at the time. Young children are egocentric and may be more interested in their own art than in the artwork of others. Cognitively, they will be unable to fully empathize with the lives, plights, and historical times of famous artists. Still, an introduction to the foundations of good art and our artistic heritage is warranted.

The art critique can focus on the following:

• What is it?
  Is it a painting, drawing, batik, weaving, or print?
  What are its physical properties? Is it big, small, square, round, solid, moving, or framed?
  What is it made out of? Did the artist use paper, paint, metal, clay, or yarn?

• What do you see when you look at this work of art?

Encourage children to focus on the artist's use of line, color, shape or form, mass or volume, design, pattern, space, balance, and texture. How are these artistic elements used? What shapes do you see? What colors were used? Can anyone find lines?

• What is the artist trying to say?

Try to put the artist's picture into words. What is the message? Pretend that this is a book with pictures. What words go along with the picture the artist has given? Discuss what you see: people, animals, buildings, or events.

• How does it make you feel?

Do you feel happy, sad, mad, scared, or funny? What does the artist do to make you feel this way?

• Do you like it?

Why or why not? What is it about the work of art that makes you like or dislike it? How would you change it?

Questions 4 and 5 will evoke very different responses. Our aim is help children acquire artistic appreciation and make judgments based on accepted standards, including the artistic elements.

Aesthetics

Aesthetics is the study of beauty; not the Hollywood view of glamour, but beauty in color, form, and design. In a time of mass production with little concern for effort and quality craftsmanship, the quest for beauty is difficult. Still, there is a human need to make sense out of and appreciate one's self and one's environment, just as there is a basic need to create.

Beauty can be found in nature, in one's surroundings, and in everyday objects. Children can use their senses and their bodies in their pursuit of beauty. The eyes can visually explore art, the ears can listen to sounds and music. Three-dimensional artworks can be touched, scents can be smelled, foods can be tasted, and the body can respond through movement and dance. Young

children can learn to appreciate and have beautiful experiences.

Children need to take the time to perceive the beauty in their everyday environment. Classrooms or centers can be aesthetically pleasing places and models of beauty. The room should be clean, bright, and colorful without being chaotic, cluttered, and gaudy. It should appeal to the senses and have things to look at, listen to, touch, smell, and taste. Flowers, plants, animals, soft pillows, a rocking chair, and a piece of sculpture add an aesthetic touch to the room.

Displays (as seen in Figure 2-3) are places that children can visit to refine their senses and build aesthetic appreciation. Aesthetic displays can include nature specimens, a postcard collection, items of different textures, art books, antique tools or gadgets, machinery parts, pottery, fabric, postage stamps, foreign currency, or items of a given size, shape, or color. Centers or areas for art, music, and movement give children an opportunity to actively represent beautiful images, thoughts, feelings, and concepts through art, music, rhythm, and dance.

Aesthetics is not confined to the interior environment. Beauty abounds in nature and the community. Children can also visit exhibits of beauti-

Figure 2-3 Providing books on art and displaying works of art are ways to foster aesthetic development.

ful things in museums, churches, and galleries, and can attend concerts and performances. Artists, dancers, and musicians can also be invited in to perform and work with the children. The discussion of aesthetics continues in Unit 9.

SUMMARY

This unit focused on building a comprehensive early childhood art program. Recommended program components included experiences in sensing; making art; learning about art, artists, and their styles; and aesthetics. Although young children need not become art historians, it was recommended that they be introduced to the major artistic movements. These were identified as realistic or naturalistic, abstract, and nonobjective. Individual styles within each general category are included in Appendix C. A format for conducting an art critique was also provided.

SUGGESTED ACTIVITIES

1. Arrange to visit an art gallery, exhibit, or museum. Try to identify works of art that belong in each of the three major artistic movements or styles.

2. Use the art critique to analyze and discuss a work of art. Research the artist and era.

3. Begin a collection of art postcards, photographs, prints, posters, or books. Visit thrift shops, used book stores, and library sales.

4. Arrange to accompany a group of young children on an informal field trip to a local art museum, gallery, or artist's studio. Visit in advance to know what is available. Or, arrange for an artist to come in and model art processing and informally work with the children.

REVIEW

A. List the components of a complete early childhood art program.
   1.
   2.
   3.
   4.

B. Identify and briefly explain the major artistic movements.
   1.

   2.

   3.

C. List the major points or questions for conducting an art critique.
   1.
   2.
   3.
   4.
   5.

Unit 3

Art and the Developing Child

OBJECTIVES

After studying this unit, the student will be able to

- Discuss how art fosters child development
- Use an art example to portray a wholistic model of development
- Discuss the developmental progression in a child's use of scissors and how to meet the needs and abilities of young cutters
- Identify safety factors related to children's art
- Critique the use of food in art activities

INTRODUCTION

This unit provides a developmental overview of the young child: physically, socially, emotionally, cognitively, and creatively. According to our wholistic model of child development, these aspects influence and are influenced by one another. Ideally, we can act on this knowledge in planning art activities. Our present analysis attempts to answer the following question: How does art foster the development of the whole child? Our purpose is twofold: First, to help understand how art can foster a child's development, and second, to use what we know about art and child development in planning our art program and justifying it to ourselves and others. Providing a justification is more than giving a defensive reply: "Art is important, and that's why we spend a lot of time doing it!" If art is important (and it is), we should be able to provide a rationale. Relating art to a child's development provides one rationale.

DEVELOPMENTAL MODEL

One way to get a working knowledge of young children is to build a model for studying development in the following areas:

- Physical—including large muscle or gross motor, small muscle or fine motor, perceptual-motor or eye-hand coordination, and sensory development

- Social—including a development of the self and relations with others (Figure 3-1)

- Emotional—including feelings about self and emotional expression as well as personality and temperament

- Cognitive—including thinking, problem solving, reasoning, and learning

- Creative—including original thinking, imagination, and verbal and nonverbal expression

This model of development is depicted in figure 3-2. Still, this neat division or separation is too simplistic. A pie or pizza can be neatly cut into five pieces or slices, but a child's development cannot. Aspects of development interact; they are interdependent and interrelated. It is impossible to study a child's physical development in isolation. Physical development is influenced by and also directly influences social, emotional, cognitive, and creative development. For example, five-year-old Joey has been mainstreamed midyear into a regular kindergarten classroom. Muscular dystrophy has left him physically confined to a wheelchair. It influences what he can and cannot do physically. However, it is not the

Figure 3-1   Art can be a physical and social experience.

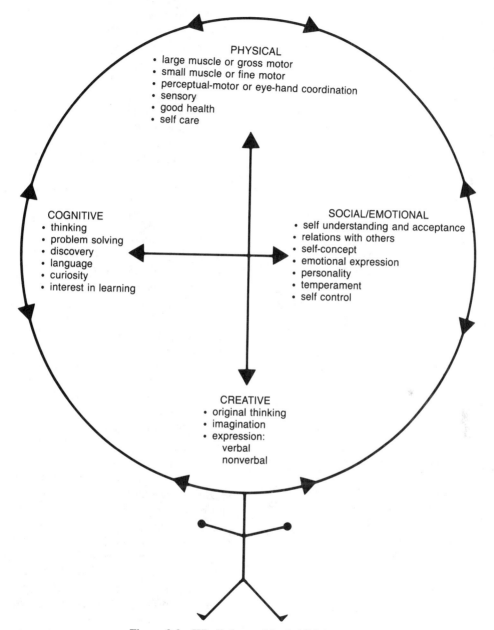

Figure 3-2   Wholistic model of child development

only influence on his overall development. Joey's physical state effects and is also affected by his social, emotional, cognitive, and creative functioning. Initially Joey was treated as an out-

cast. He was shunned by his peers and misunderstood by his teacher. Slowly, he withdrew. Emotionally, Joey began feeling sorry for himself, wishing he was like his peers. His self-concept suffered, and he began to doubt his own personal worth. Cognitively, he began to avoid school tasks, shunned class discussion, and refused to work. Creatively, however, Joey channelled his energies into making original pictures of outer space. Interestingly, Joey always drew himself as the space captain, with massive, powerful legs and strong arms. As in Joey's case, development is uneven, reflecting developmental spurts and lags. Fortunately, Joey's teacher recognized the problem and her lack of knowledge and enrolled in a course on mainstreaming. She worked closely with Joey, his mother, his peers, and his resource teacher. The students openly discussed handicaps and how all people have strengths and weaknesses, assets and limitations. Over time, the children accepted Joey and welcomed him into their activities. In fact, they became over-protective, and Joey regressed to an earlier stage of helplessness. Continual discussion, support, and encouragement helped Joey become more in-dependent. He began to show improvement in his schoolwork and eagerly reported to his mother what he was learning. Joey became very well liked by his peers, and his self-concept im-proved.

DEVELOPMENTAL PROFILE

Providing a detailed description of child devel-opment is beyond the scope of the present chap-ter. Instead, a general overview of a young child's physical, social, emotional, cognitive, and creative development will be presented.

Physical Development

Young children are physical beings character-ized by much activity and energy. Physical de-velopment depends on adequate rest, exercise, sleep, and good nutrition. Young children are in-trinsically motivated to make an effect on their environment. They do this primarily through mo-tor activity and sensory exploration.

Infants develop prehension or grasping and a pincer grasp that allows them to hold objects be-tween their fingers and opposing thumb. Older infants can hold a stubby crayon and be guided into making marks on paper. Young children are more adept with large muscle or gross motor skills than with small muscle or fine motor skills. They will master easel painting with large brushes before they can use a small brush with watercolors. By age three most preschoolers can hold a crayon with their fingers, as opposed to the earlier clenched-fist grip. Young children are good doers, talkers, and movers. They have diffi-culty sitting still, listening, and remaining silent.

Art and Physical Development Art activities provide experience and practice in developing and refining gross motor or large muscle skills. Art involves physical and manipulative activity. While easel painting, children use their entire arms and upper torsos in making large, sweeping motions with paintbrushes. Large, long-handled, wide-bristle brushes facilitate this movement. The muscles of the hand are developed while working with clay—tearing, rolling, twisting, coiling, pounding, pinching, and flattening it. Whole hand and arm motions are involved in hand painting, with paint spread and worked with the fingers, whole hand, nails, knuckles, fist, palm, and back of the hand. These gross motor or large muscle skills are perfected before fine motor or small muscle skills. Using the smaller watercolor brush with its shorter handle and narrow point involves greater precision and fine motor control. All the manipulative move-ments involved in art help develop the hand and finger muscles that are needed to properly hold and use a pencil. Although making children into early printers or writers is not the main purpose of art, art does facilitate the development of this skill.

Scissoring is another physical activity that in-volves a patterned "open-close" rhythmical movement. Cutting with scissors on a line fosters eye-hand coordination and visual acuity, with the eyes and scissoring hand working together. Children do not develop this important skill with-out some guidance and practice.

CUTTING WITH SCISSORS

Cutting with scissors is a difficult developmental task for many young children. Using scissors gives children a feeling of power and mastery. Scissors, once a taboo or "no-no," now become an acceptable tool if used properly. Some guidelines for helping children cut and select proper equipment include the following:

1. Tearing paper is a good starting point for young children. Torn pieces can be pasted on paper or cardboard to form a collage as seen in Figure 3-3. Tearing paper is itself an important skill that need not be eliminated when a child learns to cut.

2. Cutting thin, pliable Play Doh is a good introduction to using scissors.

Figure 3-3 Tearing paper is an alternative to cutting with scissors.

3. Snipping or fringing paper is a beginning step in using scissors with paper. Give children a narrow ¼- or ½-inch-wide paper strip. Show them how to make a single cut or snip into the paper. Children enjoy snipping off small pieces that can be pasted. Small snips into a wider 1-inch strip will produce fringe. Hole-punched computer paper sides are ideal for snipping and fringing.

4. With practice, the young child will be able to make repeated snips in a sequence or line. Draw a thick, straight line on paper, and show children how to follow it while cutting. It does not matter if the children stray from the line. The aim is to help them coordinate repeated snips into a continuous cutting action.

5. Advanced cutters can practice cutting wavy, bending, or angular lines. Children can also practice cutting out geometric shapes.

6. Cutting along interior lines, such as the eyes in a mask or paper bag puppet, is too difficult. It is also potentially dangerous, since children are prone to begin the hole by poking with the point of the scissors.

7. Rules for the proper use of scissors need to be established, discussed, and posted in words and/or pictures. Rules include:
   - Scissors are used only for cutting paper.
   - Walk when carrying scissors. Running with scissors is very dangerous. If you fall while running with scissors, you could get poked or stabbed, or hurt someone else.
   - There is a right way to hold and pass scissors. Hold the closed points in your own hand, pointed toward you, when carrying scissors or passing them to someone else.

8. A scissors rack provides safe storage for

scissors. Metal stands are commercially available at a modest cost. Scissors are easy to get and return to their upright position. Scissors that are merely placed in a box tend to tangle together. An egg carton or coffee can with a plastic lid can substitute for a metal scissors rack. Over time, however, the holes will tear from repeated use, and the makeshift rack will need to be replaced.

9. A variety of types of scissors are commercially available. There are different scissors for different cutting needs and abilities. For example, smaller 4-inch scissors with rounded tips are safe for use by young children. Their blades are fairly dull. Their metal handles may also pinch or irritate the skin.

10. Scissors with rubber-coated finger holes are more comfortable and will not hurt.

11. Plastic safety scissors are lightweight, inexpensive, comfortable, and easy to use.

12. Squeeze-type scissors have an easy-grip, continuous-loop handle. A gentle squeeze with two hands, the fingers and palm of one hand, or the thumb and fingers of one hand will cut. The two blades are blunt and fairly small. They are good for snipping and fringing. Extensive cutting will take more squeezing and hand activity than when using scissors with longer blades.

13. Some young children, including those with exceptionalities or poor fine motor coordination, have more difficulty learning to cut than others. Merely observing someone else cut or trial-and-error practice may not be enough. Try using double-handled training scissors with four rubber-coated finger holes. The teacher and child cut together as one. Over time, these children may graduate to using a single pair of scissors.

14. Both right- and left-handed scissors should be made available. It is very difficult and frustrating for a "lefty" to hold and cut with scissors designed for a "righty."

15. Children's 5-inch pointed metal scissors are longer, heavier, and sharper. The more skilled cutter in kindergarten and the primary grades may prefer these.

16. Some young children have difficulty holding the scissors in the air and working both blades. Children who find scissors heavy or awkward can rest the bottom blade on the table and let only the top finger do the work.

17. Some papers are easier to cut than others. Very lightweight papers, including tissue and cellophane, are flimsy, difficult to cut, and will tear. Cardboard, posterboard, and wallpaper are too thick and resistant for most children's strength and scissors. Manila, butcher paper, newspaper, newsprint, and drawing paper are recommended for beginning cutters. Skilled cutters can move on to construction paper.

ART POISONING?

Many art supplies used by young children can be considered toxic. Examples include rubber cement, permanent felt-tip markers, pottery glazes, enamels, spray paints, lead-based supplies, and wheat wallpaper paste, among others.

These toxic materials can be inhaled, ingested, or absorbed through the skin. Young children are at high risk for many reasons.

1. They are still growing and have a very rapid metabolic rate. They will absorb toxic

materials into their bodies more readily than an adult will.

2. Their brain, lungs, and nervous system are still forming and thus are at risk.

3. Young children have lowered body defenses.

4. Their lower body weight puts them at high risk, since a given quantity of a toxic material will be more concentrated in their bodies.

5. Young children may be impulsive, engage in thumb sucking and nail biting, have frequent hand-to-mouth contacts, and neither understand nor follow the necessary precautions.

ART SAFETY

Art can be a safe and pleasurable experience if guidelines are established and followed. Suggested guidelines for teachers include the following:

1. Use judgment in providing staplers, staples, sharp scissors, tin cans, glitter, spray paint, toothpicks, hotplates, needles, pins, knives, etc. Some young children are responsible and can be trusted to use these items at an early age with some supervision. Others may be too young (in developmental age or maturity) to understand the need for proper handling.

2. Take the time to discuss any potential hazards and dangers. Be honest and positive without dwelling on all the fatal possibilities. Focus on educating rather than frightening children.

3. Try out the art activity in advance. Is it safe? Can your particular group of children properly use the tools involved?

4. Demonstrate and model the proper way to use the tools. "This is the way to use a hole puncher. Sally, now you show me how to use it." "Good, you used it the right way."

5. Supervise all art activities. Aides and parent volunteers can assist in supervision. Some activities will require closer and more direct supervision than others. Remember to anticipate the level of supervision needed when planning.

6. The Arts and Crafts Materials Institute has developed a voluntary program designed to promote safety in children's art materials. Look for and purchase only those art products bearing their labels: AP for Approved Product or CP for Certified Product. The list of art products with AP and CP label ratings is found in table 3-1.

7. A table of art products to avoid and possible substitutes is found in table 3-2.

8. The label "nontoxic" is very misleading. According to present criteria, only materials that are acutely toxic merit being labeled toxic. Therefore "nontoxic" embraces a wide range of dangers from minimally to acutely toxic. Tests to determine toxicity are done on adult animals. A product considered nontoxic when tested on an adult rat may provoke a very different reaction in a young child.

9. Refuse donated art supplies unless the ingredients are known.

10. Do not use old art supplies. Older materials may be highly toxic. They may have been produced when ingredients were not listed on the label and criteria for toxicity were absent.

11. Insist that children clean up and wash their hands after doing art.

12. Food and drinks remain at the snack table or kitchen area and are not taken to the art center.

13. Children with open cuts, sores, or wounds that are not properly covered should not do art activities that involve potentially toxic supplies.

14. Parents of children with allergies, asthma, and other medical problems should consult their pediatrician regarding any limits on their child's use of art supplies.

15. Post the number of your local or state Poison Control Center. Call your local hospital for the number. Have the product in hand when you dial so that you can quickly read off the ingredients from the label and take prompt action.

For further information contact:
Art Hazards Information Center
Center for Occupational Hazards
5 Beekman Street
New York, New York 10038
(212) 227-6220

Art Materials: Recommendations for Children Under 12

Do Not Use	Substitutes
Dusts and Powders	
1. Clay in dry form. Powdered clay, which is easily inhaled, contains free silica and possible asbestos. Do not sand dry clay pieces or do other dust-producing activities.	1. Order talc-free, premixed clay. Wet mop or sponge surfaces thoroughly after using clay.
2. Ceramic glazes or copper enamels.	2. Use water-based paints instead of glazes. Teachers may water-proof pieces with shellac or varnish.
3. Cold water, fiber-reactive dyes or other commercial dyes.	3. Use vegetable and plant dyes (e.g. onionskins, tea, flowers) and food dyes.
4. Instant paper maches (create inhalable dust and some may contain asbestos fibers, lead from pigments in colored printing inks, etc.).	4. Make paper mache from black and white newspaper and library or white paste.
5. Powdered tempera colors (create inhalable dusts and some tempera colors contain toxic pigments, preservatives, etc.).	5. Use liquid paints or paints the teacher pre-mixes.
6. Pastels, chalks or dry markers that create dust.	6. Use crayons, oil pastels or dustless chalks.
Solvents	
1. Solvents (e.g., turpentine, toluene, rubber cement thinner) and solvent-containing materials (solvent-based inks, alkyd paints, rubber cement)	1. Use water-based products only.
2. Solvent-based silk screen and other printing inks.	2. Use water-based silk screen inks, block printing or stencil inks containing safe pigments.
3. Aerosol sprays.	3. Use water-based paints with brushes or spatter techniques.
4. Epoxy, instant glue, airplane glue or other solvent-based adhesives.	4. Use white glue or school paste.
5. Permanent felt tip markers which may contain toluene or other toxic solvents.	5. Use only water color markers.
Toxic Metals	
1. Stained Glass projects using lead came, solder, flux, etc.	1. Use colored cellophane and black paper to simulate lead.
2. Arsenic, cadmium, chrome, mercury, lead, manganese, or other toxic metals which may occur in pigments, metal filings, metal enamels, glazes. metal casting, etc.	2. Get ingredient information or Material Safety Data Sheets on products which are uncertified to be certain they are free of toxic metals.
Miscellaneous	
1. Photographic chemicals.	1. Use blueprint paper and make sun grams.
2. Casting plaster. Creates dust and casting hands and body parts has resulted in serious burns.	2. Teacher can mix plaster in ventilated area or outdoors for sand casting and other safe projects.
3. Acid etches and pickling baths.	3. Should not use techniques employing these chemicals.

Table 3-1 (Courtesy of Center for Occupational Hazards, *Children's Art Supplies Can Be Toxic*, Peltz and Rossol, 1986.)

PRODUCTS AUTHORIZED TO BEAR THE CP CERTIFIED PRODUCTS SEAL,
THE AP APPROVED PRODUCT SEAL
AND THE HL/NT HEALTH LABEL/NON-TOXIC SEAL OF

THE CERTIFIED PRODUCTS AND CERTIFIED LABELING BUREAU OF

THE ART AND CRAFT MATERIALS INSTITUTE, INC.
(formerly The Crayon, Water Color and Craft Institute, Inc.)
715 Boylston Street, Boston, MA 02116   (617) 266-6800

NON-TOXIC

NO HEALTH
LABELING REQUIRED

SEPTEMBER 1986

Products bearing the CP Certified Products Seal, the AP Approved Product Seal or the Health Label/Non-Toxic Seal (HL/NT below) of The Art and Craft Materials Institute, Inc. are certified in a program of toxicological evaluation by a medical expert to contain no materials in sufficient quantities to be toxic or injurious to humans or to cause acute or chronic health problems. This program is reviewed by the Institute's Toxicological Advisory Board. These products are certified by the Institute to be labeled in accordance with the voluntary chronic hazard labeling standard ASTM D-4236. In addition, products bearing the CP Seal meet specific requirements of material, workmanship, working qualities and color described in the appropriate Product Standard issued by the Institute or other recognized standards organizations. **Purchase products that bear the Institute's CP, AP or HL Health Label Seals!**

PRODUCTS AND MANUFACTURERS	BRAND NAMES	CP SEAL	AP SEAL	HL/NT SEAL
ADHESIVES				
Polymer				
Binney & Smith	CRAYOLA ART & CRAFT GLUE		•	
Ceramichrome, Inc.	ED'S GLUE			•
Rich Art Color Co.	RICH GLU WHITE GLUE			•
The Slomons Group	DRAPE 'N SHAPE			•
The Slomons Group	QUIK			•
The Slomons Group	SOBO			•
The Slomons Group	STITCHLESS			•
The Slomons Group	THIK 'N TACKY			•
The Slomons Group	VELVERETTE			•
The Slomons Group	WOODWIZ			•
School Paste				
Binney & Smith	CRAYOLA WHITE		•	
Dixon Ticonderoga	HOLDTU			•
Dixon Ticonderoga	STIXIT	•		
Rich Art Color Co.	RICH ART SCHOOL PASTE			•
Glues				
Dixon Ticonderoga	PRANG ROLL-ON			•
A. Ludwig Klein & Son	#53 CEMENTING LIQUID		•	
A. Ludwig Klein & Son	DUSSELDORF THICK CEMENT		•	
AIRBRUSH COLORS & MEDIUMS				
Badger Airbrush	AEROPAQUE			•
Badger Airbrush	AEROPAQUE GLOSSY VARNISH			•
Badger Airbrush	AEROPAQUE MATTE VARNISH			•
Badger Airbrush	AEROPAQUE PEARLS			•
Badger Airbrush	AIRTEX			•
Dick Blick Co.	DICK BLICK WATER			•
Chartpak	AQUA DYE ♦			•
Delta/Shiva	SHIVAIRTEX			•
Salis International	DR. PH. MARTIN'S SPECTRALITE			•
Salis International	DR. PH. MARTIN'S SPECTRALITE CLEANER		•	
Salis International	DR. PH. MARTIN'S SYNCHRO-MATIC TRANSPARENTS			•
BLOCK PRINTING INKS & MEDIUMS				
Oil Base				
Delta/Shiva	SHIVA OIL BASE	•		
Graphic Chemical&Ink	GRAPHIC			•
Hunt Manufacturing	SPEEDBALL			•
Hunt Manufacturing	SPEEDBALL MEDIUM			•
Water Soluble				
Dick Blick Co.	DICK BLICK			•
Cardinal School	CARDINAL			•
Delta/Shiva	SHIVA WATER BASE			•
Dixon Ticonderoga	PRANG	•		
Graphic Chemical&Ink	GRAPHIC			•
Hunt Manufacturing	SPEEDBALL			•
Hunt Manufacturing	SPEEDBALL DRIER			•
Hunt Manufacturing	SPEEDBALL REDUCER #1			•
Hunt Manufacturing	SPEEDBALL REDUCER #2			•
NASCO International	NASCO BULK-INK			•
Pyramid of Urbana	PYRA-PRINT WATER BASE			•
Rock Paint Distrib'g	PEACOCK			•
Triarco Arts & Crafts	TRIARCO TRI-INK			•

PRODUCTS AND MANUFACTURERS	BRAND NAMES	CP SEAL	AP SEAL	HL/NT SEAL
BRUSH CARE PRODUCTS				
Martin/F. Weber Co.	PRISCILLA'S BRUSH CREME		•	
CERAMICS, SPECIALTY PRODUCTS				
American Art Clay	AMACO AMACOTE			•
American Art Clay	AMACO ENAMELING OIL			•
American Art Clay	AMACO GUM SOLUTION			•
American Art Clay	AMACO KILN WASH			•
American Art Clay	AMACO PLASTER SEPARATOR			•
American Art Clay	AMACO RESIST RITE			•
American Art Clay	AMACO WAX RESIST			•
American Art Clay	REWARD SP-650 BLACK LAVA			•
American Art Clay	REWARD SP-608 FROSTED PECAN			•
American Art Clay	REWARD SP-MAGIC MENDER			•
American Art Clay	REWARD SP-REWARD MEDIA			•
American Art Clay	REWARD METALLIC POWDERS			•
American Art Clay	REWARD SP-SNOW FLUFF			•
American Art Clay	REWARD SP-TEXTURITE			•
American Art Clay	REWARD SP-651 WHITE LAVA			•
Ceramichrome, Inc.	BRUSH 'N BLEND			•
Ceramichrome, Inc.	BRUSH-ON SEALER			•
Ceramichrome, Inc.	CLAY CARVE			•
Ceramichrome, Inc.	DECO-WEB			•
Ceramichrome, Inc.	DRAPE			•
Ceramichrome, Inc.	GLAZE CONDITIONER			•
Ceramichrome, Inc.	LIQUID KILN WASH			•
Ceramichrome, Inc.	LIQUID MENDER			•
Ceramichrome, Inc.	MASTER-STROKE			•
Ceramichrome, Inc.	MEDIA			•
Ceramichrome, Inc.	NON-FIRED SNOW			•
Ceramichrome, Inc.	PLASTICIZER			•
Ceramichrome, Inc.	SCULPTURE PASTE			•
Ceramichrome, Inc.	STAIN MEDIA			•
Ceramichrome, Inc.	THIXENER			•
Ceramichrome, Inc.	TRANSFER-IT			•
Ceramichrome, Inc.	WAX-TEX			•
Duncan Enterprises	BRUSH ON GLOSS SEALER			•
Duncan Enterprises	CASCADE			•
Duncan Enterprises	GOLDMINE BLACK			•
Duncan Enterprises	GOLDMINE BLUE			•
Duncan Enterprises	HI GLOSS SEALER			•
Duncan Enterprises	MATTE SEALER			•
Duncan Enterprises	PATCH-A-TACH			•
Duncan Enterprises	PATTERN BASE			•
Duncan Enterprises	SNOW			•
Duncan Enterprises	THICKENER & TEXTURIZER			•
Duncan Enterprises	WHITE BROCADE			•
Duncan Enterprises	WHITE FROTH			•
Gare, Inc.	DRIPPIT			•
Gare, Inc.	FINGER MINI-METALLICS			•
Gare, Inc.	FIXALL			•
Gare, Inc.	HI-LO			•
Gare, Inc.	MIXIT			•
Gare, Inc.	NO FIRE SNOW			•
Gare, Inc.	PORCELAIN PROP			•
Gare, Inc.	SHADE-IT			•
Gare, Inc.	SOFT TOUCH PASTELS			•
Gare, Inc.	TEXTURE POWDER			•
Gare, Inc.	WAX RESIST			•

♦ Some products in this line do not bear the CP, AP or Health Label/Non-Toxic Seal.

Table 3-2 (Courtesy of The Art and Craft Materials Institute Inc.)

CERAMICS, SPECIALTY PRODUCTS (Continued)

PRODUCTS AND MANUFACTURERS	BRAND NAMES	CP SEAL	AP SEAL	HL/NT SEAL
Mayco Colors	BLUE LACE MENDER		*	
Mayco Colors	MAYCO MASK		*	
Mayco Colors	MAYCO MEDIA		*	
Mayco Colors	TEXTURE POWDER		*	
Mayco Colors	WAX RESIST		*	

CHALKS

Charcoal

PRODUCTS AND MANUFACTURERS	BRAND NAMES	CP SEAL	AP SEAL	HL/NT SEAL
Dick Blick Co.	DICK BLICK		*	

Extruded Colored (For Chalkboard)

PRODUCTS AND MANUFACTURERS	BRAND NAMES	CP SEAL	AP SEAL	HL/NT SEAL
Binney&Smith (Canada)	CRAYOLA SANIGENE		*	
Dixon Ticonderoga	HYGA-COLOR		*	
J. L. Hammett Co.	HAMMETT'S		*	
NationArt, Inc.	3B BLACKBOARDBEST		*	
NationArt, Inc.	OMYACOLOR		*	
NationArt, Inc.	ROBERCOLOR		*	
School Mate, Inc.	SCHOOL MATE		*	
Weber Costello	OMEGA		*	
Weber Costello	RITEBRITE		*	

Extruded Sightsaving (For Chalkboard)

PRODUCTS AND MANUFACTURERS	BRAND NAMES	CP SEAL	AP SEAL	HL/NT SEAL
Binney & Smith	CRAYOLA ANTI-DUST		*	
Binney & Smith	CRAYOLA E-Z-SYTE		*	
Binney&Smith (Canada)	CRAYOLA SANIGENE		*	
Dixon Ticonderoga	FORSYTHE		*	
Dixon Ticonderoga	VELVATEX		*	
J. L. Hammett Co.	HAMMETT'S		*	
NationArt, Inc.	3B BLACKBOARDBEST		*	
NationArt, Inc.	OMYACOLOR		*	
NationArt, Inc.	ROBERCOLOR		*	
School Mate, Inc.	SCHOOL MATE		*	
Weber Costello	ALPHASITE		*	
Weber Costello	RITEBRITE		*	

Extruded White (For Chalkboard)

PRODUCTS AND MANUFACTURERS	BRAND NAMES	CP SEAL	AP SEAL	HL/NT SEAL
Binney & Smith	CRAYOLA-AN-DU-SEPTIC		*	
Binney & Smith	CRAYOLA ANTI-DUST		*	
Binney&Smith (Canada)	CRAYOLA SANIGENE			*
Dixon Ticonderoga	DOVERCLIFF		*	
Dixon Ticonderoga	HYGIEIA		*	
J. L. Hammett Co.	HAMMETT'S		*	
NationArt, Inc.	3B BLACKBOARDBEST		*	
NationArt, Inc.	OMYACOLOR		*	
NationArt, Inc.	ROBERCOLOR		*	
School Mate, Inc.	SCHOOL MATE		*	
Weber Costello	ALPHA		*	
Weber Costello	RITEBRITE		*	
Weber Costello	WEBCO			*

Extruded Colored (For Paper and Crafts)

PRODUCTS AND MANUFACTURERS	BRAND NAMES	CP SEAL	AP SEAL	HL/NT SEAL
Binney & Smith	CRAYOLA COLORED ART		*	
Dixon Ticonderoga	PRANG PASTELLO		*	
Dixon Ticonderoga	PRANG POSTER PASTELLO		*	
Weber Costello	ALPHACOLOR		*	

Molded Colored (For Chalkboard)

PRODUCTS AND MANUFACTURERS	BRAND NAMES	CP SEAL	AP SEAL	HL/NT SEAL
Binney & Smith	CRAYOLA COLORED			*

Molded White (For Chalkboard)

PRODUCTS AND MANUFACTURERS	BRAND NAMES	CP SEAL	AP SEAL	HL/NT SEAL
Avalon Industries	AVALON NU-CHALK			*
Binney & Smith	CRAYOLA		*	
Binney & Smith	CRAYOLA ENAMELED		*	
Binney&Smith (Canada)	CRAYOLA SWAN			*
Dixon Ticonderoga	COLORART		*	
Dixon Ticonderoga	PRANG SIDEWALK		*	
Dixon Ticonderoga	WALTHAM		*	

Molded Colored (For Paper and Crafts)

PRODUCTS AND MANUFACTURERS	BRAND NAMES	CP SEAL	AP SEAL	HL/NT SEAL
Avalon Industries	AVALON NU-CHALK			*
Binney & Smith	CRAYOLA COLORED DRAWING		*	
Binney & Smith	CRAYOLA COLORED POSTER			*
Binney&Smith (Canada)	CRAYOLA COLOREX			*
Binney&Smith (Canada)	CRAYOLA GOODHUE		*	
Dixon Ticonderoga	AMBRITE		*	
Dixon Ticonderoga	EXCELLO SQUARES		*	
Dixon Ticonderoga	FREART		*	
Dixon Ticonderoga	LECTURERS		*	
Dixon Ticonderoga	PRANG COLOR CHALK			*
Dixon Ticonderoga	PRANG FLUORESCENT		*	
Dixon Ticonderoga	PRANG LECTURERS		*	

CLAYS

Modeling (Permanently Plastic, Non-Hardening)

PRODUCTS AND MANUFACTURERS	BRAND NAMES	CP SEAL	AP SEAL	HL/NT SEAL
American Art Clay	AMACO PLAST-I-CLAY			*
American Art Clay	PERMOPLAST		*	
Avalon Industries	AVALON		*	
Avalon Industries	COLOR CRAFT		*	
Binney & Smith	CLAYOLA		*	
Binney & Smith	CRAYOLA CLAYTIME CLAY			*
Dixon Ticonderoga	PRANG		*	
Leisure Craft	LEISURE CLAY		*	
NationArt, Inc.	PLASTICOLOR		*	

Modeling Dough

PRODUCTS AND MANUFACTURERS	BRAND NAMES	CP SEAL	AP SEAL	HL/NT SEAL
American Art Clay	AMACO		*	
American Art Clay	SUPER DOUGH		*	

Papier Mache

PRODUCTS AND MANUFACTURERS	BRAND NAMES	CP SEAL	AP SEAL	HL/NT SEAL
American Art Clay	CLAYCRETE		*	

Powdered Sculpting & Modeling Mediums

PRODUCTS AND MANUFACTURERS	BRAND NAMES	CP SEAL	AP SEAL	HL/NT SEAL
American Art Clay	SCULPTAMOLD		*	

Self-Hardening

PRODUCTS AND MANUFACTURERS	BRAND NAMES	CP SEAL	AP SEAL	HL/NT SEAL
American Art Clay	AMACO MARBLE			*
American Art Clay	AMACO MEXICAN POTTERY			*
Duncan Enterprises	DOLL COMPOSITION BODY			*
Produits Chimiques	DARWI		*	

Ceramic

PRODUCTS AND MANUFACTURERS	BRAND NAMES	CP SEAL	AP SEAL	HL/NT SEAL
American Art Clay	AMACO VERSA #20			*
American Art Clay	AMACO WHITE SCULPTURE #27			*
American Art Clay	AMACO BUFF FIRING #46			*
American Art Clay	AMACO INDIAN RED #67			*
American Art Clay	AMACO TERRA COTTA #77			*
American Art Clay	AMACO MOIST			*
American Art Clay	AMACO NEVO' (RED)			*
American Art Clay	AMACO STEWARTS #			*
Bennett Pottery	CORAL REEF			*
Gare, Inc.	PORCELAIN #			*
Gare, Inc.	STONEWARE			*

Ceramic Casting Slip

PRODUCTS AND MANUFACTURERS	BRAND NAMES	CP SEAL	AP SEAL	HL/NT SEAL
American Art Clay	AMACO SLIP #15			*
Ceramichrome, Inc.	PORCELAIN CASTING SLIP			*
Gare, Inc.	SLIP			*

CRAYONS

Hard Molded

PRODUCTS AND MANUFACTURERS	BRAND NAMES	CP SEAL	AP SEAL	HL/NT SEAL
Binney & Smith	ARTISTA II		*	

Molded

PRODUCTS AND MANUFACTURERS	BRAND NAMES	CP SEAL	AP SEAL	HL/NT SEAL
Avalon Industries	COLOR CRAFT		*	
Binney & Smith	CRAYOLA		*	
Binney & Smith	CRAYOLA EASY OFF			*
Binney & Smith	CRAYOLET			*
Binney & Smith	PEACOCK			*
Binney & Smith	CRAYOLA SO-BIG		*	
Dixon Ticonderoga	AMERICAN CRAYON		*	
Dixon Ticonderoga	COLORART			*
Dixon Ticonderoga	PRANG		*	
Dixon Ticonderoga	PRANG WIPE-OFF WASH-OFF		*	
J. L. Hammett Co.	ART UTILITY		*	
Pentel of America	GL1-16 PLASTIC			*
Pentel of America	PTC-25 SOFT			*
Sargent Art	SARGENT		*	

Oil Pastels

PRODUCTS AND MANUFACTURERS	BRAND NAMES	CP SEAL	AP SEAL	HL/NT SEAL
Dixon Ticonderoga	SKETCHO		*	

Pressed

PRODUCTS AND MANUFACTURERS	BRAND NAMES	CP SEAL	AP SEAL	HL/NT SEAL
Dixon Ticonderoga	COLOR CLASSICS		*	
Dixon Ticonderoga	CRAYOGRAPH		*	
Dixon Ticonderoga	KANTROLL		*	
Dixon Ticonderoga	KINDOGRAPH		*	
J. L. Hammett Co.	ART UTILITY		*	
Sargent Art	SARGENT		*	

Water Color

PRODUCTS AND MANUFACTURERS	BRAND NAMES	CP SEAL	AP SEAL	HL/NT SEAL
Dixon Ticonderoga	PRANG PAYONS		*	
Weber Costello	ALPHACOLOR		*	
Winsor & Newton	REEVES PAINTSTIX		*	

\# Some products in this line do not bear the CP, AP or Health Label/Non-Toxic Seal.

(Table 3-2 continued)

PRODUCTS AND MANUFACTURERS	BRAND NAMES	CP SEAL	AP SEAL	HL/NT SEAL
DRAWING & LETTERING INKS & MEDIUMS				
Non-Waterproof				
Hunt Manufacturing	OSMIROID			•
Hunt Manufacturing	SPEEDBALL			•
Technical				
Hunt Manufacturing	SPEEDBALL TECHNICAL BLACK	•		
Salis International	DR. PH. MARTIN'S TECH			•
Steig Products	FW WHITE TECHNICAL			•
Steig Products	PEN-OPAKE TECHNICAL WHITE			•
Waterproof				
Duro Art Industries	DURO INDIA			•
Hunt Manufacturing	SPEEDBALL BLACK			•
Hunt Manufacturing	SPEEDBALL PIGMENTED			•
Hunt Manufacturing	SPEEDBALL SUPER BLACK INDIA			•
Salis International	DR. PH. MARTIN'S BLACK STAR HICARB			•
Salis International	DR. PH. MARTIN'S BLACK STAR MATTE			•
Salis International	DR. PH. MARTIN'S PERMADRAFT			•
Steig Products	CALLI BLACK			•
Steig Products	CALLI COLORED			•
Steig Products	FW INDIA			•
Steig Products	FW WATERPROOF			•
Steig Products	LUMA PEARLESCENT			•
Steig Products	RE-WHITE CORRECTION FLUID			•
Steig Products	TRUE FLOW INDIA			•
Winsor & Newton	ARTISTS' DRAWING ♦			•
ETCHING INKS & MEDIUMS				
Grounds				
Graphic Chemical&Ink	GRAPHIC HARD TRANSPARENT			•
Graphic Chemical&Ink	GRAPHIC SOFT TRANSPARENT			•
Inks				
Graphic Chemical&Ink	GRAPHIC			•
Martin/F. Weber Co.	WEBER			•
Daniel Smith, Inc.	DANIEL SMITH, INC. ♦			•
Mediums				
Graphic Chemical&Ink	GRAPHIC SURESET			•
Martin/F. Weber Co.	MARTIN/F. WEBER PLATE OIL			•
FIXATIVES				
Salis International	DR. PH. MARTIN'S TECH COLOR FIX			•
GESSOS & PAINTING GROUNDS				
Binney & Smith	LIQUITEX GESSO			•
Duro Art Industries	DURO GESSO			•
Golden Artists Colors	GOLDEN BLACK GESSO			•
Golden Artists Colors	GOLDEN GESSO			•
Hunt Manufacturing	SPEEDBALL ACRYLIC ARTISTS GESSO			•
Martin/F. Weber Co.	MARTIN/F. WEBER ECONOMY GESSO			•
Martin/F. Weber Co.	PERMALBA GESSO			•
GLAZES, UNDERGLAZES & OVERGLAZES (CERAMIC)				
Glazes				
American Art Clay	AMACO ALLIGATOR ♦			•
American Art Clay	AMACO CRYSTALTEX ♦			•
American Art Clay	AMACO ENGOBES ♦			•
American Art Clay	AMACO F SERIES			•
American Art Clay	AMACO HIGH FIRE ♦			•
American Art Clay	AMACO LOW FIRE CRACKLE ♦			•
American Art Clay	AMACO MAJOLICA GLOSS ♦			•
American Art Clay	AMACO MATT ♦			•
American Art Clay	AMACO OPALESCENT ♦			•
American Art Clay	REWARD BRUSH & WIPE ♦			•
American Art Clay	REWARD OLD WORLD CRACKLE ♦			•
A.R.T. Studio Clay	NERO (CONE 5) ♦			•
A.R.T. Studio Clay	NERO (CONE 6) ♦			•
Ceramichrome, Inc.	ART ♦			•
Ceramichrome, Inc.	GLOSS ♦			•

PRODUCTS AND MANUFACTURERS	BRAND NAMES	CP SEAL	AP SEAL	HL/NT SEAL
Glazes (Continued)				
Ceramichrome, Inc.	KRACKLE ♦			•
Ceramichrome, Inc.	LAVA FOAM			•
Ceramichrome, Inc.	OK DINNERWARE MATT			•
Ceramichrome, Inc.	SPECIALTY ♦			•
Ceramichrome, Inc.	SPECKLED ♦			•
Duncan Enterprises	ART ♦			•
Duncan Enterprises	CERAMIC CRACKLETONE			•
Duncan Enterprises	CERAMIC CRYSTALS ♦			•
Duncan Enterprises	CERAMIC CRYSTALTONE ♦			•
Duncan Enterprises	GALLERY OPAQUE ♦			•
Duncan Enterprises	GLOSS ♦			•
Gare, Inc.	GARE ♦			•
Gare, Inc.	STONEWARE			•
Mayco Colors	ART ♦			•
Mayco Colors	CLEAR GLOSS			•
Mayco Colors	CLEAR MATT			•
Mayco Colors	CRACKLE ♦			•
Mayco Colors	SPECIAL EFFECTS ♦			•
Mayco Colors	STONEWARE			•
Underglazes				
American Art Clay	AMACO LIQUID			•
American Art Clay	AMACO DECORATING CRAYONS			•
American Art Clay	AMACO SEMI-MOIST DECORATING COLORS			•
American Art Clay	REWARD DESIGNER VELVETS ♦			•
American Art Clay	REWARD LEADFREE DINNERWARE ♦			•
American Art Clay	REWARD SUPER ONE-STROKES ♦			•
American Art Clay	REWARD TRUTONE ♦			•
American Art Clay	REWARD VELVET ♦			•
Ceramichrome, Inc.	ANTIQUE			•
Ceramichrome, Inc.	BEAUTY FLO OPAQUE			•
Duncan Enterprises	COVERCOAT			•
Duncan Enterprises	DUST AWAY			•
Duncan Enterprises	E Z STROKE			•
Duncan Enterprises	FIRED ANTIQUE			•
Duncan Enterprises	RED STROKE ♦			•
Gare, Inc.	GARE			•
Mayco Colors	FIRED ANTIQUES			•
Mayco Colors	MAYCO			•
Mayco Colors	ONE STROKE			•
Overglazes				
Duncan Enterprises	GOLD			•
GRAPHIC MASKING LIQUIDS				
Hunt Manufacturing	SPEEDBALL RED RUBY			•
LITHO INKS & MEDIUMS				
Graphic Chemical&Ink	GRAPHIC			•
MARKERS				
Solvent Base				
Chartpak	AVP AUDIO VISUAL ♦	•		•
Chartpak	OPAQUING PEN			•
Dixon Ticonderoga	WHITE SYSTEM			•
Water Color				
Berol U.S.A.	BEROL 8500			•
Binney & Smith	CRAYOLA COLORING	•		
Binney & Smith	CRAYOLA DRAWING	•		
Chartpak	AQUA ♦			•
Chartpak	AVW AUDIO VISUAL ♦			•
Chartpak	CHIZ'L I ♦	•		
Chartpak	CHIZ'L II ♦			•
Chartpak	NRBP			•
Chartpak	TECHMARKER ♦			•
Dixon Ticonderoga	PRANG		•	
Dixon Ticonderoga	PRANG BRUSH PENS			•
Sanford Corp.	MR. SKETCH SCENTED INSTANT			•
Steig Products	STEIG LIGHTFAST			•

♦ Some products in this line do not bear the CP, AP or Health Label/Non-Toxic Seal.

(Table 3-2 continued)

PRODUCTS AND MANUFACTURERS	BRAND NAMES	CP SEAL	AP SEAL	HL/NT SEAL
MEDIUMS & VARNISHES, ACRYLIC/POLYMER				
Mediums				
Binney & Smith	LIQUITEX GEL	*		
Binney & Smith	LIQUITEX MATTE	*		
Binney & Smith	LIQUITEX MODELING PASTE	*		
Binney & Smith	LIQUITEX POLYMER	*		
Binney & Smith	LIQUITEX RETARDING	*		
Dick Blick Co.	BLICKRYLIC GEL	*		
Dick Blick Co.	BLICKRYLIC POLYMER	*		
Dick Blick Co.	BLICKRYLIC RETARDER	*		
Dick Blick Co.	STROKEMASTER GEL	*		
Dick Blick Co.	STROKEMASTER GESSO	*		
Dick Blick Co.	STROKEMASTER GLOSS	*		
Dick Blick Co.	STROKEMASTER MATTE	*		
Dick Blick Co.	STROKEMASTER MODELING PASTE	*		
Dick Blick Co.	STROKEMASTER RETARDER	*		
Cardinal School	CARDINAL ACRYLIC GEL	*		
Cardinal School	CARDINAL ACRYLIC POLYMER	*		
Cardinal School	CARDINAL ACRYLIC RETARDER	*		
Ceramichrome, Inc.	DECO ART EXTENDER			
Chroma Acrylics	JO SONJA ALL PURPOSE SEALER		*	
Chroma Acrylics	JO SONJA FLOW		*	
Chroma Acrylics	JO SONJA RETARDER		*	
Chroma Acrylics	JO SONJA TANNIN BLOCKING SEALER		*	
Chroma Acrylics	JO SONJA TEXTILE		*	
Chroma Acrylics	JO SONJA TEXTURE PASTE		*	
Delta/Shiva	SHIVA GEL	*		
Delta/Shiva	SHIVA GESSO	*		
Delta/Shiva	SHIVA GLOSS	*		
Delta/Shiva	SHIVA MODELING PASTE	*		
Delta/Shiva	SHIVA RETARDER	*		
Alois K. Diethelm AG	LASCAUX MODELING PASTE A & B	*		
Alois K. Diethelm AG	LASCAUX PAINT & VARNISH	*		
Duro Art Industries	MATTE	*		
Duro Art Industries	POLYMER GEL	*		
Duro Art Industries	POLYMER GLOSS	*		
Golden Artists Colors	ACRYLIC FLOW RELEASE	*		
Golden Artists Colors	FILM MODIFIER	*		
Golden Artists Colors	FLUID MATTE	*		
Golden Artists Colors	GEL	*		
Golden Artists Colors	MATTE	*		
Golden Artists Colors	MODELING PASTE	*		
Golden Artists Colors	POLYMER 100, 500, 700	*		
Golden Artists Colors	RETARDER	*		
Hunt Manufacturing	SPEEDBALL GEL	*		
Hunt Manufacturing	SPEEDBALL GLOSS	*		
Hunt Manufacturing	SPEEDBALL MATTE	*		
Hunt Manufacturing	SPEEDBALL MODELING PASTE	*	*	
Lefranc & Bourgeois	FLASHE		*	
Martin/F. Weber Co.	PERMALBA GEL	*		
Martin/F. Weber Co.	PERMALBA GLOSS	*		
Martin/F. Weber Co.	PERMALBA MATTE	*		
Martin/F. Weber Co.	PERMALBA MODELING PASTE	*		
Martin/F. Weber Co.	PERMALBA RETARDER	*		
Mayco Colors	HI-GLOSS SEALER	*		
Mayco Colors	MATT SEALER	*		
NASCO International	BULKRYLIC GEL	*		
NASCO International	BULKRYLIC POLYMER	*		
NASCO International	BULKRYLIC RETARDER	*		
Pyramid of Urbana	PYRA-CRYLIC GEL	*		
Pyramid of Urbana	PYRA-CRYLIC POLYMER	*		
Pyramid of Urbana	PYRA-CRYLIC RETARDER	*		
Rock Paint Distrib'g	PEACOCK GEL	*		
Rock Paint Distrib'g	PEACOCK POLYMER	*		
Rock Paint Distrib'g	PEACOCK RETARDER	*		
Royal Talens	REMBRANDT CASEIN TEMPERA BINDER		*	
Royal Talens	REMBRANDT GLOSSY		*	
Royal Talens	REMBRANDT MAT		*	
Royal Talens	REMBRANDT RETARDER		*	
Salis International	DR. PH. MARTIN'S SPECTRA-LITE COLOR EXTENDER	*		
Triarco Arts & Crafts	TRI-CRYLIC GEL	*		
Triarco Arts & Crafts	TRI-CRYLIC POLYMER	*		
Triarco Arts & Crafts	TRI-CRYLIC RETARDER	*		
Utrecht Mfg. Co.	ACRYLIC GEL	*		
Utrecht Mfg. Co.	ACRYLIC MATTE	*		
Winsor & Newton	FLOW IMPROVER		*	
Winsor & Newton	GEL		*	
Winsor & Newton	GESSO PRIMER		*	
Winsor & Newton	GLOSS		*	
Mediums (Continued)				
Winsor & Newton	MATT			*
Winsor & Newton	RETARDER			*
Zipatone, Inc.	AQUA-TEC GESSO		*	
Zipatone, Inc.	AQUA-TEC MATTE		*	
Zipatone, Inc.	AQUA-TEC MODELING PASTE		*	
Zipatone, Inc.	AQUA-TEC POLYMER		*	
Varnishes				
Binney & Smith	LIQUITEX MATTE		*	
Dick Blick Co.	STROKEMASTER MATTE		*	
Chroma Acrylics	JO SONJA POLYURETHANE		*	
Alois K. Diethelm AG	LASCAUX TRANSPARENT		*	
Golden Artists Colors	MATTE		*	
Golden Artists Colors	POLYMER		*	
Martin/F. Weber Co.	AQUATOLE		*	
Winsor & Newton	GLOSS			*
Winsor & Newton	MATT			*
Zipatone, Inc.	AQUA-TEC MATTE		*	
Zipatone, Inc.	AQUA-TEC POLYMER		*	
MEDIUMS & VARNISHES, ALKYD & OIL				
Driers				
Delta/Shiva	SHIVA SICCATIVE	*		
Oils				
Dick Blick Co.	LARD	*		
Delta/Shiva	SHIVA LINSEED	*		
Delta/Shiva	SHIVA SUN-THICKENED STAND	*		
Duro Art Industries	LINSEED	*		
M. Grumbacher, Inc.	LINSEED			*
M. Grumbacher, Inc.	PALE DRYING			*
M. Grumbacher, Inc.	POPPYSEED			*
M. Grumbacher, Inc.	STAND			*
M. Grumbacher, Inc.	SUN THICKENED LINSEED			*
Hunt Manufacturing	SPEEDBALL LINSEED	*		
Martin/F. Weber Co.	WEBER LINSEED	*		
Martin/F. Weber Co.	WEBER PROCESS THICKENED LINSEED	*		
Martin/F. Weber Co.	WEBER STAND	*		
Royal Talens	TALENS PURIFIED LINSEED			*
Royal Talens	TALENS STAND			*
Winsor & Newton	LINSEED - COLD PRESSED			*
Winsor & Newton	LINSEED - DRYING			*
Winsor & Newton	LINSEED - REFINED			*
Winsor & Newton	LINSEED - SUN BLEACHED			*
Winsor & Newton	POPPY - SUNBLEACHED			*
Winsor & Newton	STAND LINSEED			*
Winsor & Newton	SUN-THICKENED LINSEED			*
Zipatone, Inc.	BOCOUR LINSEED	*		
Painting Mediums - Liquids				
Chroma Acrylics	ATELIER FLOW			*
Chroma Acrylics	ATELIER GESSO			*
Chroma Acrylics	ATELIER GLOSS MEDIUM/VARNISH			*
Chroma Acrylics	ATELIER MODELING COMPOUND			*
Delta/Shiva	SHIVA PAINTING, HEAVY	*		
M. Grumbacher, Inc.	HYPLAR HYSLO			*
Lefranc & Bourgeois	COLOURLESS PAINTING			*
Painting Mediums - Gels				
Delta/Shiva	SHIVA SIGNA-GEL	*		
M. Grumbacher, Inc.	M. G. GEL			*
Winsor & Newton	OLEOPASTO			*
Winsor & Newton	WIN-GEL			*
Varnishes				
Delta/Shiva	SHIVA GLAZING	*		
Delta/Shiva	SHIVA OIL MATTE	*		
Lefranc & Bourgeois	BALL OF BLACK			*
Lefranc & Bourgeois	BLACK SATIN FOR ETCHING			*
Lefranc & Bourgeois	BLACK STOPPING-OUT			*
Lefranc & Bourgeois	DUROZIEZ HARLEM DRYING			*
Lefranc & Bourgeois	FINEST DAMMAR			*
Lefranc & Bourgeois	J. G. VIBERT PAINTING			*
Lefranc & Bourgeois	J. G. VIBERT RETOUCHING			*
Lefranc & Bourgeois	SOFT BLACK			*
MEDIUMS & VARNISHES, WATER COLOR				
Duncan Enterprises	THIN N SHADE			*
M. Grumbacher, Inc.	MISKET			*

Some products in this line do not bear the CP, AP or Health Label/Non-Toxic Seal.

(Table 3-2 continued)

PRODUCTS AND MANUFACTURERS	BRAND NAMES	CP SEAL	AP SEAL	HL/NT SEAL
MEDIUMS & VARNISHES, WATER COLOR (Continued)				
Salis International	DR. PH. MARTIN'S COLOR-OUT FRISKET		*	
Salis International	DR. PH. MARTIN'S MASK LIQUID		*	
Steig Products	COLORFLEX		*	
Steig Products	LUMA LIQUID MASK		*	
Steig Products	WAX-GRIP		*	
Winsor & Newton	AQUAPASTO			*
Winsor & Newton	ART MASKING FLUID			*
Winsor & Newton	ART MASKING FLUID COLOURLESS			*
Winsor & Newton	PREPARED SIZE			*
Winsor & Newton	WATERCOLOUR MEDIUM			*
MEDIUMS, MULTI-PURPOSE				
Dick Blick Co.	MULTI-GEL		*	
Salis International	DR. PH. MARTIN'S PHOTO-ACE		*	
PAINTS				
Acrylics, Artists				
Binney & Smith	LIQUITEX		*	
Dick Blick Co.	BLICKRYLIC		*	
Dick Blick Co.	STROKEMASTER		*	
Cardinal School	CARDINAL ACRYLIC	*		
Ceramichrome, Inc.	DECO ART		*	
Chroma Acrylics	ATELIER			*
Chroma Acrylics	JO SONJA ◊		*	
Color Craft	CREATEX POSTER/FABRIC	*		
Delta/Shiva	SHIVA SIGNATEX		*	
Duro Art Industries	DURO		*	
Golden Artists Colors	FLUID		*	
Golden Artists Colors	GOLDEN		*	
Hunt Manufacturing	SPEEDBALL		*	
M. Grumbacher, Inc.	HYPLAR COLORS			*
Martin/F. Weber Co.	PERMALBA		*	
Martin/F. Weber Co.	PRISCILLA'S BASECOAT		*	
NASCO International	BULKRYLIC		*	
Pyramid of Urbana	PYRA-CRYLIC		*	
Rock Paint Distrib'g	PEACOCK		*	
Royal Talens	DECORFIN			*
Royal Talens	REMBRANDT			*
Triarco Arts & Crafts	TRI-CRYLIC		*	
Utrecht Mfg. Co.	UTRECHT ◊		*	
Winsor & Newton	ARTISTS' COLOURS ◊			*
Zipatone, Inc.	BOCOUR AQUA-TEC		*	
Acrylics, Washable				
Chroma Acrylics	CHROMACRYL	*		
Duncan Enterprises	DOLL COMPOSITION PRIMER		*	
Duncan Enterprises	MASK N PEEL		*	
Duncan Enterprises	NATURAL TOUCH DRYBRUSHING		*	
Duncan Enterprises	PREP COAT		*	
Duncan Enterprises	ULTRA METALLICS		*	
Koh-I-Noor	TOP COLOR		*	
Rich Art Color Co.	RICH CRYL		*	
Alkyds				
Winsor & Newton	LONDON ◊		*	
Caseins				
Delta/Shiva	SHIVA COLORS		*	
Ceramic Stains, Water Base				
American Art Clay	REWARD PEARLETTE		*	
American Art Clay	REWARD SUNBURST		*	
Ceramichrome, Inc.	BISK-CHROME METALLICS		*	
Ceramichrome, Inc.	BISK-CHROME OPAQUES		*	
Ceramichrome, Inc.	BISK-CHROME PEARL		*	
Ceramichrome, Inc.	BISK-CHROME TRANSLUCENT		*	
Ceramichrome, Inc.	OPAQUE ACRYLICS		*	
Ceramichrome, Inc.	SOFTEE STAINS		*	
Duncan Enterprises	LIQUID PEARLS		*	
Duncan Enterprises	OPAQUE		*	
Duncan Enterprises	WATER BASE TRANSLUCENT		*	
Gare, Inc.	ACRYLIC		*	
Gare, Inc.	BISQUE		*	
Gare, Inc.	BISQUE METALLICS		*	
Gare, Inc.	BISQUE PEARLS		*	

PRODUCTS AND MANUFACTURERS	BRAND NAMES	CP SEAL	AP SEAL	HL/NT SEAL
Ceramic Stains, Water Base (Continued)				
Gare, Inc.	GARE STROKES		*	
Gare, Inc.	GARE-TIQUES		*	
Gare, Inc.	WATER BASE TRANSLUCENT		*	
Mayco Colors	FINAL TINT ◊		*	
Mayco Colors	LIQUID METALLICS ◊		*	
Mayco Colors	OPAQUES		*	
Mayco Colors	PEARLS		*	
Mayco Colors	WATERBASE TRANSLUCENTS		*	
Mayco Colors	WOODGRAIN		*	
Designer Colors (Gouache)				
Lefranc & Bourgeois	LINEL 35GT ◊			*
Lefranc & Bourgeois	LINEL 650 ◊			*
Turner Colour Works	TURNER DESIGN	*		
Winsor & Newton	DESIGNERS' ◊			*
Winsor & Newton	PROCESS ◊			*
Dyes				
American Art Clay	BATIKIT COLDPRINT DYE THICKENER			*
Enamels				
American Art Clay	AMACO ARO		*	
American Art Clay	AMACO ART		*	
American Art Clay	AMACO COUNTERENAMEL		*	
Thompson Enamel	LEAD FREE OPAQUES		*	
Thompson Enamel	LEAD FREE TRANSPARENTS		*	
Fabric				
Decart, Inc.	DEKA-PERMANENT			*
Finger Paint, Dry				
Binney & Smith	CRAYOLA		*	
Finger Paint, Liquid				
Avalon Industries	COLOR CRAFT		*	
Binney & Smith	CRAYOLA		*	
Dick Blick Co.	STROKEMASTER		*	
Dixon Ticonderoga	PRANG		*	
J. L. Hammett Co.	ART UTILITY		*	
Palmer Paint	PALMER		*	
Rich Art Color Co.	RICH ART		*	
Sargent Art	SARGENT		*	
Weber Costello	ALPHACOLOR		*	
Oils				
Binney & Smith	LIQUITEX ◊		*	
Binney & Smith	LIQUITEX TEXTURE WHITE UNDERPAINT			*
J. Blockx Fils	BLOCKX ◊			*
Daler-Rowney	GEORGIAN ◊		*	
Delta/Shiva	SHIVA ARTISTS OIL PAINTSTIKS			*
Delta/Shiva	SHIVA PERMASOL			*
Delta/Shiva	SHIVA PICTOR ARTIST			*
Delta/Shiva	SHIVA SIGNATURE			*
Duro Art Industries	DURO		*	
M. Grumbacher, Inc.	FINEST ◊			*
M. Grumbacher, Inc.	GAINSBOROUGH ◊			*
M. Grumbacher, Inc.	GOLDEN PALETTE			*
M. Grumbacher, Inc.	PRETESTED			*
Hunt Manufacturing	SPEEDBALL		*	
Lefranc & Bourgeois	401 EXTRA-FINE ARTIST'S ◊			*
Lefranc & Bourgeois	104 FINE ◊			*
Fratelli Maimeri	BRERA			*
Martin/F. Weber Co.	MISTY COLOR		*	
Martin/F. Weber Co.	PERMALBA		*	
Royal Talens	AMSTERDAM			*
Royal Talens	REMBRANDT ◊			*
Royal Talens	VAN GOGH			*
Utrecht Mfg. Co.	UTRECHT ◊		*	
Winsor & Newton	ARTISTS' PROFESSIONAL ◊			*
Winsor & Newton	ARTISTS' UNDERPAINTING WHITE			*
Winsor & Newton	LONDON ◊			*
Winsor & Newton	REGENCY			*
Winsor & Newton	WINTON ◊			*
Zipatone, Inc.	BOCOUR BELLINI ◊		*	
Pigments, Dry Ground				
Winsor & Newton	ARTISTS' ◊			*

◊ Some products in this line do not bear the CP, AP or Health Label/Non-Toxic Seal.

(Table 3-2 continued)

PRODUCTS AND MANUFACTURERS	BRAND NAMES	CP SEAL	AP SEAL	HL/NT SEAL
PAINTS (Continued)				
Tempera, Cake				
Binney&Smith(Canada)	CRAYOLA	*		
Dixon Ticonderoga	PRANG	*		
Weber Costello	ALPHACOLOR	*		
Winsor & Newton	REEVES TEMPERABLOCK		*	
Tempera, Liquid				
Avalon Industries	COLOR CRAFT	*		
Avalon Industries	SPECTRUM		*	
Binney & Smith	ARTISTA II	*		
Binney & Smith	CRAYOLA	*		
Binney & Smith	CRAYOLA FLUORESCENT		*	
Binney & Smith	TEM-PRA-TONE	*		
Dick Blick Co.	BLICK CITY	*		
Dick Blick Co.	STROKEMASTER	*		
C2F, Inc.	PRO ART		*	
Cardinal School	CARDINAL SCHOOL	*		
Chroma Acrylics	CHROMACRYL TEMPRA I	*		
Chroma Acrylics	CHROMACRYL TEMPRA II	*		
H. S. Crocker Co.	SIERRA	*		
Delta/Shiva	SHIVA PROFESSIONAL ARTISTS		*	
Dixon Ticonderoga	AMERICAN CRAYON	*		
Dixon Ticonderoga	COLORART	*		
Dixon Ticonderoga	PRANG	*		
J. L. Hammett Co.	ART UTILITY	*		
J. L. Hammett Co.	HAMMETT SCHOOL TEMPERA	*		
Leisure Craft	LEISURE TONE	*		
NASCO International	NASCO COUNTRY SCHOOL	*		
Palmer Paint	LIQUID TEMPRA	*		
Palmer Paint	ULTRA TEMPRA	*		
Pyramid of Urbana	PYRAMID PPC		*	
Rich Art Color Co.	LIQ FRESCO/RICH GEL	*		
Rich Art Color Co.	RICH ART SCHOOL		*	
Rock Paint Distrib'g	PEACOCK	*		
Sargent Art	GOTHIC	*		
Sargent Art	SARGENT	*		
Sax Arts & Crafts	TRUE COLOR	*		
Sax Arts & Crafts	VERSATEMP		*	
Triarco Arts & Crafts	TRIARCO		*	
Utrecht Mfg. Co.	UTRECHT		*	
Weber Costello	ALPHABRITE	*		
Weber Costello	ALPHACOLOR	*		
Weber Costello	WEBCO		*	
Tempera, Powder				
Avalon Industries	COLOR CRAFT	*		
Avalon Industries	SPECTRUM		*	
Binney & Smith	ARTISTA II	*		
Binney & Smith	CRAYOLA	*		
Dick Blick Co.	BLICK CITY	*		
Dixon Ticonderoga	AMERICAN CRAYON	*		
Dixon Ticonderoga	COLORART		*	
Dixon Ticonderoga	PRANG	*		
J. L. Hammett Co.	ART UTILITY	*		
Palmer Paint	PALMER DRY TEMPRA	*		
Rich Art Color Co.	FRESCO		*	
Sargent Art	GOTHIC	*		
Sargent Art	SARGENT	*		
Weber Costello	ALPHABRITE	*		
Weber Costello	WEBCO		*	
Vinyls				
Lefranc & Bourgeois	FLASHE ‡		*	
Water Colors, Dry Pan				
Daler-Rowney	ROWNEY ARTISTS ‡		*	
M. Grumbacher, Inc.	SEE FOR YOURSELF		*	
Winsor & Newton	REEVES WATER COLOUR TABLETS		*	
Winsor & Newton	SKETCHERS			
Water Colors, Semi-Moist				
Avalon Industries	COLOR CRAFT	*		
Binney & Smith	ARTISTA II/PEACOCK	*		
Binney & Smith	CRAYOLA	*		
Binney&Smith(Canada)	CRAYOLA		*	
Dixon Ticonderoga	AMERICAN CRAYON		*	
Dixon Ticonderoga	COLORART		*	
Dixon Ticonderoga	KOPY KAT	*		
Dixon Ticonderoga	PRANG	*		
J. L. Hammett Co.	ART UTILITY	*		
Salis International	DR. PH. MARTIN'S BLEED PROOF WHITE		*	

PRODUCTS AND MANUFACTURERS	BRAND NAMES	CP SEAL	AP SEAL	HL/NT SEAL
Water Colors, Semi-Moist (Continued)				
Salis International	DR. PH. MARTIN'S FLO-2 WHITE		*	
Salis International	DR. PH. MARTIN'S GRAPH-X WHITE		*	
Salis International	DR. PH. MARTIN'S RADIANT CONCENTRATED		*	
Sargent Art	SARGENT (22 SERIES)	*		
Sargent Art	SARGENT (66 SERIES)		*	
Steig Products	INKABLE WHITE		*	
Steig Products	LUMA BRILLIANT CONCENTRATED		*	
Steig Products	LUMA SOLAR CHROMATIC		*	
Steig Products	LUMA WHITE HIGH OPACITY		*	
Steig Products	PRO BLACK		*	
Steig Products	PRO WHITE RETOUCH WHITE		*	
Steig Products	Q WHITE RETOUCH WHITE		*	
Steig Products	STEIG WHITE		*	
Winsor & Newton	ARTISTS' PROFESSIONAL ‡			*
Water Colors, Tube				
Binney & Smith	LIQUITEX ‡		*	
Daler-Rowney	ROWNEY ARTISTS ‡			*
Delta/Shiva	SHIVA TRANSPARENT ‡		*	
M. Grumbacher, Inc.	ACADEMY			*
Hunt Manufacturing	SPEEDBALL PROFESSIONAL		*	
Lefranc & Bourgeois	AQUARELLE 600 ‡		*	
Martin/F. Weber Co.	WEBER			*
Pentel of America	SW-15 WATER COLOR DYES		*	
Utrecht Mfg. Co.	UTRECHT ‡		*	
Winsor & Newton	ARTISTS' PROFESSIONAL ‡			*
Winsor & Newton	LONDON ‡			*
PASTELS				
Oil Pastels				
Pentel of America	PHN-36 OIL PASTELS			*
Pentel of America	PTA-50 OIL PASTELS			*
Pentel of America	PTS-15 PENTEL DYE STICKS		*	
Sakura Color Products	CRAY-PAS		*	
Sakura Color Products	CHUBBIES		*	
Sakura Color Products	DELUXE STICKS		*	
Sakura Color Products	FOR ARTISTS' USE		*	
Sakura Color Products	JUMBO		*	
Sakura Color Products	JUNIOR		*	
Sakura Color Products	LARGE SIZE		*	
Sakura Color Products	SQUARE STICKS		*	
Sakura Color Products	SQUARE TYPE		*	
Sakura Color Products	SUPER		*	
Soft Pastels				
Royal Talens	REMBRANDT		*	
PHOTO EMULSIONS				
Hunt Manufacturing	SPEEDBALL (BLUE)			*
RESTORATION/CONSERVATION PRODUCTS				
M. Grumbacher, Inc.	RETOUCH			*
Martin/F. Weber Co.	WEBER ADHESIVE PREPARATION			*
Winsor & Newton	WINTON PICTURE CLEANER			*
SCREEN PRINTING INKS & MEDIUMS				
Acrylic				
Hunt Manufacturing	SPEEDBALL PERMANENT		*	
Textile				
Decart, Inc.	DEKA-PRINT			*
Hunt Manufacturing	SPEEDBALL NO-HEAT		*	
Hunt Manufacturing	SPEEDBALL TEXTILE WATER-SOLUBLE		*	
Water Soluble				
Hunt Manufacturing	SPEEDBALL WATER-SOLUBLE		*	
Accessories, Water Base				
Hunt Manufacturing	SPEEDBALL DRAWING FLUID (BLUE)			*
Hunt Manufacturing	SPEEDBALL SCREEN FILLERS		*	

‡ Some products in this line do not bear the CP, AP or Health Label/Non-Toxic Seal.

(Table 3-2 continued)

PRODUCTS AND MANUFACTURERS	BRAND NAMES	CP SEAL	AP SEAL	HL/NT SEAL
SOLVENTS				
Solvent Base				
Winsor & Newton	ARTIST'S ACRYLIC VARNISH REMOVER			*
Winsor & Newton	OIL OF SPIKE LAVENDER			*
Detergent Cleaners				
Winsor & Newton	ART GEL			*
Winsor & Newton	ARTGUARD			*
Winsor & Newton	ART WIPES			*

* Some products in this line do not bear the CP, AP or Health Label/Non-Toxic Seal.

Courtesy The Art and Craft Materials Institute Inc.

(Table 3-2 continued)

Social Development

Infants begin life as asocial, egocentric beings with little regard for the needs of others. Through socialization they are introduced to a wider arena of family, relatives, and significant others. Their individual desires are slowly curbed in response to the needs of others. Young children are egocentric and may need assistance in learning how to share; wait patiently; take turns; listen to others; and respect the property, rights, and ideas of others. They can also express empathy in appreciating the plight of others hurt or in trouble.

According to Erikson (1963), it is important for parents and caregivers to help

- infants develop a sense of trust rather than mistrust

- toddlers develop a sense of autonomy rather than doubt or shame

- preschoolers develop a sense of initiative rather than guilt

Young children are struggling with their freedom. At times they will be independent and autonomous. At other times they will be dependent, seeking comfort, security, and reassurance. Young children are talkers and socializers. They learn language and social skills from interacting with others, observing significant models, and witnessing the effects of their behavior upon others. For example, a young child who constantly snatches toys from others may find that they refuse to include her in their play.

Young children are interested in themselves: who they are, what they look like, what they know, and what they can do. Their interest also extends to their peers and the immediate community. They enjoy being part of a social group other than their family.

Art and Social Development Art helps children learn about themselves and others. Children validate their uniqueness by making a personal statement through art. "This is my chalk mark," says Deidra. It is a part of her, an extension of her self, and unlike others. Missy finds out that she prefers using clay to pasting. She likes to work intently alone, away from the noise and social interaction. Missy is independent. Art helps children become comfortable with themselves, learning what they like and dislike and what they can and cannot do. Yet Missy rarely has the art center all to herself. The classroom is a social setting, and she is learning how to interact positively with others. The art center has rules that protect the welfare of both the group and the equipment. In turn, children learn responsibility for cleanup and proper return of materials to their rightful place. This is difficult for Missy, who is an only child and is used to getting her own way at home. Slowly, she is learning to share materials, take turns, and wait patiently.

Emotional Development

Most young children like themselves—who they are, what their name is, what they look like, and what they can do. It is our job to help them continue to feel good about themselves. The concept of one's self is in a very formative stage during early childhood. Young children need an abundance of opportunities to experience mastery, success, and acceptance and to witness their own competence: "Look, teacher, I did it all by myself. Good for me!" Young children may transfer their parental attachment to their teacher or caregiver. They may express love and affection, and be overly possessive. They may be jealous of their peers and expect or demand a caregiver's total time, interest, attention, and praise.

Art and Emotional Development   Art is an emotionally pleasurable experience. Most children express happiness, joy, and pride in their art. In turn, this results in positive mental health and an expression of feelings. Young children are emotional beings, and art allows intense involvement. Art helps children nonverbally express those objects, ideas, people, places, experiences, events, and feelings that are emotionally significant. Often, a child is unable or unwilling to verbally discuss highly emotional topics or feelings about self, family, and friends. Art, however, allows these feelings, fantasies, fears, and frustrations to surface and be expressed (see Figure 3-4). It allows children the opportunity to represent in fantasy what cannot happen in reality. Negative feelings and impulses can be released in a positive, acceptable way through art. For

Figure 3-4 Through art children can represent and master unpleasant experiences.

example, anger against another cannot be physically expressed in the classroom, but it can be portrayed and expressed through art. "Show me in your picture how mad you are right now" (see Figure 3-5).

ART THERAPY

Art, play, music, dance, literature, dramatics, and puppetry are vehicles for psychotherapy. Although therapy with adults is largely verbal, children profit from nonverbal forms.

Qualified therapists look for some of the following in art:

- An expressive use of colors. Red, bright orange, or black may be used repeatedly to symbolize objects of emotional importance.

Black may be used to represent fear or death, red for rage or love.

- Personal meaning behind the repeated use of a symbol. Art therapists try to "crack the code" or discover the link between the artistic symbol and the unconscious. What meaning lies behind a child's repeated portrayal of a charging horse, monster, knife, or blood?

- An exaggeration, distortion, or overemphasis of objects reflecting emotional signifi-

Figure 3-5   Art allows children to express how they feel.

sibling when drawing the family. Art allows children to accomplish in fantasy what they cannot do in reality. For a child with sibling rivalry, it may mean the elimination of that sibling, at least on paper.

- Placement provides clues to emotional significance. Objects that are drawn large and in the center of the paper are important. Children with low self-concepts may draw themselves off in a corner or in the far background. They may also be hidden behind larger objects of emotional significance placed in the center foreground. Painful fear-evoking content may also be reduced in size and safely "tucked away" in a far corner of the picture.

- Defense mechanisms that protect the ego appear in art. Harmful or painful thoughts and experiences that are repressed in reality may be safely uncovered and expressed

cance. Perhaps this is why young children first draw themselves as a large head with protruding arms, mounted on stick legs. They like their face and how they look, so they draw it big. Arms and legs help them do things and get around, so they are also emphasized. Refer to the self-portrait (Figure 3-6) drawn by a four-year-old. Note the "wound" on the face. At the time she had a bruise from a fall and was very vivid in pointing it out, representing and exaggerating it in her self-portrait.

- The omission or underemphasis of objects also provides emotional clues. For example, children with low self-concepts often omit themselves or make themselves tiny by comparison with others. Children with intense sibling rivalry may simply omit that

Figure 3-6   Children include, distort, and exaggerate what is personally meaningful to them.

through art. The child who has been abused may portray herself with unusual colors or designs on her body. Identification may be reflected in a child's repeated use of a symbol with which to identify. The aggressive child identifies with the soldier or the marauding tiger. The fearful child becomes the scared witch, at least on paper.

There are inherent dangers in the use of art therapy. First, it requires extensive training. Second, one needs many samples of a child's artwork over a long period of time to recognize patterns, rather than making a snap judgment or rash interpretation. For example, it would be naive to assume that a child's preoccupation with the color red indicates a fixation with blood, violence, fire, or rage. There are many possible explanations. Red may simply be the child's favorite color, the nearest color, or the only one available. Although they are untrained in art therapy, early childhood educators can use art to help children nonverbally express their feelings and emotions. Our aim is to provide a vehicle for emotional expression and release rather than analysis or interpretation.

Art enhances a child's self-concept and feelings about self. Since art guarantees success, children experience mastery, which further enhances a positive self-concept. It is important for young children to have a positive self-concept, since it is a prerequisite to learning. Children who do not feel good about themselves do not learn. Their energy and attention are focused on fear of failure and self-doubt. It is a lot wiser to focus our attention on developing a positive self-concept in the early years as a preventive measure rather than attempting to remediate a negative self-concept in older children who may have given up on themselves, learning, and life.

Cognitive Development

The early years are a time of very rapid cognitive development. By age two, the brain has reached 75 percent of its adult weight. By age five, the brain has attained 90 percent of its adult weight. The early years provide an opportunity for mental stimulation and challenge. Young children are self-motivated, curious explorers who are eager to learn about themselves, others, and the world. They need concrete materials to manipulate; problems to solve; people, places, and events to experience; and a time to discuss and ask questions. Books and the media may provide important vicarious, second-hand information, but they are no substitute for direct experience.

According to Piaget, young children's thinking is action-oriented and largely nonverbal. He believed that thinking precedes the development of language. Language enhances thinking, but is not its source. Children understand and know more than they can verbalize. Likewise, what a child can say or discuss may not be an accurate indicator of intelligence. A young child's understanding and representation of the world proceeds through stages.

Overview of Piaget's Stages of Development

During Piaget's *sensory motor stage* (birth to age two), infant thinking is limited to sensory impressions and motoric behaviors. A toy rattle is something to be held, shaken, dropped, stared at, listened to, smelled, and tasted. There is no thinking about the rattle apart from these sensory and motoric actions.

Toddlers attain significant cognitive achievements as they leave the sensory motor stage (birth to age two) and enter the *pre-operational stage* (ages two through seven). Representation frees toddlers from a reliance on action-based thinking. They can now form mental images, symbolize, and think about their world in the absence of direct action.

Preschoolers in Piaget's pre-operational stage (ages two through seven) are using symbols, including play, art, and language, to represent their

Figure 3-7   Children draw what they know.

world. They continue to construct and refine their concepts of time, space, classification, seriation, and number. Preschoolers in Piaget's preoperational stage think in ways that are qualitatively different from adult logic or reason.

Children in the primary grades have entered Piaget's stage of *concrete operations* (ages seven through eleven). An operation is an internalized action. Older children have attained several important cognitive operations, including reversibility, conservation, classification, and seriation as well as addition, subtraction, multiplication, and division, that help them think in more logical terms. Their thinking, however, is still bound to the concrete. They are unable to think abstractly.

Art and Cognitive Development   Eisner (1976) makes one of the strongest cases for the relationship between art and thinking, learning, and overall academic performance. Art reflects what a child knows about the world (see Figure 3-7). Children who have directly experienced a wide variety of people, places, and objects will have an array of things to choose from when doing art.

Children who have neither been to a zoo nor been exposed to pets will probably not include animals in their art. One must know about something before one can recreate it through art (see Figure 3-8).

Translating ideas, concepts, and experiences into art involves many thinking skills. One must decide what to represent and how to execute it. "To make a dinosaur, should I use clay, mark-

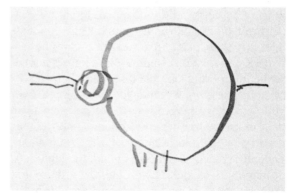

Figure 3-8   A field trip to the zoo prompted one child to make this elephant.

ers, or paint?'' thinks Nate. He must plan, organize, and make choices. Art involves concentration, staying on a task, and seeing it through to completion—all important work skills and habits. ''What steps are involved and how should I go about it?'' ponders Nate. He decides to draw an outline with pencil, trace over it with thick marker pen, cut it out, and then paint it at the easel. Art involves problem solving. Nate needs dark paint when only the three primary colors are available. He decides to mix all three together into a muddy color that he thinks is just the right color for a ''beast.'' Nate becomes upset when the muddy color runs into the white of the dinosaur's eye. Using too much water has thinned down the paint. Nate has learned about cause and effect. He hypothesizes and gets a crumpled paper towel to gently blot it out. It is impossible to document all the thinking that is going on in Nate's head while he is doing art. By the way, Nate is a bright four-year-old who is largely nonverbal. Art provides an opportunity for him to symbolize what he knows but cannot and will not discuss. Over time, he may. Through art Nate can communicate with himself and others. ''Yes, Nate, I see how hard you worked to get the eye just right,'' says his teacher. The thinking cycle moves from planning to implementing and reworking, if necessary. The author believes that the thinking side of art has been neglected in favor of identifying physical, social, emotional, and creative ends. The major benefits of art may very well be cognitive in nature.

Through art children learn about the concepts of color, shape, size, line, texture, and other artistic elements. For example, Beth knows her basic geometric shapes. She discovers that squares combine to form a rectangle. Painting red over yellow makes orange. Lines that intersect form an X or cross shape. White added to blue lightens it and makes it the perfect color for Beth's sky. Difficult spatial concepts, including right, left, up, down, over, beside, through, next to, on top of, between, and under, are represented in art. These spatial concepts will be vital to reading and comprehension at a later time.

Art serves as an index of a child's thinking. We can look at children's artwork, particularly painting and drawing, and find out what they know about their world, what they consider important, and how they choose to represent it. Detailed artwork indicates that a child knows much about that particular subject. Children who can express what they know about their world will be at an advantage later when they are expected to write and read about it. Signs (words) spoken or in print must have some referent. Art gives children the opportunity to symbolize that referent and serves as a bridge between object and sign (see Figure 3-9).

Creative Development

Creativity begins during infancy as babies invent solutions to problems and engage in novel

Figure 3-9 Young children are concrete learners. Art helps them symbolize their experience.

Figure 3-10   Art fosters creative expression.

actions. According to Torrance (1965), young children are at their peak of creative functioning, which declines with age. Young children are highly imaginative. Imagination is strongly related to creativity. Rewarding a child's sense of autonomy and initiative (Erikson, 1963) enhances creative functioning.

Art and Creative Development   As seen in Figure 3-10, art allows children to express their own creative uniqueness, originality, and individuality. Children's artistic expressions may be vaguely similar yet still significantly different from all others. Art is the perfect medium for young children, who are so highly imaginative. Their fantasy can be given form through art. Art is an open-ended activity that encourages discovery, exploration, experimentation, and invention. All of these skills are vital to creativity. Gene thinks about what will happen if he uses two paint brushes at a time. He tries it out and is pleased with the double-stroked result. He asks

his teacher to help him tie a rubber band around three paint brushes. Through active experimenting he invents a new way to paint.

FOOD FOR THOUGHT: FOOD FOR ART?

Opinion is divided on the use of food in art projects. Breakfast cereal and macaroni are often strung on string or yarn for necklaces. Beans and popcorn are glued on paper. Rice is used in collage. Younger children enjoy hand painting with pudding, frosting, or whipped topping. Infants and toddlers like to use applesauce. The above activities are enjoyable and may serve important developmental and sensory ends. The author, however, advises against the use of food in art for several reasons.

1. Food is expensive. If parents want to donate, they can bring in junk recyclable materials, ingredients for cooking, or other

more crucial and perhaps costly supplies such as wooden blocks, books, or puzzles.

2. Food is a precious commodity that many take for granted and waste.

3. There is such a pressing need for food in Third World countries that the casual use of food in art can be questioned on moral and ethical grounds.

4. The use of food in an art activity may offend some cultural groups who use that food item for religious or ethnic celebration.

5. Foods like frosting, pudding, and whipped topping are highly caloric and contain an abundance of sugar.

In summary, there are many sound alternatives to the use of food in art. Small straw sections can replace macaroni for stringing. Sand rather than rice can be glued. Styrofoam squiggles can replace beans in a collage activity. Be creative in identifying alternatives to food in art activities.

SUMMARY

We have moved from an overview of wholistic child development to links between art and a child's development. This unit explained how art fosters a child's physical, social, emotional, cognitive, and creative development. Art was viewed as a developmentally appropriate and important activity. Knowledge of a young child's physical needs and abilities suggested strategies and materials for helping the child learn to cut with scissors. Although art is pleasurable and multisensory, potential art hazards do exist. Guidelines for identifying toxic art supplies and suggested alternatives were provided. Although art fosters emotional expression and release, it was not recommended that art therapy be attempted without adequate training. The relationship between creativity and art has long been recognized, but the link between art and thinking may be as strong. Although the use of food in art activities appears to be creative, objections were raised. It was recommended that the teacher discover alternatives to the use of food in art.

SUGGESTED ACTIVITIES

1. Observe a young child actively involved in an art activity. Record what the child says and does. How did this art experience help the child physically, socially, emotionally, cognitively, and creatively?

2. Observe children aged three, four, and five using scissors. Using the guidelines in this unit, what recommendations can you make for each with respect to tools, paper, activity, or teacher input?

3. Use the guidelines and criteria for safe art materials to double-check an art supply cabinet or closet. State your findings and recommendations.

4. Arrange to work with a difficult or troubled young child. Ask the child to draw or paint how he or she is feeling. Encourage the child to discuss or talk about the picture. Encourage emotional expression without formally attempting art therapy.

REVIEW

A. Fill in the aspects of a child's development.
   1.
   2.
   3.
   4.
   5.

B. At your midyear open house, a few parents wonder why so much time is devoted to art in your preschool program. Using the wholistic model of child development, what could you say to justify your art program?

C. A parent is alarmed because her five-year-old is always drawing ghosts and graveyards. She fears that her child is abnormal or emotionally disturbed. What are some possible explanations for this child's art?

D. Suggest a nonfood art activity for each of the following:
   Activity: Alternative:

   1. printing with cut vegetables

   2. gluing breakfast cereal on a self-portrait for facial features

   3. sprinkling powdered gelatin over white glue for sparkling lines

   4. making ice cream for snack and finger painting with it

Unit 4

Children Are Unique Individuals

OBJECTIVES

After studying this unit, the student will be able to

- Discuss how individual differences express themselves
- List five guidelines for working with young children with exceptionalities and/or multicultural backgrounds
- Discuss how art can help exceptional and multicultural children

INTRODUCTION

Young children are unique individuals, and few will totally conform to our developmental norms for what is normal, typical, or average. Instead, they come to us with a variety of differences resulting from background, family, and individual factors. This may prove both fascinating and frustrating as we strive to meet their individual needs, interests, and abilities. Exceptionalities and multicultural backgrounds may be the most extreme form of individual difference. Direct contact and knowledge can overcome any stereotypes and help set only positive expecta-

tions. Art is an excellent activity for children, who profit from nonverbal symbolic expression, social interaction, and mastery. Knowing young children, valuing individual differences, and acting on this information will help us to provide appropriate art activities that enhance the wholistic development of each and every child in our care.

GOING BEYOND NORMAL, TYPICAL, AND AVERAGE

A working knowledge of child development can be a very useful tool. Knowing the needs, interests, and abilities of young children at a given age or stage can help us design developmentally appropriate art activities. We can act on what we know. This knowledge of child development, however, will give us only a general pattern of what is "normal, typical, or average." Few children conform to the norm or can be considered typical or average. How boring life and caregiving would be if each of us were cloned to be normal, typical, or average! Children are unique individuals. Their physical, social, emotional, cognitive, and creative development will reflect individual differences resulting from both heredity and environmental influences. Chronological age can be very misleading. Although our knowledge of child development tells us that children learn to skip at age 5, Leslie at 5½ cannot. Her own timetable for physical development does not match the norm. In terms of skipping she may not be typical of the average five-year-old. She need not be labeled slow, immature, or developmentally delayed. If Leslie's overall physical profile departs radically from the norm, however, referral and remediation might be warranted.

VALUING INDIVIDUAL DIFFERENCES

Individual differences are the spice of life; they make teaching young children both fascinating and challenging. Within any one age group there will be a wide range of commonalities in terms of physical, social, emotional, cognitive, and creative needs, interests, and abilities. There will also be significant individual differences. Obviously, it would be much simpler to work with a group of three-, four-, or five-year-olds with similar, if not identical, developmental characteristics. But the aim of early childhood education is to foster the development of unique individuals, not to mass-produce robots.

Differences in development and learning that result from heredity, environment, or the interaction of both are expressed in the following ways:

- Background: race, culture, and social class
- Family: family size, siblings, birth order, divorce and remarriage, parental educational and occupational levels, nutrition, parental teaching style, and the possibility of child abuse or neglect
- Individual: sex, personality and temperament, motivation, learning style, and personal interests

Identifying and discussing every factor that can potentially influence the development of individual differences is clearly beyond the scope of this section. Further, background, family, and individual influences interact and may produce different effects on different individuals.

PROVIDING FOR YOUNG CHILDREN WITH INDIVIDUAL DIFFERENCES

The greatest expression of individual differences will be for children with

- exceptionalities
- multicultural backgrounds

SOME GENERAL GUIDELINES FOR WORKING WITH EXCEPTIONAL YOUNG CHILDREN

1. Accept the child unconditionally, including disabilities, handicapping conditions, and limitations. Accept the child "as is," not as what we might like him or her to be, do, or look like.

2. Build on the child's strengths and capitalize on what he or she can do. Slowly, work on weaknesses and deficiencies.

3. Adapt the physical environment to meet the child's needs. Rearrange classroom space and furniture. Remove any potential hazards or obstacles. See Figure 4-1.

4. Encourage independence and wean the child from overdependence upon you. Ex-

Figure 4-1   All children should have access to art.

pect the child to do some things independently, and reward him or her for doing them.

5. Treat all children equally. Being handicapped is no excuse for behavior that continually violates classroom rules. Handicapped children need and want to be treated like everyone else.

6. Be informed and educate your students about specific handicapping conditions. Discuss these in an open and honest way, giving children time and space to express their feelings and fears. For example, children need to know about a seizure and what they can do for a child who is having one.

7. Provide multisensory stimulation. Incorporate an array of things for the children to visually inspect, listen to, touch, smell, and taste. Capitalize and build on sensory strengths.

8. Allow ample time, practice, and repetition for learning. Handicapped children will have developmental delays and will need

time and additional practice if learning is to occur.

9. Help the handicapped child to be successful and experience mastery. Systematically break down complex tasks into smaller, manageable steps.

10. Help children develop a positive self-concept by feeling good about themselves. Help them to view themselves as unique individuals with one or more significant individual differences that just happen to be more noticeable or extreme.

PROVIDING FOR YOUNG CHILDREN WITH MULTICULTURAL BACKGROUNDS

Multicultural backgrounds include racial, ethnic, and cultural differences. Racial differences are expressed in skin color. Cultural differences are expressed in foods, dress, language, customs, values, and celebrations. Like exceptional-

Figure 4-2   Art helps all children make a very personal statement.

ities, racial and cultural differences extend, enhance, and enrich society.

SOME GENERAL GUIDELINES FOR WORKING WITH YOUNG CHILDREN WITH MULTICULTURAL BACKGROUNDS

1. Accept the child unconditionally, including ethnicity. Accept the child "as is," not as what we might prefer in the way of looks, skin color, dress, or customs.

2. Value, accept, respect, and encourage the child's native language and ethnicity as a strength and as an expression of a unique individual difference.

3. Build on the child's strengths and what he or she can do. Provide instruction in the child's native language. Slowly, work to help the child to become bilingual and proficient in standard English.

4. Help the child to feel comfortable in school. The sights, sounds, and surroundings may be unfamiliar and overwhelming to some children who have nothing to compare it with. See Figure 4-2.

5. Treat all children equally. Ethnic children need and want to be treated fairly. Guidelines, rules, and rewards should apply to all children.

6. Be informed about ethnic differences. Take a course on multicultural education. Eat at ethnic restaurants, sample ethnic foods, visit ethnic stores and shops, participate in ethnic celebrations, learn a second language, travel to a foreign country, become bilingual.

7. Discuss and study similarities and differences among people. It is important for children to focus on human similarities as a framework for the individual differences resulting from culture and ethnicity. Some examples include

> What are some things that all people need? We all need housing and food. Where he came from, Lin lived on a houseboat with his parents and grandparents. What do you think it would be like to live on a boat? Now he lives in an apartment. How many of you have ever lived in an apartment? I did while I was going to school. So even though Lin talks different than we do, he is still a lot like us. He has his own language and a place to live, just as we do. We are going to help Lin learn our language, and he will teach us his.

8. Involve the parents. Some ethnic parents may have great reservations about school. Some may be embarrassed about their lack of standard English. Others may be ashamed of their minimal level of education. Some will place great value on their child's education and may have unrealistically high expectations. All will be proud of their culture and willing to share their ethnicity if encouraged and invited. Help them to feel comfortable. Let them know that they have something very special that the children would like to know more about. For example, Lin's mother was invited in to cook a rice dish with the children for a snack. Others could come dressed in native costume or bring in cultural artifacts. Their presence and participation will make their child feel good about being in school.

9. Help ethnic children to be successful and experience mastery. Many of them are experiencing *culture shock*. They are aware of their language and cultural differences. They need an abundance of things they can do successfully rather than an endless list of things they need to remediate.

10. Help ethnic children to feel good about themselves just the way they are. They may be different, but differences are OK.

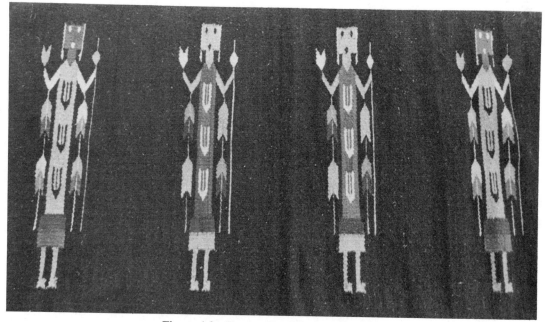

Figure 4-3 Every culture has its own art.

We are all different. Being different does not mean being bad or wrong. Ethnic children have a language, culture, customs, and individual worth. It just happens to be different from the white middle-class culture of many schools.

Art is recommended as a basic activity in multicultural classrooms. Since art is a form of nonverbal expression, there is no language prerequisite and no need to understand verbal directions. Children can discover on their own or observe each other. Art time is a good opportunity for children who do not speak standard English to hear and informally practice standard English. The setting for art is usually relaxed, and the child may feel less inhibited about speaking. Art time is also a good time for standard-English-speaking, monocultural children to hear and practice other languages. Ethnic children enhance and enrich any classroom. Art is also a good vehicle for teaching about cultures. All cultures have their respective art forms (see Figure 4-3). For example, Japanese children practice origami. Although it is difficult, most children can learn some simple paper folds.

SUMMARY

Few children match the developmental norms for what might be considered normal, typical, or average at a given age or stage of development. One goal of early childhood education is to foster the development of children as unique individuals. Our aim is not to clone children who are typical or average. A child's uniqueness is expressed in individual differences resulting from background, family, and individual influences. Young children who have a handicapping condition or who speak nonstandard English provide an additional challenge.

Art is a developmentally important activity for all children, regardless of developmental ability, disability, lag, or difference.

SUGGESTED ACTIVITIES

1. Observe in a room of same-age children. Note the expression of individual differences within the same age range. Record your findings.

2. Observe or volunteer to work with young exceptional children who have been mainstreamed.

3. Observe or volunteer to work in an early childhood bilingual or multicultural program.

REVIEW

A. List the major ways in which differences in development and learning are expressed.
   1.
   2.
   3.

B. List general guidelines for working with exceptional young children.
   1.
   2.
   3.
   4.
   5.

C. List general guidelines for working with children from multicultural backgrounds.
   1.
   2.
   3.
   4.
   5.

Unit 5

Understanding Creativity

OBJECTIVES

After studying this unit, the student will be able to

- Explain creativity as a product, process, skill, set of personality traits, and set of environmental conditions
- Compare and contrast creativity with conformity and convergent thinking
- Discuss the relationship between creativity and intelligence

INTRODUCTION

What or who do you associate with creativity? Do you think of architecture by Frank Lloyd Wright, a play by Shakespeare, a painting by Picasso, Henry Ford's Model T, or the *Nutcracker Suite?* These are classic examples of the creative works of some very creative individuals. You probably had other examples. Children were not included in this list. Were they included in yours? Let us focus on creativity and see how it specifically relates to young children. Consider the following:

- Jenny, age four, puts all the small building blocks into a large plastic pot. She pretends to cook beef stew over her play stove.

- A preschool teacher asks her group of three-year-olds to name an object you need to take outside with you on a rainy day. Shana replies, "A rainbrella."

- A kindergarten teacher has cut three white circles of different sizes. She pastes them vertically from smallest to largest and makes a snowman. William, however, seriates and pastes his on top of each other. He proudly states, "That's how my snowman looks when I fly over him in my airplane."

These three young children have not created masterpieces. Still, creativity is reflected in Jenny's play, Shana's answer, and William's picture. Gifted and talented adults and young children are capable of creativity.

BEGINNINGS OF CREATIVITY

Creativity begins in infancy as babies manipulate toys, explore space, discover their body parts, test hunches about their immediate world, and even solve problems. For example, Lea wants a toy rattle that she has accidentally kicked to the foot of her crib. Through trial-and-error behavior she discovers that she can get the toy by tugging at the blanket it rests on (see Figure 5-1).

There are many possible examples of creativity in adults and young children. Merely identifying examples, however, does not help us understand the nature of creativity. Just what is creativity? How will we know if something or someone is creative? One way to attempt to understand creativity is by defining it.

DEFINING CREATIVITY

There are many ways to define creativity. Perhaps this has added to the confusion, misunder-

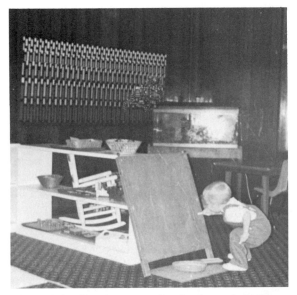

Figure 5-1 Creative expression begins early in life.

standing, and mystique surrounding it. People have different definitions for the same term. How would you define creativity? Some generally accepted definitions include

- The ability to see things in new ways
- Boundary breaking and going beyond the information given
- Thinking unconventionally
- Making something unique or original
- Combining unrelated things into something new

How does your definition compare with these? Torrance (1963), a pioneer in creativity, has chosen to define creativity as the process of sensing problems or gaps in information, forming ideas or hypotheses, and communicating the results. For example, two five-year-olds, Missy and Eric, want to build a school, but they have no blocks or pieces of wood. They consider using shoe boxes, which are fairly durable and stackable, for a base.

Although our attempts to define creativity may provide us with some general feel for the concept, there are other ways to better understand and explain creativity.

EXPLAINING CREATIVITY

Although there is no single definition of creativity, there are different ways to explain it. Creativity can be explained as a

- product
- process
- skill
- set of personality traits
- set of environmental conditions

Creativity as a Product

The light bulb was Edison's creative product. Bell invented the telephone. Both creators made a unique product that revolutionized society. Other creative products could include a musical score, medical cure, work of art, scientific principle, or law. Gifted creators include Mozart, Plato, Galileo, Newton, and Einstein, among others. Focusing exclusively on revolutionary products restricts creativity to a very small core of gifted elite. Most of us are truly uncreative by comparison.

According to this view, creative functioning is not accessible to the masses. Only a very small percentage of the general population, the gifted elite, can be considered creative as judged by their unique works.

This product view of creativity automatically excludes children, because few, if any, produce something that is truly novel or that contributes significantly to the advancement of society. Still, most adults would consider young children capable of creativity. For example, from a product perspective, there is nothing unique about mixing red and blue paint at the easel and creating pur-

ple. Either young children are uncreative or the product explanation for creativity is too narrow. Perhaps the product explanation should be qualified to state that the object created must be unique or new to the creator. If so, the swirling of purple paint may be considered creative for Brad, a toddler who has not yet discovered that red paint mixed with blue makes purple. Modifying a product explanation to reflect personal originality extends creativity to the activities of young children.

Creativity as a Process

A process approach to creativity holds that a person can engage in the creative process even though it may not result in a finished product. All people are capable of creative processing (see Figure 5-2). Creative processing includes thinking, speaking, playing, writing, dancing, singing, playing a musical instrument, experimenting with objects, transforming materials, and manipulating ideas and objects. Therefore, the art work

Figure 5-2 Creative processing by painting with a twig

of young children can be considered creative according to this process explanation. Artists, whether young or old, engage in the same processes when pounding clay, drawing, mixing colors, painting, weaving, and making a collage. In the early years, children's creative functioning emphasizes a process orientation. The emphasis is on making and doing rather than on completing a project. For example, children may paint but end up throwing the picture away or not claiming it to take home. The primary satisfaction is in the processing, the smearing with paint, rather than in what it turns out to be. Other young children, however, may also be product-oriented. Three-year-old Lisa delights in finishing her art projects and often insists on taking several examples home. Some children may have learned that a completed art product will bring praise from adults. Pictures that look like something may even get taped to the refrigerator door. Hopefully, young children will not abandon a creative process orientation in favor of making art products that look like something solely to please adults. This is not the essence of creativity. Artistic processing may not produce a souvenir. Evidence of a finished art product often justifies a child's existence in school. The finished picture shows what he or she did today. Young children should engage in artistic processing and product making for themselves. The child who fails to bring home a finished painting may be no less productive or creative than the one who insists on finishing a picture.

The product and process explanations for creativity are not mutually exclusive. Choosing the creative process over the product or vice versa should not be an either-or decision. The process and product are complementary. If it were not for the creative process, the production of creative products would be impossible. Creative products are built up through creative processing. Rome was not built in one day! It is unfair to acknowledge only the creative product. If the creative product remains the sole criterion for assessing creativity, it is obvious that creativity must be reserved for the gifted elite.

Creativity as a Skill

Although all children are capable of creativity, the potential to create remains dormant without practice. Creativity requires practice to flourish. With practice, the potential to create becomes a reality. For example, the skill of playing tennis is quickly lost without practice. Good tennis players practice frequently. So too the skill of creativity requires exercise to grow. Without practice, the ability to write, make music, sing, dance, and paint would cease. Creativity as a potential and skill requires exercise.

When a discussion of creativity arises, many adults are prone to reply, "I'm just not creative." Everyone seems to have a friend or relative who is creative, but not all people believe themselves to be creative. In part, this relates to the old idea of a creative elite and a product explanation for creativity. Still, all people evidence some degree of creativity, whether in writing, sewing, cooking, making crafts, pursuing hobbies, home decorating, or even teaching! It is important to find a creative outlet and practice the process or skill involved. What is your creative outlet?

Still, why do some adults feel themselves uncreative when by contrast young children are considered highly creative? What has happened between early childhood and adulthood? Research on creativity suggests that the child reaches a peak of creative functioning during the early childhood years. Torrance (1965) plots the degree of creative functioning versus age. Creativity peaks at about 4 to 4½ years of age and is followed by a sharp drop upon entrance into the elementary school. Perhaps the push for conformity, accountability, and academics in the elementary school accounts for this sharp drop. Yet this drop is not inevitable. Environmental conditions and practice can keep the spirit of creativity alive.

Creativity as a Set of Personality Traits

This approach attempts to identify the personality profile of highly creative individuals. Researchers have identified highly creative individuals and attempted to identify personality traits that these individuals share. Some of these personality traits include

- an openness to the new and unexpected
- a tolerance for ambiguity
- a willingness to experiment and take risks
- impulsivity
- curiosity
- a preference for complexity
- being highly intuitive
- sensitivity
- flexibility
- introversion
- individualism
- nonconformity, daring to be different
- independence
- playfulness
- a sense of humor
- prefers being alone, may be unsocial

The list of personality traits is extensive, and not every highly creative individual will possess all the traits. Also, the list of personality traits will vary depending on the researcher. Torrance (1962) has identified the following seven indicators of creativity that may be useful in identifying and explaining the behavior of the highly creative young child.

Curiosity The child's questioning is persistent and purposeful. Curiosity can be either verbal— "What is that?" or "Why?"—or nonverbal—manipulation and active exploration.

Flexibility If one approach fails, the creative child will try a variety of different approaches.

Sensitivity to Problems The child is quick to see gaps in information, exceptions to the rules, and contradictions in what is seen and heard.

Redefinition The child sees hidden meaning in statements that others accept at face value. New uses are found for familiar objects. The child sees connections between things that appear unrelated to others.

Self-Feeling The child has a feeling of self-importance and individuality. Self-direction permits the child to work alone. Merely following directions or conforming results in boredom.

Originality The child has surprising, uncommon, interesting ideas.

Insight The child has access to realms of the mind that the less creative visit only in their dreams. Much time is spent toying with ideas and possibilities.

Attempting to identify the one typical personality pattern of the highly creative individual may be impossible. There is too much variation among creative individuals. Still, a set of global traits may provide some assistance in identifying these individuals and understanding the nature of creativity.

Creativity as a Set of Environmental Conditions

If creativity is an inherent potential, there must be things that can be done to enhance or retard its development. Environmental conditions include people, places, objects, and experiences. Children do not create out of a vacuum. They need a source of inspiration or an experiential background from which to draw. For example, a child who has never visited an airport or been aboard a plane will have difficulty discussing these concepts or incorporating them into block play, dramatic play, movement, art, and other creative activities. By contrast, a child who has visited an airport and flown on a plane will be able to discuss these experiences and use them as pivots for creative expression. Parnes (1967)

Figure 5-3 Parents can discuss art with their children.

draws an analogy between a kaleidoscope and creativity. The more numerous and colorful the pieces in the drum of a kaleidoscope, the greater the variety of resulting shapes, colors, and patterns. Likewise, in creative expression, the greater one's background of experiences with people, places, and objects, the greater the range of possibilities to draw from in creative activity.

Home Environment   Obviously, the home environment is a critical factor in a child's development of creativity. Is there a home environment that optimizes the development of creativity? In MacKinnon's (1962) study of creative adults, he found the following family variables operating during their childhood:

- Parents respected their child.
- Parents had confidence in their child's ability.
- Parents granted their child unusual freedom to explore and make decisions.

- Discipline was almost always consistent and predictable.
- Family values stressed integrity, quality, intellectual and cultural efforts, success, and ambition.

The above factors and behaviors can be practiced in home and school settings to foster children's creative development (see Figure 5-3).

OBSTACLES TO CREATIVITY

Just as a stimulating environment and family factors can enhance creativity, negative conditions can restrict it. Four environmental conditions that provide potential obstacles to creativity include

- parents
- school
- sex role
- society, culture, and tradition

Parents

Parents often have certain expectations for their children. Unfortunately, creative children may not conform to these expectations. Highly creative children often question authority, limits, adult logic, and explanations. These children act and behave differently. Parents may view these creative behaviors as misbehavior. They may perceive and treat their creative child as odd, immature, abnormal, or naughty. Parents may need to be informed and educated about the nature of creativity through classroom observation, readings, and informal sessions in which they discuss creativity and engage in creative processing themselves.

School

The teacher may not understand, encourage, or value the creative child. Too often the creative child must operate in a school situation based entirely on conformity and convergent thinking. The child is taught that black is the color of night when he or she has experienced it as purple-blue or licorice. With the current emphasis on academics in early childhood education, there is a concern that less time will be spent on creative activities. It is also possible that some children feel confined in noncreative classrooms and "shut down" or rebel to protect their creative integrity. It is important for teachers to understand, value, and encourage creativity by providing an abundance of curricular activities to foster it.

Sex Roles

Sex roles limit boys and girls to certain types of behavior on the basis of biological sex. Creative functioning, however, transcends sex role barriers. Forcing children to conform to sex roles denies them their optimal development as individuals. We do children a disservice when we expect boys to be active, independent, and rugged and girls to be passive, dependent, and gentle. If sex roles were to dictate, boys would be denied access to quieter expressive activities and girls would be denied access to more active ma-

nipulative experiences. Either way someone loses, since both types of experience are vital to creative processing.

Society, Tradition, and Culture

Society, tradition, and culture are distinct concepts, but each dictates a certain set of behaviors, values, and attitudes. These are transmitted to children at a very early age in the form of expectations. Unfortunately, creative children may operate with a different agenda. Problems arise for highly creative children in a milieu where adults have all the answers and children are expected to fit into a rigid behavioral mold or pattern. Often, the rationale includes "That's the way it's done in our family" or "If it was good enough for me, it's good enough for you." It is important to respect, reinforce, and uphold the expectations of society, tradition, and one's culture without sacrificing individuality in the process.

COMPARING AND CONTRASTING CREATIVITY

Another way of attempting to understand and explain creativity is through comparison and contrast. One way to learn about a concept is by comparing and contrasting it with other concepts that are either similar or different.

Creativity vs. Conformity and Convergent Thinking

Convergent or noncreative thinking and behavior based on conformity are built into our educational system and reflected in our school goals. There are facts and bodies of knowledge that we want all children to possess. For example, children need to know that up is the opposite of down, that a triangle has three sides, that wheels are round, that STOP on the traffic sign does not mean to run, and that there are five pennies in a nickel. This type of knowledge involves memory and convergent thinking in that all children are expected to come up with the one right answer. Beyond this, conformity in school often entails behaving in a certain way, with an emphasis on sitting still, speaking only when spoken to, obeying, not challenging authority, not questioning, compliance, and doing what is generally expected. Obviously, conformity is important if groups of people are to get along, whether in school or in the wider society. When it is carried to extremes, however, an emphasis on conformity and convergent thinking can kill the creative spirit.

Creativity vs. Intelligence

Creativity can also be compared and contrasted with intelligence. It has sometimes been erroneously assumed that a high IQ is needed to be creative. The research, however, indicates that high scores on tests of creativity do not correlate with high scores on IQ tests. A high IQ says something about intelligence, but it cannot guarantee high creativity. This is easy to understand, since answering items on an IQ test requires remembering bits and pieces of factual information and involves convergent or noncreative thinking. Thus, it is possible for a child with a high IQ to be quite uncreative compared with other children of average intelligence. It does seem, however, that some basic level of intellectual functioning and an average IQ near 100 is required for creativity. For example, a child must have some basic knowledge of the properties of a milk carton and transportation before he or she can creatively transform an empty milk carton into a moving van. Therefore, using tests of intelligence to screen highly creative children must be done judiciously. They are merely one of many tools, including teacher observation and parental reports, that can be used. According to Torrance (1962), if we were to identify children as gifted solely on the basis of IQ tests, we would eliminate approximately 70 percent of the most creative. In summary, although some amount of intelligence is a prerequisite for creativity, a high IQ does not guarantee high creativity. In turn, average intelligence does not necessarily mean mediocre creative ability. Intelligence is merely one factor influencing creativity.

Since children's thinking is a vital concern of early childhood educators, it may be interesting to further pursue the relationship between intelligence and creativity. It appears that the profile for the highly intelligent child and that for the highly creative child do not match. Nor does the profile for the child of low intelligence match the profile for the child of low creativity. Wallach and Kogan (1965) studied the interplay of intelligence and creativity in school-age children. Four patterns emerged.

1. High intelligence and high creativity
   These children were flexible and could act serious at one time and playful at another. They could easily adapt to different learning environments. They were very self-confident and displayed high attention and concentration for school tasks. They also engaged in attention-getting and disruptive behavior.

2. Low intelligence and high creativity
   These children were frustrated and had a difficult time in traditional schools. This probably tended to make them feel unworthy and inadequate. They were cautious, lacked self-confidence, and engaged in disruptive behavior.

3. Low intelligence and low creativity
   These children did not appear to understand what school was all about. They spent their time in either intense physical activity or passive retreat.

4. High intelligence and low creativity
   These children were devoted to achieving in school. They had high attention spans and high self-confidence. They were unlikely to act up in school, and were well liked by their teachers.

Teachers were later asked to identify their ideal pupil from these four profiles. Which one would you select? Teachers overwhelmingly selected children characterized as highly intelligent but low on creativity. The behavior problems that could arise from creativity (or its stifling), as in 1, appear to outweigh any advantages or assets. It may be understandable why teachers in this study favored high intelligence over high creativity. Highly intelligent children follow directions, work independently, listen, pay attention, obey, and conform. On the other hand, the highly creative child is often viewed as a problem requiring individual attention. Referring back to the general personality profile, highly creative children tend to be daydreamers, independent, nonconforming, impulsive, outspoken, challenging, and questioning individuals who test limits. It comes as no surprise that Getzels and Jackson (1962) also found that teachers favored high IQ but less creative children because they were easier to manage.

CREATIVITY AND CHILD DEVELOPMENT

What is the relationship between creativity and a child's development? Are there any developmental benefits to a child's creative functioning? Whatever the form that creativity may take, the child develops large and small muscle skills through handling and manipulating the appropriate tools or apparatus. Musical instruments are played, paint is mixed and spread, clay is pounded, and the body moves to music and song. Creative expression can enhance physical development. Socially, it can also help children come to terms with themselves and others. At times creativity involves solitary thinking or grappling with a problem. At other times social skills, including sharing, taking turns, and entertaining other points of view, are practiced. Creative expression fosters emotional development and positive mental health by validating the uniqueness of the individual. Juan, age three, made a clay dinosaur with two legs and an oversized head. He was proud of his accomplishment, and it did not matter if dinosaurs had four legs. Juan felt good about himself and the dinosaur he had created. Creativity fosters success and mastery, since there is no one right way involved. In turn, successes accumulate and enhance a positive self-concept. Children feel worthy and competent, knowing that they can have an effect on their environment. Creativity fosters mental or cognitive development. It involves a wide range of higher-level thinking skills, including observation, problem solving, discovery, analysis, hypothesizing, predicting, testing, and communicating, among others (see Figure 5-4). In the

Figure 5-4 Rocky's Rock Restaurant makes a personally creative statement.

school setting, creativity can enhance and reinforce learning in the traditional curricular areas of math, science, social studies, listening, speaking, pre-reading, pre-writing, and other expressive arts. Beyond individual development, creativity advances civilization and society by addressing and attempting to solve the global problems of hunger, poverty, disease, war, and pollution.

SUMMARY

The mystery surrounding creativity was addressed in this unit. Creativity can be viewed as making a unique product. Children, however, may make or create things that are new or original only to them. These were considered creative on the basis of their creative processing, which may or may not result in a finished product. Creativity was also viewed as a skill requiring practice. Environmental conditions can either foster or hinder creativity, and an optimal home environment was identified. Creativity was also compared and contrasted with conformity, convergent thinking, and intelligence. It was found that a high IQ did not guarantee a high degree of creativity.

SUGGESTED ACTIVITIES

1. Identify or develop at least one thing you do creatively. Practice and continue to refine it. Document your own creative development, including setbacks, frustrations, and successes, with a diary or journal.

2. Make a resource list of local businesses and contacts that are good sources of free (or inexpensive) and recyclable materials. Include the name, address, phone number, and contact person.

3. Spend one morning observing a teacher's use of time, space, and curriculum as well as his or her teaching behavior. List specific recommendations for how each could be modified to further enhance creativity.

4. Write your own definition of creativity. Ask five other individuals to do the same. Note similarities and differences.

REVIEW

A. What is the relationship between creativity, convergent thinking, and intelligence?

B. Name three different ways of understanding creativity.
   1.
   2.
   3.

C. Pretend that you are speaking to your parent group on creativity. They ask you for vital things that they can do at home to enhance their child's creativity. Specifically, what do you recommend?

       1.

       2.

       3.

D. List major obstacles to creativity.

       1.

       2.

       3.

       4.

       5.

E. Are young children more process- or product-oriented in their creative expression? Explain your position.

Unit 6

Creative Thinking

OBJECTIVES

After studying this unit, the student will be able to

- Discuss creativity as a function of the brain
- Discuss creativity as a mental operation
- Identify and explain the four components of divergent thinking and production

INTRODUCTION

There are many ways of being creative. These outlets or modes of creativity include play; the expressive arts: art, music, movement, dance, drama, and mime; and thought and language. For example, play is an excellent opportunity for creative expression. A young child building with blocks relies on past experiences in transforming pieces of wood into a train, airport, or castle. Putting on an oversized coat helps four-year-old Beth become a business executive, queen, or pilot. Children can use their bodies to creatively move like animals, robots, or astronauts. They can also use paint, markers, clay, and paper to give form to their innermost thoughts and substance to their experiences. Young children also

creatively transform standard English. Darrell, age three, felt that "carage" made more sense than garage. Tanya, age four, announced to her preschool class that Santa Claus has a team of "snowdeer," not reindeer. Swiss made no sense to five-year-old Kyle, shopping with his grandmother. He insisted on having "hole cheese" in his sandwiches. Young children also engage in creative thinking, although this particular mode is often given less emphasis and less of a role in the early childhood curriculum.

Just what is creative thinking? Creativity has been identified as a cognitive process or way of thinking. DeBono (1970) identified two types of thinking: vertical and lateral. Vertical thinking involves learning more about something or arriving at a conventional, accepted, convergent answer. For example, when Ms. Bell asked her pre-schoolers, "What time of the day do we eat breakfast?" Lin answered, "In the morning." But if the object is to find unusual, divergent, creative solutions for problems, lateral thinking is appropriate. Lateral thinking is the way of using one's mind or mental processes that leads to creative thinking or products. For example, Katie, who was playing alone at the sandbox, decided to creatively use sticks and twigs to keep her company.

Creativity and the Brain

Creativity can also be discussed as a function of the brain. According to Galin (1976), the human brain houses two separate but interacting thinking systems, or hemispheres. The right and left hemispheres are joined by the corpus callosum, a thick branch of nerves that serves as a communication system between them. The hemispheres have different specializations. The left hemisphere houses the thinking abilities traditionally associated with school: reading, writing, math, and rational and logical thinking. The right hemisphere specializes in nonrational, intuitive thinking and spatial relations—in short, creative ways of processing information. Dominance is not established at birth, and it is imperative that children be provided with experiences that capitalize on and integrate the functioning of both sides of the brain. Although schools are set up to emphasize conformity and convergent thinking, or left-brain functioning, Galin (1976) believes that at an early age the right-brain or creative function is dominant. Early childhood educators are in a key position to open the vistas of thinking for young children by planning experiences that engage both left- and right-brain functioning.

Creativity as a Mental Operation

Guilford (1977) was one of the original investigators of creativity as a mental process or operation. He conceptualized a Structure of the Intellect consisting of three dimensions: contents, products, and operations. Operations include knowing, discovering, or being aware (cogni-

tion); retrieving information from storage (memory); the generation of multiple responses (divergent production); coming up with the one right answer (convergent production); and judging the appropriateness of information or decisions (evaluation).

Divergent Production

Creative thinking can be loosely equated with divergent thinking and production. Divergent production involves the following four components.

- *Fluency* involves the generation or production of a large number of possibilities. Young children demonstrate fluent thinking when they respond to "How many things can you think of that roll?" or "Name as many things as you can to do with an empty shoe box." Fluency involves coming up with as many different ideas as you can.

- *Flexibility* involves the ability to mentally "shift gears" and come up with a different strategy or approach to thinking. The flexible thinker is able to shift classes or categories in giving responses. For example, when asked, "Name as many things as you can to do with an empty paper cup," Nan, age five, answered, "Drink water, drink soda, drink juice, have some pop in, hold coffee, and pour milk." Although Nan's responses are fairly fluent, her thinking is inflexible. She is unable to surmount the concept of "cupness." Her answers are inflexibly tied to the idea that a cup is something that holds some

Figure 6-1   Open-ended drawing

Figure 6-2   Completed drawing by a six-year-old

kind of a liquid to drink. April's answers included, "Wear it on your head as a hat, use it for playing catch, use it as a house, and talk into it." At age four, April's responses evidence flexible thinking in that she has surmounted the idea of "cupness" to think in novel ways.

- Assessing *originality* or uniqueness, however, is difficult, since a subjective judgment is involved. We might all agree that thirty different things to do with a shoe box would be fluent for a three-year-old. However, we might not agree on the degree of originality of each response.

- *Elaboration* is the ability to spell out details and to make an idea fancy.

Not all creative thinking activities provide the opportunity to assess all four components of divergent production. The following sample item from a test of creativity will help us practice informally evaluating a child's thinking for originality and elaboration. In the following example,

children are asked to complete an open-ended drawing similar to the one in figure 6-1. Obviously, there is no one right way to complete this picture, and many possibilities exist. How would you complete it? Carefully examine the finished product in figure 6-2. What can you say about this six-year-old's originality and elaboration? The author would rate this low on both originality and elaboration. The completed picture is rather stereotyped, unimaginative, mundane, and not very original. Details are minimal, and the picture lacks elaboration. From only this one sample, the author is not in a position to make a strong statement about this child's level of creativity. It does indicate, however, that this particular child needs practice and encouragement in divergent production. On the other hand, consider a drawing completed by a different six-year-old (figure 6-3). What can you say about this six-year-old's originality and elaboration? The author believes that this completed drawing evidences a high degree of originality and elaboration.

Not every creative activity will or should lend itself to evaluation for fluency, flexibility, originality, and elaboration. Fluency and flexibility may be more appropriate to games of creative thinking. Originality and elaboration can be applied to children's art; see figure 6-4. The informal rating scale (figure 6-5, page 63), adapted from Guilford's (1967) work, can be used to assess divergent production. Again, our intent is not to grade or label creativity, or to include it on a child's report card. Discretionary use of the following instrument will help us keep track of

Figure 6-3   Completed drawing by a six-year-old

Figure 6-4 This five-year-old's drawing of a park is detailed and elaborate.

progress as we strive to reach our goal of young children who demonstrate fluency, flexibility, originality, and elaboration in their creative processing and production.

ACTIVITIES FOR CREATIVE THINKING

Sample items taken from tests of creativity (Torrance, 1966) and modified for use with young children provide suggestions for activities to foster creative thinking. Some general guidelines are in order. You may want to try out these activities yourself first. Record and evaluate your responses. Allow yourself and your children plenty of "think time" to grapple with the problem posed. The activities can be conducted with individual children or with small or large groups. Creative thinking games can be played at any time during the day and can easily become part of

one of the following routines: arrival time, opening activity, group time, circle time, snack time, story time, transition time, indoor recess, indoor rainy day activity, and predismissal time, among others. Explain the nature of these creative thinking games. You are looking for unusual responses, and there will be no one right answer. This may be unsettling to some children. Participation should be voluntary, and some children will feel more comfortable with these activities than others. Try to reward and encourage thinking rather than acceptable answers. Children may get silly, and some answers may bear no relation to the question asked. These children may simply be testing your commitment to creativity and suspending conformity. Initially, the games should be kept short. Stop when the children show signs of restlessness or disinterest. Since the games are so open-ended, they may

Low	FLUENCY	High

- few different
- many different

FLEXIBILITY

- lacks variety
- rigid
- limited range

- wide variety
- flexible
- wide range

ORIGINALITY

- stereotyped
- unimaginative
- common

- unique
- imaginative
- unusual

ELABORATION

- lacks detail
- unelaborate
- simple

- very detailed
- elaborate
- complex

Figure 6-5 Rating scale (Source: Guilford, J. P., *Way Beyond the IQ*, Buffalo, N.Y.: The Creative Education Foundation, Inc., 1967.)

create some initial mental discomfort, especially to children who have been led to believe that all questions have one right answer. The key being used is *N/Pre* for Nursery/Preschool, ages three and four; *K* for Kindergarten and five-year-olds; and *Pri* for six-, seven-, and eight-year-olds in the primary grades. As always, the ages listed are tentative. What is recommended for a typical five-year-old may be quite appropriate for a very verbal and creative three-year-old in your group. Conversely, what appears to be an activity appropriate for three-year-olds may challenge a group of developmentally young five-year-olds. The activities assume some degree of verbal fluency. Older children could print their responses. There is no upper age limit on the thinking games.

Finish My Picture (N/Pre, K, Pri)

Ask the children to complete one of the pictures in figure 6-6. The pattern could be drawn on the board at child level or runoff as a ditto. The advantage of using a ditto is that children may be less prone to copy and that later they can share their products with one another. In this way they come to see that there are many, many possible responses.

Picture Possibilities (N/Pre, K, Pri)

Draw one of the line or pattern pictures in figure 6-7 on the board or on a transparency for the overhead projector. Allow the children time to think about possible meanings. Ask them to give

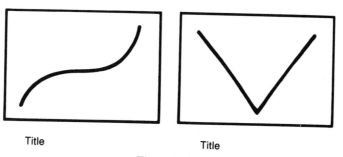

Title   Title

Figure 6-6

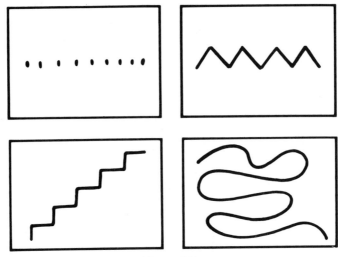

Figure 6-7

you a possible title or interpretation. "What do you see in this picture?" "What else could it be?"

What Would Happen If? (N/Pre, K, Pri)

Ask the children to listen very carefully as you ask them one of the following. What would happen if . . .

- refrigerators ate food?
- bathtubs could talk?
- you could be invisible?
- cars could drive by themselves?
- toys were real?
- dreams came true?
- you never had birthdays?
- pets went to school?

Young readers might enjoy using the tape recorder to tape their responses. Print the above sentences on index cards and place them in a learning center.

Unusual Uses (N/Pre, K, Pri)

Bring in each of the following items. Encourage the children to inspect each one carefully and

to handle them. Ask them to think of many things to do with these items.

- shoe
- shoe box
- cork
- dish
- newspaper
- balloon
- juice can
- napkin
- golf tee
- brick
- paper clip
- rubber band

Just Suppose (N/Pre, K, Pri)

Ask the children to listen carefully to a short story. Have them "just suppose" an end to your story. Examples might include

- Just suppose you found $1 million. What would you buy?

- Just suppose you met a moon child in an empty field. What would you say or do?

- Just suppose you could be somebody else. Who would you be?

- Just suppose you could be the teacher. What would you do?

- Just suppose you found a magic flying carpet. Where would you go?

- Just suppose you could be invisible for one whole day. What would you do, and where would you go?

- Just suppose you could be any animal. Which would it be?

Your Own Book Ending (N/Pre, K, Pri)

Assemble a small group of children for story time. Ask them to listen quietly while you read a class favorite. *Where the Wild Things Are* by Sendak is one possibility. Slowly read the story, stopping just before the end. Close your book. Ask the children to think up a different way to end the story. Some children may insist on giving back the predetermined ending. Encourage them to come up with their own even though it will be different from the book ending. As children gain experience at supplying their own endings, you can stop reading earlier in the story and require them to supply a greater part of the creative ending.

Tell Me About My Picture (N/Pre, K, Pri)

Seat a small group of children in a close circle. Hold up an interesting picture you have clipped from a magazine. Try to find pictures that are vague and have a variety of possible meanings. Ask the children to examine the picture carefully and

- Give different names or titles for the picture. What else could we call it? What else could this story be about? What happened to cause this? What might happen next?

- Tell your very own story about this picture.

Beginning writers can be encouraged to dictate or even print their own story lines. Individual children might enjoy taping their own story at a learning center.

How Many Ways (N/Pre, K, Pri)

Seat a small group of children in a close circle. Ask them to listen very carefully as you ask the following questions. How many different ways can you . . .

- celebrate your birthday?

- scare your brother or sister?

- get into trouble?

- make a new friend?

- be happy?

- go on a vacation?

- spend Saturday?

- surprise Grandma or Grandpa?

- earn some money?

- be naughty?

Descriptives (N/Pre, K, Pri)

Seat a small group of children in a close circle. Hold up one of the following objects. Encourage each child to inspect it carefully as it is passed around the circle. Ask the children to tell you many different words that describe a

• flag	• sock
• umbrella	• gerbil
• cereal box	• lunch box
• key	• pencil
• toy	• coin

Encourage children to use descriptive terms, including references to color, shape, size, use, form, texture, weight, composition, and so on.

Make Up a Story (N/Pre, K, Pri)

Seat a small group of children in a close circle. Ask the children to listen very carefully to the beginning of a story. Then, ask them to finish your story. Three very simple story starters are:

- Once upon a time there was a little girl who wanted her very own horse. But her Mommy said there was no money to buy one. So one day the little girl . . .
- One morning Marco was waiting for the school bus. He waited and waited, but it didn't come. So Marco decided to . . .
- Kitten wanted to go to school. But Billy said, "Kittens don't go to school. They stay at home." So one day Kitten . . .

Encourage children to make up their own beginnings to share with their friends.

Picture Guess (N/Pre, K, Pri)

The open-ended designs in figure 6-8 can be sketched on the board one at a time. Ask the children to study the shape carefully. Allow plenty of "think time," and do not encourage quick shouting out. Have the children tell you many different things each of the pictures could be.

Make It Better (N/Pre, K, Pri)

Seat a small group of children in a close circle. Hold up a familiar toy, such as a stuffed animal or race car. Encourage each child to inspect it carefully as it is passed around the circle. Ask the children

- How could we make it a better toy?
- What could we do to make it more fun to play with?

What Would . . . If It . . . ? (K, Pri)

Seat a small group of children in a close circle. Ask them to listen very carefully to your question and then think up their own answer. Here are some sample questions.

- What would taste better if it were sweeter?
- What would be more fun if it went faster?
- What would be scary if it were bigger?
- What would be happier if it could escape?
- What would be funny if it were alive?

Figure 6-8

What All (N/Pre, K, Pri)

Seat a small group of children in a close circle. Ask them to think of many things that

- are round
- make noise
- sink
- are wet
- smell
- have horns
- squeak
- ring
- shine
- roll
- are green
- hurt
- are square
- stick
- fly

Pretend (N/Pre, K, Pri)

Seat a small group of children in a close circle. Ask them to carefully listen to a "pretend" sentence. Examples might include

- Pretend you didn't have a paint brush. What else could you use to paint the walls?

- Pretend you didn't have a present. What else could you take to a friend's birthday party?

- Pretend you didn't have a friend to play with. What else could you do?

- Pretend you didn't have any money for your play store. What else could you use?

SUMMARY

There are many ways to express one's creativity. Play, the expressive arts (art, music, movement, dance, dramatics, and mime), language, and thought are just a few that are relevant to early childhood. Creativity or divergent production was viewed as a thinking skill or mental operation within Guilford's Structure of the Intellect. Creative thought and production are characterized by fluency, flexibility, originality, and elaboration. A rating scale and sample activities are provided for the adult reader to use with young children.

SUGGESTED ACTIVITIES

1. Do several of the creative thinking activities. Record your own responses. Use the rating scale to informally evaluate your divergent thinking and production. Record your strengths and weaknesses in fluency, flexibility, originality, and elaboration.

2. Do one of the creative thinking activities with a small group of young children. Record their responses. Practice using the rating scale to evaluate their creative thinking.

3. Check out tests of creative thinking from the library and review them. Begin a card file of creative thinking activities. Be creative and modify the test items rather than merely copying them.

REVIEW

A. List the major mental operations.
   1.
   2.

3.

4.

5.

Place an * in front of the one that is generally equated with creativity.

B. List the components of divergent thinking and production.

1.

2.

3.

4.

C. Match each term with its description.

1. elaboration   coming up with many possibilities

2. originality   the uniqueness of an idea

3. flexibility   making an idea rich or fancy

4. fluency   coming up with very different responses

Unit 7

Art and the Early Childhood Curriculum

OBJECTIVES

After studying this unit, the student will be able to

- Compare and contrast different ways of viewing the early childhood curriculum
- Identify the major early childhood curricular areas
- Discuss how art fosters learning in other early childhood curricular areas

INTRODUCTION

Curriculum means different things to different people. Two major ways of viewing the curriculum are as an overall program or as subject areas. Each view will be discussed in this unit. Art is merely one of many curricular areas. How can art reinforce and extend learning in the other curricular areas? Integrating art throughout the early childhood curriculum will be the focus of this unit.

ART AND THE EARLY CHILDHOOD CURRICULUM

Curriculum means different things to different people. The word *curriculum* is used to refer to an educational program, activity, or set of activities and to guidelines set by a school district office, state, corporation, or professional organization. In its widest sense, curriculum refers to what happens in schools or centers. Two major ways of viewing the early childhood curriculum include

- curriculum as program
- curriculum as subject matter, content, or academic area

Curriculum as Program

To some, curriculum means the total program, such as an infant, toddler, preschool, Montessori, Head Start, or kindergarten program. In this view, curriculum refers to all the things children learn in school or center. This is a very broad view of curriculum. It would include learning how to wait one's turn, sit in a circle for group time, and share toys as well as learning about colors and shapes. In this view, children learn through specifically planned learning experiences as well as through incidental learnings. For example, Mel's parents are pleased that he enjoys his day-care program and is making friends. However, they are concerned that he has become more verbally and socially aggressive, behaviors that they had never observed before he attended day care. Children who are in groups for long periods of time learn these behaviors as ways to cope and protect themselves. Children learn much more than is planned and intended in any curriculum or program.

Curriculum as Subject Matter, Content, or Academic Area

A second way to look at curriculum is to view it as a separate subject, content, or academic area of study. The present text focuses on art in the early childhood curriculum. Traditionally, the school curriculum has centered around the following curricular areas:

1. math
2. science
3. language arts/communication arts/literacy:
   - speaking
   - listening
   - (pre)-reading
   - (pre)-writing
4. social studies
5. expressive arts
   - art
   - music
   - movement

See figure 7-1 for a visual portrayal of this model of the early childhood curriculum.

Just as child development cannot be dissected into neat divisions, the curricular areas are not separate entities. The model indicates that the curricular areas interact and influence each other. Children do not simply "switch channels" or "change gears" to move from mathematical to scientific thinking. Knowledge and skills are not neatly compartmentalized according to subject area. This is why math and science, communication and language arts, and the expressive arts are depicted with overlapping circles. Experiences such as cooking and play are highly recommended because they cut across and involve learning in many, if not all, of the curricular areas. Although the separation will work for our present analysis, children are wholistic individuals who learn in wholistic ways. For example, they engage in creative thinking and problem solving that may cut across the areas of math and science, art, and social studies.

ART AND MATH

Children naturally quantify art materials, equipment, and supplies. "There are four jars of paint out, but only three brushes. There are more jars than brushes." The teacher asks, "How many more brushes do we need to make them equal?" Some paintbrushes have longer handles and wider bristles than others. "My red crayon is longer than your blue one." "Yes, but mine is fatter and wider than yours." "This paste cup has less than the others," states Evie. Her teacher asks, "What can you do to make them the same?" Evie gets the large paste container and adds more.

Children quantify as they create. "There, now my bug has six legs, just enough," announces Ty

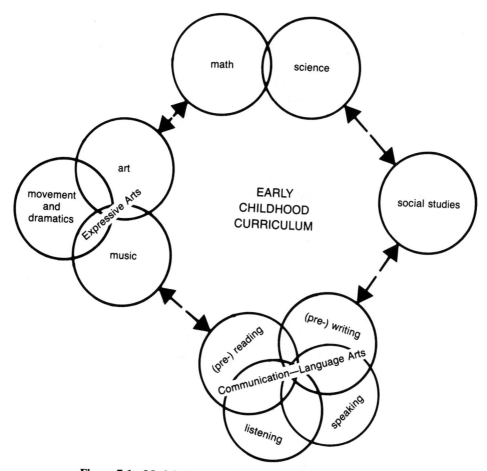

Figure 7-1   Model of early childhood curriculum development

as he coils a final leg out of clay. Marcy adds a second eye to her self-portrait. She carefully counts fingers and toes as she paints them on one by one. Some children use geometric shapes in composing their picture. "A tall brown rectangle with a green circle on top. Now, I'll color in my tree," announces Tess.

Some activities that incorporate art with math include:

Geometric Shape Picture (N/Pre, K, Pri)

Older children can cut an array of circles, squares, triangles, and rectangles of different sizes. These can be creatively arranged and

pasted to form a picture. Teachers may want to cut out the geometric shapes for younger children. Cutting for children is warranted in this activity. Children see how common objects, people, vehicles, and animals are made up of geometric shapes and can be constructed from them.

There are two ways to vary this activity. Teachers can cut shapes out of flannel, including circles, squares, triangles, and rectangles that vary in color and size. Children can creatively arrange these shapes on a larger piece of flannel that forms the background. Some teachers pin or tape pieces of flannel to a bulletin board or chalkboard. Others cover a large piece of cardboard with flannel. A second variation is to use magnetic tape. Wide strips of magnetic tape can be cut into geometric shapes, or small pieces of magnetic tape can be glued to the back of poster board or cardboard shapes. In turn, these shapes can be creatively arranged on a cookie sheet.

Cube Art (K, Pri)

Older children may enjoy making a picture or design using graph paper. Graph paper with large squares is recommended. This activity will take time and patience and is not recommended for very young children. The paper may need to be cut in half or quarters if children become overwhelmed by all the squares on the paper.

Lines, Arcs, and Circles (N/Pre, K, Pri)

Young children enjoy using the tools of the mathematician: ruler, compass, and protractor. Specific instruction in the proper care and use of these instruments should be given. Model different ways of using a ruler, compass, protractor, and pencil to produce interesting designs and patterns. Children may want to color in the spaces between or connect forms with thin markers.

Variety of Paper Shapes (N/Pre, K, Pri)

Art can be done on round, square, triangular, diagonal, rectangular, and odd-shaped pieces of paper. Each unique shape poses a new challenge to the child artist. Wide, sweeping strokes are appropriate on a big rectangular sheet of paper. A smaller, detailed picture may fit better on a smaller six-sided sheet.

Teachers can point out and discuss the different shapes of the paper provided. For example, "I put out some different paper today. What shape could we call it?" (holding up a piece of round paper). Since it is round with a hole cut out of the center, the children decide that circle, wheel, and doughnut are appropriate terms.

Teachers can also discuss how a large square sheet can be cut into smaller square pieces of paper. Four small squares make one larger square. Cutting the large diamond-shaped sheet

of paper in half makes two triangular pieces of paper. In this way, children are slowly introduced to fractions through an integrated art activity.

Geoboard (N/Pre, K, Pri)

Children can practice making geometric shapes with rubber bands on a geoboard. See figure 7-2 for a geoboard pattern. Find a piece of wood. Carefully hammer in rows of evenly spaced nails.

Use short nails with wide heads or upholstery tacks. A one-inch space between rows and columns of nails is recommended. The total number of rows and columns will depend on the size of your board. Eight rows and eight columns are recommended.

Encourage the children to see

- How many nails can you fit under just one rubber band?

- How many nails do you need to include to make a circle (square, rectangle, diamond, triangle, etc.)?

- Does it take more or less nails to make a square, triangle, circle, or rectangle?

- How many different shapes can you make using ten nails?

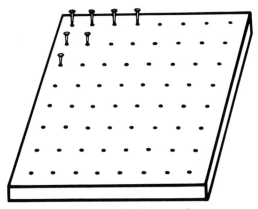

Figure 7-2 Geoboard

String Design (N/Pre, K, Pri)

Children can make abstract linear designs with string on a wooden frame. Find an old picture frame. Lay the frame down flat and hammer in a row of nails on each of the four upright sides. Encourage children to connect the nails using string, rope, or yarn. The result will be a creative linear design. Children can note the designs, patterns, shapes, and angles produced.

Tangram (N/Pre, K, Pri)

The tangram is an old Chinese puzzle consisting of seven angular shapes that can fit together to make a square. (See figure 7-3 for a tangram pattern.) The shapes can also be creatively combined to make pictures and designs. You may want to reproduce, cut out, mount on poster board, and laminate the individual pieces to ensure durability. Time invested in protecting the pieces will pay off in the long run. When laminating, remember to cut out the individual pieces first, then laminate them to avoid frayed ends. Covering the pieces with clear contact paper is also recommended.

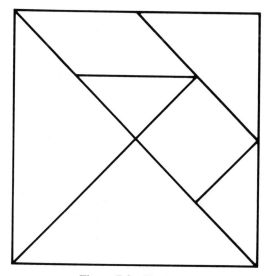

Figure 7-3 Tangram

ART AND SCIENCE

Art activities help children discover scientific principles. Powdered tempera dissolves in water. Adding water to dry tempera or watercolor cakes produces a liquid. Over time, wet paint dries. Placing wet paintings in the sun will hasten the drying process. Clay remains moist if it is kept wrapped. On Monday morning Ms. Carlson announces, "Someone left their clay work out on the table over the weekend. What has happened to it?" "It turned hard," answers Juan. "Yes, it got hard and brittle when exposed to the air for three days," explains his teacher. "Also, someone left a wax crayon on the radiator. What has happened to it?" "Yes, it melted. Why?" "Yes, the heat from the radiator melted the wax. What would happen if we left our crayons out in the sun on a hot summer day?" The possibilities of scientific thinking, hypothesizing, predicting, observing, questioning, discussing, and explaining are endless.

Too much water makes paint runny and uncontrollable. Little or no water produces a thicker, intense stroke. Pressing hard or lightly produces different effects. Children are learning about force. Children learn about resistance when they discover that they can cut paper but not cardboard with their scissors.

Some activities that incorporate art with science follow.

Food Groups Collage (N/Pre, K, Pri)

After studying the major food groups, children can be encouraged to find pictures of foods in magazines. These can be cut and pasted onto poster board sheets, one for each of the major food groups.

Nature Art (N/Pre, K, Pri)

Young children and nature go hand in hand. Children enjoy taking short nature walks and collecting nature specimens. These can be creatively arranged and glued onto a paper plate, cardboard, or construction paper.

Children also enjoy making nature rubbings.

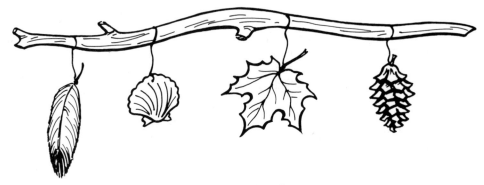

Figure 7-4 Mobile

Thin white paper can be placed over leaves, flowers, bark, stones, or other objects. Children can gently rub one side of an unwrapped crayon over the specimen. The texture and outline of the item will leave an impression. Children can also take their crayon and paper outdoors and make rubbings as they find them. Overlapping produces a different, more complex impression.

Children can also make nature prints. Paint can be brushed on a leaf or an acorn can be lightly dipped in paint. The items can then be carefully pressed onto white paper. Gently lifting the item results in a print. Repeated prints result in a pattern. Separate prints can be creatively combined into a new design.

Color Mixing (N/Pre, K, Pri)

Children can discover the principles and joys of color mixing. Provide paint and a separate brush and container for each of the primary colors: red, blue, and yellow. Encourage children to mix any two colors in equal parts or dabs and see what happens. What color did you make? What happens if three colors are mixed together? This activity can also be done using food coloring, a Styrofoam egg carton, and an eye dropper.

After this tempera paint activity has been successfully completed, white paint can also be provided. What happens if white is mixed with red, blue, or yellow? What happens if white is added to your mixture of red and yellow, red and blue, or blue and yellow? Let's find out.

Mobile (N/Pre, K, Pri)

Mobiles help children learn about balance, motion, and the effects of air and wind. A tree branch makes an excellent support or base for a mobile. (See figure 7-4.) Acceptable nature items include shells, pine cones, feathers, leaves, and anything else that can be hung with thread, string, or fishing line. Items for a mobile can also be suspended from a coat hanger, yardstick, dowel rod, or broom handle.

Advanced mobile makers can experiment with different levels or planes. This provides an opportunity to experiment with weight, placement, space, and balance. A coat hanger mobile with several levels is shown in figure 7-5.

Figure 7-5 Coat hanger mobile

Ecology Construction (N/Pre, K, Pri)

Children can assist in the cleanup of litter, both indoors and outdoors. Recycled items can also be brought from home. Children can discuss the importance of avoiding needless waste, not littering, and recycling. Such items as scrap paper, boxes, containers, and plastic packaging can be recycled into a construction activity. For example, boxes and bottle tops inspired one preschooler to construct a robot.

ART AND THE LANGUAGE/COMMUNICATION ARTS AND LITERACY

Art gives children the opportunity to represent what they know nonverbally or graphically. With encouragement, they may also choose to talk about what they have created. Children read their artwork just as adults read words from a book. At times children enjoy having their titles or story lines printed on their pictures. They can be encouraged to read along with the teacher. Older children may attempt to print their own words as a story line. They may invent letters and misspell. This is to be expected; it is an important step that children go through as they become writers and readers. Scribbling, mark making, and painted strokes are important steps in the development of printing and writing.

Art gives children an opportunity to include art vocabulary in their discussions with peers and adults. Teachers can introduce and model the use of these terms as they talk with children about their art. Children recognize colors, shapes, textures, lines, and movement in their own art and that of others. Lines can be thick, intersecting, crisscrossed, wavy, horizontal, vertical, diagonal, curved, or broken. Paint can be dry, wet, dripping, sticky, tacky, runny, slick, or crackled.

Some activities that incorporate art with the language/communication arts or literacy follow.

Art Talk (N/Pre, K, Pri)

Encourage children to talk about their art, but do not require that art be followed by verbalization: "What would you like to tell me about your picture?" or, "Your colors and shapes make an interesting design; what words could you use to tell about it?" Labels, titles, and story lines can be recorded. For example, Marie asks a parent volunteer, "Can I tell you about my bunny picture?" Marie's words are carefully printed across the top of her paper. The parent points to each word as she reads the story back to Marie. She encourages Marie to read along. Marie says she's done for now but will trace over the letters with a pencil tomorrow. Ned prefers to talk his story into the tape recorder. His teacher will listen to it, transcribe it, and read it back to him.

Puppets (N/Pre, K, Pri)

Making a puppet is an art activity that can evolve into a speaking activity. For example, Tami, a shy four-year-old, makes an animal puppet out of a folded paper plate. She hides behind a bookshelf and lets her animal speak to and answer questions from two other children. Tami's puppet is a prop that gives her the psychological boost to speak in a group. After all, it is the puppet, not Tami, who is speaking.

Consonant Collage (K, Pri)

One kindergarten class had been studying words that begin with the letter sounds. They practiced these sounds at concept time. They hunted through magazines for pictures of things that start with these sounds. The "b" page had pictures of a book, bicycle, bird, boy, Big Bird, bag, and Band-Aid. Pictures of a dog, duck, doll, doughnut, dishes, and dancers were pasted on the "d" page. By the end of the year, the children hoped to complete a collage page for each of their sounds.

Art Words (N/Pre, K, Pri)

Children at the clay table were trying to think of something new to make. Their teacher suggested that they form the letters in their names. Some also made their initials, ABCs, and simple words out of rolled clay.

As a variation, children could use paint to finger paint their names or letters of the alphabet. Getting the actual feel and direction of making a "b" and "d" may help some older children who are learning to print and who tend to reverse these letters.

Children also enjoy using squirt bottles to paint their names, letters, or words. Find a bottle with a pointed tip and a fairly small opening so that the paint will not merely run out. For example, bottles that hold white glue are a recommended size and shape for young hands.

Listen and Draw (N/Pre, K, Pri)

Mrs. Banks enjoys reading books to children. She wants children to listen attentively, appreciate literature, and get the main idea. She knows how important these skills will be when they learn to read. She often asks her children to draw a picture about the story she has just read. Sometimes she stops short of the ending and asks them to draw how they think the story will end. The pictures clearly reveal which children were listening and which might need additional practice in this area.

The creative teacher will invent many variations on this activity. For example, children can be encouraged to listen and then draw what the teacher requests. For example, "Please draw three cats of any color with long tails sitting by a tree." Children need to listen, remember, and represent. The details requested must be minimal and within the memory range and drawing ability of young children. Details such as "inside of," "behind," "checkered," or "star-shaped" may be too difficult to represent.

ART AND SOCIAL STUDIES

Art helps children get in touch with themselves and others. Representing oneself through self-portraits and human figure drawings increases one's awareness of self, body parts, and others.

Through art one takes on and identifies with the role of artist. A study of artists can be part of a lesson on community helpers. Children can visit a museum or gallery. An artist can come in and model artistic processing and work with the children. This can also be a brief introduction to history and culture, since artists and their different styles have been around since prehistoric times. Different cultural groups have their own art forms. Some include

- Mexican pinata
- Mexican Gods-eye
- Chinese pen and ink
- Ukrainian egg painting
- Indian sand painting
- African masks
- Colonial American candlemaking

Some activities that incorporate art and social studies follow.

Me Book (N/Pre, K, Pri)

Children can illustrate pages of their "All About Me" book. Sample activities include drawing one's face, body, senses, likes, dislikes, house, family, and friends.

My Twin (N/Pre, K)

After learning about "me," children can lie down on a long sheet of butcher paper. Encourage children to slightly spread out their arms and legs. The teacher can carefully trace around the outline of each child. Children can cut and color their twin, paying attention to color of hair, eyes, and clothing. A full-length mirror should be handy. Do not, however, expect a mirror image or realistic likeness.

My 3-D Twin (N/Pre, K)

Using two sheets of butcher paper, follow the directions for the previous activity. Children can color or paint in their front and back. Slowly staple both sides together while gently stuffing with crumpled newspaper. As with the previous activity, expect children to take creative liberty. Since this tends to be a long activity, you may want to split it into several sequences. For example, separate sessions to trace, cut, color, stuff, and staple may be warranted. Art projects or activities need not be hurriedly completed in one session.

Family Flag (K, Pri)

Briefly discuss how flags are symbols for countries. In our country, the United States, we use stars and stripes and the colors red, white, and blue. Let children carefully examine the flag. Encourage them to make their own flag for their family. "What can you put on your flag that tells us about you and your family?" Family members and things that remind them of their family can be included.

Murals (N/Pre, K, Pri)

Making a mural is a good activity to wrap up or synthesize something. It is an activity that can be repeated with different areas or concepts being studied. For example, after a field trip to the bakery, children can draw a mural to represent what they experienced—people baking, decorating baked goods, rolling and kneading dough, selling bakery products, stocking shelves, and so on. After studying a unit on the farm, children can represent what they have learned about the farm in a mural. If a farm mural does not contain animals, vehicles, and buildings related to the farm theme, the teacher might conclude that perhaps the children did not learn much about the farm. The teacher might want to review key concepts in discussing the farm mural. Or, it might simply be that the bus ride over and the picnic lunch were more meaningful.

Holiday Sentiments (N/Pre, K, Pri)

Art, child-directed and initiated, is the perfect gift for a child to give. It may be nonverbal, but it conveys personal meaning and love. After studying any of the major holidays, children can be encouraged to plan and implement an artistic

Figure 7-6 Children can make their own unique holiday greeting card.

representation of the joy, hope, love, and fellowship associated with that particular holiday. A simple but personalized greeting card or collage may result (see Figure 7-6).

ART AND THE EXPRESSIVE ARTS

Art is merely one mode of creative expression. Music and movement are two other expressive arts that are vital to early childhood. Both art and movement involve nonverbal expression. What children represent in art can also be represented through movement. Liz is fascinated with unicorns. She attempted to make one out of clay. Its long horn was prominent. During a "Guess what I am" movement session, she pretended to be a unicorn, moving on all fours while indicating something sticking out of her forehead. Just as music can foster artistic expression through a certain mood, tone, tempo, or beat, it can also trigger spontaneous movement.

Some activities that incorporate art with the other expressive arts follow.

Musical Painting (N/Pre, K, Pri)

Encourage children to hand paint or color to different types of music. These might include slower classical, pop show tunes, and rock music. Discuss how paint strokes, movement, and design are related to the tempo of the music.

Costumes and Props (K, Pri)

Children can design, paint, or color masks, costumes, scenery, and props related to a play or movement activity. For example, children can design paper-plate masks for the different characters in "The Gingerbread Boy." A mural can be decorated and used as scenery.

SUMMARY

Curriculum means different things to different people; it can mean the overall program or a particular subject area. In this second view, art is merely one curricular area. A discussion and suggested activities emphasized the relationship between art and math, science, communication/language arts or literacy, social studies, and the other expressive arts.

SUGGESTED ACTIVITIES

1. Interview two different teachers regarding their views and definitions of curriculum. Do they agree or disagree? Do their views match those in the unit?

2. Devise an activity that integrates art with one or more of the early childhood curricular areas.

3. Implement one of the integrated art activities with an individual or small group.

REVIEW

A. Identify the two major ways of viewing the early childhood curriculum.
   1.
   2.

B. List the major early childhood curricular areas.
   1.
   2.
   3.
   4.
   5.

C. Match each art-related activity with a curricular area that it attempts to incorporate or integrate.

_____ counting the number of children at the art center to see if there are too many

1. speaking

_____ explaining to another child the steps involved in making a print of one's finger painting

2. writing

_____ doing a Thanksgiving collage of people and things we are thankful for

3. science

_____ Zak painting XZo across his picture for his name

4. social studies

_____ Larry finding that quickly stirring water into powder tempera makes colorful bubbles

5. math

Unit 8

Children's Artistic Development

OBJECTIVES

After studying this unit, the student will be able to

- Discuss and critique the different explanations for the development of children's art
- Match the corresponding artistic accomplishments with Kellogg's and Lowenfeld and Brittain's stages
- Overview artistic development from birth through age eight using the author's sequence

INTRODUCTION

Children's art has a mysterious quality to it. The flow of lines, shapes, colors, and overall design may make more sense to the child artist than to the adult observer. Why do children scribble? What does their art mean? Why do they draw stick figures when they know people do not look that way? Theories and stages attempt to provide answers to these questions. This unit surveys and critiques a physical, emotional, perceptual, cognitive, general developmental, and cognitive developmental explanation for children's art. The author has used the stages identified by Kellogg and by Lowenfeld and Brittain in proposing one general sequence to account for the development of art from birth through age eight.

EXPLAINING CHILDREN'S ART

Appreciating children's art may be easier than understanding it or attempting to explain it. Beyond the sheer enjoyment, adults have been trying to make sense out of children's art for de-cades. Researchers, teachers, parents, art educa-tors, and those interested in child development are concerned with the content, motive, process, and product. Their interest focuses on the fol-lowing:

- What children choose to include or repre-sent (content)

- How children create (process)

- Why children create (motive)

- What they create as a result (product)

The *content* refers to the subject matter or object being represented. This might include a pet ani-mal, person, feeling, mood, wish, dream, or im-pulse. The content of children's art is often very personal or idiosyncratic. For example, a wide stroke of black paint may represent a tree trunk. On the other hand, it may represent a child's creative exploration with paint and brush and not be intended for public communication. Too of-ten, adults are prone to search for public meaning where there is none. The *process* refers to the actions and skills involved in creating an art product—cutting and tearing paper, rolling clay, painting, or marking with crayons. Not all art processing results in the creation of a finished art product. Many young children process for its own sake. The *motive* refers to the reason under-lying a child's art. For example, adults may ex-plore why a child filled a paper with wide strokes of black paint. Does the child's preoccupation with the color black signify some underlying emotional problem? Is the mark characteristic of a lack of maturation? Does the solitary mark rep-resent social isolation? Or, is the child represent-ing the concept of one? The *product* refers to the final outcome. Examples include black paint smeared across a paper, a clay dinosaur, a paper bag puppet, or a geometric design done in water-color. The finished product may or may not bear any resemblance to the content or subject matter.

In analyzing the what, why, and how of chil-dren's art, there is a risk of misinterpretation or of reading too much into this art. After studying children and their artwork for an extended pe-riod of time, however, trends and patterns do emerge. A skillful observer can note these trends and patterns and begin to make some generaliza-tions about what, why, and how children create.

THEORIES OF ARTISTIC DEVELOPMENT

Theories of artistic development attempt to ex-plain what, why, and how children create. The theories are similar yet different. All theories of artistic development attempt to do the same thing—explain a child's artistic development. Each, however, takes a different slant, perspec-tive, or focus. Some theories do a better or more complete job of explaining than others.

Why does one need a theory of artistic devel-opment? A theory provides the overall structure or foundation for what we do with children. Dif-ferent theories suggest different educational practices. For example, there is much debate about the roles of theory and practice in the prep-aration of early childhood educators. We all want teachers who are competent practitioners. Some-one who is long on theory but short on practice would not do a good job in the classroom. Our aim is to translate theory into practice. A theory can be our blueprint or road map, steering us to sound, developmentally appropriate practice. Theory can also help us justify how, why, and what we do with children.

There are numerous theories and explanations that attempt to explain the development of child art. They can be grouped into the following six categories:

- Physical

- Emotional

- Perceptual

- Cognitive

- General developmental
- Cognitive developmental

Physical Explanation for the Development of Child Art

A physical explanation for the development of child art holds that the content, process, product, and style of children's art are indicative of their limited physical development. The young child is limited in eye-hand coordination, fine motor control, small muscle development, manual dexterity, and visual acuity. Young children mark aimlessly, scribble, and draw unrecognizable shapes because they are physically incapable of anything else. Young children's drawing often appears immature and unintelligible to some adults.

It is obvious that the physical development of a young child does affect artistic expression. For example, one cannot expect a toddler to draw a detailed still life in realistic fashion. Yet, a child may simply choose to scribble or explore with the media, just as an adult may choose to doodle. Accomplished artists who have mastered the techniques of realism often opt for an impressionistic, expressionistic, or abstract style. Adult primitive art with its simplistic quality conveys purposeful intent rather than limited physical development and lack of coordination.

Emotional Explanation for the Development of Child Art

An emotional explanation for the development of child art holds that the content and style of children's art is indicative of their emotional make-up, personality, temperament, and affective state. Objects, emotions, people, and events of significance are often emphasized in children's drawings and paintings through an exaggerated, distorted, and expressive use of color, size, shape, line, texture, and overall treatment. For example, when a child draws her father as a "Superman" caricature with bulging muscles, a huge red heart, and a wide smile, this may signify her love, respect, admiration, and identification

rather than distortion due to faulty vision or limited physical development.

Perceptual Explanation for the Development of Child Art

A perceptual explanation for the development of child art holds that the content and style of children's art reflects their perceptual development. A perceptual explanation is not identical to a physical one, since perception is not synonymous with vision. Vision, the mechanistic recording of reality, involves projecting images upon the retina. Perception is influenced by the neurophysiological structure, personality, and prior learning. The perceptual explanation holds that a child draws what he or she perceives rather than what he or she sees. The task of art is to create the structural equivalent of the perceived three-dimensional object on the two-dimensional canvas. This can be a monumental task for the artist regardless of age.

The development of child art provides support for a perceptual explanation. The young child's first attempts at drawing are scribbles with a minimum of line and shape; they gradually increase in complexity and clarity. Some children, however, draw or paint less than they actually perceive. For example, a child may choose to paint the stripes of a tiger with wide, sweeping strokes and ignore the head or other extremities. It is also possible that the medium can limit one's expression of the perceptual image. For example, using a wide-bristle brush dipped in watered-down paint might limit the number of details that appear in one's painting. The size of the paper also places constraints on what can be fit into the picture.

Cognitive Explanation for the Development of Child Art

A cognitive explanation for the development of child art holds that the content and style of children's art is indicative of general intelligence and a function of conceptualization. Children can draw or paint only what they know. One's con-

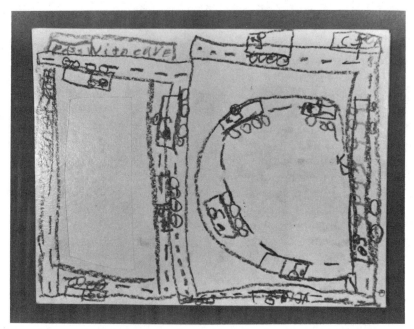

Figure 8-1   Children draw the world as they know and interpret it.

cept of an object will determine how that object will be represented. For example, when one draws an apple, one's concept of an apple is determined by one's experiences with its color, taste, size, shape, and smell and by related experiences in picking apples, polishing apples, planting apple seeds, climbing apple trees, paring apples, bobbing for apples, mashing apples for cider, and baking and eating an apple pie. Observation of young children involved in art supports a cognitive explanation. Young children rely on memories, images, experiences, and concepts when they draw or paint. Detailed drawings will reflect concepts with which the child has had extensive experience. For example, it would be expected that an urban child will have a less developed concept of a silo, tractor, and barn than a child living on a farm. The differences will appear when each child draws or paints a farm scene. One would expect the child living on a farm to execute a picture with greater detail and elaboration (see Figure 8-1).

Goodenough (1926) devised the Draw-A-Man test, a reliable nonverbal measure of intelligence. It is assumed that the child's drawing of the human figure is a reflection of that child's concept of a man. Indices of conceptual maturity include appearance of limbs and location, size, and relationship of body parts (see Figure 8-2). If a child has a well-defined concept of a man, reflected in an accurate drawing with properly located body parts, this would indicate a high level of intelligence on the Goodenough measure. The problem with this normative approach is its neglect of individual differences, experiences, and motivational, attitudinal, and environmental factors that can either foster or inhibit concept formation. Ears may be particularly relevant to a young girl with pierced ears. A child living in an area where both sexes sport long hair may be oblivious to ears. A related problem with the human figure drawing test is that some children choose to omit body parts out of whim rather than lack of knowledge. The human figure drawn without ears may

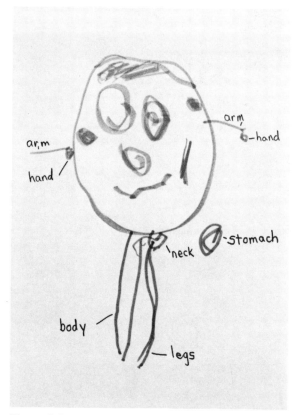

arm

hand

arm

hand

stomach

neck

body

legs

Figure 8-2 The young artist is not concerned with proper placement of body parts.

be simply the result of creative expression and personal preference. It is also possible that the child may have run out of paint, patience, or interest.

Concept formation and perceptual analysis are reciprocal processes. Knowledge of an object can improve one's ability to accurately observe its details. In turn, careful observation can lead to increased knowledge of the object.

General Developmental Explanation for Child Art

A fifth explanation for the development of child art is more global. It provides a general developmental explanation that incorporates social, cultural, personality, and environmental factors as well as elements of former explana-

tions. General developmental explanations make use of a stage sequence approach in attempting to explain the artistic expression of the child in "wholistic" fashion.

Theories have given us ages and stages to help understand a child's artistic development. Like theories, there are many stage sequences for the development of children's art. Knowing stages will help us do the following:

- understand where a child is developmentally

- set appropriate but flexible expectations, neither too high nor too low

- plan a developmentally appropriate art program

- serve as a framework for evaluation and for conferences with parents

- appreciate the process and products of art during the early years

Rhoda Kellogg (1969) has amassed over a million paintings and drawings of children from the United States and thirty other countries over the past few decades. Her stages appear in figure 8-3.

According to Kellogg, some twenty basic scribble patterns make up the first stage of development. These basic scribbles are the foundation for future graphic art, pictorial and nonpictorial. As the child proceeds from scribbling to picture making, he or she passes through stages: placement, shape, design, and pictorial. More specifically, the twenty basic scribbles are subsequently drawn according to some seventeen different placement patterns by the age of two. By the age of three, these diagrams or gestalts contain shapes, including the circle, cross, square, and rectangle. One basic diagram, the "mandala," dominates the child's visual thinking at this time and serves as a basic artistic referent in future drawing. Children use mandalas to draw people, flowers, and the sun. Gestalt psychology has shown the mandala, a crossed circle, to be a universal pattern that the brain is predisposed to utilize in all visual perception (see Figure 8-4 on page 90).

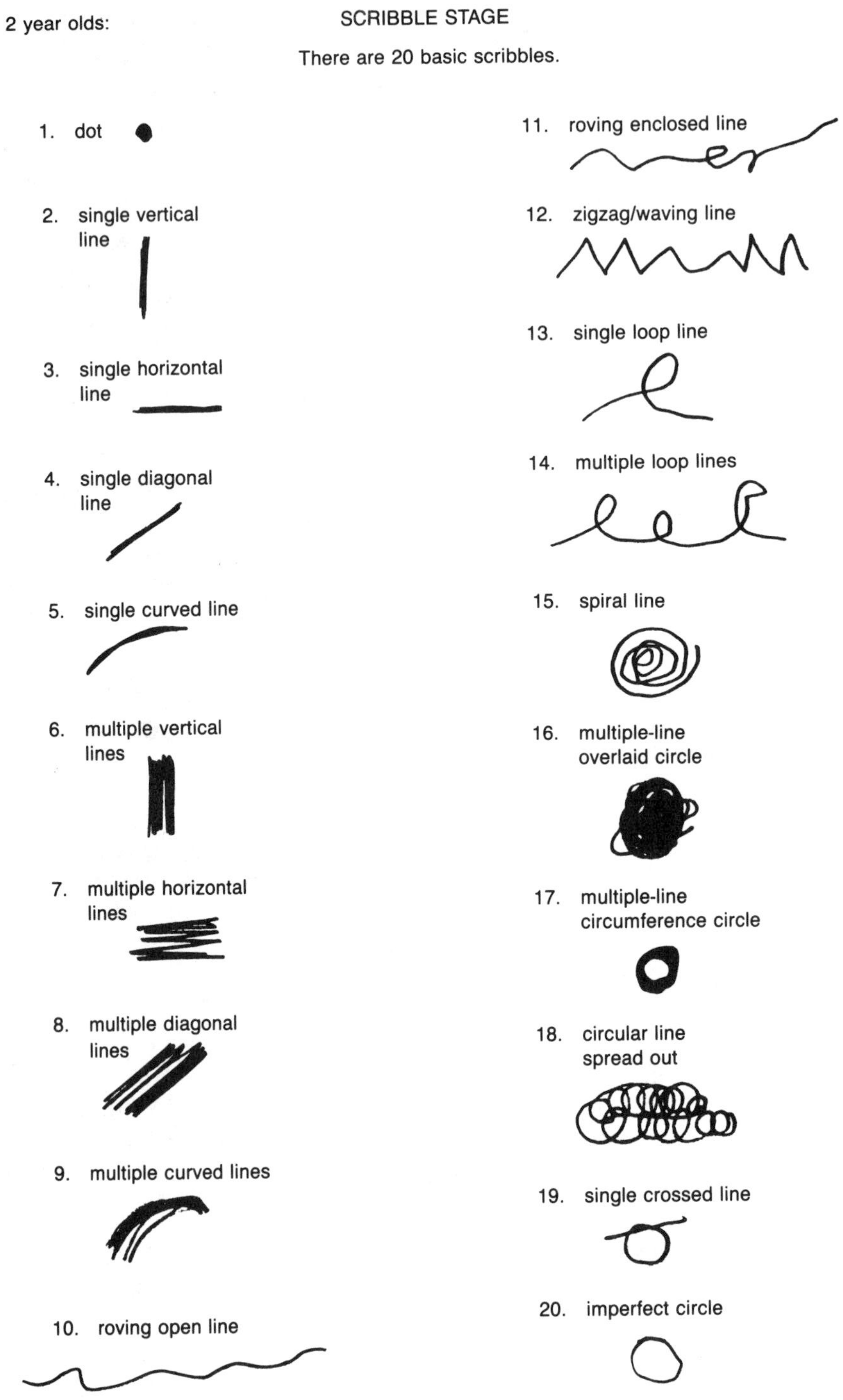

2 year olds:

SCRIBBLE STAGE

There are 20 basic scribbles.

1. dot ●

2. single vertical
    line

3. single horizontal
    line

4. single diagonal
    line

5. single curved line

6. multiple vertical
    lines

7. multiple horizontal
    lines

8. multiple diagonal
    lines

9. multiple curved lines

10. roving open line

11. roving enclosed line

12. zigzag/waving line

13. single loop line

14. multiple loop lines

15. spiral line

16. multiple-line
     overlaid circle

17. multiple-line
     circumference circle

18. circular line
     spread out

19. single crossed line

20. imperfect circle

Figure 8-3   Kellogg's stages

2–3 year olds: PLACEMENT STAGE

Scribbles become more controlled and the child becomes
concerned with placement. There are 17 different placements.

Some include:

all over

central

bottom/top

diagonal

right/left

top/bottom quarter

3 year olds: SHAPE STAGE

Former scribbles drawn at 2 produce overall "gestalts" or
forms. These gestalts or forms contain the following
implicit shapes:

Later, the above implied shapes are drawn as single outline
forms called DIAGRAMS.

(Figure 8-3 continued)

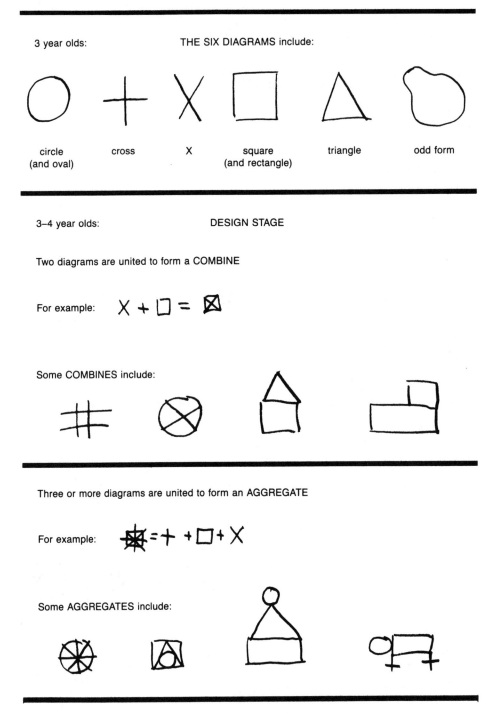

3 year olds: THE SIX DIAGRAMS include:

circle   cross   X   square   triangle   odd form
(and oval)   (and rectangle)

3–4 year olds: DESIGN STAGE

Two diagrams are united to form a COMBINE

For example: X + □ = ⊠

Some COMBINES include:

Three or more diagrams are united to form an AGGREGATE

For example: ✳ = + + □ + X

Some AGGREGATES include:

(Figure 8-3 continued)

4–5 year olds   PICTORIAL STAGE

Their structured designs begin to look like objects that
adults can recognize. The pictorial stage can be divided
into two phases:

1.   early pictorial
2.   later pictorial

(Figure 8-3 continued)

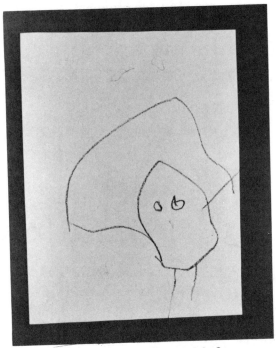

Figure 8-4 An early mandala figure

With the ability to draw diagrams or mandalas, the child moves into the design stage. Two diagrams are put together to make "combines," or structured designs (see Figure 8-5). Three or more united diagrams constitute an "aggregate." Between the ages of four and five most children arrive at the pictorial stage, in which their structured designs or aggregates begin to represent objects. Kellogg likens the development of stages in child art with primitive art. Her normative approach supports the position that all children everywhere draw the same things, in the same way, at the same age. The development of artistic ability in the individual appears to recapitulate the artistic development of the human species.

Kellogg's (1979) stages in drawing a human figure are depicted in figure 8-6.

Lowenfeld and Brittain (1987) are interested in the creative and mental growth of children. Their theory and stages of artistic development are widely recognized and accepted. Their ages, stages, and characteristics appear in table 8-1.

A General Overview of Artistic Development (Birth to Eight)

The author has attempted to combine the different stages of artistic development suggested by Kellogg, Lowenfeld and Brittain, and others into one workable general sequence. The levels or stages are overlapping, and ages are approximate. Schirrmacher's sequence of early childhood art includes:

I Scribbling and Mark-Making Stage (birth to two and up) Scribbling and mark making are forms of nonverbal self-expression. They set the stage for later art. Scribbling and mark making are to drawing as babbling is to speech and crawling is to walking. These marks or scribbles are random as the young child motorically explores and processes with tools. What can I do with this crayon, pencil, chalk, or marker, ponders the young artist. Scribbling and marking are pleasurable, involving visual and tactile stimuli. Holding and moving the tool produces an interesting visual account. The young scribbler or mark maker moves from uncontrolled movements to greater control and purposeful placement of scribbles and marks. From the age of two on, the child artist's marks and scribbles will be more organized, deliberate, planned, and repeated. Some will be given names, although there will be no resemblance to any real object (see Figure 8-7).

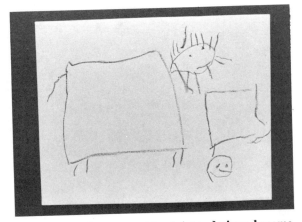

Figure 8-5 Shapes combined into designs become mandala figures.

1. Scribbling:

2. Drawing a single shape:

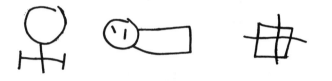

3. Combining single shapes into designs:

4. Drawing mandalas, mandaloids, and sun figures:

5. Drawing a human figure with limbs and torso:

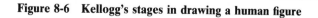

Figure 8-6   Kellogg's stages in drawing a human figure

II Very Personal Symbol and Design Stage (two to four and up) Scribbles, marks, and a concern for the placement of lines and geometric shapes are built up into very personal symbols and designs. For example, a crude circle with a line on each side becomes a stick-figure rendition of a human figure. Actually, this stick figure is a schema, a generalized symbol or form concept that will be used to represent any and all human figures, regardless of age, sex, or build. A square box becomes a schema for any and all buildings. A circle atop a line is the ''lollipop'' schema used to portray trees and flowers. Eisner (1976) would call these examples of pictographs or simplified flat, two-dimensional shapes. The child adds,

Figure 8-7 Scribbling and mark making produce very personal symbols and designs.

Table 8-1 STAGES OF ARTISTIC DEVELOPMENT by Lowenfeld and Brittain

Age: Stage and Characteristics:

2–4 years I Scribbling: The Beginnings of Self-Expression

Scribbling is a developmentally and artistically important kinesthetic, manipulative, and expressive behavior.

1½–2½ substage IA: Disordered and Random Scribbling

- large muscle, whole arm movements
- kinesthetic pleasure, pure processing
- whole-hand grip on marking tool
- may not look at paper while marking
- accidental, random motoric mark making
- haphazard lines
- swing of arm coming in contact with paper results in mark
- uses shoulder motion
- may scribble beyond confines of paper
- exploration—what can I do by moving these tools on paper?
- lines made with simple movements
- tight grip with rigid wrist position
- minimal movement with fingers in marking

2, 2½–3 substage IB: Controlled Scribbling

- smaller marks, better control and organization
- marking motions are repeated
- uses wrist motion with greater control
- stays within drawing area of paper
- variety of lines and direction appear
- better visual and motoric control over where to make lines
- watches intently while scribbling
- more intricate loops and swirls appear
- wider range of scribbles

3, 3½–4 substage IC: Named Scribbling

- spends more time mark making
- gives names to scribbles
- relates scribbles to things in environment
- name of scribble may change in the process
- holds marking tools with fingers, better fine motor control
- greater variety of lines

(Continued)

- increased concentration
- more intentional placement of marks
- awareness and intentional use of empty space
- scribbles do not match name or label given except to child artist
- moves from sheer physical expression to making marks that stand for something else by giving them a name

4–7 years II Preschematic

A schema is a generalized symbol that represents a specific concept. For example, a child's stick-figure drawing is used to represent all people.

- child makes first representational attempts
- symbolic representation built up from former scribbles
- appearance of recognizable geometric shapes
- placement and size random and out of proportion
- random floating spatial arrangement
- may turn or rotate paper while drawing
- distortion and omission of parts in human figure drawing
- head-feet representation of human figure as in figure 8-8
- head-feet representation of human figure
- over time, arms, body, fingers, toes, clothes, hair, and other details appear
- objects drawn as isolated entities; no relationship
- art as personal self-expression rather than for public communication
- very personal idiosyncratic symbols
- can copy a square at age four, triangle at five
- relative size appears at end of stage
- child learns that what is known or experienced can be symbolically represented by mark marking
- children draw how they feel or think about an object, leading to omission, exaggeration, and distortion
- color used randomly, not realistically
- schemas or symbols begin to be recognizable to others

- children enjoy talking about their art
- draws things that are important, relevant, or personally meaningful, e.g., family, pets, or friends
- objects drawn facing forward

7–9 III Schematic: Achievement of a Form Concept

- form concept is developed and repeated
- drawing reflects a child's concept, not perception of an object
- bold, direct flat representation
- two-dimensional spatial representation
- baseline appears to portray space
- skyline may also appear at top
- drawing reflects what a child knows
- subjective portrayal of space
- x-ray drawing appears simultaneously, showing exterior and interior view
- representation of space shows a frontal and aerial view depicted simultaneously
- human figure made up of geometric shapes is repeated and refined
- detailed and decorative
- move to greater conformity or "stiffness" in drawing things the way they should be

9–12 IV Dawning Realism: The Gang Age

There is a greater awareness of details. Older children are more self-conscious about their art. The plane replaces the baseline. Objects are drawn smaller and less distorted.

12–14 V Pseudo-Naturalistic/Realistic Drawing

Young adolescents are very self-critical of their drawing. Detailed human figures with sexual characteristics appear. Cartoons, caricatures, and action figures are also popular. Depth and proportion appear. End of spontaneous art.

14–17 VI Artistic Decision: Adolescent Art

For some adolescents, natural artistic development does not extend beyond the former stage unless they are given further instruction. Some pursue naturalistic style, while others use art for a personal statement. They may copy an artistic style in forming their own personal style.

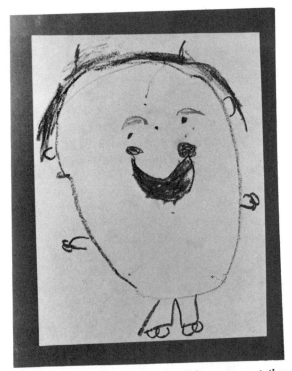

Figure 8-8 Preschematic art: head-feet representation of the human figure

omits, distorts, exaggerates, or streamlines these very personal symbols. The result is a shorthand abbreviated form with little concern for actual color, shape, or size. Spatial arrangement is random, and the child may simply rotate the paper to fit objects in. The very personal symbol or design may not be recognizable to the observer. Children in this stage are still very much process-oriented. They delight in playing with colors, shapes, and forms. They enjoy talking about their creations, which have design quality.

III Attempts at Public Representation (approximately four to seven) Older preschoolers are beginning to customize and individualize their personal symbols and schemas. Their symbols become recognizable to others. There is greater concern for detail, planning, and realistic render-

ing. Children may move from a process to a product orientation. Some are very concerned that the observer recognize the content or subject matter. For example, a human is no longer drawn as a head on sticks. Women begin to have long hair and may wear dresses and make-up. If a child's father has a beard, he will be given one in the picture (see Figure 8-9). Houses are no longer drawn as a triangle atop a square. In drawing one's own house, attention will be given to adding significant details, such as windows, placement of front door, steps, porch, fence, sidewalk, and landscaping.

IV Realism (primary grades and up) Older children in the primary and elementary grades strive for photographic realism in their art (see Figure 8-10). They are very concerned with size, placement, shape, color, perspective, proportion, depth, shading, and the use of details to approximate reality. Art, however, is not the same as photography. Art involves an artist's personal rendering, and some children will become frustrated and may give up art when their products do not match reality. Others continue to repeat perfected stereotypic symbols. A child's passion for race cars, princesses, unicorns, or horses will be endlessly repeated and refined. Still, others will abandon their quest for realism and pursue impressionistic, expressionistic, and abstract styles in their art.

In sum, the developmental explanations, including Kellogg and Lowenfeld, use some form of stage sequence to account for the development of child art. In viewing the child as a whole, they also recognize physical, social, emotional, perceptual, and cognitive factors that influence artistic expression. Yet a general developmental explanation must also account for social, cultural, religious, individual, and environmental factors in tracing the development of child art. A child's culture and religion might affect his or her drawing ability depending upon whether or not the culture values art. A child with an unfulfilled need for acceptance might draw realistic pictures in order to win the praise of a teacher who dis-

Figure 8-9   Early attempts at representing the human figure

Figure 8-10   The older artist strives for realism.

likes abstract art. Environmental factors include home and family, who might constantly punish a child for manipulating, experimenting, exploring, and getting messy. A normative comparison might label this child uncreative or developmentally delayed in artistic expression without allowing for environmental effects.

Cognitive Developmental Explanation for Child Art

It would appear that an explanation that incorporates the best of cognitive and general developmental explanations would account comprehensively for the development of child art. Since early childhood educators have been educated in Piaget's theory, it would seem feasible to see whether this theory can be applied to the realm of art. A comprehensive theory that explains all sectors of child development would be more useful than separate theories that explain different behaviors.

Piaget on Child Art

What can Piaget tell us about children's art? His theory and stages of intellectual development claim to be comprehensive, encompassing, and universal. Artistic expression is, at least in part, a cognitive activity. It follows that a cognitive developmental theory such as Piaget's should explain the development of child art. The task, however, is a difficult one, since Piaget himself believed that it is more difficult to establish regular stages of artistic development than of mental functions. He notes that general development is one of progression, whereas artistic development is one of retrogression. The artwork of the young child appears more creative than that of the older child. In reviewing the theories

of children's artistic development, it appears that Piaget accounts for physical, emotional, perceptual, cognitive, and individual factors within his cognitive developmental framework.

Piaget's theory is cognitive in that his interest was in how children think. It is developmental in that his focus was on how children's thinking changed over time. He believed that all children progress through four major stages of development, which proceed in invariant sequence. Cognitive development proceeds from sensory-motor, concrete activity to symbolic, higher-order conceptual functioning.

Piaget holds drawing or the graphic image to be a form of the semiotic or symbolic functions and as such a representational activity that is considered to be halfway between symbolic play and the mental image. It is like play in its functional pleasure and autotelism (assimilation) and like

Table 8-2   Stages of Art Compared with Piaget's Stages of Cognitive Development

PIAGET'S STAGE	KELLOGG'S STAGE	LOWENFELD'S STAGE
Sensory motor (0–2)	Scribbling (2)	
Preoperational: (2–7)		
• Preconceptual (2–4)	Placement (2–3)	Scribbling (2–4): • disordered and random • controlled • named
	Shape (3): • Gestalts • Diagrams	
	Design (3–4): • Combines • Aggregates	
• Intuitive (4–7)	Pictorial (4–5) • Early • Late	Preschematic (4–7)
Concrete operations (7–11)		Schematic (7–9)
		Dawning realism (9–12)
Formal operations (11–adult)		Pseudo-realism (12–14)
		Artistic decision (14–17)

the mental image in its effort at imitating the real (accommodation). The first spontaneous attempts at artistic expression can be seen as a series of endeavors to reconcile the tendencies inherent in symbolic play and those that characterize adapted behavior. Through drawing, the child attempts to simultaneously satisfy the need for assimilation and to adapt himself or herself to objects and others through accommodation. According to Piaget and Inhelder (1969), the very first form of drawing does not seem imitative but is more like pure play. It is this play of exercise or scribbling that toddlers do when given a pencil, crayon, or marker. Soon, however, the young child realizes forms in these aimless scribbles and tries to repeat them from memory. There may be little or no likeness between these scribbles. As soon as this intention exists, Piaget and Inhelder believe, drawing becomes imitation and image.

Lowenfeld and Brittain's stages of artistic development appear to parallel Piaget's stages of cognitive development. A comparison of Piaget with Kellogg and Lowenfeld and Brittain is found in table 8-2.

SUMMARY

Children's art has a fresh, spontaneous quality that is easier to appreciate than to explain. Theories have attempted to explain what, why, and how children create. Different theories have different explanations for the content, motive, process and product of children's art. A physical explanation holds that young children scribble and draw unrecognizable marks because they lack motor coordination and control. An emotional explanation states that children distort, add, omit, and exaggerate through art those things that have high emotional value to them. A perceptual explanation holds that children rely on their perceptions when drawing. Since a young child's perceptions lack clarity and refinement, their artwork will reflect this. A cognitive explanation holds that children draw what they know. Children who lack experience and sensory involvement with people, places, and things will have little to include in their art. A general developmental explanation using a stage sequence approach incorporates the former explanations while addressing the whole child and individual differences. Kellogg's stages move from scribbling to placement, shape, design, and pictorial. Lowenfeld and Brittain's stages include scribbling, preschematic, schematic, dawning realism, pseudo-naturalism, and artistic decision. The author has attempted to capture the essence of these stages and provide a general developmental sequence for early childhood art from birth through age eight.

SUGGESTED ACTIVITIES

1. Collect several art samples from children (later infancy to age eight). Attempt to sequence them according to Kellogg's, Lowenfeld and Brittain's, and the author's general sequence. Which system works best for you? Why?

2. Recall the physical explanation for children's art. Check out books on art history. Note the similarities and differences between children's art and adult abstract and primitive art.

3. Collect several samples of art from one young child over an extended period of time. Note patterns or growth over time. Attempt to explain the what, why, and how of children's art using different theories of artistic development.

4. Ask children aged two, three, four, five, and six to draw a picture of themselves using crayons or markers. Ask their permission to keep or borrow the pictures. Try

to sequence them according to Kellogg's stages in the development of human figure drawing. Does your data support her stages?

REVIEW

A. Match the artistic term with an appropriate example:

_____ product   1. "I get so mad sometimes, and that's why I make scribbles all over my paper."

_____ content   2. Jim looks in the mirror and smiles. He runs back to the easel and works on his self-portrait.

_____ motive   3. Amy folds, tears, and staples a sheet of scrap paper. She crumples it up and tosses it in the wastebasket on the way to lunch.

_____ process   4. Keely paints several lines and shapes. She says, "See my pretty, pretty design."

B. Identify the major theories or explanations for children's art.
   1.
   2.
   3.
   4.
   5.
   6.

D. Match the age range with its appropriate stage according to Lowenfeld and Brittain.
   1. 1½–2, 2½   _____ Named scribbling
   2. 2, 2½–3   _____ Schematic
   3. 3, 3½–4   _____ Pseudo-naturalistic/realistic
   4. 4–7   _____ Disordered and random scribbling
   5. 7–9   _____ Preschematic
   6. 9–12   _____ Dawning realism
   7. 12–14   _____ Controlled scribbling

E. Identify the author's general stages of artistic development:
   0–2 and up   _____
   2–4 and up   _____
   4–7   _____
   primary grades and up _____

Unit 9

Aesthetics

OBJECTIVES

After studying this unit, the student will be able to

- Define and provide a rationale for aesthetics in early childhood education
- Discuss the aesthetic attitude, process, and response
- Discuss the teacher's role in aesthetics

INTRODUCTION

What is aesthetics, and why should it be addressed in early childhood? This unit attempts to answer these two basic questions. Our concern for the young child's aesthetic development and education stems from our wider concern for the whole child. Young children are aesthetic experts. They demonstrate the aesthetic attitude in their spontaneity, wonder, and amazement at things that adults may take for granted. What is the teacher's role in aesthetics? Teachers can be aesthetic models in the way they dress, behave, and communicate. The indoor and outdoor environment can also be aesthetically pleasing and stimulating.

AESTHETICS

Aesthetics is an abstract concept that means "perception" in Greek. Hopefully, this chapter will not be Greek to the reader. Although we may feel it is important that children learn something about aesthetics, we may not be quite sure what all the term entails. Aesthetics is not synonymous with art. Aesthetics includes art, and the other expressive arts like music and dance, but it also goes beyond them. Just what is aesthetics? Aesthetics

- is a nondiscursive and metaphorical way of knowing and experiencing.

- involves the love and pursuit of beauty as found in art, movement, music, and life.

- is an awareness and appreciation of the natural beauty found in nature and one's surroundings.

- is a basic human response to life.

- means being a beholder of beauty and savoring beautiful things in the world around us.

- involves being connected with one's experiences.

- links knowing and feeling, the cognitive and affective.

Some examples of aesthetic experiences include

- seeing and touching the delicate petals of a rosebud.

- listening to and moving to the beat of an ethnic folk song.

- stopping to savor the aroma of freshly baked bread.

- sitting in wet sand and splashing in the waves upon the shore.

- slowly sipping hot cider while marveling at all the different colors crackling in a campfire.

- admiring the linear design and pattern in a skyscraper.

The type of beauty that aesthetics pursues is the type taken for granted in our everyday lives, rather than the artificial Hollywood-type definition of beauty.

RATIONALE

Why are aesthetics and aesthetic education important in early childhood? There are five reasons. First, our humanistic concern for the whole child motivates us to provide for all aspects of child development. Second, it is our belief that children who marvel at beauty in the world around them will be able to appreciate the beauty of letters, words, numbers, stories, poems, formulas, books, symbols, and people of other cultures. Third, children with the aesthetic sense will develop into adults who know and value good design and can use this as wise consumers in choosing vehicles, clothing, home furnishings, and entertainment as well as on a wider level in planning cities, highways, and attempting to solve problems of pollution, war, poverty, and urban blight. Fourth, it is important for children to value the arts and directly participate in a variety of the arts. Fifth, aesthetic experiences foster concept development.

What is aesthetics? Aesthetics is a branch of philosophy concerned with an individual's pursuit of and response to beauty. Aesthetics involves

- attitude

- process

- response

Aesthetic Attitude

The aesthetic attitude involves:

- openness or childlike freshness

- spontaneity

- intense focusing on the here and now

- a sense of joy, wonder, marvel, or excitement

- willingness to perceive as if experiencing something for the very first time

- commitment or willingness to "stop and smell the roses"

Young children constantly demonstrate the aesthetic attitude. They are sensory gluttons who need to look at, listen to, touch, smell, and taste everything they come in contact with. This may prove embarrassing to some adults: "Nina, please don't touch the daisies.'' Over time Nina may decide not to wonder at flowers. She may learn to take them for granted. Or, as her mother told her, ''If you've seen one, you've seen them all.'' Unfortunately, Nina's mother has lost the aesthetic attitude. The author observed a preschool field trip to the library. The children were stopping to watch and listen to the sights and sounds at a construction site. The teacher was hurrying them up, urging them to walk faster to get to their destination. A rich sensory experience was lost. We live in a too fast-paced world. We rush from home to work. In the process we may ignore rainbows in the sky, colorful patterns in rain puddles, or daisies growing alongside the freeway. The aesthetic experience takes time. It means being frozen for the moment and totally caught up in the here and now.

Aesthetic Process

The aesthetic process is intrinsically motivating. Children sense and perceive for the sheer joy of it. The aesthetic process involves active engagement rather than passive taking in. It means using all the senses to ravish an object or experience, getting completely lost or totally consumed. Examples of the aesthetic process include:

- listening attentively to music rather than merely hearing a song.

- visually exploring or quietly contemplating a work of art rather than merely glancing at it.

- manipulating and feeling a peacock's feather rather than quickly touching it.

Aesthetic processing takes time and a commitment to flow with the experience. Children are more aesthetically proficient than adults. They are sensory gluttons who thoroughly examine their world with all their senses. Adults can learn much about aesthetics from watching children explore the world.

Aesthetic Response

The aesthetic attitude and process result in a response or reaction on many different levels. Our affective response may involve a sense of wonder, appreciation, surprise, a feeling of being moved or touched, awe, exhilaration, or being carried away. We may get lost in the aesthetic experience and totally caught up or consumed for the instant. At the physiological level our response may result in a smile, grin, laugh, perspiration, shiver, chill, heavy sigh, or even ''goose bumps.''

Our reaction will also entail a mental response in the form of a decision, judgment, or evaluation. One may ask

- Was this personally enjoyable, and why?

- Is this work of art, music, or dance good, and why?

- Do I like it, and why?

Our intent is not to make children art critics. They can, however, learn to apply simple criteria to discuss and critique works of art. They can learn to separate what is good or bad from what they like or dislike. For example, a young boy may not like ballet, but he can still appreciate the beauty and grace of the movements. Over time, children will slowly construct their own personal preferences and tastes. They need not follow the crowd in believing that what is popular or current must be good. They will come to identify with and value the arts. Hopefully, they will grow up reading good books, listening to a variety of music, and with tolerance for different artistic styles. Life will offer more than being passively entertained by TV.

Expose Not Impose

As early childhood educators, our task is to expose rather than impose. Expose children to a wealth of sensory experiences and variety in each of the arts. Encourage them to critique, develop personal preferences, and value art, music, movement, dance, and literature. Children can

Figure 9-1 Exposing children to a variety of art forms and styles

use accepted criteria, including the artistic elements, as standards in developing their own preferences. Expose children to a wide variety of art forms and styles without imposing your own preferences. For example, a teacher may not like abstract art, but that does not mean that it is junk or bad, or that realistic art is better. Help children see that art can be good in terms of design or composition even though one may not like it (see Figure 9-1).

TEACHER'S ROLE IN AESTHETICS

What can early childhood educators do to foster aesthetic development? Aesthetics does not come neatly packaged in a kit, series of books, text, unit, or set of materials to purchase. Still, it is important and within our reach. There are guidelines for making the teacher, children, and classroom aesthetically alive. Some of these include:

Teacher as Aesthetic Model

It is important that the teacher personally invest the time to become aesthetically responsive. Teachers can model their own aesthetic awareness and sensitivity. The way one dresses is an aesthetic statement. One need not dress like a fashion model, however, to make this statement. First and foremost clothing should be neat, comfortable, and appropriate for stooping, moving, playing, and sitting on the floor. We can reflect an appreciation of color and color harmony in choosing articles of clothing and accessories. For example, a young girl is proudly showing off her new sweater. Her teacher asks her to identify the colors. Nikki replies, "It has red and blue." Her teacher replies, "My dress has red and blue in it, too. And I wore my white earrings. I wore the same colors that are in our flag." Or, "Jim, you mixed blue and yellow in your picture and made green. I wore blue slacks with a yellow blouse and my green belt. We match.''

Teacher's Inner Beauty

The teacher's inner beauty can be demonstrated by positively relating to all children and valuing their uniqueness. Find something unique and beautiful in each child, and let that child know. Convey beautiful messages. Children appreciate being talked to in regular tones. There is no need to artificially raise the pitch of one's voice and speak in a "syrupy sweet" manner. Refer to oneself as I rather than as Miss Jones or Teacher, as in "Miss Jones doesn't like it when the children are not paying attention" or, "Teacher will just have to get some more apple juice for snack, won't she?" Talk to children in a natural voice rather than in a condescending or patronizing tone. Unfortunately, the elderly are often subjected to this same vocal treatment.

Provide for a Wide Variety in the Arts

Children can be exposed to different examples within a variety of the arts. For example, different types of music can be informally introduced

Figure 9-2 An aesthetically pleasing use of classroom space

throughout the day: slow lullabies or waltzes during rest, classical as background music during snack, and a march or rock-and-roll during clean-up.

Aesthetic Classroom

The classroom can be an aesthetically pleasing and sensory rich environment (see Figure 9-2). Cartoon characters in bright competing colors can be removed from the walls and replaced with aesthetically pleasing artwork, wall hangings, tapestry, weavings, posters, stained glass panels, or prints. Signs on the doors of the classrooms or learning centers can be tastefully constructed, with care taken in the choice of color, material, placement, and printing. Aesthetic centers for experiencing art, music, and movement can be arranged. Aesthetically pleasing displays can be set up with

- beautiful things around a given color, shape, pattern, texture, or design theme, e.g., all things that are square, yellow, checkered, or soft (see Figure 9-3).
- flowers, plants, nature specimens, or seasonal fruits and vegetables, e.g., harvest corn
- machine and appliance parts, gears, tools, and mechanical things
- musical instruments
- postcards and souvenirs
- ethnic costumes and artifacts
- an array of artwork, including drawings, paintings, pottery, ceramics, sculpture, weaving, stitchery, batik, collages, watercolors, and prints
- art: books, postcards, prints, posters
- antique kitchen gadgets and farm tools
- special collections of postage stamps, cookie cutters, baskets, ceramic animals, stuffed animals, license plates, fans, hats, coins, music boxes, arrowheads, minerals, rocks

Figure 9-3 The classroom should be a beautiful environment.

Art Visitors

Invite professional artists, musicians, dancers, crafts people, volunteers, and parents who have some interest and skill in one of the arts. Remember to include this when you survey parents at the beginning of the year concerning any interests and skills that they might volunteer. Get to know the artists, musicians, and dance companies in your area. Remember to provide brief training just as you would with any volunteer. Some may feel more comfortable answering questions or modeling their art or craft. Others may enjoy directly working along with the children.

Art Trips

If no one is willing or able to come into the classroom, it may be possible to take children on a field trip. Art abounds in nature, and a simple outdoor walk qualifies as a recommended field trip. Most communities have at least one of the following to visit:

- museum
- art gallery
- exhibit
- concert
- play
- children's theater
- ballet
- recital
- performance

Figure 9-4   An aesthetically pleasing display of nature items

- planetarium
- artist's studio

It is wise to first attend by yourself to make sure that your particular group will profit from this experience. Field trips involve a great deal of planning, energy, and often expense, and they need to be well thought-out. In arranging the field trip, try to match what the experience has to offer with your group's developmental needs, interests, and abilities. For example, most toddlers would not sit still through an hour of chamber music. See if there is someone on the staff who has experience in giving tours to young children. Some museums have special children's rooms and exhibits. Others may have collections that they loan out. Many libraries have art prints that may be rented or checked out.

Sensory Literacy

Help the children become sensory literate. This can be done in two ways. First, help them to stop, sense, and heighten their awareness of the experience at hand. For example, ask the mother of a newborn to let the children at least look and listen. Touch may come weeks later with a supervised bath. Second, stimulate their senses. An array of sensory experiences appears in the following unit.

In a sense, the teacher and classroom quietly whisper, "Beauty, it is all around you. Together we will take the time to get involved."

SUMMARY

Aesthetics and young children go hand in hand. Babies begin by exploring and marveling at their world. Over time, children will internalize adult "don'ts" and learn not to look, listen, touch, taste, or smell. They will take their senses and the world of lines, shapes, colors, and design for granted. Our task was identified as a multipurpose one. We need to stimulate their senses; be an aesthetic model in dress, behavior, and communication; and set up a sensory rich and appealing learning environment. Our discussion focused on a rationale for including aesthetics in early childhood. First, it was seen as a part of a child's wholistic development. Second, it will help children see the beauty of line and shape in the world of letters, words, and numbers they will encounter. Third, it was believed that children who grow up with the aesthetic sense will become wise consumers and concerned citizens who will advocate for beauty in the community and workplace. Fourth, it will help children understand and appreciate a wide range of arts. Fifth, sensory data fosters thinking and concept formation.

SUGGESTED ACTIVITIES

1. Reflect on your most recent or vivid aesthetic experience. Sketch it or attempt to put it in words. Describe how you felt and your reaction.

2. Critique the use of indoor classroom space for its aesthetic appeal. Make specific recommendations.

3. Set up an aesthetically pleasing display of objects that have sensory appeal.

4. Arrange an aesthetic experience through a simple field trip such as a nature walk.

REVIEW

A. Explain aesthetics as
   1. attitude
   2. process
   3. response

B. List aspects of the teacher's role as it relates to aesthetics.
   1.
   2.
   3.
   4.
   5.

Unit 10

Sensory Stimulation

OBJECTIVES

After studying this unit, the student will be able to

- Discuss the relationship between sensing, perception, feeling, thinking, and concept development
- List and briefly explain the different senses
- Construct a multisensory activity

INTRODUCTION

Young children use all their senses to process their aesthetic experiences. They are sensory gluttons who are intrinsically motivated to look, touch, listen to, taste, and smell everything they come in contact with. They respond on both affective and cognitive levels. For example, they not only experience pleasure in looking at and smelling a flower but also enhance their concept of what a flower is. Hopefully, young children with the aesthetic sense will grow up to be wise consumers and planners for a better future that includes beauty and peace.

FROM PERCEPT TO CONCEPT

Perception is the ability to receive sensory impressions from one's surroundings and relate them to what one knows. Sensing, perception, thinking, and concept development are closely related. The aesthetic experience merges the cognitive with the affective response. Thinking and feeling come together. For example, when they hear bells chime in a church for the first time, young children may perceive the sound, smile with amazement, think about it, and relate it to the doorbell or clock chimes at home. The process can be depicted as:

Senses	+	Perception	+	Feeling	+	Thinking	=	Concepts
visual		look		enjoy		compare		color
auditory		listen		marvel		contrast		tone
tactile		touch		joy		analyze		texture
olfactory		smell		happy		classify		scent
gustatory		taste		amazed		describe		taste

The world has much to offer. A child with a sensory handicap or deficit may miss stimuli. Often, such children develop strengths in other areas. For example, children who are blind often develop a strong sense of touch or hearing. A child who does not invest the time in perceptual activity or who lacks sensory stimulation is also at a disadvantage. For example, a child who has never touched, looked at, smelled, or listened to an elephant will be at a loss when asked to discuss or read about them.

MORE THAN FIVE SENSES

Children use their senses to thoroughly explore their environment. Traditionally, the five senses include:

- visual
- auditory
- tactile
- olfactory
- gustatory

To this basic list Montessori (1967) would also add the following senses:

- chromatic
- thermic
- sterognostic
- baric
- kinesthetic

Figure 10-1   Many experiences are multisensory.

Each of the above senses will be explained and exemplified with activities. The Appendix contains an incomplete list of books on the senses.

Multisensory Experiences

Most experiences involve more than one sense (see Figure 10-1). Cooking is a good example of a multisensory experience. Making popcorn involves looking at and touching the kernels before, during, and after popping; listening to the sound of popcorn popping; smelling the scent of melted butter being poured over hot popcorn; and lastly eating the popcorn in big handfuls. Children would also enjoy moving like popcorn popping. Start off as small, compact kernels that slowly expand and puff up as they get hotter. A coconut has a distinctive color, shape, covering, texture, and taste. Children can look at the outside of a coconut and discuss its color, size, shape, and covering. "What do you hear when you shake it? What do you think is inside? What can we do to find out? How can we open this coconut? What words describe how it looks and feels? Does it smell? I also have a bag of shredded coconut. How are the two similar? How are they different? Let's cut the coconut in half and look inside. Now what do you see and smell?

Scrape off a piece of the white inside. How does it taste? Does it taste the same as the flakes of coconut in the bag?'' The line of questioning, discussing, and experiencing is endless. The same process could be done with an artichoke, melon, pineapple, or baking cookies.

Visual

The visual sense involves looking and seeing. Ideally, it involves a thorough visual exploration rather than a passing glance or quick look. Vision and discriminating between letters and words will be required for reading.

The indoor classroom should be a visually rich, appealing environment with nature specimens, artifacts, and objects to visually explore. Samples of children's art as well as art posters or prints can be displayed on the walls. A science center or discovery table can display a collection of seashells, antique kitchen items, or postcards to visually explore.

Some recommended materials to encourage visual exploration include

- prism

- magnifying glasses: hand-held and three-legged stool or stand

- safety mirror: both hand-held and full-length

- lenses: concave and convex (making things bigger or smaller)

- microscope and slides

- telescope

- kaleidoscope

- binoculars

- camera

- cellophane color paddles

- sunglasses

- flashlight

- mirror

- view master and reels

Water play with bubbles is a simple visual activity. Provide a tub of water, liquid dishwashing soap, and rotary eggbeaters. Food coloring is optional, and children love the effect. A related activity is blowing bubbles outdoors. Children enjoy trying to catch them. Encourage them to note the transparent quality of bubbles as well as the rainbow of colors present. A simple recipe for homemade bubbles is

Iridescent Soap Bubbles

1 cup of water
2 tablespoons of liquid dishwashing detergent
1 tablespoon of glycerine (available from drugstore)
½ teaspoon sugar

Other visual activities include:

New View (N/Pre, K, Pri) Encourage children to view their indoor and outdoor environment from new perspectives. For example, What do you see . . .

- when you lie on the floor and look up?

- when you lie on the floor on your right or left side?

- if you lie on your back outdoors on the grass? What appears in the sky? What shapes do you see in the clouds?

- if you climb to the top of the jungle gym and look down or up?

- if you balance on your hands and stand on your head?

- when you are swinging on the swing? What colors and shapes appear?

Nature Walk (N/Pre, K, Pri) Take magnifying glasses when going on a nature walk. Look for interesting shapes and designs in nature. Stop to

- look at moss, berries, insects, fungus, mushrooms, nests, tree stumps, shadows, birds, spiderwebs, ant hills, or the pattern in rust on a building.

- listen to birds chirping, leaves rustling, wind blowing, dogs, cats, squirrels, twigs cracking, and acorns or nuts falling.

- touch tree bark, damp moss, dry leaves, sand, and cold mud.

- smell evergreen trees, pinecones, pine needles, damp earth, dry leaves, and crisp, cold air.

Collect interesting specimens to bring back to the science table. Some teachers may prefer to leave the natural environment intact and not remove bugs, leaves, or twigs.

Focus Scopes (N/Pre, K, Pri) It is sometimes difficult to notice design and detail in an environment that is alive with color, shape, sound, and movement. Children may need help focusing their visual sense. This is why magnifying glasses, cameras, binoculars, and telescopes are recommended. An empty tissue roll makes a very good focus scope. The outside can be decorated or covered with contact paper to enhance its appeal. Encourage children to explore the indoor and outdoor environment by very slowly exploring with their focus scope. Pay attention to small things that might be missed by just looking. Focus scopes can also be covered with cellophane at one end and used like color paddles. Children can also join their fingers to make a frame to focus their vision.

Peek Frames (N/Pre, K, Pri) Find an interesting picture in a magazine. Look for color and design and cut off any words. Find sheets of construction paper that are the same size or larger than your picture. Peek frames can be used in many ways. Neatly cut a 1-inch round hole out of your sheet of construction paper. Place this sheet over your picture. Ask the children, "What do you see through my little window? Let's think of many different things that the picture might be." Peek frames can have more than one opening.

The hole can also be torn into and slowly peeled larger to foster continued guessing and heighten suspense. This activity forces children to focus their visual sense on a small area of design, color, or shape. The idea is not to guess the one right answer but to use the visual clues to come up with many possibilities.

Look and Match (N/Pre, K) Children enjoy matching objects or pictures that are the same. Find pairs of some of the following:

- magazine pictures

- fabric scraps

- wallpaper samples

- tile or linoleum samples

Younger children will enjoy matching pairs that are quite distinct. Older children can be challenged with subtle variations in color or design, such as those found in wallpaper sample books.

Masterpiece Match (N/Pre, K, Pri) Children would enjoy matching pairs of art postcards. Art postcards are available from art museums. See Appendix E for other sources. Try to find pairs of postcards that are similar but not identical—for example, a family done in realistic and abstract styles. The subject matter may be identical, but the treatment is different. Older children may also enjoy playing a "memory" game with the postcards. You will need at least six pairs of postcards. Arrange them face up on the floor. Turn them over. Older children may not need to see them turned right side up. Next, encourage children to turn over a pair. If they match, the child gets another turn. If one child gets all the pairs correct in sequence, this might indicate that there are too few pairs.

Eyes Spy (N/Pre, K) This activity involves both looking and listening and can be played with a large group. Focus on an item in the room that has a distinct color or shape. "Eyes Spy. I see something in the room that is bright red. What could it be?'' Children may need additional clues. "It is bright red only on the front. The back side is white. What could it be?'' Or, "Eyes Spy triangle. I see something on the wall that has a triangle shape. What could it be?'' Children enjoy being the leader for this activity. Encourage them to use color and/or shape clues rather than merely saying, "I see the round clock on the wall that ticks. What is it?''

Watch the Waves (N/Pre, K) Capture a wave in a bottle. Find a large plastic bottle. Add mineral oil and some water that has been colored with blue food coloring. Cover tightly. Tilt, tip, and watch the waves.

Auditory

The auditory sense involves hearing and listening, which are two very different processes. Children who hear do not always listen. Our world is a noisy one, with people talking, appliances, stereos, traffic, and televisions. Children are exposed to much auditory stimulation, and learn at a very early age to tune much of it out. Casual hearing is appropriate much of the time. Music, literature, or teacher's directions warrant concentrated listening. Our aim is to help children know when to switch from passive hearing to active listening. Recommended objects that foster active listening include

- stethoscope
- tape recorder with tapes of stories, rhymes, and poems
- record player with music and story records
- rhythm instruments
- tuning fork
- music boxes
- bells
- metronome

Some activities include

Quiet Time (N/Pre, K, Pri) Quiet Time can be used as a relaxation technique after a noisy activity. It is a good routine to quiet the children. Gather children and have them sit quietly. They may giggle at first but will improve with practice. Encourage them to close their eyes and listen. "What do you hear? Think about the sounds but do not talk yet. Let's keep on listening to the noises inside our body and around the classroom.'' Wait a few seconds or minutes, depending on the group. Children may hear their heart beating, blood flowing, stomach grumbling, throat swallowing, lungs breathing, or classroom pet moving about.

Sounds Around Us (N/Pre, K) Tape-record distinct sounds, including

- toast popping out of a toaster
- clock ticking
- whistle blowing
- vacuum cleaner in operation
- horn honking
- bell ringing
- blender or electric mixer in operation
- running water
- toilet flushing
- water going down the drain
- animal sounds
- traffic sounds
- telephone ringing
- alarm clock ringing
- door slamming
- siren wailing
- baby crying
- ball bouncing
- someone jumping rope

Some more difficult sounds might be

- sticks or twigs cracking
- someone walking on leaves
- a match being struck
- a refrigerator door being closed
- tape pulled off a dispenser
- coins being dropped
- wind blowing
- car ignition being turned on and off

Pause between sounds. Play the sounds back and encourage the children to quietly listen (not just hear) and guess what made the sound. Children may want to close their eyes to help focus exclusively on the sounds without any distracting visual stimuli. Younger children who know but cannot verbalize may enjoy hearing the sound and pointing to a corresponding picture or sketch that you provide.

Sound Detectives (N/Pre, K)   Encourage children to close their eyes and listen very quietly while you perform some action. They must actively listen and attempt to guess what you have just done. Some actions include

- clapping hands
- jumping
- snapping fingers
- rubbing hands together
- blowing a kiss
- yawning
- stamping feet
- bouncing a ball several times
- stapling papers
- dropping a pencil
- writing on the chalkboard

- whistling
- opening and closing a book
- walking on tiptoe
- shutting a door
- turning on a water faucet

Children enjoy taking turns being the leader in this game. Encourage them to think up new actions, not merely repeat what was just done.

Sound Containers (N/Pre, K)   Active listening involves being able to discriminate among sounds. Auditory discrimination involves listening to sounds and deciding which ones are similar and which are different (see Figure 10-2). Hearing similarities and differences will help children with speaking, phonics, and reading. Find a matched set of at least six opaque boxes or containers. Small milk cartons or soda pop cans are

Figure 10-2   Michelle listens for the same or different sounds.

fine. Plastic toy eggs or egg-shaped pantyhose containers are also recommended. Cover half of the set in one color and half in another—e.g., three red and three blue. Since the cues can only be auditory, it is important that the children cannot see what is inside. Separate your set into three, four, five, or six pairs. Fill each pair with an equal amount of one of the following:

- marbles
- salt
- rice
- cotton balls
- paper clips
- wad of papers
- toothpicks
- string
- pennies
- tacks
- ribbons

First, test the items chosen to make sure each pair has identical sounds. Pairs must be significantly different from each other. For example, a pair filled with salt and a pair filled with sugar will probably sound identical. With very young children or those with auditory problems, limit the set to two or three very distinct pairs. Slowly add to your collection as the children begin to master the task. Cleverly and inconspicuously mark or code your pairs on the bottom to foster a quick check.

Water Sounds (N/Pre, K, Pri) Children can listen to sounds and make music in containers filled with water. Find a set of at least three identical glass bottles or jars. Fill one to the top with water, another halfway, and the third a half inch from the bottom. Different amounts of water will make sounds of different pitch when the bottle is struck with a metal spoon. Practice making

sounds that vary in volume (soft and loud) depending on how lightly you strike. Which makes the highest pitch? Which makes the lowest pitch? Encourage children to seriate the sounds from low to high or vice versa. The children will enjoy playing music on the bottles. They may want to incorporate their water sounds with music made on other rhythm instruments. Additional bottles with different water levels can gradually be added.

Listen Along (N/Pre, K, Pri) Children enjoy being read to. Reading to them is one way to encourage an interest in and love of reading. Get animated and stress words and phrasing. Encourage children to hear words that rhyme in poems. Storytelling with props, such as puppets or a flannel board, allows you to get dramatic with the story line while making continual eye contact. It also allows the children to get involved.

Tactile

The tactile sense involves feeling and touch. For our purposes the tactile sense may operate in conjunction with the visual sense. Activities that involve touching and feeling texture will be categorized as tactile. Those involving touching to identify, recognize, and name an object without looking will be categorized as sterognostic and covered in a later section.

Sandpaper Feel (N/Pre, K) Different grades of sandpaper, from rough/coarse to fine/smooth, can be used in this activity. Make a pair of strips for each grade of sandpaper. Start with fine and very coarse and add in-between gradations as the children master this activity. Cut the sandpaper into 2-inch-wide strips about 4 inches long. Mount the sandpaper strips on sturdy cardboard or a piece of wood. Encourage children to trace down the strip with an index finger and feel the texture. Ask them to find another strip of sandpaper that feels the same. What word describes how it feels? Is it rough or smooth? Older children might enjoy seriating the sandpaper strips from smooth to rough or vice versa.

Fabric Feel (N/Pre, K) Children can wear blindfolds or agree to close their eyes for this activity. Provide identical pairs of some of the following:

- burlap

- velvet

- silk

- netting

- corduroy

- denim

- cotton

- gauze

- fur

- terrycloth

- vinyl

- wool

- carpet

Remember to make the sizes the same so that the only clues will be tactile. Encourage children to discuss their matched pairs. How do they feel? What word tells us? Are they soft, smooth, rough, wrinkly, or bumpy?

How Does It Feel? (N/Pre, K) Discuss with children how different things feel hard or soft (see Figure 10-3). Encourage them to give examples. Neatly print "hard" and "soft" on separate sheets of paper. Encourage children to say the words after you. Place a picture of something hard and something soft on the corresponding papers. Encourage children to put the following items under the proper heading:

- cotton

- velvet

- stone

- coin

Figure 10-3   How does it feel?

- feather

- plush stuffed animal

- wet sponge

- dry sponge

- powder puff

- sandpaper

- rubber squeeze toy

- tree bark

- cactus

- yarn ball

- plastic

- emery board

- tin foil (over cardboard)
- plastic wrap (over cardboard)
- steel wool

Young children will enjoy sorting the actual objects. Older children will enjoy cutting pictures of hard and soft objects out of magazines and pasting them onto the corresponding sheet. They may also expand their tactile vocabulary to include rough, smooth, slick, bumpy, prickly, fuzzy, furry, porous, and coarse.

Texture Collage (N/Pre, K) Children enjoy pasting or gluing objects with varied textures into a collage. The group can also work on a thematic collage containing both pictures from magazines and actual objects that are rough, smooth, sharp, fuzzy, or furry. Provide pieces of sturdy cardboard when pasting or gluing heavy objects.

Olfactory

Although animals rely heavily on the sense of smell, people do not. We use our sense of smell on a very limited basis to smell food or perfume or cologne, or to react to unpleasant odors. Children use their sense of smell more than adults. For example, they enjoy scratching and sniffing stickers. Still, they may refuse to try a food based solely on its smell or color (visual cue). Green, yellow, and orange vegetables hold little olfactory or visual appeal for some children. Some activities to stimulate the olfactory sense include:

Scent Bottles (N/Pre, K) Find a set of identical bottles or containers with lids or tops. Glass baby food jars, pill vials, empty spice bottles, or film containers are ideal. Make two, three, four, five, or six pairs. Color-code the lids in each set, for example, six green and six orange. Place a ball of cotton in each pair if you are using liquid scents or extracts. Make air holes in the lids if solids are used. Pieces of nylon stocking can be placed over the opening and secured with rubber bands (see Figure 10-4). Fill each pair with one of the following:

- cinnamon
- mustard
- garlic
- coffee
- pepper
- sawdust
- baby powder
- perfume
- vanilla
- lemon peel
- pine
- tea

Figure 10-4 The nose knows.

- onion

- cloves

- peppermint

- talcum

- bath crystals or bath salts

Cotton balls soaked in clear liquids or extracts provide no visual clues. Scents need to be fresh and will have to be replaced from time to time. Remind children to replace the lids or tops after use. Items like coffee or tea cannot be used in clear containers, since the cue will be visual rather than olfactory. Remind children to smell without inhaling or tasting. Match up pairs that smell the same. Use a word to describe how each smells. Is it sweet, sour, spicy?

It Smells Good Enough to Eat (N/Pre, K)   The olfactory and gustatory senses work together. Generally, foods that smell good taste good. This activity can be done with a small group as a lead-in to snack. Encourage children to close their eyes while you hold a piece of food on a toothpick under their nose. Pause long enough for them to get a good sniff without making skin contact. A piece of banana is one example. Next, hold a different food, such as a pineapple chunk. Do they smell the same or different? Encourage children to match up an array of fruits or vegetables on a plate in front of them with your standard. The finale to the activity is being able to eat the samples for snack.

The classroom can also be an olfactory-rich environment. Teachers can add scents and aromas. A bowl or dish of rose petals, pine needles, sachet, incense, dried orange rinds, scented soaps, or potpourri provides a lovely fragrance. Flowers such as roses, mums, and carnations, scented candles, and perfume samples also encourage children to stop and smell. The following recipe can be used to produce a cinnamon scent in your room:

Soak several whole cinnamon sticks in cinnamon oil.

Dry.

Tie together with dried flowers in a bundle.

Add a pretty ribbon or lace.

The fragrance of cinnamon should last for months.

To make a simmering stove-top potpourri mixture, follow this recipe:

Combine whole allspice, whole cloves, cinnamon sticks, and pieces of dried orange peel. Put a tablespoon or two in 3 cups of water and place in a pot. Bring to a boil on the stove and simmer. Add more water as needed.

Children enjoy sticking whole cloves into oranges that have been pierced with holes. Tie with pretty ribbon and hang. They can also be taken home as gifts if the children have had a good deal of input into making them.

More importantly, the classroom should be free of stale, musty smells. Spraying with a disinfectant spray or air freshener may eliminate or mask stale odors. Fresh air and a routine airing out are essential.

Gustatory

Eating and quiet time spent enjoying home-cooked meals have become a luxury in many households. Many children may never see their parents cook a meal. Meals are now quickly eaten on the run or even skipped. Convenience foods may be bland, precooked, or low in nutritional value. Eating occurs out of habit and routine rather than for its gustatory or taste appeal. Eating may be something that is done at different times by different family members, perhaps in front of television, or merely something children do before getting ready for bed. Perhaps this is why most early childhood educators value snack time and cooking as a time to talk, socialize, and share food and experiences. Some recommended gustatory activities include:

Snacks and Cooking (N/Pre, K)   These two activities are vital in any early childhood program. Snacks should be more than crackers and sugary juice. Although they are moderately expensive, nutritious snacks provide their own characteristic look, color, shape, texture, taste, smell, and sound when eaten. Recommended snacks include

- banana slices
- pineapple wedges
- peanut butter
- orange slices
- carrot sticks
- apple wedges
- cheese chunks
- celery stalks
- grapes
- melon balls
- pear halves
- grapefruit sections
- cauliflower
- cucumber slices
- sunflower seeds, raisins, and nuts
- strawberries

Cooking experiences using nutritious ingredients with much child input are also highly recommended. For example, children can be actively involved in making fruit salad: washing and dividing the fruit, reading the recipe, mixing, and measuring ingredients. Baking bread is another multisensory cooking activity that involves learning across many, if not all, of the early childhood curricular areas. To bake bread one must read a recipe and measure ingredients. Children are actively involved in kneading dough. Is it magic or science that makes the dough rise? Bread baking has a wonderful aroma, and the bread has an equally good taste when it is topped with homemade butter. Cooking with apples provides unlimited possibilities for learning and eating. Apples can be cut, peeled, pared, or baked, or the slices can be spread with peanut butter or dipped in melted cheese. Using the following recipes, one can also make

Apple Juice

½ cup seeded apples
1 cup water
1 teaspoon sugar

Put ingredients in blender and blend thoroughly. Chill and serve. Will serve two, so vary recipe given the size of the group.

Applesauce

Cut several apples. Place in electric frying pan or covered skillet. Cover apples with cider. Put lid on pan and bring to a boil. Reduce heat and simmer until apples are soft. Let cool. Take turns grinding in a food mill. Add sugar and cinnamon to taste.

Dried Apples

Peel and core several apples, and cut them into rings or slices.

Place them in salted water for 15 minutes. Dry for 2 weeks.

* Dried grapes become raisins using this recipe.

Taste Party (N/Pre, K)   Children can sample an array of foods and classify them as sweet, sour, hot, cold, or salty. Bitter, bland, and spicy may be difficult for young children. They can be added as children master the basic tastes. Each child will need his or her own spoon. Using an eyedropper, place a drop of a sweet substance, e.g., sugar water, onto each child's spoon. Encourage them to think about the taste before guessing. They should wipe their spoon and take a drink of water from their own cup between tests. Repeat the procedure using salt water. Sample tastes include

- sugar water
- salt water
- cocoa
- chocolate
- cinnamon
- nutmeg
- brewed tea
- orange
- lemon
- honey
- vinegar water
- syrup

Solids can also be introduced at a taste party. Try using

- chocolate chips
- carrot cubes
- apple squares
- banana slices
- cheese chunks
- cinnamon candy
- cottage cheese
- melon balls

Remember to check for food allergies before any taste test or food experience.

Chromatic

Montessori views the chromatic sense as a subset of the broader sense of vision. The chromatic sense involves the ability to identify, match, and discriminate among colors. Activities for the chromatic sense involve:

Color Games

a. Matching (N/Pre, K) Very young children enjoy matching colored shapes cut out of construction paper (see Figure 10-5). Begin with red, blue, and yellow and add more colors as children master this task. Or, glue colored shapes in a vertical column on a sheet of cardboard or file folder. Draw an outline of identical shape next to each color. Cut out a second set of colored pieces. Encourage children to place the second set next to its match. Paint samples obtained from hardware or paint stores can also be used. Select bright enamels rather than pale pastels. Older children may enjoy matching color

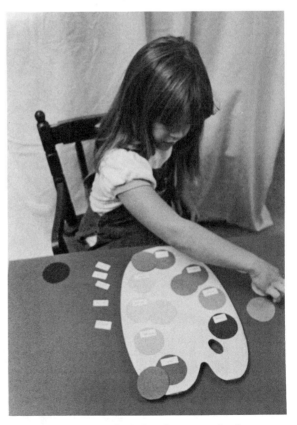

Figure 10-5   Refining the sense of color

names. Later they can match a color name printed on an index card with a color cue.

b. Seriating (N/Pre, K) Not all colors are created equal. Colors come in different shades, tints, tones, intensities, and values. Black added to red will turn it into a darker shade, perhaps scarlet. White added to red will turn it into a lighter tint, such as pink. To make a color game for seriation, first find color charts or paint strips that have variations in tint or shade. Begin with very obvious gradations: light green, medium green, and dark green. Glue an identical set to a piece of cardboard or a file folder and let children first match the shapes in order. Later, they can lay them out in a trainlike array from darkest to lightest. Gradually increase the number of colors or add more difficult gradations in color as children become more proficient. This seriation activity can also be made self-correcting or self-checking. For example, place each of the five shades of red on its own index card. The cards can be coded 1 through 5 or A through E in small numbers or letters on the back side. Or, a simple picture, such as a caterpillar, can be drawn on the back. When the colors are put in proper sequence, the picture will be complete when the cards are turned over. The caterpillar should appear whether the cards are seriated from darkest to lightest or lightest to darkest.

Color Our World (N/Pre, K, Pri) Viewing objects through pieces of cellophane will distort their color. Color paddles are sturdy pieces of cellophane or translucent plastic. They are commercially available, or it is easy to make a set. Individual sheets of cellophane wrapping paper or term paper covers can be mounted or framed in cardboard to form a sturdy holder. Provide at least the primary colors. Color paddles can be used individually or together. For example, viewing the room through red over blue will make it look purple.

Create Colors (K, Pri) Provide round pieces of tissue paper in the three primary colors for each child. Tissue paper is difficult to cut, and you may have to provide ready-cut pieces for younger children. Cut a large piece of wax paper for each child. Children can arrange any two pieces of tissue paper on the wax paper. Make sure the two primary colors have some overlap. Add the third colored circle, making sure it overlaps the other two. Carefully place a second sheet of wax paper on top. Press with a warm iron. Older children should be able to press their own provided they have direct supervision. The heat will melt the wax and seal the round shapes. Hold the picture up to the light or display it on the window. Notice how purple appears where red and blue overlap, orange where red and yellow overlap, and green where blue and yellow overlap. What color appears in the very center, where red, blue, and yellow overlap?

Color Show (N/Pre, K, Pri) You will need an overhead projector for this activity. Project on a blank wall or white sheet. Find a flat glass dish and place it on the illuminated projector. Add several drops of water. Add a few drops of food coloring. Start with one primary color. Wiggle the dish and swirl the beads of food coloring with a toothpick. Add a second primary color. Repeat the process and watch the colors mix. What has happened? Continue with your color show by adding new colors or starting over with a different combination of primary colors. A squirt of black ink will also make an interesting pattern in water. Adding a very small drop of black ink to food coloring will make shades.

As a variation on this activity, fill three Zip-Lock plastic storage bags with water. Add a different primary food color to each. Do not fill them to the top or bulging. Lock securely. Hold them up and let children view their surroundings through different colors.

Thermic

The thermic sense deals with one's perception of temperature. How do things feel: hot, cold, warm, lukewarm, or tepid? Our thermic sense responds when we touch a hot stove, eat frozen ice cream, or take a cold shower. Recommended materials include a thermometer and barometer. Activities for the thermic sense include:

Fingers Swim (N/Pre, K) Fill three shallow or low bowls with water. One bowl should contain hot water, a second cool, or room-temperature water, and a third cold or melted ice water. The bowls of water should look the same but feel very different. Encourage children to put one or two fingers into one bowl and tell you how it feels. Is the water hot or cold? Pairs of bowls can also be used. Can you find water in another bowl that feels just the same as the water in this one? Since the bowls are open, the hot and cold water will return to room temperature very quickly. Encourage children to discuss which feels like the water they use in the bathtub, to swim in, to water the lawn, to drink on a hot day, or in soup.

Temperature Jars (N/Pre, K) This activity must be prepared fresh each time. It works best with a very small group. Locate three pairs of identical glass jars. Baby food jars are ideal. Fill each pair with equal amounts of one of the following:

- hot (but not scalding) water
- cold or melted ice water
- tepid/lukewarm or room-temperature water

Begin by having children hold one of a pair in one hand. Ask them, "How does it feel? What word describes it? Is it hot, warm, cold, or cool?" Encourage them to use their other hand to find a match that feels the same. Remember that this activity must proceed fairly quickly, since the water in all the jars will quickly return to room temperature. As children master this activity, intermediate temperatures, including finer grades of warm and cool, can be added.

How Does It Feel? (N/Pre, K) Encourage children to discuss how they feel when they directly experience some of the following:

- being in snow
- being out in the rain
- being in front of an air conditioner or fan
- being near the stove or oven
- being near the fireplace
- taking a bath
- having your hair washed and rinsed
- when opening the door of the refrigerator or freezer
- walking barefoot on sand at the beach in the summer
- playing outside in summer with the sun shining
- walking barefoot in mud
- splashing in the waves at the beach
- having your hair dried with a hair dryer
- fanning a piece of paper in front of your face
- sucking on a Popsicle
- holding an ice cube

Encourage children to use thermic terms such as hot, warm, cold, freezing, cool, and burning when discussing their reaction.

Thermic Moves (N/Pre, K) Encourage children to use their bodies to show what happens to water under different temperature conditions:

- Pretend you are a drop of water in the ocean. Some one picks you up with their shovel and carries you home in their sand pail.
- They leave you outside, and it is getting colder and colder. Winter is coming, and soon it will snow.
- It is freezing cold, and you turn into an ice cube. Someone picks you up and rolls you in

the snow. They keep rolling until they get a big ball of snow. They make two more big balls and stack them into a snowman. You are up near the snowman's head and very proud.

- Slowly, the sun starts to shine. It is getting warmer and warmer. You are beginning to melt, slowly, very slowly.

- All that's left of the snowman is a big puddle of water.

- Someone scoops you back into the sand pail and brings you inside. She pours the water into a pot and puts it on the stove. She turns the heat on. It feels good being warm inside. The water comes to a boil and starts to jump around because it is so hot.

- They pour you into the dishpan, and you help make bubbles and clean the dishes.

Thermic Cooking (N/Pre, K) There are many simple cooking experiences that include heating or freezing ingredients. Two simple ones include:

Popsicles

1 cup of hot water
2 cups of lemonade
1 package Jell-O (any flavor)

Mix and pour into ice cube trays. Insert a toothpick or Popsicle stick in each. Freeze. Children and adults enjoy these because the Jell-O slows down the melting process and eliminates much of the mess.

Snow Sherbert

Snow (fresh, clean, and white)
1 egg
½ cup sugar
1 teaspoon vanilla
1 cup milk

Mix ingredients. Slowly add snow. Stop when it reaches the consistency of sherbert.

Sterognostic

Being able to recognize objects through tactile-muscular exploration without the aid of vision is the sterognostic sense. Touching and feeling a pinecone involves the tactile sense. But closing one's eyes while touching and handling a pinecone to identify it involves the sterognostic sense. Whereas the tactile sense usually involves visual clues, the sterognostic sense does not. Activities for the sterognostic sense include:

Feely Bag (N/Pre, K) Place a magazine tub at the bottom or toe of an old large sock. Children enjoy working an arm through the sock to find the object in the tub. Use objects made of wood, metal, paper, plastic, cloth, cork, glass, rubber, and leather (see Figure 10-6). Encourage children to verbally describe

- how the object feels: Is it rough, smooth, or bumpy?

- the size of the object: Is it big or little?

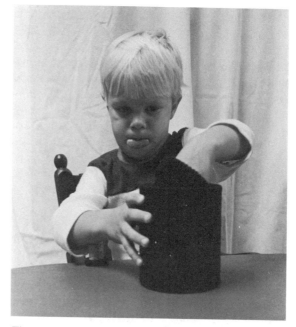

Figure 10-6 Identifying an object by touching without looking

- the shape: Is it round, square, triangular, flat, or solid?

- what the object is made of: Is it made of wood, paper, rubber, glass, or metal?

- the length of the object: Is it long or short?

- the weight of the object: Is it heavy or light?

Children can also guess the object's

- color

- function or purpose: What is it used for?

- name: What is it called? What do you think it is?

As with all questioning, it is important for children to attempt to justify their answer. Asking them, "How do you know?" or "Why do you think so?" encourages them to go beyond random guessing. For example, "I think it's money 'cause it's round, small, and feels like a penny."

Young children may prefer to match the object they touch with its picture or a sample of the actual object. Toddlers will enjoy merely putting things in and out of the Feely Bag.

Blindfold Game (N/Pre, K) Children can be blindfolded or agree to keep their eyes closed. The child can be given an object—e.g., a doll—to thoroughly touch and feel without the aid of vision. The child can use these sterognostic cues to guess what the object is. Young children do tend to peek or tell each other the answer. This is to be expected.

Baric

Recognizing objects as heavy or light and gradations in between involves the baric sense. An activity for the baric sense involves

Weight Jars (N/Pre, K) Find a set of six baby food jars and spray paint the insides the same color or cover them with identical wrap. Separate them into pairs—e.g., three brown and three

yellow—and fill one of each pair with plaster of paris or some other self-hardening and weighted substance

- to the very top

- to the middle

- one-half inch full

Encourage children to hold one jar in one hand and find another jar that weighs the same. Children should be encouraged to use both hands like a balance scale, with one jar in each hand. Put the matched pair aside. Keep going until the children have decided that the three pairs weigh the same. Subtly coding each matching pair on the bottom will aid in checking. Encourage children to talk about weight. Which pair is heavy/light? Which pair is the heaviest/lightest? Children can order or seriate from heaviest to lightest or vice versa. Older children may enjoy using a set of ten with finer gradations in weight.

Kinesthetic

The kinesthetic sense involves a whole-body, sensory-motor muscular response. When we talk about children learning by doing or being actively involved, we are referring to their kinesthetic sense. For example, young children learn about animals by observing, listening, smelling, touching, and using their body to act like them. Moving on all fours like a tiger will help the child form a strong concept of that animal, which is necessary for talking about, reading, or making art objects related to tigers. Some activities for the kinesthetic sense include:

Musical Moves (N/Pre, K) Record on tape or find albums of different types of music, including

- jazz

- classical

- waltzes

- calypso

- Latin rhythms
- rock-and-roll
- Irish jig
- polka
- marches
- electronic
- tango
- Broadway show tunes
- country
- soul
- Hawaiian
- African
- zither
- Mexican hat dance
- flamenco
- any and all ethnic

Each piece of music has its own characteristic mood, tempo, and rhythm. Therefore, each will suggest a certain type of bodily expression through movement. This activity combines listening with the kinesthetic sense of body movement. Play different samples of music and encourage children to move the way the music makes them feel. The teacher may want to model and move along with the group. However, encourage children to come up with their own way of moving rather than imitating the teacher's moves. Turning the lights off may help set the tone. Moving with the aid of scarves or pieces of fabric may help some children. Other shy or insecure children may prefer to merely watch, not participate. Reassure them, but also encourage their eventual participation. Over time and with repeated practice children will become more comfortable and confident in their creative movement.

Listen and Move (N/Pre, K, Pri) Children can also move in response to taped sounds. Tape-record some of the following:

- a waterfall
- birds chirping, soaring, or flapping their wings
- feet marching
- a jet soaring
- sounds of laughter
- animals growling
- waves pounding against rocks
- popcorn popping
- a car engine trying to start on a cold day
- toast popping out of a toaster
- a chain saw starting up
- skating on ice
- people swimming in a pool
- water coming to a boil
- teakettle whistling
- jumping off a diving board

This movement activity is more sophisticated than the former. It will take more thought on the part of older children to translate what they know about a waterfall into bodily movement.

Shapes Movement (N/Pre, K) Young children will enjoy crawling through openings of different shapes. Find a large cardboard appliance carton. Cut a large geometric shape out of each side. Use a circle, square, triangle, and rectangle. Make sure that each shape is large enough for your biggest child to fit through easily. Mark and reinforce the edges of each cut-out shape with different colored cloth tape. Children can take turns listening to your directions and crawling through the appropriate shape; for example, ''Go in the square and come out the triangle." This activity involves listening, sequencing, shape recognition, and body movement. Make the directions longer and more difficult for older children; for example, "Go in any four-sided figure, come out a red shape (marked with colored cloth tape), and walk around all the shapes two times."

Squeeze, Mash, and Taste (N/Pre, K) Children will enjoy the movement and physical activity needed to:

- squeeze oranges, lemons, limes, or grapefruits on a reamer for juice
- mash apples for cider
- mash tomatoes for juice
- mash carrots for cookies or cake
- mash strawberries for natural ice cream
- mash bananas for yogurt

The finished products can be sampled for snack. Juices that look the same do not always taste the same. Adding sugar to lemon juice changes it from sour to sweet.

Artistic Dramatic Play (N/Pre, K) Children may enjoy pretending that they are artists. Think of what an artist might wear and do. Items to include would be an old white shirt, a beret, an easel, an art supply box (e.g., a suitcase), a palette, brushes, goggles, and a sketch book. Place these in the dramatic play center.

Keep on Movin' (N/Pre, K, Pri) Find a large open space and help children locate their own personal space in which they can move without touching another child. "Today, we are going to pretend that our room is filled up with some very different things. Listening and thinking about the different things will help us move. For example, what if the room was filled from the floor to the ceiling with balloons and we had to move? How would we do it? Show me with your body how you would move. How would it feel on your body? How would you move to get through?" Other examples include

- Jell-O
- snow
- mashed potatoes
- ice
- sand
- water
- peanut butter
- honey
- frozen yogurt
- ice cream
- cotton candy
- syrup
- glue
- rubber tires
- pillows
- jelly beans

Gingerbread Children (N/Pre, K) Read the children's classic tale of the Gingerbread Boy. Encourage children to take turns acting out the different parts. Cooking can also be coordinated.

Gingerbread Children

1 box butterscotch pudding mix
½ cup shortening
½ cup brown sugar
1 egg
1½ cups flour
1½ teaspoon ginger
½ teaspoon cinnamon
½ teaspoon baking soda

Cream shortening and sugar. Add egg and let children take turns mixing well. Add dry pudding mix, flour, and spices. Mix well. Distribute individual balls to children. Roll thin and flat, and cut with cookie cutter. Or, mold like clay into ginger-bread child. Bake on greased cookie sheet at 350° for 10 minutes. Will make about a half dozen.

SUMMARY

Sensory stimulation was viewed as involving more than the five senses. Montessori identified the chromatic, thermic, sterognostic, baric, and kinesthetic as vital senses. Materials and activities for each of these senses were provided. Senses, however, do not operate in isolation, and a multisensory approach was advocated. The relationship between sensing, perception, feeling, thinking, and concept formation was identified.

SUGGESTED ACTIVITIES

1. Select one of the sensory activities from this unit and implement it with young children.

2. Plan and implement a multisensory cooking experience.

3. Observe in a Montessori classroom. Focus on the sensory materials and how children use them.

REVIEW

A. Match the sense with its key descriptive terms.

1. auditory   _____ touch
2. olfactory   _____ smell
3. chromatic   _____ weight
4. visual   _____ color
5. gustatory   _____ hearing
6. kinesthetic   _____ looking
7. baric   _____ temperature
8. thermic   _____ tactile-muscular
9. tactile   _____ movement
10. sterognostic   _____ taste

B. Use the example of a young child eating cotton candy for the first time to explain the following equation:

Senses + Perception + Feeling + Thinking = Concept Formation

Unit 11

The Elements of Art

OBJECTIVES

After studying this unit, the student will be able to

- List and briefly explain the artistic elements
- Discuss the categories and physical properties of color
- Devise an art activity that will help children learn about the artistic elements

---

INTRODUCTION

Some people have difficulty separating whether a work of art is good or bad from how they feel about it. Liking a work of art does not make it good. Although artistic tastes and preferences are personal, we can use accepted criteria to talk about, analyze, and critique art. The artistic elements are one accepted criterion. They include line, color, shape or form, mass or volume, design or composition, pattern, space, balance, and texture. A work of art can be critiqued in terms of how successfully the artist has used one or more of the artistic elements. Art activities to help children learn about, appreciate, and use the artistic elements will be provided in this unit.

AESTHETIC CRITERIA

What does one look for in an aesthetic experience? How does one analyze, let alone critique, a dance, musical score, or work of art? The various expressive arts have their own criteria. In dance, one might match up an individual dancer's movement with the music. Do the movements flow? Evaluating a musical score on the basis of rhythm, tempo, and one's emotional response is appropriate when listening to music. The visual arts have their own criteria or artistic elements (see Figure 11-1). These include

- line

- color

Figure 11-1 Can you identify artistic elements in works of art?

- shape or form
- mass or volume
- design or composition
- pattern
- space
- balance
- texture

Each of these will be explained and illustrated with activities. Some were discussed previously in the section on senses. Please refer to Appendix F for books on the artistic elements—line, color, and shape in particular.

Line

What is a line (see Figure 11-2)? A line

- is a visible mark made by an artistic tool, such as a crayon, moved across a surface, such as paper.

- is a continuation of a dot.

- usually suggests direction, movement, rhythm, or form.

- does not exist in nature. Nature produces edges. Artists produce lines to represent edges.

- helps the artist define shapes and contours or represent edges.

- is something we use to make letters, words, numbers, symbols, and signs.

Lines can be used in many different ways. Lines have their own dimensions, including size, direction, length, width, and weight. They also have their own personality. Lines can be

- long or short (length).

- tall or short (height).

- thick, fat, heavy or thin, skinny, light (weight). Heavy lines may convey a feeling of force, weight, boldness, or strength. Thin lines may add a delicate, light, or timid touch.

- big or little (size).

- horizontal, vertical, or diagonal (direction). Horizontal lines suggest calm, quiet, and a sleeping, restful position. Vertical lines suggest stability and strength. Think of the lighthouse in the middle of the sea, an upright steel girder, or a rocket blasting off. Diagonal lines suggest tension and activity, as in climbing uphill or skiing downhill.

- up or down (direction).

- forward or backward (direction).

Figure 11-2   Art can be made using lines.

Line Design (N/Pre, K)   Children can make abstract line designs using string and a frame. Secure a wooden picture frame. Hammer small nails a few inches apart around the frame. By pulling the string taut from nail to nail, the child can create a line design. Different colors of yarn will add the element of color to the linear design. A cardboard frame can also be used. Cut 1-inch-long slits on all four sides. Encourage children to connect the slits with yarn. The result will be a line design.

Dancing Lines (K, Pri)   This activity is a variation of drawing to music. Play a short passage of music and ask the children to respond by making a line with a marker, brush, or paint. For example, a march might suggest a forceful, patterned up-and-down line. A waterfall might suggest thick vertical lines, whereas water dripping from a faucet might suggest a vertical dotted line. What kind of a line is suggested by the following taped sounds:

- water boiling
- rocket blasting off
- siren blaring
- sawing wood
- ice skating music
- a polka
- thunder
- hopping on one foot
- jumping rope
- a creaking swing in motion

- to the right or to the left (direction).
- continuous or broken, dotted.
- open or closed.
- jagged or smooth.
- patterned or irregular.
- straight or curved, zigzag or wiggly. Curved lines suggest graceful movement, as in a dance or in nature. Zigzag lines suggest energy, as in a bolt of lightning.
- controlled or uncontrolled and spontaneous.
- dark or light.
- parallel or perpendicular, intersecting or crossed.
- fast or slow.
- plain or fancy.
- sharp or soft.

Art activities that will help children learn about lines include:

Line Art (N/Pre, K)   Children can make their own line art by dipping cut pieces of string into a small bowl of white glue. Gluey string can be creatively arranged in a linear design on a black sheet of construction paper. Colored yarn can be glued onto white drawing paper. Let dry.

Squeeze and Sprinkle (N/Pre, K)   Children can be encouraged to make a linear design using a small bottle of white glue. Before it dries, have them sprinkle sand, salt, glitter, or crushed eggshells to highlight their line design. Let dry.

Lots of Lines (N/Pre, K, Pri)   Children can cut line strips out of construction paper. Encourage them to make some thick, thin, wide, fat, short, and long. Provide cut strips of paper for very young children who lack scissoring skills. Children will enjoy arranging their cut paper lines into a design and gluing them onto a piece of colored construction paper.

Stick Art (N/Pre, K)   Children can make line designs using toothpicks, Popsicle sticks, or pipe cleaners. Each of these can be spread with glue and pressed onto cardboard or sturdy paper. The arrangement will be a linear design with angles. Children may bend the pipe cleaners into nonlinear forms. This is to be expected. Arrange and let dry.

Color

A world ablaze with color provides a beautiful backdrop for our daily lives. What is color? Color

- is based on the passage of light. It is the visual sensation of light caused by stimulating the cones of the retina. As the light source changes, so does the color. With no light there is no color.

- comes from the sun. We see colors because of the way certain objects reflect color rays to our eyes. For example, we see a banana as yellow because the banana absorbs all the color rays except yellow and reflects the yellow rays back to our eyes.

- makes each of us respond with feeling. Some of us have favorite colors. Children develop their color preferences and palettes early in life. These influence the colors that we use to select articles of clothing, home furnishings, and cars, and to do art.

Colors can be categorized as

1. Primary
   Red, blue, and yellow are the three primary colors. They are called primary because they are used to produce the other colors.

2. Secondary
   Mixing two primary colors in equal amounts results in a secondary color. For example,
   Red + Yellow   = Orange
   Yellow + Blue   = Green
   Red + Blue   = Purple/Violet

3. Intermediate
   Mixing an adjoining primary and secondary color in equal amounts results in an intermediate color. For example,
   Yellow + Orange   = Yellow-Orange
   Red + Orange   = Red-Orange
   Red + Violet/Purple   = Red-Violet
   Blue + Violet/Purple   = Blue-Violet
   Blue + Green   = Blue-Green
   Yellow + Green   = Yellow-Green

4. Complementary
   Complementary colors are opposite each other on the color wheel. They provide a dramatic visual contrast. Examples include red and green, yellow and purple, and blue and orange.

5. Neutral
   Neutral refers to pigments that do not have a particular color. Black and white are considered neutrals.

Please refer to the Color Wheel (on the back cover), which identifies colors as primary, secondary, and intermediate.

Colors have recognizable physical properties, including

1. Hue
   Hue refers to the color name. Hue is color in its pure, unmixed form. For example, red and blue have different hues.

2. Value

   Value refers to the relative lightness or darkness of a hue. It refers to the amount of light that a surface reflects back to the eye. For example, the value of a hue such as yellow is lighter than that of a darker hue such as purple. Red and blue can have the same value (dark) but different hues.

3. Intensity

   Intensity refers to the purity of light reflected from a surface. Terms like bright and dull refer to color intensity. Pure colors are most intense or bright, and mixing a color with others dulls its intensity.

4. Tint

   Adding white to any color lightens its value and results in a tint. For example, adding white to red makes pink.

5. Shade

   Adding black to any color darkens its value and results in a shade. For example, adding black to red makes maroon.

Colors also have thermal qualities that have a psychological impact on the viewer. Colors make us feel. Colors can

1. Be Warm

   Warm colors, including red, yellow, and orange, remind us of hot or warm objects, such as the sun or fire.

2. Be Cool

   Cool colors, including blue, green, and purple/violet, remind us of cold or cool objects, such as water, ice, grass, and shade.

3. Give the Illusion of Size and Space

   Light colors make objects appear to be larger than they actually are. Dark colors make objects appear to be smaller than they actually are. For example, painting a room off-white will make it look larger. Painting the same room a dark tan will make it look smaller. Light colors make ob-jects look closer. Dark colors make objects look farther away.

Adult artists are more consciously concerned with how the viewer will be affected by their choice of color. An artist might use red, yellow, and orange to convey the sense of heat in painting a Fourth of July picnic. Blues and greens could be used to paint a ship adrift at sea. Light colors would be used to paint a portrait. Dark colors might be used to hint at the presence of crowds in the far background. Color has many possibilities and personalities. Some of these include

- light or dark (value)

- bright or dull (intensity)

- warm or cool (thermal quality)

- opaque (oils, acrylics, thick tempera) or transparent (watercolors, thinned tempera)

- primary, secondary, or intermediate

- pure or mixed

Some activities for color have already been mentioned in the sections on the visual and chromatic sense. Others include:

Color Sort (N/Pre, K) Children enjoy sorting different objects by color. Provide a muffin tin or egg carton. Very young children can use only a few openings. Older children can be challenged with a dozen openings. Cut circles of different colors and place one in the bottom of each opening. Use pieces of construction paper, small yarn balls, or pom-poms for the children to sort. Children can use metal tongs to pick up the yarn balls or pom-poms and place them in the matching opening.

Wheel of Colors (N/Pre, K, Pri) Use a round, clean pizza cardboard. Glue on pie-shaped wedges of different colors. Find as many pinch-type clothespins as you have color wedges. On each of the clothespins, use markers to color it a corresponding color. For example, a red pie wedge will have a clothespin marked with red. Encourage children to clip each clothespin to the matching color. Older children may enjoy using a separate set of clothespins that have color names written on them. The color names can be matched with the corresponding colors.

Color Cooking (N/Pre, K) A sweet snack should be the exception rather than the rule. When used, however, they can be turned into an educational experience. Children can learn the principles of color mixing by frosting cookies, graham crackers, or cupcakes. Begin with clear icing or vanilla frosting in three small bowls. Put blue, red, or yellow food coloring into one of the bowls. Children can frost some of the goodies with the primary colors. Mix any two of the primary colors to get purple, orange, or green frosting. This can be done in conjunction with holidays.

- red and green during Christmas
- pink, white, and red for Valentine's Day
- green for St. Patrick's Day
- purple and yellow for Easter
- orange and black for Halloween
- red, white, and blue for the Fourth of July
- orange, brown, and yellow for fall and Thanksgiving

A recipe for a drink that reinforces color:

Orange Drink

6-ounce can of concentrated orange juice
1 cup milk
½ cup water
10 to 12 ice cubes
1 teaspoon vanilla

Pour in blender. Blend until frothy.

A recipe for a snack that reinforces color:

Edible Color Blocks

1 envelope Knox gelatin
⅓ cup cold water
1 small box Jell-O (experiment with colors and flavors)
1 cup boiling water

Dissolve Knox gelatin in cold water. Dissolve Jell-O in boiling water. Mix everything together. Pour into rectangular pan. Cool. Cut into shapes.

Color Mixing (N/Pre, K, Pri) Children will enjoy experimenting with mixing colors. Find six baby food jars. Six sections of a Styrofoam egg carton can also be used. Fill three with several drops of water. Add one of the primary colors of food coloring to each. This leaves three empty for color mixing. An eyedropper can be used to mix equal parts of any two colors. What new color do you get? Repeat the process using two different colors.

A variation on this task includes additional materials. Provide a color mixing directions card as follows:

Red + Blue   =

Blue + Yellow =

Red + Yellow =

Provide a separate eyedropper for each of the primary colors. Label three jars red, blue, and yellow. Label three other jars red + blue, blue + yellow, and red + yellow. Young children need directions using actual color swatches rather than the color words. Older children can do the color mixing by reading the color names.

Hand Painting (N/Pre, K) Finger, or more appropriately hand, painting is a good opportunity to learn about color mixing. Provide one primary color and encourage the children to use their entire hand in moving the paint about. Next, add a second primary color. What happens when they mix? What color did you make? This may be enough color mixing at one sitting for young children. At a different time, repeat the above process using the primary color that was not originally involved.

Color Clay (N/Pre, K) Teachers can use one of the recipes for homemade clay or play dough listed in Appendix H. Start with three uncolored balls. Add a few drops of food coloring of one of three primary colors to each ball. Knead. Divide the primary-colored balls in half. Use half to experiment with color mixing. What happens if balls of red and blue, blue and yellow, or red and yellow are mixed together? What new color of clay do we get? The result will be different-colored clay balls.

Made in the Shade (N/Pre, K, Pri) Children can learn to make tints and shades of a color. Individual finger paint sets or tempera paints can be used. Begin with the three primary colors. Add a small dab of white to each. What happens? What color did you get? Is it lighter or darker than the one you started with? Mix the three secondary colors and repeat the process. Repeat the process adding a very small dab of black. Adding white will produce tints of red, yellow, blue, and the secondary colors. Adding black will produce shades.

Color Helpers (N/Pre, K) Discuss with children how community helpers often wear a certain color. Fire fighters wear red. Police officers wear blue. Doctors, nurses, veterinarians, ambulance drivers, paramedics, and hospital workers wear white or green (in surgery). Cooks and chefs also wear white.

Color Day (N/Pre, K) Declare a day of the week to have a specific color. For example, every Friday is color day. This Friday's color will be green. Encourage children to wear something green. Activities, songs, stories, and snack can be focused on the color green. Some color-coordinated snacks include

- red: apples, cherries, strawberries, ketchup
- yellow: banana, scrambled eggs, mustard
- green: grapes, celery, lettuce
- orange: carrots, cheese, pumpkin bread
- purple: grape juice, grapes
- brown: whole wheat bread, peanut butter, chocolate milk or pudding
- blue: blueberry muffins
- white: cottage cheese, milk, plain yogurt, rice, mayonnaise

Color Stories (N/Pre, K) Please see Appendix F for an incomplete list of books related to color. *Caps for Sale* is an excellent one to read and act out. Children will enjoy stacking the red, blue, brown, and gray caps. They can take turns being the peddler or monkeys.

Shape or Form

Shape and form are terms that are appropriate for critiquing two-dimensional art that has length and width (see Figure 11-3). Specifically, what is a shape or form? Shape or form

- refers to the outside form of an object.
- is the edge of an enclosed space.
- is defined by a line or outline, or by contrasting color or texture in the surrounding area.
- represents positive space or figure.
- is created by connecting lines.

Shape and overall form have their own qualities and personalities. Some characteristics include

- simple or complex

Figure 11-3 Michelle learns about shape by painting on round paper.

- circular or angular
- geometric, including circle, square, rectangle, or triangle, or nongeometric, including irregular, free-form, organic, or amorphic
- active or quiet
- clearly defined or vaguely defined
- tall or short
- big and large or small and little
- open or closed
- solid, heavy, massive or open, light
- proportional or nonproportional
- concave or convex
- transparent or opaque
- hard or soft
- abstract or realistic
- symmetric or asymmetric
- precise or vague

Activities that help children learn about shape include:

Sandpaper Shapes (N/Pre, K) Geometric shapes, including circles, squares, triangles, rectangles, diamonds, and so on, can be cut out of pieces of sandpaper and mounted on sturdy cardboard. Children will enjoy using their fingers and hands to feel the shapes. Older children can progress to feeling only the outlines of shapes done in sandpaper.

Bean Bag Shapes (N/Pre, K) Children will enjoy manipulating and tossing beanbags that have been cut into geometric shapes. Shape beanbags can vary in size, shape, and color. They can be sorted and classified as well as tossed in a basket or dropped in a pail.

Puzzling Shapes (N/Pre, K) Geometric shapes can be carefully drawn with a ruler on poster board. Use a different color for each shape for younger children. Older children will not need the color clue. Cut each shape into a number of pieces. Color-code the pieces on the back if necessary. Laminate the individual pieces and trim the excess. Match the number and sizes of the pieces with your age group. For example, a square cut in half diagonally may challenge a toddler but might bore a kindergartner.

Sew a Shape (N/Pre, K) Trim the raised edges off Styrofoam meat trays. Cut each into a different geometric shape. Sturdy cardboard could also be used. Use a hole punch to carefully punch an inner outline of the shape. Encourage children to sew the shape by following the line of holes that outlines the shape. They can use a shoelace or thick yarn rather than thread. Use a large plastic needle or tape the beginning end to get it through the holes. Tie a large knot, button, or bead at the end so that it will not pull through. Some children will sew with an over-under, in-and-out motion as one would do with needle and thread. Others may prefer to loop or lace around the edge. Either of these is preferred to randomly connecting the holes without any notice of shape.

A piece of pegboard with the outline of a shape drawn through the holes could also be used. The children could use golf tees rather than yarn to complete the outline of the shape.

Safety Shapes (N/Pre, K) An awareness of shape serves many purposes beyond mere aesthetic beauty. Different shapes are used on signs that help people live, walk, and drive safely. The same is true for colors. Even if one cannot read a sign, the shape and color tell us what to do. Take a short neighborhood walk and look for safety signs, such as STOP. Safety shapes include the octagon, triangle, diamond, and circle. Children may want to make red, green, and yellow circles and paste them in proper order against a black background to make a traffic light.

Shape Stamps (N/Pre, K) Children enjoy placing objects on an inked stamp pad and stamping that impression on a piece of paper. Find items that have round, square, rectangular, and triangular shapes. The round edge of a plastic hair roller is ideal for a round shape. Find hair rollers in different sizes. Encourage children to creatively combine the shapes into a design or picture.

Shape Spatter Paint (N/Pre, K, Pri) Cut geometric shapes out of sturdy cardboard. Place a sheet of paper into the lid of a box. Place one shape on the paper. Place a thin screen over the top. Dip an old toothbrush in paint. Carefully brush across the screen, making sure that the paint is spattering around the edge of the shape. Remove the screen and carefully lift up the shape. The outline of the shape will appear on the paper. Repeat the process, creatively combining shapes at a different sitting as a separate activity.

There are many standard activities that are appropriate for learning about color as well as shape. Some of these include:

Signs (N/Pre, K) Signs or displays of colors and color names as well as shapes and their corresponding names help children learn these concepts. A color caterpillar can have a body made up of different-colored sections. Each circular ball of the body is a different color. A shape train can have a regular locomotive but cars of different geometric shapes. The names can be neatly printed above or below the items in each. Remember to post these at children's eye level rather than high up at adult level.

Manipulative Games (N/Pre, K, Pri) Traditional games can be specifically designed and adapted to learn about shapes and color. Recommended examples include

- bingo
- lotto
- dominoes
- card games, including old maid, rummy, hearts, and fish

Browse through the aisles of a toy store or the pages of a toy catalogue, noting board games and manipulative materials. Then, creatively adapt your own version.

Match and Memory (N/Pre, K, Pri)   Make pairs of colors or shapes on index cards. Encourage children to match pairs. Older children enjoy turning all the color or shape cards over and trying to remember where the pairs are. If the two cards that are turned up match, the player gets another turn.

Classify (N/Pre, K, Pri)   Children can be challenged to find different ways to classify an array of cards. Index cards can be grouped on the basis of color, shape, and size. Older children will enjoy playing with a total deck of twelve cards per color. For example,

• Red: circle, square, rectangle, triangle; small, medium, large.

If you use this formula for each of the three primary colors, you will end up with a total of thirty-six cards.

Gone Fishing (N/Pre, K)   Draw an outline of a fish on a series of index cards. Add a color or shape to each. Staple a paper clip at the mouth of each fish shape. Find a paper towel roll to use as a fishing rod. Tie a length of string to one end and a small magnet at the other. Spread the fish out on the floor on top of a piece of blue construction paper for the water. Encourage children to catch a fish and name the color or shape.

Partner Match (N/Pre, K)   This is a good activity for the entire group. Give each child an outline of a geometric shape or color to hold. Older children may enjoy working with shapes of different colors. Gather children in a circle holding up their shapes. Have them carefully look around to find someone who is holding the same shape, then take turns finding the partner whose shape matches. Exchange and repeat.

Flip-Flop Books (N/Pre, K)   Find a small book of index cards that are bound with spiral wire binding. Neatly cut each card in half. Actually, you will have too many cards, so you may want to carefully remove some. Or you can use the book to cover color, shape, and other concepts. Open up the book to any page. You will have a top and bottom section on the right and left sides, four index-card sections. For example, for the red page in the color book, find or draw something red in the upper half of the right page. Carefully print the word *red* in red marker on the bottom half of the right page. Find or draw something else that is red, but carefully divide it up between the top and bottom halves of the left side. Encourage children to flip-flop through the various pages, top and bottom, until they find a match. For example, the red balloon (top right) with the word in red (lower right) matches the completed picture of a red apple on the left.

Mass and Volume

Mass and volume are terms that are appropriate for critiquing three-dimensional art, which has height, length, and width. What a circle is to two-dimensional shape or form, a sphere is to three-dimensional mass or volume. What is mass or volume? These are terms that refer to a solid body. An artist such as a sculptor can portray mass or volume in many different ways. Mass or volume can be portrayed as

• open or closed

• heavy, bulky, massive or light, delicate

• solid, impenetrable, blocklike or open, penetrable

• opaque or transparent

• geometric or organic

• static or dynamic

• angular or curved

• hard or soft

- large or little, big or small

- stationary or moving

Design or Composition

Throughout this book design has been used as a polite way to describe anything and everything young children create in art. A scribble of lines, a splash of colors, and an array of shapes have been referred to as designs. Adult artists use design in a different sense, as in overall composition. Design or composition is the overall mark of success, the standard of achievement, and the frosting on the cake. Design and composition as artistic criteria attempt to address the following questions:

- Did the artist pull off or accomplish what he or she originally set out to do? Was the artist successful?

- Do line, shape, color, texture, and form blend and work together as a unified whole? Is the arrangement of these artistic elements pleasing and satisfying?

- Does the finished work impart a sense of overall order, coherence, equilibrium, and organization?

- Did the artist strike a balance between monotony and chaos or unity and variety?

- Is there a focal point, emphasis, center of interest, or dominant spot that attracts and holds attention? Does it make the viewer want to return and admire again and again?

With a good design or composition, the answer to the above questions would be yes. Adult artists walk a fine line between unity, variety, and contrast. It is difficult to create a unified work that hangs together while adding novelty, variety, contrast, and an element of surprise to make it interesting. Child artists, who are less concerned with their finished products, may have little concern for design and composition. We can, however, use the principles of design and composition to talk about works of art and make

children aware of the planning and energy that often accompany the making of art.

Overall design and composition, although less directly relevant to early childhood art than some of the other criteria, do form an arch or backdrop for the other criteria.

Pattern

Pattern surrounds us. Fence posts, steps, rungs of a ladder, railroad tracks, and spokes on a wheel all suggest a repetitive pattern. Pattern

- refers to the treatment given to a surface.

- suggests flow, rhythm, motion, or movement.

- suggests regularity and repetition.

- can be made with forms, shapes, lines, colors, textures, or symbols that move across a surface in a recurring sequence.

Patterns have their own identity. They can be

- ornate and fancy or plain

- regular or irregular

- symmetrical or asymmetrical

- sequenced or alternating

Activities for learning about patterning include:

Sponge Painting (N/Pre, K, Pri) Cut different geometric and abstract shapes out of household sponges. Encourage children to identify a pattern, e.g., circle-square-circle, and repeat that pattern on their paper. The pattern can be arranged in horizontal, vertical, or diagonal fashion (see Figure 11-4).

Pattern Printing (N/Pre, K, Pri) Provide an array of items to print with. Examples include cookie cutters, lids, corks, and bottle tops. Encourage children to identify a pattern and repeat it on their paper. Encourage them to come up with different ways to repeat their pattern hor-

Figure 11-4   Making shapes with sponges dipped in paint

izontally, vertically, or diagonally by dipping their items in paint and making a pattern.

Pattern Picture (N/Pre, K, Pri)   Shapes cut out of wallpaper, fabric scraps, or gift wrap can be glued or pasted in a repetitive sequence. For example, a pattern could consist of scraps of white burlap, foil, gift wrap, and white burlap glued in a row. A different pattern sequence could follow below, or the same pattern could be repeated.

String a Pattern (N/Pre, K)   Children can use wooden beads and a shoelace to create a pattern and series of repeated patterns. Children may enjoy repeating a pattern that a teacher begins. Others enjoy making a pattern as it appears on an index card. Remember to tie a large knot at one end. The lacing end should be pointed and reinforced with tape.

Space

An artist's ultimate space is determined by the size of the canvas, be it paper, cardboard, wood, or a shoe box. Within the overall space, the artist must deal with the problem of arranging elements. How many shapes or symbols will be used? Where will they be placed? How much room will be left? How much blank space will remain? Basically, there are two types of space

1. Positive Space
   Positive space is the space taken up with lines, colors, shapes, and forms. Subject matter, content, and design occupy positive space.

2. Negative Space
   Negative space is the space left between or surrounding subject matter, symbols, or shapes.

Positive space refers to the shape, and negative space is what is left empty. In figure 11-5, the white star occupies positive space and the black background represents negative space.

Artists use space in different ways. Some artworks are completely filled with vibrant colors and exciting designs (positive space), with little white paper (negative space) showing. Other works may highlight one object or symbol by surrounding it with much negative space.

Some of the different ways artists can use space include

- positive or negative

- unoccupied, empty, sparse or occupied, filled, dense

Figure 11-5   Example of positive and negative space

- vertical, horizontal, or diagonal

- symmetrical or asymmetrical

- ordered or random

- balanced or unbalanced

Activities for helping children learn about space include:

Stencil (K, Pri) A stencil can be cut out of cardboard. Use an X-acto knife or safety razor blade to cut out a simple shape, for example, a star. The cutout star is positive space. The surrounding area is negative. Children can securely hold the star on a piece of paper. They can use their drawing or printing hand to mark around the star, using chalk, crayon, or paint. Chalk is preferred because of its ability to creatively combine with other colors. Also, it does less damage to the stencil than paint. Children can also use the surrounding piece that the star was cut from. Instead of chalking away from the star stencil, they now stroke inward.

Balance

When the forms appear to be in proportion to each other, the picture is said to have balance, equilibrium, or harmony. *Balance* involves how an artist uses positive and negative space (see Figure 11-6). Basically, there are two ways of achieving balance

1. Symmetrical or formal
   With this type of balance, the shapes are evenly or equally balanced around some point, e.g., up or down, right or left, horizontally, vertically, radially, or diagonally. Think of two children of the same weight balanced on the two ends of a seesaw. This is symmetrical or formal balance. Symmetrical balance is often evident in the artwork of children. For example, a house painted on the right side symmetrically balances a large tree on the left. This type of balance is not bad or wrong; it is merely obvious, and gets boring with repeated use.

2. Asymmetrical or informal
   With this type of balance, the objects are not evenly or equally balanced from a

Figure 11-6 How is this painting balanced?

point. For example, a house painted near the upper left corner can be asymmetrically balanced with half of a large tree emerging from the right edge of the paper. The balance is unusual and intriguing.

There are many ways to achieve balance. A dark color may balance lighter ones. A massive shape may be balanced with a few smaller ones.

Texture

Texture refers to the surface quality of a work of art. How does it feel? Layers of paint, dried finger paint, and a fabric collage all have texture or a certain feel to them. Texture is a term that is appropriate to discussing and critiquing collage, construction, assemblage, and other three-dimensional art activities. Texture can be actual or implied. Young children work with actual textures. Adult artists use both. Implied texture involves technical proficiency in skillfully using the medium to suggest wood grain or peeling rust that does not actually exist on the canvas.

As mentioned in the previous unit on the senses, there are many possible textures. Some terms that relate to texture in art include

- rough, bumpy, or smooth
- hard or soft
- coarse or fine
- wet, sticky, or dry
- raised or lowered
- flat or layered
- dull or shiny
- pebbled
- granular
- rubbery
- slippery, slick
- spongy
- furry, fuzzy
- sharp

Art activities to help children learn about texture include:

Texture Collage (N/Pre, K, Pri) Provide an array of textured objects. Encourage children to glue or paste an array of textured items onto a piece of sturdy paper or cardboard. See Appendix A for artistic junk to include. Since nature items have such a variety of textures, they can be included.

Texture Rubbings (N/Pre, K, Pri) Go on a texture hunt with the children. Both indoor and outdoor environments offer a wealth of textures. For example, placing a piece of white paper over the bark on a tree and rubbing with the side of a crayon will produce an impression or rubbing. The same thing will happen if you rub over cement, wood grain, coins, a license plate, corrugated cardboard, or an embossed greeting card. Encourage children to overlap and creatively combine their rubbings. Older children might enjoy sketching a very simple picture containing large objects, such as a house and a tree. Later, they can finish their picture with rubbed areas. For example, one could rub with a dark crayon over bark in the area sketched for a tree trunk.

These artistic elements are used in Unit 14 as a basis for talking with young children about their art. They can also be used as part of a wider framework for critiquing a work of art, as discussed in Unit 12.

SUMMARY

Artistic elements are the building blocks of artistic expression. Artists process with line, color, and shape until these elements are successfully combined into a harmonious design or overall composition. Children go through the same steps, but on a more informal and often unplanned basis. These elements are the criteria for making, understanding, appreciating, and critiquing art. Our intent is not to turn children into art critics. This would be developmentally inappropriate. It is our intent, however, to use the vocabulary of the artistic elements so that children can learn to value and directly participate in the arts. They will come to know good art when they see it and be able to use the artistic elements in justifying their evaluation.

SUGGESTED ACTIVITIES

1. Visit an art museum or check out books with art prints. Use the artistic elements in analyzing a work of art.

2. Implement an art activity involving one or more of the artistic elements.

3. Complete the Color Clock activity.

REVIEW

A. List the major artistic elements discussed in this unit:
   1.
   2.
   3.
   4.
   5.
   6.
   7.
   8.
   9.

B. Complete the following color equations:
   Red + _____   = Orange
   Yellow + Blue   = _____
   _____ + _____ = Purple

C. Put the proper color term: P for Primary
                               S for Secondary
                               I for Intermediate
                               N for Neutral

   in front of each color:
   _____ yellow-orange   _____ blue
   _____ green   _____ blue-green
   _____ yellow-green   _____ orange
   _____ red   _____ red-violet

_____ black   _____ yellow
_____ red-orange   _____ white
_____ blue-violet   _____ purple/violet

D. Match the following columns related to color:
   1. The colors that are used to produce all   _____ neutral colors
      other colors.
   2. Orange, green, and purple.   _____ complimentary colors
   3. Mixing a primary and a secondary color   _____ secondary colors
      results in this.
   4. These colors are opposite each other on   _____ primary colors
      the color wheel.
   5. Black and white are examples.   _____ warm colors
   6. A pure, unmixed color.   _____ hue
   7. Lightness or darkness of a color.   _____ value
   8. Brightness or dullness of a color.   _____ intensity
   9. Adding white will produce this.   _____ tint
   10. Adding black will produce this.   _____ shade
   11. Red, yellow, and orange are examples.   _____ cool colors
   12. Blue, green, and purple are examples.   _____ intermediate colors

E. Match the following columns related to artistic elements:
   1. Has hue, value, and intensity.   _____ texture
   2. Can be symmetrical or asymmetrical.   _____ balance
   3. Can be positive or negative.   _____ space
   4. A recurring, repeated sequence.   _____ pattern
   5. Refers to the integrated whole.   _____ mass/volume
   6. Refers to three-dimensional art.   _____ design/composition
   7. A visible mark made by moving an   _____ shape/form
      artistic tool across a surface.
   8. Refers to the surface quality of a work of   _____ color
      art.
   9. Refers to two-dimensional art.   _____ line

COLOR CLOCK

1. Get white paper.

2. Use watercolors.

3. Draw a large clock.
   -black-in center
   -blob of paint

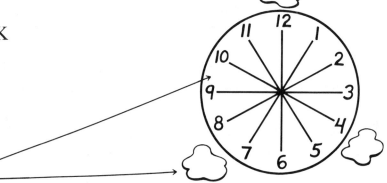

4. Fill-in (with blob of paint)
 12 = yellow (primary)
 4 = red (primary)
 8 = blue (primary)

5. Mix (secondary colors)
 12 + 4 = 2 (add blob and name of color to clock)
 4 + 8 = 6 (add blob and name of color to clock)
 8 + 12 = 10 (add blob and name of color to clock)

6. Mix (intermediate colors)
 12 + 2 = 1 (add blob and name of color to clock)
 2 + 4 = 3 (add blob and name of color to clock)
 4 + 6 = 5 (add blob and name of color to clock) P.S. Mathematically
 6 + 8 = 7 (add blob and name of color to clock)   incorrect!
 8 + 10 = 9 (add blob and name of color to clock)
 10 + 12 = 11 (add blob and name of color to clock)

7. Dry and turn in.

Unit 12

Adult's Role in Children's Art

OBJECTIVES

After studying this unit, the student will be able to

- Use the continuum of approaches to identify three different ways to teach art
- Discuss the teacher's role as a model and participator in early childhood art
- Identify ways in which a teacher can be a creative individual and art specialist in the center or classroom

INTRODUCTION

There are many different ways to approach the teaching of art. This unit will identify and critique teacher-directed, guided, and child-directed approaches. What is the teacher's role in children's art? Adults can stimulate children to make art by being a model and participant. Adults can model creativity in their daily lives and actively participate in art activities themselves. Although it is important to be an art specialist and to know about art, an adult does not need to be a talented artist to provide creative art experiences for children.

The different approaches to working with young children reside along a continuum. Teacher direction and child direction are two opposite points along the continuum. See figure 12-1. Both points are valid at certain times for certain children and certain activities. The role of facilitator or guide is a compromise and midpoint position between these two opposite roles.

A facilitator or guide is readily available without directly monopolizing the activity, as is the case with direct instruction. A facilitator or guide is a keen observer who knows when to subtly step in, intervene, ask a question, or pose a problem. Children who need assistance know that

Teacher Directed	Guided	Child Directed
• direct instruction	• facilitate	• complete freedom
• teacher intervention		• nonintervention
• structured		• unstructured

Figure 12-1   Continuum of approaches

their teacher is a resource person who is available to share facts, knowledge, skills, abilities, time, and attention.

APPROACHES TO TEACHING ART

The major approaches to teaching are also applicable to teaching art. The three approaches are:

- Teacher-directed
- Child-directed
- Teacher-guided

Some art projects are structured and teacher-directed. The teacher has an idea of what to make and how to go about it. Specific directions are given to ensure a recognizable product. Often, there is little input from the children. For example, a teacher distributes a piece of paper with an outline of a tree. The children are instructed to use a dark color, such as black or brown, to color in the trunk and green for the top. They also cut or tear small circles from red construction paper. These are pasted onto the green top. The completed apple trees look nearly identical. Generally, this approach is used when art is approached with the entire group or small groups of children. Most craft projects are teacher-directed.

An opposite approach is to be unstructured and completely child-directed. A teacher may distribute pieces of paper and encourage children to make whatever they want or encourage them to visit the easel or art center. In this approach, children have much input and choice. There is

very little structure. Some children do very well with this approach. They may have a bank of ideas to represent through art. They may also see endless artistic possibilities at the easel or art center. Many children, however, are uncomfortable with this approach. It may be too loosely structured. Some children quickly tire of inventing their own daily art program. They look to the teacher for some structure, guidance, or possibilities.

A teacher-guided approach offers the best of the two former approaches: subtle structure with much child direction and input (see Figure 12-2). Some examples include

- A teacher supplies the theme.
  "Children, it's getting very close to summer. Today, we will make a picture that reminds us of this season." Although the theme is given, there is no specified product. Children are free to use paint, crayons, markers, or clay to make their own version of what summer means to them.

- A teacher introduces new materials at the art center.
  "Today I put some spools and buttons near the easels and art table. I want you to look at them and think of how they might be used in art. Try out different ways of using them." Children are free to use them as brushes, make a stamped impression, or paste them to a collage so long as the rules for art are upheld.

- A teacher extends or builds upon an existing activity or suggests a new technique.
  "I've noticed how much we enjoy easel painting with our long-handled brushes. I found these small tree branches outside and am leaving them at the easels. Let's see if we could use them to paint with." Or, "Let me show you another way of doing watercolor by first wetting your paper." Or, "I see how much you enjoy your paper bag puppet. If you like, I could show you how to sew one out of cloth." Or, "Did you enjoy

Figure 12-2 A facilitator or guide gives help when needed.

your paper weaving? Would you like to learn how to weave on a loom with yarn?''

- A teacher poses a problem.
  "Let's see how many different shapes we can cut out of paper for pasting." Or, "How could we use these empty boxes and ribbon?" Or, "What will happen if we try painting on newspaper or the colored pages in this magazine?"

- A teacher extends art into other areas.
  "There seems to be a lot of excitement in your picture. Would you like to share it by telling me a story?" Or, "The dog you painted looks so happy, let's work together and write a poem about it." Or, "Perhaps you would like to plan a play for your ferocious dinosaur."

Different approaches may work for certain activities and certain children. Young children will not automatically discover how to use a watercolor set. They will need some direction and instruction in its use and care. They need not, however, be told what to make or what it should look like. For example, Emily is having difficulty deciding what to include in her summer picture. Her teacher senses her frustration and asks her to name things that remind her of summer. Emily answers, "Sun and swimming." Her teacher further structures the task by asking Emily to choose one. With the teacher's subtle guidance, Emily chooses the sun and now must decide if she should use paints, watercolor, crayons, markers, or clay to represent it.

Teacher as Model

Children learn in different ways. Some profit best by listening to a teacher. Others may learn by simply observing what a teacher does. For example, it would be more beneficial for a teacher to simply demonstrate how to sew or weave than to verbally tell children all the steps involved. Rather than telling children to "walk quietly," showing them how to quietly walk is more effective. In these cases, the teacher serves as a model or demonstrator. Simply modeling or demonstrating a new activity will draw a small group of curious observers, who can be eased into participating. For example, a teacher who models different ways to work with clay and clay tools will soon find the clay table filled with willing sculptors. One way of learning how to be a good teacher is to observe others modeling good teaching.

Teacher as Participator

Children enjoy playing, both by themselves and with other children. They also enjoy an adult's participation in their activities. There are times when a teacher would be most welcome as a participator or player in one of the centers. For example, Kevin was standing at the easel with a puzzled look on his face. "I don't know what to make. What should I make?" The aide moved to the other side of the easel and started to process with the brushes and paint. "Let's see. I think I will try different lines and shapes today." Kevin replied, "Me too. I'm going to make lots of colored shapes." At other times, children will not welcome a teacher's presence and may even ask him or her to leave. "No big people, just kids!" states a group of block builders. Their wishes should be respected. It is important that all children have a teacher's participation in their activity. The close contact is valuable, especially since the children are being met on their terms. This stands in opposition to a teacher-directed activity, where children are simply drawn or assimilated into the existing activity.

Teacher as Creative Individual

A teacher must also be a creative, unique individual. Creative teachers encourage creativity in their children. They model creativity. "I don't have a paper cutter. What else can I use to make paper strips for our weaving?" "We don't have an easel to take outdoors. How else can we have art outside?" Children come to see that problem solving and creative solutions are a necessary and vital part of daily living.

The Creative Teacher Develops

FROM	TO
1. viewing children in terms of groups on the basis of sex, age, or ability.	1. viewing children as unique individuals.
2. viewing highly creative children as a threat, nuisance, or menace.	2. seeing creativity as an asset.
3. stressing conformity in thinking and behavior.	3. encouraging creative thinking and different ways to do things.
4. looking for children to give the one right answer or best idea.	4. considering many possible solutions and ideas.
5. viewing self as uncreative.	5. seeing how all people have the potential to be creative.
6. a teacher-centered program.	6. a child-centered program that values child input and decision making.
7. a structured program, planned in detail.	7. subtle planning that allows for diversion and sudden twists and turns.
8. equating creativity with art, music, and movement.	8. seeing creativity as a skill that cuts across the program.
9. adding creative activities here and there.	9. weaving creativity throughout the entire program.
10. confining creativity to a certain day, time, or slot.	10. including creativity throughout the entire day.

Creativity is something we strive for. We may not be very creative during our internship, student teaching, or first year of actual teaching. Hopefully, however, we have been successful and slowly move toward our lofty goal of becoming creative early childhood educators.

Teacher as Art Specialist

It is also important for us to be art specialists. We need to know about art, artists, artistic elements, and developmentally appropriate art activities. Just as one need not be a hockey player to enjoy viewing a game or be a musician to appreciate a concert, one need not be a gifted or talented artist to provide art experiences for children. It is more important that teachers display artistic sensitivity, awareness, and discovery than that they develop an endless list of art activities. Encouraging children to use all their senses, to experiment, to explore, and to represent what they know about the world does make one an art specialist.

SUMMARY

This unit focused on the teacher's multifaceted role with respect to children's art. A teacher can model and participate in art activities. Knowing about art will help one become an art specialist and provide creative experiences for children. It was recommended that the teacher be a creative individual who demonstrates creative thinking and expression on a daily basis. Different approaches to teaching art were also identified. Teacher-directed and child-directed were opposite positions. Being a guide or facilitator was recommended as providing a good balance between child input and subtle teacher direction.

SUGGESTED ACTIVITIES

1. Observe a teacher involved in an art activity. Use the continuum of teaching approaches to decide whether the activity was teacher-directed, teacher-guided, or child-directed.

2. Use the continuum of teaching approaches to plan a single art activity in three different ways:
   • structured and teacher-directed
   • unstructured and child-directed
   • teacher-guided

3. Practice using a guided approach in working with children during art. Be a facilitator as you respond to children.

4. Practice being a model and participator as you interact with children making art. Record your reactions.

REVIEW

A. Fill in the indicated three points along a continuum of approaches to teaching.
   X _____ X _____ X _____
   1. _____   2. _____   3. _____

B. Fill in the approach to teaching next to its corresponding activity:
   1. _____ The children are free to explore at the art tables or easels.
   2. _____ The teacher encourages children to design their own Valentine's Day card for their parents. She provides paint and paper.
   3. _____ Children cut out the outline of a heart traced by their teacher. The teacher writes, "I Love You Mom and Dad" across the front.

Unit 13

Planning, Implementing, and Evaluating Art

OBJECTIVES

After studying this unit, the student will be able to

• Describe the PIE cycle in curriculum development
• Identify the major developmental goals in early childhood education
• Compare and contrast strategies for integrating art into the early childhood curriculum

INTRODUCTION

It is time to move beyond our knowledge of child development and translate this into curriculum. Actually, it is as easy as PIE—Plan, Implement, and Evaluate. Goals will give direction to our long-range planning; objectives are useful for our daily work with children. Our values and beliefs will influence our goals and the experiences chosen to meet these goals. Our wholistic model of child development will serve as a framework to ensure that our program is child-centered and developmentally focused. Taking into account

management concerns and devising effective procedures will help us implement our activity. Evaluation helps us check on our effectiveness as teachers and providers. Different teachers use different strategies in teaching. Four strategies for planning and providing art experiences will be portrayed.

TEACHER AS PLANNER AND CURRICULUM DEVELOPER

All teachers are planners and curriculum developers. Some build their own curriculum;

others follow a prescribed one. Curriculum development involves planning what to teach and how to teach it. A unit on dinosaurs may send the beginning teacher to the library to do some research. Learning activities must be organized. Centers must be stocked with materials, equipment, and supplies that are relevant to the curricular theme. Teaching without a curriculum or plan is like traveling cross-country without a map. It does a disservice to the children and hinders professional development. Without a curriculum, the teacher operates in a random, disorganized way. Quality teaching requires planning and curriculum development.

One way of planning and developing a curriculum is to ask oneself a series of questions. These might include

- WHO?
  Who am I as a teacher? What types of things do I know about and do well? What special interests or skills do I have? What do I value and believe about early childhood? Who are my children—ages, needs, interests, abilities, likes, dislikes, family, culture, background?

- WHAT?
  What do I want my children to learn, know, or be able to do?

- WHY?
  Why am I planning this activity? Why should my children know, learn, or be able to do it? Why is this important or relevant?

- HOW?
  How will I carry out this activity? How will I present it? How will I motivate the children or capture their interest? How will I know if I have been successful? How will I know if the children have learned anything?

- WHERE?
  Where will this activity take place?

- WHEN?
  When will this activity take place?

We need to act on what we know about children and their development in developing curriculum and planning activities. We need to translate theory into practice. How do we begin? Basically, planning is as easy as PIE. The three key components of early childhood curriculum development are

- P lanning
- I mplementing
- E valuating

Developing an early childhood curriculum is a lot like taking a trip. Planning helps us decide where we want to go. Do we want to take the fastest or the scenic route? What do we need to take along? All of these concerns are taken into account during our planning. Implementing is similar to actually taking the trip. We think we have done a good job of planning and now are ready to depart. Implementing our trip involves reading the map, stopping as planned, and allowing for unexpected diversions. Was the trip worth it? Did it cost too much or take too long? Were the benefits appropriate to the expense? Would you do it again? How could you improve on the trip? All of these questions attempt to evaluate the trip.

Teachers follow the same steps in developing curriculum. Planning involves deciding what we want children to learn and be able to do. Planning is a continuous, ongoing process. It involves acting on what we know about children and their development in setting appropriate goals and objectives. All planning is influenced by the values and beliefs one holds about children and education.

Implementing involves two major processes. First, management concerns must be considered. Second, effective procedures for carrying out one's activity must be established.

Evaluation attempts to assess the effectiveness of what was done. It attempts to answer the following question: How do I know if what I set out to do was ever accomplished?

Figure 13-1 What happens when different brushes are introduced?

The three PIE components can be illustrated with the following example. A teacher could devise an art activity that would help children discover that different types of brushes can be used in painting (planning); see figure 13-1. Different brushes are located, identified, introduced, labeled, and displayed at the art center (implementing). Evaluation could entail observing the different ways children used the brushes and their ability to use many different brushes for painting. The PIE model for planning and curriculum development is depicted in figure 13-2.

GOALS

A goal is something to strive for. For example, being creative is a lifelong pursuit and goal. Few reach their creative potential. A goal is like the brass ring on the merry-go-round. We reach out for it but rarely capture it. Still, goals give direction or focus to what we do with children on a monthly or yearly basis. Translating goals into more manageable objectives helps us plan for the week, day, and hour. Try as one may, however, one can never plan completely. At times plans will change because of unexpected or unforeseen events. The relationship between long-term and short-term planning and between goals and objectives is depicted in figure 13-3.

The Goals of Early Childhood Education

What are some of the goals of early childhood education? Our wholistic model of child development can help us further identify goals for early childhood. These might include:

1. PHYSICALLY (to develop):
   - large-muscle or gross motor coordination
   - small-muscle or fine motor coordination
   - perceptual-motor or eye-hand coordination
   - sensory awareness
   - self-care

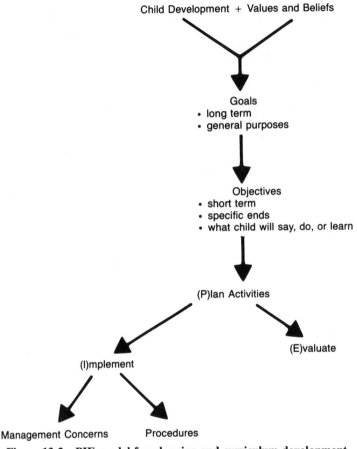

Child Development + Values and Beliefs

Goals
• long term
• general purposes

Objectives
• short term
• specific ends
• what child will say, do, or learn

(P)lan Activities

(E)valuate

(I)mplement

Management Concerns   Procedures

Figure 13-2   PIE model for planning and curriculum development

2. SOCIALLY (to develop):
   • self-understanding and acceptance
   • positive relations with others
   • positive self-concept

3. EMOTIONALLY (to develop):
   • a positive self-concept
   • positive and appropriate emotional expression
   • self-control

4. COGNITIVELY (to develop):
   • a wide range of thinking skills, including problem solving and discovery

   • concepts, skills, and learnings in the curricular areas
   • language

5. CREATIVELY (to develop):
   • original thinking
   • imagination
   • verbal and nonverbal expression

If these are important developmental indicators, and if our program is child-centered, it follows that these can serve as goals or aims that can influence what we do with the children in our care. For example, creative expression, both

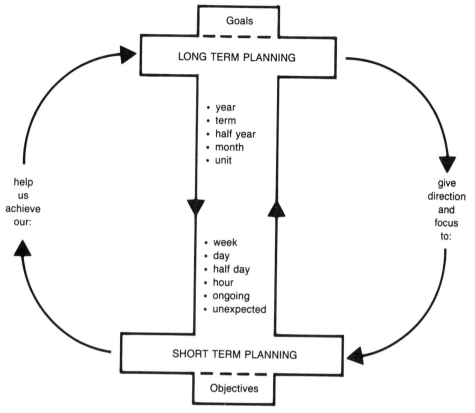

Figure 13-3   Planning cycle

verbal and nonverbal, is an important aspect of creative development. Art is one way to nonverbally express one's creativity. Art activities help us reach our goals for creative development.

VALUES AND BELIEFS

Goals also reflect our values and beliefs about children—how they develop and learn, what they should know, and the purpose of schooling and life. Teachers who value early academic performance and competition may view early childhood as a time to push children ahead by filling their heads with facts. They will set goals that stress competition and early academic accomplishment, and select activities in reading, writing, and counting to meet these goals. Teachers who view early childhood as a time for discovery and social interaction will set goals for developing curiosity and provide socializing experiences in play to meet these goals. Different values and beliefs lead us to set different goals and activities. There are no right or wrong, good or bad beliefs. Some values and beliefs may, however, suggest educational practices that are not in line with what we know about young children. The key is to consistently match up what we value and believe about children and schooling with an appropriate curriculum, one that is firmly grounded in child development. Although one may value and believe in the formal teaching of reading in the early years, our working knowledge of child development suggests that this practice is developmentally inappropriate.

OBJECTIVES

Objectives are the bridge between goals and activities. They are specific and short-term intended outcomes. As a result of a given activity, we expect children to be able to say, do, or demonstrate what they have learned. Objectives can be worded loosely or in precise behavioral terms. Regardless of the wording, teachers need to be able to set objectives and develop activities to meet them. For example, Karen Thomas wants her four-year-olds to interact with others, to be creative, to be successful at what they do, and to develop fine motor control. These are some of her goals. Her objective is for children to creatively experiment with different ways of painting. She plans to bring in an old toothbrush and shaving brush for her proposed art activity.

Referring to figure 13-2, Ms. Thomas must still address how she will implement and evaluate this proposed activity. She must consider some concerns related to classroom management.

- Where should this activity take place—indoors, outdoors, at the easel, on the floor, or at a table? These are space considerations.

- When will this activity take place—before or after snack, in the morning or afternoon? Will it be offered as an additional free choice activity, or will it be added to the ongoing art center? How much time will be allotted? These are time considerations.

- What is needed? Ms. Thomas has already found two different types of brushes. She will also need to think about paints, paper, and smocks.

- How many children can do this activity at one time? Will everyone get a chance in one session, or will it continue throughout the week? Will children self-select to do this activity, or will she need to systematically rotate them through? These are considerations related to grouping.

- How will this activity be supervised? Will it need the constant supervision of an adult? Probably not.

Ms. Thomas will also need to think through her procedures.

- How will she introduce the activity? Would a story, book, or picture be appropriate? How can she capture the children's interest and get them motivated? She chooses to introduce her activity with questions during morning circle time. "Children, today I brought in two things to show you" (holding up a toothbrush and a shaving brush). "Yes, they are both brushes. Each has a special name and use." "Yes, this one is a toothbrush. How many of you have one and use it? Good. What about the other one?" Jamie says his grandfather has one, but he doesn't know its name. "Jamie, what does he use it for?" "Yes, for shaving. It's called a shaving brush. You use it to mix shaving soap and water and put it over your whiskers and beard before you shave." The children giggle. "Well, I have a different idea. I wonder if we could use them in our art center?" Children gasp and groan. "Let's quietly think of how we could use these new brushes to paint." Stephanie says, "You could use the toothbrush to paint up and down just like when brushing your teeth." Lacey says, "You could just make touches of paint on your paper." "That's very good thinking. I bet there are many, many different ways to use them as we paint. Remember to try out some different ways when you get your turn."

Actually, there is no definite teacher-directed procedure, since this is a creative discovery lesson. Ms. Thomas also reminded them to creatively explore while upholding the rules.

Evaluation was ongoing. Ms. Thomas checked to see whether the brushes were being used in different ways. They were. Some children used a pulling, pushing, swirling, dabbing, dotting, stamping, swirling, or circular motion. The finished products also revealed differences. From this she concluded that her activity was a success. She had met her objective. This activity helped children become more creative and versatile in their painting. As a follow-up activity she planned to bring in two additional types of brushes from home to increase the possibilities. As a recommendation, she noted that she should bring in two of each, since it was very difficult for the children to wait their turn. Also, the child with the brushes was very engrossed and spent more time than she had planned. Even though her activity was successful as planned, she knew it could be improved upon.

Karen Thomas is an experienced preschool teacher for whom planning and curriculum development now come very easy. She relies on very brief plans that work for her. This was not always the case. She began teaching by writing very detailed plans. She was afraid of leaving something out. She believes that her prior experience in writing out lesson plans, although it was time-consuming at the time, has helped her become the professional early childhood educator she is today.

A lesson plan format that closely follows our model for planning and curriculum development is given here.

LESSON PLAN

Activity:

PLANNING

   Goals:

   Objectives:

IMPLEMENTATION

   Management concerns:

   Procedures:

EVALUATION

STRATEGIES FOR INCLUDING ART IN THE EARLY CHILDHOOD CURRICULUM

Although we have introduced goals, values, and beliefs, we have yet to systematically deal with the nuts and bolts of daily planning and curriculum development. Let us continue by studying general ways to include art in the early childhood curriculum. Some strategies include:

Teaching Art as a Separate Activity

A teacher may find, hear about, or read about something that sounds like a good art activity that the children would enjoy. For example, Mr. Kent was glancing through a magazine in the director's office when he got the idea for painting or printing with sponges of different geometric shapes. The children had not done this activity before. He felt it would encourage creative processing with different shapes to make new forms. The activity would also help his four-year-olds and young five-year-olds with their fine motor skills. The activity was developmentally appropriate and sounded enjoyable. He planned to do the activity the following morning, since he had not yet planned an art activity. Further, he planned separate activities for the morning, but did not try to integrate or relate them. His daily lesson plan is found below.

TEACHER: Mr. Kent
CLASS: four- and five-year-olds
DATE: Monday

Areas/Activities:

ART: painting and printing with sponges cut into different geometric shapes
MUSIC: sing a "silly song"
I know an old man who had a black dog . . .
MOVEMENT: alphabet march in a circle
CONCEPT: Science (for Monday)
sort and discuss attributes of nature specimens. Bring in pinecones, leaves, grass, twigs, stones, acorns, and so on
GROUP: discuss weekend activities
encourage Ariel to discuss her hospital stay
SNACK: vegetable slices and cottage cheese dip
double-check for allergies to milk products
PLAY: continue work on airport (block corner)
restock shelves in grocery store (housekeeping)

Mr. Kent wished he had discovered this art activity last week, when they were studying geometric shapes in concept time. He did not think to find a song or movement activity that would tie in. Mr. Kent's approach is not bad or wrong. It is fragmented, with the different learning experiences left without integration or relation to each other.

Art Can Be Used to Extend or Reinforce Learning in Another Curricular Area

For example, Mrs. Gomez's four-year-old kindergarten had also been studying geometric shapes during math concept time. She tried to find an art activity that would tie in. She cut sponges into geometric shapes and encouraged the children to print with them. During group or circle time, the children had a "show and tell" session during which they discussed the different shapes they invented and also named the shapes used. Art extended and reinforced what the children were learning in math. Her lesson plan for the day is found below. The arrows indicate integration between the different activities. Group time and art extended or reinforced the concept of geometric shapes discussed during math concept time.

DAILY LESSON

Mrs. Gomez
4 K's
Monday

Welcome:	• do calendar
	• sing good morning song
	• read Little Red Hen
Blocks:	• take large hollow blocks outside (with Mrs. Raines if nice day)
Dramatic Play:	• introduce doctors and nurses, tools, careers
	• encourage hospital play
Table Toys:	• put out legos, new puzzles, flannel boards
Concept Time:	• math (Monday)—discuss geometric shapes
↕	
Creative Arts:	• sponge painting with geometric shapes
↕	
Group Time:	• show and tell with geometric shape pictures

Art Becomes a Superactivity Integrating Several Curricular Areas

For example, Ms. Lansky's kindergarteners were reviewing geometric shapes. She planned to devote all day Monday to this review. She included the following activities in her superactivity. Note the curricular areas in parentheses indicating integration.

- Children counted and classified the different sponge shapes on the basis of color, shape, and size (math).

- They observed a dry sponge being submerged in water. They noted differences between wet and dry sponges. They put the wet sponge in the sun to predict and observe what would happen (science).

- They took a field trip outdoors to identify geometric shapes in nature (science).

- They played shape bingo (visual discrimination, pre-reading).

- They discussed things that are hard and soft and the many uses of sponges (speaking, creative thinking).

- They listened to a story on shapes (listening).

- They printed their name or initials with rectangular shapes dipped in paint (pre-writing).

- They created their own geometric shape picture (art).

- They listened to a march and participated in a shapes dance (music and movement).

- They moved like dry stiff sponges, sponges in a bubble bath, sponges being squeezed dry, wet sponges lying in the sun on a beach (movement).

- They discussed diving for sponges and people who dive for a living (social studies).

Ms. Lansky's approach to planning helped children integrate and coordinate all experiences related to learning about geometric shapes, as well as incidental learning on sponges. See figure 13-4. Ms. Lansky's only objection was that she felt the children's enthusiasm for and interest in studying shapes and sponges were more than she had expected and planned for in one day's flow of activities.

Art as an Integrated Part of an Extended Unit of Study

Miss Susan enjoys teaching four-year-olds through the use of units. Her units are organized around a theme, such as geometric shapes. Her units are planned for days and even weeks at a time, depending on the level of interest and involvement of her particular group. She believes that a unit approach provides a focus for all of her planning. Each activity relates to her theme. In turn, everything children experience during the unit is somehow related to the theme under study.

Miss Susan begins by sketching out a flowchart. See figure 13-5. She writes her theme of shapes in the center and merely writes in anything and everything related. At this point she is more concerned with terms, concepts, and understandings than with actual activities. Items on her flowchart will suggest activities. Miss Susan brainstorms with her fellow teachers sometimes, using a blackboard in working and reworking her flowchart. She may have more on her flowchart than will appear on her plan. Some concepts may be too difficult or may not translate into a specific early childhood activity.

The second step is moving from flowchart to general plan of activities. Miss Susan decides to allow one week for the study of shapes. She bases this on the interests of her particular group and her experience with teaching this theme in the past. Although she does not teach shapes exactly the same way every year, she does use her flowchart and plans as a general guide. Slowly, she is accumulating a wealth of flowcharts and thematic plans. Her weekly plan for shapes is found in figure 13-6.

Activity: Geometric Shapes (integrated curriculum)
Grade: Kindergarten
Teacher: Lansky

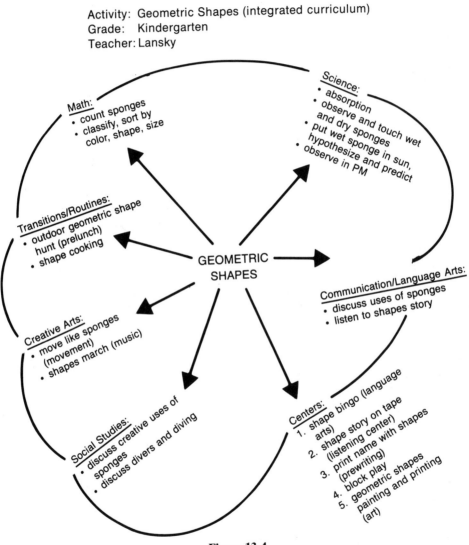

Figure 13-4

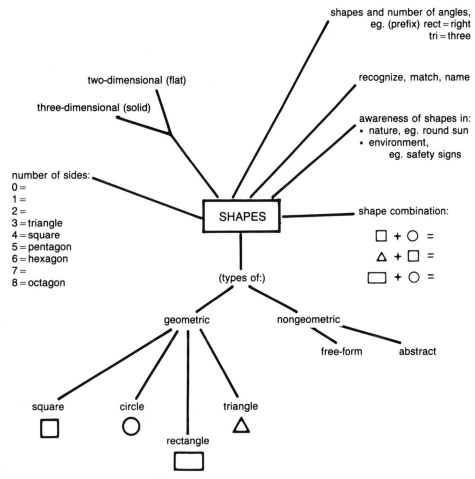

Figure 13-5   Flow chart on shapes

THEME: SHAPES

	MONDAY	TUESDAY	WEDNESDAY	THURSDAY	FRIDAY
EXPRESSIVE ARTS	Making shapes out of clay	Making shapes using self and others	Sing shapes song: I'm a little circle . . .	Sponge painting and printing with sponges cut into shapes	Make, bake, and frost shape cookies
LANGUAGE ARTS	Read and discuss story on shapes	Locate shapes in our ABCs	Match word with its shape	Play shape bingo and dominoes	Dictate story: "If I were a ○, □, △, □, I would . . .
MATH	Count number of square shapes on flannel board	One-to-one correspondence with: ○, □, △, □'s	Classify items by shape	Seriate circles	Conservation game: more, less, same ○, □, △, □ shapes
SCIENCE	Outdoor shapes hunt Shapes in nature	Indoor shapes hunt: I spy . . .	Sink and float: Does an item's shape make a difference?	Test out: Can all shapes roll? fall? slide?	Blow up balloon Discuss shape deflated and inflated
SOCIAL STUDIES	Discuss facial features as shapes	Draw self using geometric shapes	Show filmstrip on housing. Discuss shapes of: igloos, pyramids, teepees	Discuss shapes in foods: round pizza, square sandwich, triangular half-sandwich	Identify shapes in safety signs

Figure 13-6

Let us compare all four strategies. Mr. Kent taught art and all other areas as separate activities. There was no integration or tie-in. Mrs. Gomez used art and group time to extend and reinforce what children were learning during math concept time. Ms. Lansky planned a superactivity, focusing on geometric shapes and sponges, that integrated the day's activities. Miss Susan planned for a week around the theme of shapes. Separate activities throughout her day were all related to a study of shapes (see Figure 13-7).

SUMMARY

This unit focused on curriculum development by presenting a PIE model for planning, implementing, and evaluating. Goals based on what we know about children and their development as well as our values give direction to our planning. Breaking goals down into short-term objectives assists in daily planning. Implementing raises management and procedural concerns about carrying out activities. Evaluation addresses the match between what we set out to do and what actually happened. The unit ended by comparing and contrasting different strategies for integrating art into the early childhood curriculum.

Figure 13-7 An activity to help children learn about shapes.

SUGGESTED ACTIVITIES

1. As a group, brainstorm your goals for early childhood education. Are they developmental in focus? Do you agree? How do they reflect different values and beliefs? Can you reach consensus? What might this indicate about the state of early childhood education?

2. Observe how different teachers use planning, implementing, and evaluating in their programs.

3. Use the lesson plan format to write up and implement an art activity.

4. Divide the class into four groups. Each group is responsible for very general daily planning for teaching the concept of primary colors using one of the four strategies discussed at the end of this unit.

REVIEW

A. Complete the cycle of curriculum and development

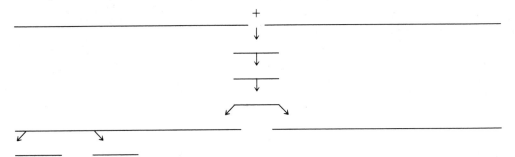

B. Identify the components of the PIE approach to curriculum development.
   1. P _____
   2. I _____
   3. E _____

C. List strategies for including art in the early childhood curriculum.
   1.
   2.
   3.
   4.

Unit 14

Responding to Children's Art

OBJECTIVES

After studying this unit, the student will be able to

- Critique different approaches to talking with children about their art
- Use the artistic elements to analyze and discuss children's art
- Discuss the teacher's role as troubleshooter in children's art

INTRODUCTION

Adults can respond both verbally and nonverbally to children's art. What should one say to a child artist? Should a teacher praise, judge, question, or correct? This unit will overview and critique different strategies. Art Dialogue, a strategy using the artistic elements, will be presented as a preferred approach. Although the art program will run smoothly most of the time, individual children may have difficulty on occasion and will need direct intervention. The role of the teacher as troubleshooter will be portrayed.

TEACHER AS RESPONDER

Teachers can respond and react to children's art both nonverbally and verbally. Often, we are unaware of our nonverbal communication. A smile conveys approval, while a frown or puzzled look conveys disapproval. For example, a teacher may verbally say that she likes a child's abstract artwork, but her wrinkled forehead and squint convey quite the opposite. Posture and overall body language also communicate a message. Giving a cold stare to a child who is making a creative mess communicates one's preference for order and neatness. Hands on hips or crossed arms while staring down at a child conveys a cold, aloof message. Stooping down to eye level or sitting close to a child conveys warmth, respect, and acceptance. Young children are physical beings who use their bodies to express what they feel. In turn, they are sensitive to the nonverbal messages conveyed by adults. One goal for early childhood educators is to develop positive nonverbal communication and establish congruence between our nonverbal and verbal messages to children.

ART DIALOGUE*

Verbal comments that teachers traditionally make concerning children's art take the following six approaches:

- complimentary

- judgmental

- valuing

- questioning

- probing

- correcting

The impact of each of these on the child artist will be analyzed, and an alternative to the six traditional approaches will be presented.

With the complimentary approach, teachers tell children that their art is nice, pretty, lovely, or beautiful. Specific comments include, "That's a beautiful painting," "Oh, how lovely," "Pretty, a very pretty picture," or "Yes, very nice." In turn, the child will often smile, say "thank you," and walk away. The opportunities for rich verbal dialogue are limited. A second limitation is that these terms become vague and overworked platitudes. For example, the term "nice" is used so freely, as in "Have a nice day!" that it conveys very little meaning or sincerity. What is the criteria for a "nice" picture? Is an abstract picture "not nice"? The term "pretty" is another example. Not all children's art is pretty. A solid mass of black paint may be dark, massive, thick, layered, or rectangular, but it is not pretty. The terms "nice" and "pretty" are empty ones and should be replaced with terms that provide specific feedback to the child.

With the judgmental approach, the teacher tells children that their art is good or great. Specific comments include "Very good" and "That's great work." Since most teachers do not want to judge and rank children's art as good, better, or best, they may simply tell all children that any and all of their art is good. In turn, these judgmental terms become overworked and meaningless. A teacher may lose credibility with the judgmental approach. How can one child's impulsive scribble and another's detailed portrait both be good? Is the teacher not telling the truth? Or could it be that the teacher is not really looking, but merely rubber-stamping them in production-line fashion with the same empty judgment?

With the valuing approach, the teacher tells children that she likes or even loves their art. Specific comments include "I like that a lot" and "Oh, I just love it." Obviously, it is important to tell children that you recognize all the time and effort they have spent processing with the medium. You can appreciate how hard a child worked to get a clay dinosaur to stand up. Rewarding and encouraging the child for processing, however, is different from putting the teacher's seal of approval on the finished product. Children create to express themselves. They should not make art to please a teacher. Unfortunately, many children create art that is personal and as a result devalued. Stereotypic, impersonal art is often the type valued by adults. A classic example is the square house flanked by trees with a triangle roof and a smoking chimney. Often there are two windows with parted curtains and a smiling sun in the sky. Adults understand and may even encourage the making of stereotypic art. This type of picture gets praised and displayed at home on the door of the refrigerator.

---

* This section has been adapted from the original work by Robert Schirrmacher "Talking with Young Children about Their Art," *Young Children* 41 (1986):3–7.

The stereotypic symbols or schema convey public meaning. Although they may reflect a developmental landmark in attaining realism, they are not better than children's abstract art.

With the questioning approach, a teacher directly and bluntly asks children, "What is it?" or "What is that supposed to be?" An older or very verbal child may answer. Some children may not be able to verbalize what they have represented on a very personal level. It may be difficult for a child to respond, "I just painted how I feel inside when I'm mad." Young children may not know why or what they have painted. In response, they may shrug their shoulders, cast their eyes downward, say "I don't know," or walk away. Some teachers continue their questioning. "Well, is it a _____ or is it a _____?" A child may verbally play along just to end the interrogation.

Much of young children's art is private, egocentric, and not intended to look like something. According to Smith (1983), it is unwise and even harmful to ask "What is it?" of a child who is making nonrepresentational art. According to Kamii and DeVries (1978), for young children who engage in nonrepresentational art, art may have primary value as a physical knowledge activity. Motoric hand and arm movements result in brushing, dabbing, swirling, and smearing paint. The finished product or end result is of no consequence. Other children may be hurt or insulted that their teacher did not immediately recognize their splash of thick blue paint as the ocean.

With the probing approach, the teacher attempts to draw from children some hint, title, or verbal statement about their art. Typical comments include, "Please tell me all about it" or "What can you say about this?" This approach is less forward and abrasive than the previous one. It is supported by an integrated approach to curriculum development (Unit 7) in which children's art is used as a lead-in to other curricular areas. This probing approach has merit, but it should be used sparingly. Children cannot and need not always verbalize, dictate a story, or write about their art. Also, there is a tendency for this approach to grow stale with repeated use. A young boy once told his peers not to show their artwork to the new student teacher because "she will make you tell a real long story about it and then you have to wait while she writes it across your picture." Encouraging but not mandating that children talk about their art is sound practice (see Figure 14-1).

ART DICTATION

Many children will want to talk about their art. Some will provide a title, labels, or sentence to accompany it (see Figure 14-2). Some teachers elect to very neatly print these words across the picture. The author, however, recommends using a separate piece of paper for two reasons. First, adult artists rarely have words written

Figure 14-1 Children enjoy inventing their own spelling. Teachers can also record children's talk about their art.

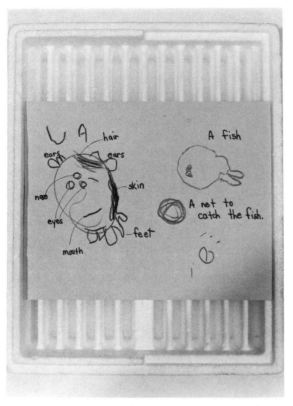

Figure 14-2   A teacher can label as a child dictates.

Figure 14-3   This artist has taken creative liberty. There is no need to correct.

across their canvas. Second, often there is little blank space, and the words have to be written too small or squeezed in. Using a separate piece of paper has a few advantages. It allows a separate story to be stapled or taped to the bottom. A blank sheet allows you to print in fairly large letters. Therefore, it will be easier for the child to see and read back. Lastly, it allows room for the child to trace over the letters and words. Leaving blank space between lines provides room for the child to attempt to copy the letters, words, and sentences.

The correcting approach attempts to provide children with specific feedback that will enable them to improve their art or make it "better" by more closely approximating reality. For example, a child shows her teacher a drawing of a green spider. The teacher replies, "Very good, but remember to draw legs on your spider. Spiders have many legs. And remember when you color that most spiders are black." This teacher's intentions were good but misdirected. Art, and child art in particular, is not a copy of the real world. Photography, not art, copies reality. Instead, the child artist freely chooses to creatively improvise. For example, children know what their face looks like. Still, their self-portrait may reflect a face that lacks ears or eyebrows. Lowenfeld (1968) warns that a teacher's corrections or criticism only discourage children and do not foster their artistic growth (see Figure 14-3).

So what is a teacher to say or do? Nothing? Smile or nod approvingly? Eisner (1976, 1982) recommends that teachers shift from searching for representation in child art and focus on the abstract, design qualities or "syntax," such as shape and form. Children's art is related to the work of adult artists in the use of these artistic fundamentals. Discussing the formal elements of the visual arts is vital to the development of aesthetic awareness and aesthetic potential. Even very young children can understand artistic terms such as shape, pattern, line, design, and color.

Merely knowing about the artistic elements will not suffice. Teachers can use the aesthetic

Figure 14-4 **"You have been working hard. I see colorful lines that cross, circles, and squares."**

elements of art as a framework for verbally responding to children's art. One need not be an artist to understand and implement this approach. There are different ways of identifying and organizing the artistic elements. Consensus is lacking on the one best list or approach. Hardiman and Zernich (1981) emphasize the following seven artistic elements:

- color
- line
- mass or volume
- pattern
- shape or form
- space
- texture

Their list is both manageable and developmentally appropriate for talking with young children about their art (see Figure 14-4). It will serve as the framework for the alternative approach advocated in this section.

Saying, "That's interesting" allows you to buy time and structure a more specific comment. For example, "That's a very interesting picture. Yes, I see lots of color and moving lines."

Teachers can also say "I like the way you . . .

- are working so hard."
- are being so creative."
- are trying to come up with your very own idea."
- are not giving up."
- are trying new ways."
- are putting things away."
- are sharing at the art center."

Teachers can also verbally reflect the way a piece of art makes them feel. For example, "Robbie, your bright colors make me feel so happy." Or, "The big bright yellow sun makes me feel so warm all over." Or, "All those lines racing around your paper make me feel like moving around."

Teachers are being responsive when they carefully examine children's art and provide a rich dialogue in which the artistic elements are pointed out and discussed. No one piece of children's art will contain all of the artistic elements. Texture is useful in describing collage or painting, where surfaces are rough, smooth, nubby, or layered. Mass or volume in three-dimensional art is a useful term in describing a child's clay work, sculpture, construction, or assemblage.

A teacher may want to comment on other qualities that are not formally considered artistic elements. It is also important to comment on the amount of time, effort, and planning, and on the handling of the materials and media. A child's unsuccessful attempts or disappointments with the media should also be discussed. For example, a child tries to paint a rainbow with watercolors, but the colors run together. A teacher could say, "I know you worked hard at trying to keep your colors separate. Watercolors get very wet, and colors sometimes run. What could you do differently next time?" Or, "Try using less water next time."

A teacher may want to relate art to life. "You

have drawn so many colorful flowers they remind me of my backyard flower garden." Or, "I see so many squares and rectangles in your picture. Remember when we went on our field trip downtown and saw all those tall buildings that looked like squares and rectangles." Or, "How is your robot like the ones you see on TV?"

At times it may be wise to wait and say nothing. This serves two purposes. First, it gives the teacher time to study the child's art and reflect on the artistic elements evidenced before speaking. This will eliminate an impulsive, curt response like, "That's nice." Second, it will give the child an opportunity to talk first if he or she so chooses. This provides a lead-in and agenda for a teacher's comments.

It is also important to help parents respect and encourage their children's artistic processing and production. Perhaps a letter similar to the one below will help.

Dear Parents,

This is one of many pieces of artwork your child will be bringing home this year. Please consider it a personal gift from your child and thank him/her. Use magnets to proudly display it on the refrigerator door where all can see it.

Do not worry if you cannot figure it out. Its beauty may reside in your child's use of colors, lines, and shapes. Do not ask, "What is it?" Consider it a design. Encourage your child to discuss it if he or she chooses.

Your child would probably enjoy doing art at home. Art supplies make good gifts. Keep a small box filled with the following: scissors, glue, paste, tape, crayons, markers, ruler, stapler, watercolor set, clay or Play-Doh, and paper in a variety of sizes, shapes, colors, and textures.

Your child will also enjoy doing art with you. Enjoy art together!

Your Child's Teacher

TEACHER AS TROUBLESHOOTER

Not all young artists will trust their own creative urges and impulses. Some have learned to doubt their own ability or personal worth. Others are frustrated by their inability to meet a standard of realism held by others. From time to time, all children will need a teacher's subtle guidance and direction in making art. They may need verbal and nonverbal encouragement to accept, trust, and act on their creative impulses. A teacher can act as a troubleshooter, identifying children who are artistically or creatively "blocked" and use an appropriate intervention strategy. Some examples include:

Children Who Criticize Another's Art

One child at an easel tells another at the other side, "Your picture is dumb; it doesn't look like nothing!" The second child gets upset and begins to cry. Children need to know that they cannot criticize another's art idea or work. "Tyrone has worked very hard at painting his colorful picture. Remember, pictures can be made up of bright colors without looking like anything." Or, "It is Tyrone's picture, and he can paint anything he wants. If he doesn't want it to look like something, that's okay too."

Children Who Copy and Imitate

Although imitation and copying are forms of flattery, children do not see it that way. "Teddy has spent a lot of time making his picture. Let's everyone come up with their very own idea." "Remember, it's yours—your idea, your way, and your very own picture."

Children Who are Not Progressing Artistically

Artists, whether young or old, sometimes get stuck in a rut. They continue to make the same things in the same way. A teacher can help by suggesting a new activity. "Les, try watercolor today. You have been painting at the easel for days, and it is time for a change." Or, "Les, I see how much you enjoy painting houses at the easel. What other kinds of buildings could you paint? Let's try to paint something different today.''

Children Who Refuse to Try

Some children will totally avoid involvement in art. They will stand close by but refuse to try. They may need a teacher's subtle prompting, guidance, and guarantee of success. "Here, Susan, I'll stay with you and get you started. I'll dip the brush in the paint. Now you take over. I know you can finish on your own.''

Children Who Do Not Like to Get Dirty or Messy

Some children grow up in homes where they are discouraged from getting messy or dirty. They may have been punished for playing with their food, soiling their clothes, or walking in mud. Others will come to school inappropriately dressed in expensive outfits with a warning to "stay clean.'' Young children do get messy and dirty. This is a fact of childhood. Smocks, however, can protect clothing, and hands can be washed. Children need to be reassured that they will not get in trouble for getting dirty or messy. "Your parents know we paint at school and want you to enjoy it. We will wear a smock and clean up afterwards.'' It is also important to inform parents of the importance of art and that making a mess and getting dirty is a part of the process. Encourage parents to send their children appropriately dressed for dirty and messy work.

Children Who Avoid Art

Some children will completely avoid the art area. If given the choice, they will choose other areas. It is like the child who if given a choice eats only meat and refuses any vegetables. Occasionally, this may be acceptable. However, the author believes that over time all children need to interact at all centers. One solution is to rotate children through the centers. "Joey, I know you like to go to blocks every day, but there are many other things to do at school. Today, I want you to spend some time at the art area and at least try one activity. Let me know when you are finished so we can talk.''

Children Who Do Not Know What to Make

"Teacher, what should I make?'' "I don't know what to paint.'' Some children say this hoping that someone else will give them an idea. Usually this is the case for a child who has been pampered, spoiled, or catered to at home. Try diverting the question back to the child. "Fay, that's a good question. What should you make? Since you are the artist, you need to think and come up with an idea. Try to get a picture in your head. Look around the room, outside, or in our books. There are many, many things just waiting for you to make in art.'' A list of books on color, shape, senses, and art that may also be a stimulus for making art is found in Appendix F.

Children Who Dislike Their Own Art

Some children are overly critical of their own artwork. They may tear up picture after picture because it does not turn out just right. Sometimes they are frustrated with their childlike results. Others have poor self-concepts and doubt their own ability. These children will need heavy doses of praise, support, and encouragement. "Oh, Todd, please let me have that picture. Don't throw it away. I would like to add it to my collection of children's art.'' Or, "I don't think it looks like a dumb giraffe. I see a tall yellow animal. You did a very good job of painting and worked very hard.''

Children Who Set Unreasonable Expectations

Some children may set themselves up for disappointment. They expect photographic realism that they are developmentally incapable of producing. They may want perfect pictures without smudges, smears, runs, or tears. Perhaps their parents hold unreasonably high expectations, and expect and will accept only the best. These children become their own worst critic. They need to be accepted for what they are—young artists. "Cammy, I enjoy seeing all the bright colors in your picture. It doesn't matter that the colors have run together; it helped mix new ones." Or, "Remember you are making your idea of a rainbow, not taking a picture with a camera. I think your rainbow is just as colorful as the ones I see in the sky."

Children Who Want an Adult to Do Art for Them

"Teacher, make one for me. I can't do it." Or, "Teacher, I can't draw a pig. Please make one for me." Adults should not do art for children, regardless of how much they plead. It makes them dependent on others and teaches them to distrust their own ability. "Sean, I have difficulty drawing animals too. Just try and do your best." Or, "Sean, everyone has to do their own work. I make my own pictures, and you need to make your own too. I can help you in many other ways, but I cannot make art for you. I know you are an artist, and artists just have to keep trying and practicing."

SUMMARY

This unit identified the different ways to talk with children about their art. Complimentary, judgmental, valuing, questioning, probing, and correcting approaches were critiqued. Art Dialogue, a strategy incorporating the artistic elements, was provided as an alternative to saying "pretty," "nice," "good," or "What is it?" Art Dictation was proposed for children who might want their art talk put into written form. It was recommended that teachers become troubleshooters when individual children have difficulty or appear to be artistically stuck.

SUGGESTED ACTIVITIES

1. Listen to a teacher talking with a child about his or her art. Which approach was used? If necessary, suggest alternatives.

2. Encourage one child to show you his or her artwork. Use the artistic elements as a framework for your Art Dialogue. If possible, tape-record your session. Did you use any of the traditional approaches or remarks? If so, suggest alternative statements.

3. Encourage but do not demand that a child talk about his or her art. Conduct Art Dictation.

4. Identify a child who is having difficulty or who is artistically stuck. Act as a troubleshooter.

REVIEW

A. Match the comment with the approach to talking with children about their art.
   1. correcting   _____ "I love it!"
   2. probing   _____ "I think you left something out."
   3. questioning   _____ "That's just wonderful."

4. valuing   _____ "What is it supposed to be?"
5. judging   _____ "Explain it to me, please."
6. complimentary   _____ "Yes, very, very good."

B. Fill in the artistic element that matches each comment.
   1. _____ "I see red, blue, yellow, and green all over your paper."
   2. _____ "Here your dry paint feels so smooth, but over here where they mixed it feels rough."
   3. _____ "So many lines—straight, crossing, and swirly."
   4. _____ "You worked so long and hard that your picture fills the entire sheet of paper."
   5. _____ "Your clay elephant is thick and solid, and can stand on its own."
   6. _____ "I see rows of circles, squares, and triangles."
   7. _____ "You repeated these trees across the bottom of your paper. What an interesting effect."

Unit 15

Strategies for Enhancing Children's Artistic Expression

OBJECTIVES

After studying this unit, the student will be able to

- Identify specific strategies for enhancing children's artistic expression
- Compare and contrast art circle time with show and tell
- Discuss different ways to frame and display children's art

INTRODUCTION

This unit identifies strategies for enhancing children's artistic expression. An Art Idea Book uses pictures to provide potential ideas of things to make in art. Even young artists can be encouraged to sign or mark their artwork. Matting and framing children's art communicates our interest in what they have created. Displaying their art provides an opportunity for all to share in the child's creation. Hosting an Art Party lets parents join in the celebration of children's creative expression through art.

ART IDEA BOOK

Teachers can browse through magazines for large and interesting pictures of people, places, objects, and animals. Look for vivid colors and interesting designs. Mount one or more pictures on each page of a scrapbook or photo album. Children can be encouraged to browse through

Figure 15-1   Children enjoy looking through the Art Idea Book.

the Art Idea Book when they are at a loss as to what to color, draw, paint, or make. For example, Fay's teacher directed her to the Art Idea Book. She was intrigued by a picture of circus animals and decided to make performing animals out of clay. The book need not be taken to the art center as a model to copy. The pictures are merely stimuli and suggestions (see Figure 15-1).

ART CIRCLE TIME

Circle time is a popular routine in early childhood programs. The writer prefers circle time to show and tell because it encourages language, social development, and synthesis without the use of toys and possessions from home. The focus can be on what children do during art.

Some guidelines for art circle time include

1. Set aside a specific time each day. The end of the day is an excellent time to summa-rize and synthesize the day's events and plan for tomorrow. "Let's show and talk about what we did today. Who would like to share their art with us?"

2. If possible, split the large group into smaller groups. Or, offer circle time as an option during free play time. With fewer children, the time spent waiting and listening will be compatible with their developmental level.

3. The time should initially be kept brief and slowly increased as the year progresses.

4. The teacher should remain seated with the group. Smiling, making eye contact, and nodding will nonverbally communicate your interest in the activity. The teacher may also want to encourage or gently prod the child who is shy or reluctant, or who offers only minimal utterances. Always reinforce the child's verbalizations. Saying, "Thank you for sharing that" or "You did a good job of telling us about your picture" will make the child want to verbalize in the future. Always accept what the child says, whether it is grammatically correct or incorrect. For example, three-year-old Tab says, "Sees what I did." Don't attempt to correct the child or point out the error. Instead, simply mirror the essence of what the child has said, using correct grammar. For example, "Yes, Tab, I see what you did at the art table. It's a very colorful picture." In this example, the teacher not only accepted the child's speech and modeled grammatically correct feedback, but also expanded on the child's natural language.

5. It is important to begin on time. Do not wait for everyone to be seated, quiet, and ready to begin. This wastes too much time. Instead, begin slowly. The other children will slowly join your group, especially if they sense they will miss out on something important.

6. Do not let the older, brighter, or more verbal children dominate the discussion. All children have the right to speak during circle time. It is the teacher's responsibility to encourage each child to exercise that right. We can also respect the child's right not to participate.

7. You are a model. If you appear bored, restless, or preoccupied, so will the children. Do not expect a quality circle time if you plan to file papers or hang a bulletin board at the same time. If by your actions you show children that circle time is important, they will respond accordingly. You may also want to model and share something important that you were successful at during the day. "Children, I am so pleased that we got our winter bulletin board up before the first snowfall. I worked hard cutting out my letters, and I like how they look."

8. Focus on artwork rather than on toys or possessions brought from home. Our goal is to make children so proud of their daily school accomplishments that they will want to verbally share them with their peers each day. Obviously, this is a long-range goal that takes a great deal of time, patience, practice, and encouragement.

MATTING AND FRAMING CHILDREN'S ART

Matting and/or framing children's art tells them that you value what they have done. You have invested the time and effort to "finish" their artwork. Matting and framing "finish" a picture by adding the final touches. This does not make a picture better; it merely further enhances its aesthetic quality. It is a nonverbal way of saying, "Yes, I like your picture very much!" (See Figures 15-2 and 15-3.)

Figure 15-2 Mandy draws herself as her favorite food—a pickle!

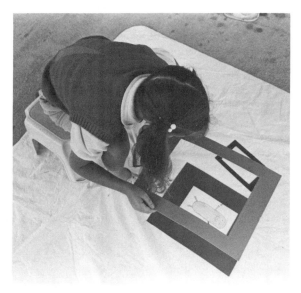

Figure 15-3 Mandy mats and frames her own art.

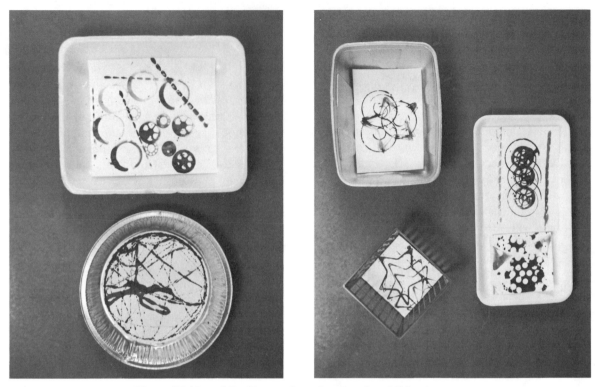

Figure 15-4A and B   Be creative when framing children's art.

There are many possible ways to frame art. Some of the ways appropriate to early childhood include:

Framing Art In . . .

A variety of lids, containers, and boxes make ideal frames (see Figures 15-4A and 15-4B). Merely match a picture to the size and shape of a container. Ask the child's permission to "crop" or trim excess white area to get a better fit between the picture and the frame. Be creative. Whoever said picture frames had to be square or rectangular? Circular swirls of paint show up very well in a round frame. Some examples include framing children's art in a

- shoe box

- lid of a box

- gift box

- large Styrofoam packing container

- pie tin

- Styrofoam meat tray

- metal ham container

- coffee can lid

- plastic storage container

- plastic berry basket

Framing Art On . . .

Children's artwork can also be glued or pasted directly onto

- construction paper

- poster board
- cardboard
- gift wrap (over cardboard)
- wallpaper

Try to pick out a color in the picture when you select a frame. In this way the two will complement, not fight each other. For example, a painting composed of large red, blue, and black shapes with smaller yellow swirls would look good framed in yellow. Black would also set off the primary colors. A finger painting composed largely of browns and greens would not be properly set off with a purple frame. Be creative and experiment with double and even triple frames. Combine wallpaper and construction paper together as multiple frames. Over time, children can select and frame their own artwork. Ideally, this will involve planning and searching at home and at school for just the right frame.

Art in a Picture Frame

Having artwork professionally framed involves great expense for both labor and materials. Garage sales and thrift shops are excellent sources of inexpensive plastic, metal, and even wooden frames.

Frames Hung in Different Positions

Framed pictures can also be hung diagonally or in a diamond position if the picture allows. For example, a picture of a street scene painted horizontally would not look good hung diagonally or at an angle.

ARTIST'S SIGNATURE

Even young artists can be encouraged to sign their art. The result may be their printed name, a letter, or a configuration of lines and shapes. It does not matter. Avoid printing a child's name across a picture without first asking the child's permission. Many children do not want their name plastered across their canvas. Many prefer to have their name printed on the back.

DISPLAYING CHILDREN'S ART

Space is at a premium in most early childhood classrooms. Although guidelines mandate square footage per child, there is rarely enough wall space to go around. Available wall space is taken up with windows, doors, restrooms, sinks, counters, and so forth. The remaining wall space holds children's names, their birthdays, the schedule, first aid procedures, notes from parents, reminders, lesson plans, a calendar, bulletin boards, chalkboards, a weather chart, a helper's chart, classroom rules, and current events. Usually, some wall space is reserved for children's work. There are many ways to provide space for displaying children's art.

Children's Art Gallery

If space allows, devote one area to a classroom art exhibit. Pictures that are matted and/or framed can be displayed in aesthetically pleasing ways. A table, shelf, or ledge allows three-dimensional products in clay or construction to be exhibited. A bookshelf could hold art books or sample prints for children to examine but not copy. The intent is to expose children to a variety of styles, not to encourage imitation. They can wonder and marvel at the beauty in nature and their surroundings and see how different artists have represented them. The classroom art exhibit or gallery is a good place to quietly escape to and reflect. It is important that children's artwork be displayed at their eye level. Since this is a children's art gallery, it is important that they share some responsibility for displaying. The pictures may not be hung in straight or well-spaced rows, but they do reflect the children's input and will be a source of pride. It is also important to respect a shy child's wishes not to have his or her art publicly displayed. Be sure to display a wide range of artwork, and not just the more realistic ones or the types you happen to prefer.

Art Kiosk

An art kiosk is a workable solution to limited wall space. A kiosk is a self-standing display with three or more sides. It can be constructed of panels of sturdy cardboard, wood, or stacked cartons. It is space-efficient in that many pictures can be simultaneously displayed on a number of sides in a few feet of floor space. A set of folding screens may serve the same purpose.

Art Rotation

Some teachers rotate children's work on a weekly basis—one week numbers, one week reading readiness, and so on. In this way, all curricular areas are covered and all children get their work up.

Shared Space

It is possible to divide display space into different areas. In this way, representative samples of all subject areas are displayed at the same time—one row of artwork, one row of visual discrimination activities, and so on.

My Own Space

It is possible to divide up the available wall space among the children. Each child can decide what he or she would like displayed. One teacher follows this practice and rotates displayed work on a weekly basis. Children keep their work in folders stored in their cubby. Every Friday they select what they want displayed for the upcoming week, then they hang it up as they enter on Monday morning.

ART PARTY

Parents can be invited to a classroom art party. Children can design and decorate the invitations. Samples of artwork from each child can be collected, framed, and displayed. The art party can be held in conjunction with open house or as a separate annual event. Children can accompany their parents and proudly point out their artwork. Perhaps the art center could be open, with parents and/or children rotating through it. This could be a good lead-in to a discussion of children's art, creativity, and child development. Although parents may find an excuse not to attend a regular night meeting, most will show up if their child is somehow directly involved. Serving simple refreshments and snacks made by the children may also boost attendance. The art party should remain just that—a celebration of children's art. It is not a contest or competition. All children win through art. Prizes, awards, trophies, and ribbons have no place at an art party.

SUMMARY

This unit provided an array of strategies for enhancing children's artistic expression. For example, an Art Idea Book provides artistic possibilities without encouraging copying and imitation. Art circle time provides children with the opportunity to show and tell about their art. Even young artists should be encouraged to sign or mark their art. Strategies for matting, framing, and displaying children's art were discussed. An art party was recommended as a strategy for encouraging family participation in the celebration of children's artistic expression.

SUGGESTED ACTIVITIES

1. Make an Art Idea Book for use with young children.

2. Ask a teacher's permission to conduct art circle time at the end of an art session. Encourage children to talk about their art using the artistic elements. Model the process for them.

3. Ask a child's permission to mat, frame, and display his or her piece of art.

4. Ask a teacher's permission to help plan, organize, and implement an art party.

REVIEW

A. List different strategies that would foster a child's artistic expression.
  1.
  2.
  3.
  4.
  5.

B. List guidelines for art circle time.
  1.
  2.
  3.
  4.
  5.

Unit 16

Evaluating Children's Artistic Development

OBJECTIVES

After studying this unit, the student will be able to

- Discuss the teacher's role as observer and how observational data assist in artistic evaluation
- Discuss the role of evaluation in art
- Identify strategies for collecting and storing children's art

INTRODUCTION

Evaluation may cause a negative reaction. Some may be suspicious of attempts at evaluating young children, let alone in the area of art. Can art be evaluated? If so, how does one go about it? This unit will look at procedures for collecting and storing art as well as an instrument for evaluating children's artistic progress. The instrument is based on our wholistic model of development. Being a keen observer of children will help teachers collect data that are essential to evaluating children's artistic development. It is crucial to note strengths and progress as well as areas of weakness or deficiency that warrant extra help.

TEACHER AS OBSERVER

At times, the teacher may decide to withdraw from direct interaction and turn to observation, a related form of nonintervention. One can gain a wealth of knowledge about children by observing them. As an observer, a teacher may observe an individual child's favorite art activity, playmate, material, or learning center. Over time, patterns emerge and analysis or interpretation can be made. The skilled observer can make statements regarding an individual child's physical, social, emotional, cognitive, and creative development. The skilled recorder enters systematic observations on note cards and includes them in the child's folder. Samples of children's work, such as art, can also be included to supplement observational data. This information can be used for conferences at a later date. At times it may be beneficial to observe and record the behavior of children in groups. One may focus on a specific child, on boys or girls, on young or older children, or on groups of children at a particular center. Who is not selecting art? Who is artistically stuck? What materials or media are preferred and which are not being used? The tasks of observation and recording allow the teacher to step out of the role of instructor or interactor and focus all attention on studying children.

TEACHER AS EVALUATOR

Curriculum development requires that the teacher be an evaluator and recorder. Evaluation tells us how children are progressing and what the effects of our educational program on their development are. Observational techniques, informal tests, and samples of children's work are three major sources of evaluative data about children that can be placed in their individual files or folders. A child's folder contains valuable information for parent conferences and meetings. It is important that a teacher be a good record keeper. Records must be dated, organized, categorized, centrally located, and periodically updated. New entries must be made at regular intervals.

Evaluation is something that is not generally associated with art. Evaluation in art is concerned with how children are progressing artistically and creatively as they process and make art products.

CHILDREN'S ART FILES AND FOLDERS

Keeping samples of children's artwork is a good way to collect evaluative data. Ask the child's permission to enter his or her name and the date on the back of the piece. Try to collect a sample at least once a week. Tell children you are saving pieces for their art file or folder. Encourage their participation in making artwork they want included. Honor their requests for pieces they insist on taking home. Encourage them to make both "take home" and "folder" pieces. Use a large manila file folder or folded piece of poster board to hold the pieces. Periodically lay the pieces out in temporal order. Look for development, progression, and mastery in the use of media and materials and in the expression of ideas, concepts, objects, and feelings. Match what is artistically rendered with a particular child's artistic and overall level of development. Use these data in reporting to parents and planning future art experiences. (See Figures 16-1A through 16-1D.)

INSTRUMENT FOR ARTISTIC EVALUATION

Our wholistic model of child development has served many purposes: to understand child development, to plan appropriate experiences, to report to parents, and to justify our program. We can also use it as a framework for evaluating children's artistic development.

Physically

1. In using artistic tools the child demonstrates
   _____ large-muscle or gross motor control.
   _____ small-muscle or fine motor control.

2. Proper use of the following artistic tools
   _____ scissors.
   _____ glue.
   _____ brushes.
   _____ crayons.
   _____ markers.
   _____ clay tools.
   _____ watercolor set.

A   B

C   D

Figure 16A–D   A girl's concept and drawing of herself develops over time.

3. Concentration and sustained involvement in art.

4. Completion of the art activity.

Socially

1. Ability to work alone at art.

2. Demonstrating self-responsibility
   _____ in getting and returning art materials.
   _____ in clean-up.
   _____ in following the rules of the art center.

3. Self-direction in using own ideas in art rather than copying others.

4. Ability to work cooperatively with others at the easel, art table, or art center.

5. Tolerance of others' art ideas, styles, and products.

Emotionally

1. Acceptance of own mistakes, errors, and unsuccessful attempts at art.

2. Self-assurance and confidence in art rather than an inhibited, fearful, overly cautious attitude.

3. Expresses feelings, moods, emotions, and personality through artwork.

4. Enjoyment and pride in own art.

5. Addition, omission, distortion, and/or exaggeration of things that are emotionally significant.

Cognitively

1. Understands art and why people have made art in the past and continue to do so.

2. Interested in talking about own art and dictating labels, titles, sentences, or stories.

3. Knows and uses art vocabulary.

4. Evidences
   _____ very personal representation.
   _____ public representation with subject matter recognizable to others.

5. Demonstrates a knowledge of colors and color mixing.

6. Reflects a knowledge of shapes, including
   _____ circle.
   _____ square.
   _____ triangle.
   _____ rectangle.
   _____ lines.
   _____ combinations of above.
   _____ other nongeometric.

7. Reflects a knowledge of people, places, objects, experiences, and events of personal importance in the environment.

8. Draws human figures.

Creatively

1. Demonstrates a willingness to discover, experiment, and explore with a variety of media.

2. Demonstrates ways of creatively combining media, materials, and artistic junk.

3. Uses detail, decoration, and elaboration.

4. Reflects originality, imagination, and creativity.

5. Makes individual and personally unique artistic statements.

Aesthetically

1. Enjoys
   _____ processing with the media.
   _____ making artistic products.

2. Uses a variety of
   _____ two-dimensional artistic media.
   _____ three-dimensional artistic media.

3. Demonstrates awareness and sensitivity through
   _____ looking.
   _____ touching.
   _____ listening.

_____ smelling.

_____ tasting.

4. Demonstrates awareness and sensitivity to
_____ surroundings.
_____ nature.
_____ environment.

5. Sees similarities and differences in artistic styles.

6. Appreciates work of artists encompassing a wide range of styles.

7. Knows the following artistic elements:
_____ color.
_____ line.
_____ mass or volume.
_____ pattern.
_____ shape or form.
_____ space.
_____ texture.

8. Uses artistic elements to discuss and appreciate
_____ nature.
_____ surroundings.
_____ environment.
_____ own artwork.
_____ artwork of others.

Personally

The child's favorite choices are numbered 1, 2, and 3.

Two-dimensional	Three-dimensional
_____ mark making	_____ sculpture
_____ painting	_____ clay
_____ printing	_____ papier-mâché
_____ watercolor	_____ construction or
_____ resist	assemblage
_____ stencil	_____ mask making
_____ paper work	_____ mobile
_____ collage	_____ stabile
_____ tie and dye	_____ weaving
_____ batik	_____ stitchery

SUMMARY

This unit recommended that samples of children's art be kept in individual files or folders. This is vital to evaluating a child's artistic progress, reporting to parents, and further planning. One way to evaluate artistic progress would be to use the instrument provided in this unit. To use the instrument, the teacher must carefully observe, record, and file his or her findings in a child's folder.

SUGGESTED ACTIVITIES

1. Working in teams, interview teachers about their views on evaluation in early childhood, how they evaluate young children, and what they use to evaluate children's artistic progress.

2. Collect samples of one child's art over an extended period of time. Lay the artwork out in temporal order. Use the evaluation instrument in this unit to make some statements about this child's artistic development. Can you make any recommendations?

REVIEW

A. Discuss the teacher's role as observer and evaluator of a child's artistic development.

B. Identify a major strategy for collecting and storing children's art.

Unit 17

The Art Center

OBJECTIVES

After studying this unit, the student will be able to

- List and discuss the five criteria for setting up an early childhood art center
- Compare and contrast two- and three-dimensional art media
- Identify potential rules and limits for successfully operating an early childhood art center

INTRODUCTION

The rationale for setting up the art program around a center format is that this allows for discovery, choice, responsibility, and independent activity. The early childhood art center should be an artist's studio, conveniently located and easily accessible, well stocked, orderly and organized, with rules and limits. These criteria or guidelines will be explained in this unit.

THE ART CENTER

The classroom art center is an area where children can go to do art. Most programs already have centers set up for manipulatives, table toys, blocks, books, and dramatic play. Others have centers for science, water play, and sand play. Although space is always at a premium, an early childhood art center is warranted. Just what is an art center, and how does one go about starting it and maintaining it? (See Figure 17-1.) The criteria for an art center would include the following. An art center is

- an artist's studio
- conveniently located and easily accessible
- well stocked
- orderly and organized
- with rules and limits

Each of these five points will be examined in detail.

Figure 17-1 Art centers come in a variety of styles.

An Artist's Studio

The art center should be an artist's studio. It is a place to experiment and explore with legitimate artistic media. It is not a place to color in coloring books or complete a workbook page. Creative self-expression is encouraged. No one right or realistic way is expected. Although subtly structured, the artist's studio reflects creative clutter. A productive level of noise and mess is expected, although the art center is never chaotic or out of control. The work of child artists appears on nearby wall space. Art books are kept at hand for reference and as a source of inspiration, but never to copy.

The child should be exposed to a variety of stimulating activities and experiences with legitimate artistic media. These will complement, broaden, and balance self-directed free expression. They will depend, in part, upon the individual child's developmental level, coordination, ability, and interest level. A balance between process and product can be built in to one's art center. The creative process of painting and ex-ploring visual symbols is as important as the finished product, e.g., a painted picture. Pounding, rolling, pinching, and stretching clay are as important as the aesthetic quality of the finished clay piece. (See Figure 17-2.)

Art Activities as Suggestions, Not Prescriptions   There is danger in merely listing or prescribing a set of art activities. These are included merely as suggestions or possibilities, not as a set of activities to fill the pages of one's lesson plans on a day-to-day basis. Teaching them directly as specific activities would negate everything we have discussed about art as a creative, discovery process. Instead, encourage children to discover many of these extensions or possibilities on their own. The activities are based on a few media (see Figure 17-3).

Mixing Media   Mixing media results in the discovery of new artistic possibilities. For example, let us assume that children have worked with crayons at the table and paints at the easel. Ask

Figure 17-2   Children experiment and explore at the art center.

Figure 17-3   Mixed media—construction paper and coloring

children, ''What would happen if we used them together? Can you paint over your coloring? Or, can you use markers along with colored pencils? Have you ever tried to do a collage over your dried hand painting?'' The possibilities for creative mixing are endless. One need not suggest specific combinations but merely reinforce experimenting with and joining different artistic media.

Varying the Tool, Method, and Media   Varying the tool will help children discover new artistic possibilities. For example, they have painted with an array of paintbrushes, flat and round. Ask them, ''Can we paint with a toothbrush? Is there a brush in your house or garage that could be used for painting? Let's think of things other than brushes that we could use for painting.''

Varying the method will also lead to new possibilities. Paint can be spread with a brush to make long, sweeping lines. There are also many other ways to apply paint. It can be dabbed, swirled, sprayed, dripped, and dribbled.

Varying the medium also increases the range of possibilities. Children can paint with water, colored water, transparent watercolors, thick opaque tempera, or tempera to which sand, salt, or sugar has been added.

Incorporate Both Two- and Three-Dimensional Art Media   Similarly, there should be a balance between two-dimensional and three-dimensional art media. Two-dimensional activities involve a relatively flat artistic surface with height and width portrayed. Three-dimensional art activities also portray depth. Some media, including work with paper, allow for both two- and three-dimensional expression. The following two- and three-dimensional art media are recommended and will be explained.

ART MEDIA

TWO-DIMENSIONAL:	THREE-DIMENSIONAL:
Mark making	
Painting	
Printing	
Stencil, spatter, and screen printing	
Watercolor and ink	
Resist	
Tearing, cutting, pasting, gluing, taping, stapling	Tearing, cutting, pasting, gluing, taping, stapling
Collage	Collage
Paper art	Paper art
Tie and dye, batik	
	Clay
	Construction, assemblage, and sculpture
	Puppets and masks
	Mobile and stabile
	Sewing and weaving

Units 18 and 19 will discuss a variety of two- and three-dimensional art activities.

Conveniently Located and Easily Accessible

An art center should be conveniently located and easily accessible, not cramped into a crowded corner. It should be located near a sink and removed from the mainstream of classroom traffic. The location of the sink and of neighboring centers will determine where the art area is placed. For example, an art center should not be placed in the middle of the room, where children will walk through it while visiting other centers. Since different activities or centers have their own noise levels, it would be wise to locate the art center near other noisy activities. For example, the art center could be located near the block area, since both centers encourage children to move, talk, socialize, and be active. It is not recommended that the art center be located adjacent to the book corner or quiet area. If your room does not have a sink, pails of water can be stored in the art area. Paper towels should also be provided.

An art center need not be restricted to the indoors (see Figure 17-4). Art can be offered as an activity during outdoor free play. An easel or art cart on wheels can be easily rolled in and out as needed. When identifying the best spot for your art center, try to select a spot that is easy to view and supervise, both up close and from a distance. The table tops should be easy to clean. A plastic-laminated table top can be easily wiped clean with a damp sponge. Try to avoid placing the art center in a carpeted area. If necessary, cover the flooring under the easel and art table with newspaper or an old shower curtain. An old washable throw rug placed under the easel would be both practical and attractive. Ideally, children will clean up after themselves. Try to reserve adjacent wall space to display children's artwork. Samples of artists' work reflecting different artistic styles can also be displayed. Our intent is not to encourage children to copy but to expose and educate them to the different ways in which people have done and continue to do art. If space permits, art books, laminated prints, and art postcards can also be kept close, but at a sufficient distance from water, paint, and other media that might soil them. Adjacent counter space can be reserved for displaying three-dimensional artwork, including clay, sculpture, construction, assemblage, and papier-mâché. Adjacent floor space can be reserved for drying paintings. Or, a commercial drying rack can be used.

Well Stocked

The art center should be well stocked with basic art media, tools, equipment, accessories, and artistic junk. An art center need not entail great expense and can operate on a modest budget if planning and economical purchasing are involved. Plan with other teachers to order in bulk. Buy only the basics. Frills and gimmicks are of-

Figure 17-4   An outdoor art center

ten expensive, quickly expendable, and not conducive to creative expression. Still, even junk must have some artistic merit. It should be sorted, organized, and arranged. For example, a crushed box filled with old newspapers and other odds and ends might overwhelm a young child. Children need to see some order and relationship between the parts and pieces and ask themselves, "How can I creatively combine these things?" This will not happen if everything is piled haphazardly or thrown into a heap. See Appendix H for list of art basics needed to set up an art center.

Orderly and Organized

The art center is orderly and organized to maximize efficiency. Children know that the paste jars are kept in a plastic tub on the middle shelf. Both the word "paste" and a picture or sketch of

a paste jar appear on the front. Labeling helps children assume responsibility for securing all art materials and returning them to their rightful place. This will help free the teacher from responding to an endless list of questions, such as, "Where's the paste? Who has the scissors? Who was the last one to use the glue? Teacher, I can't find any paper." Obviously, not all young children will be self-responsible, but self-responsibility is one goal we should aim for in early childhood.

The art center need not be chaotic or needlessly cluttered. It should be well organized and pleasantly arranged to maximize efficiency. Children know that the scissors rack is kept on the second shelf. Thus, they can secure and replace scissors on their own. Through this subtle structuring, regularity, and predictability, the ordered environment of the art center serves as a model

Figure 17-5 The art center should be orderly and organized.

for children, who are often confused by the disorder in their life and surroundings. In the art center, everything has its rightful place, and the child artists are responsible for its daily maintenance and operation (see Figure 17-5).

With Rules and Limits

An art center provides the child with unlimited opportunities for attaining self-responsibility. Children abide by reasonable rules and limits. These rules and limits should be verbally discussed in advance, with the reasons for each rule clearly explained. Children need to know both the rules and the reasons behind them. For example, children discuss the proper use of materials. Paint brushes are for painting. Waving paint brushes in the air could either splash paint or hurt someone. Rules can also be posted in writing and pictures near the art center for easy reference. Rules and limits need to be discussed, posted, and enforced. Children who break a rule can be removed from the art center. When they have had time to reflect and believe that they are ready to abide by the rule, they can return.

Rules and limits will vary from teacher to teacher, center to center, classroom to classroom, program to program, and age group to age group. The following is a very comprehensive list of guidelines from which you can select those that work best for you and your group.

A Limit on the Number of Children at the Center at Any One Time This will depend on the number and size of tables, floor space, and easels. For example, Mrs. Tull displays four Art signs on clothespins at her art center. When all have been removed, children know the art center is full. Ms. Valdez allows eight children in her larger art center. Four children can work at the tables, two at the easel, and two on the floor. When children ask if they can do art, she asks them to count the number of children or see if there is an open or vacant spot for them.

Use a Smock During Art Activities Children whose parents warn them about staying clean and avoiding messy activities may be apprehensive about doing art. Teachers can strongly recommend that parents provide "work" or "play" clothes rather than party attire. Young children need to dress appropriately for an active day at school, and this will involve getting dirty. Adding liquid detergent to paint will also make the paint easier to wash out when doing the laundry. Children should be reminded to let their paintings dry thoroughly before moving them or attempting to take them home. This will minimize smudging and smearing of paint onto clothing.

Slightly oversized children's shirts make good smocks. Cut off the sleeves, put them on backwards, and have someone button up the back. Daddy's old shirts are often too long, bulky, and awkward. The sleeves constantly need to be rolled up and often dangle in the paint. Smocks are vital during painting. They also protect clothing when children are using glue, paste, and markers. It is a good idea to wear a smock for any and all art activities. Shirt sleeves should be rolled or pushed up above the elbows. Removing sweaters is a good idea, since this will allow greater freedom of movement and eliminates the possibility of their getting stained with paint. Attractive smocks can also be made from oilcloth or vinyl cut into a large square with a head opening and worn as a poncho. Velcro or elastic can hold the sides. See figure 17-6. Or, a child-sized apron can be made, with elastic at the waist and neck. Allow about eighteen inches for the neck and about twenty inches for the waist. Adjust according to specific needs and sizes within your group. See figure 17-7.

A painting smock could be made out of an old large bath towel. Fold it in half and cut a large opening for the head. Sew up the sides, leaving ample room for the arms. Young children do not like clothing that fits snugly over their head, so make sure you use a large towel and leave plenty of extra room for it to slide on easily.

Figure 17-7　An apron

Some companies make special art sleeves that give good protection for the arms, although not the chest. Basically, they consist of elastic sewn to both the cuff and upper arm of a shirt sleeve. Make them out of durable material that will hold up to repeated washing. See figure 17-8.

The author saw one teacher effectively use a plastic trash bag as a makeshift smock. Holes for the head and arms were quickly cut at the closed end. The children enjoyed wearing their artist's costume.

Use Art Tools Properly　This is not to suggest that there is only one way to paint or draw. It does mean that brushes are for painting and scissors are for cutting paper. Teachers should discuss and model the proper care and use of all art media in advance.

Use Only What You Need　Discuss the economical use of paper, glue, paste, and so forth, and the avoidance of needless waste. Have a variety of paper sizes available. Not all children need or want to work on a large sheet of paper. Some children have a small idea that fits nicely

Figure 17-6　A smock

Figure 17-8　Art sleeves

onto a smaller paper square. Avoid putting too much paper out at any one time. Children may feel obligated to deplete the pile or believe that there is an endless supply.

Complete Your Art Activity   The writer has seen children go through a pile of papers by making a series of aimless, quick marks. Quality rather than sheer quantity should be the goal. Teachers can encourage children to take their time and finish each picture. "Jill, you have started a picture that has a lot of action and movement. But there is so much more room on your paper. Maybe you would like to keep working on it." Jill is free to accept or reject her teacher's suggestion.

Share Supplies   Items at the art center need to be shared. There may not be enough glue or staplers to go around. Children learn that the items belong to the school or center and are available for all children to use. Some children will have difficulty following this rule. They may become possessive and clutch the sharpest pair of scissors or the prettiest roll of ribbon.

Respect Others   Children learn to respect and value the ideas, styles, and work of others, just as they have come to value their own. Children cannot ridicule or criticize the ideas and work of others: "That's a dumb picture" or "That's no good; it don't look like no train!" Children's statements may be well intended, but the message hurts. It also hampers creative expression. Teachers can discuss how children can draw, color, or paint anything in any way they want. It is their decision and their rendering, not someone else's, that matters. "I'm sure James knows the sun is yellow, but he chose to paint it purple. It's his picture, and he can paint it any way he wants." Perhaps children who receive criticism or correction for their own artwork also become overly critical of others.

Children may also get possessive of available space. They may try to occupy the majority of the table. Young children who are used to having their own way and having one of everything at home will need guidance. Young children who have little space and no toys may also squander and require intervention. "The art center is for everyone, but only four at a time. This means we each have this much space [marking off with fingers] and we must share our things. If we cannot share, we will have to leave the art center."

Return Everything to Its Place When Finished   Small paper scraps are thrown in the wastebasket. Larger scraps of construction paper can be saved in a scrap paper box for collage. Smocks are hung up on a hook.

Clean Up When Done   Brushes need to be washed. Spilled glue needs to be wiped up with a wet sponge. Remind children to leave their space clean for the next artist to use. Children know that they need to wash their hands and clean up the space they occupied. They should also check the floor before they leave. In short, children learn that the art center is primarily their responsibility, with the teacher playing only a minor role in its subtle guidance, maintenance, and supervision.

SUMMARY

This unit focused on setting up an art program around a center format. By definition, an art center is an artist's studio, conveniently located and easily accessible, well stocked, orderly and organized, with rules and limits. It was recommended that the art center provide for an array of two- and three-dimensional art media and that children be encouraged to creatively mix media and invent their own activities.

SUGGESTED ACTIVITIES

1. Observe a successfully run art center. Note the teacher's role.

2. Use the criteria for an art center to informally evaluate an early childhood art center.

3. Set up an informal art center. Observe its operation for a period of several days. Play an indirect role as guide or facilitator. Document your findings in a journal or diary.

4. Evaluate an early childhood art program for its balance between two- and three-dimensional media and activities. Make recommendations if necessary.

REVIEW

A. List the criteria or guidelines for an early childhood art center:
   1.
   2.
   3.
   4.
   5.

B. Place the appropriate classification (2-d, 3-d, or Both) in front of each of the art media listed below.

   _____ mark making   _____ painting
   _____ printing   _____ ink and watercolor
   _____ resist   _____ collage
   _____ paper art   _____ tie dye
   _____ clay   _____ construction, assemblage,
                                                and sculpture
   _____ masks and puppets   _____ stabile and mobile
   _____ weaving and sewing   _____ batik

C. List major rules for successfully operating an early childhood art center.
   1.
   2.
   3.
   4.
   5.

Unit 18

Two-Dimensional Art Activities

OBJECTIVES

After studying this unit, the student will be able to

- List major two-dimensional art media that are appropriate for use with young children
- Identify developmentally appropriate two-dimensional art activities
- Construct new activities by mixing and creatively combining two-dimensional art media

INTRODUCTION

This unit is strategically placed at the end of the book. By now you should have a working knowledge of child development, curriculum development, aesthetics, and artistic theories to serve as a framework for what you do with children. The format of this unit is significantly different. It is designed as a resource of art activities and a guide. Use it sparingly as a reference rather than teaching directly from it. Suggested age ranges are included for each activity, although age and developmental stage alone are often misleading.

MARK MAKING

Mark making is a term used to refer to the variety of artistic marks that young children make. Young children begin by making scribbles or unrecognizable marks and progress to recognizable shapes and forms. Scribbling is important both in itself and as practice for later printing, writing, and drawing. Scribbling is to drawing and printing or writing as babbling is to talking and crawling is to walking. Most young children will have some experience with using crayons, pencils, markers, or pens at home.

Children need large sheets of paper to make

movements with the entire arm. Later, they will develop hand coordination and fine motor control. Crayons are recommended for the beginning mark maker. Colored pencils are too long and thin and have a soft point. They are hard to control, and the points break easily. The advanced mark maker can be given colored pencils for making precise drawings. Scribblers need crayons, but not a wide array of colors. Often, one dark color is enough for making marks. Their interest will be in making marks and strokes rather than using a variety of colors. Crayons will be peeled, sucked, and broken. Actually, scribblers need peeled crayons so that they can use both the tips and the sides and bottom to make a variety of marks.

There is no one best position for mark making. Older infants and toddlers enjoy sprawling on the floor on their tummies and marking with crayons on a large piece of paper. This setup can accommodate four mark makers at any one time, one at each side of the paper. Others may enjoy kneeling on the floor while marking. Easels are not just for painting. Some children may be most comfortable standing while making marks. Others will prefer to stand or sit at a table. The seated position is most appropriate for the older, experienced mark maker, since it requires more restricted small-muscle movement. Standing, reclining, or kneeling permit greater whole body involvement and movement while marking.

Children make marks with a variety of tools, including

- pencils
- chalk
- crayons
- markers
- paper or hole punch
- pastels

Please see the section in Appendix H that lists and discusses the basic equipment and art supplies.

Tools to accompany mark making include

- ruler
- pencil compass
- stencils
- protractors
- lids and tops (to trace)

Activities for mark making include:

Scribbling (N/Pre)

Older infants, toddlers, and preschoolers scribble. They make marks for the sheer joy of moving a tool across paper and seeing what happens. They need a variety of mark-making tools and large sheets of paper.

Crayons Crayons are a preferred medium. They are colorful, responsive to children's movements, and fairly inexpensive. They are always ready for use and do not require mixing or special preparation. Most young children will have experience with them and be automatically drawn to them. Young children will have their color preferences. Vibrant colors, such as silver, gold, and hot pink, will quickly lose their pointed tips. Young scribblers do well with only the basic primary colors. Yellow is difficult to see when used on white paper.

Crayons are composed of pigmented wax. Dark crayons contain more wax, are softer, and will leave an opaque mark. Light crayons contain less wax, are harder, and will leave a transparent mark. The older mark maker discovers that if you color dark over light, e.g., brown over yellow, the lighter color will not show. The younger mark maker, however, will not be that concerned with color mixing and planning.

Marking with crayons or scribbling will progress in stages. Young scribblers push, pull, and drag their crayon across the paper, resulting in horizontal, vertical, diagonal, and circular marks. The crayons will not be lifted off the paper, and the resulting marks will be continuous, with little or no variation. Beginning scribblers will often look away while marking, being more interested in the muscular activity itself than in the finished product. Details and small marks will be largely absent because of limited fine muscle development and control. With time, practice, and control, shapes and symbols begin to be included. Details and variations appear. Some variations on the use of crayons include

- scribbling with a crayon in each hand

- marking with a crayon in the nondominant hand—e.g., righty uses a crayon with left hand

- using two or more crayons that are tied together with a rubber band

- making notches or grooves in a peeled crayon and using it in a sideways, swirling, or up-and-down motion

- mixing colors by blending or overlaying crayons on white paper

- using crayons on colored construction paper

- varying the pressure on crayons, coloring heavily or lightly, and noticing the effects of pressure on the types of marks

- polishing crayon marks by rubbing them with a tissue to make a shiny surface

- using all sides of the crayon: the point for small dots; the flat end for larger round circles; the side for sweeping, wide strokes; and holding the crayon in the middle and rotating it to make bows or large circles

- using only dots made with a crayon to form a picture, outline, or design

Musical Scribbling (N/Pre) Children also enjoy scribbling or mark making to music. Make a mark or stroke that shows how the music makes you feel. Most of the previous suggestions also apply to musical scribbling. Make a simple doodle to music. Stop and turn the paper in a different direction. Attempt to continue the design or to complete a picture that the doodle suggests. For example, a mass of looping lines might suggest a snake. A tail and head could be added. Or, it could be spaghetti, with the child drawing a fork and plate.

Drawing or Sketching (K, Pri)

Older children develop from random scribbling to more purposeful drawing or sketching that is often systematically planned out in advance. Some children may enjoy drawing or sketching

- each other

- objects in the room

- a very simple display, such as two stuffed animals

- school or center experiences, such as a field trip or outdoor play

- people, places, and things at home

- numbers, letters, and words

- using only geometric shapes

- a new animal made up of two very different ones, for example, a "turtlephant" with a turtle's head and an elephant's body

- items brought for show and tell

Chalk and Pastels (K, Pri)

Older children will appreciate the possibilities of marking with chalk. It is messy, but the colors produced are beautiful and the possibilities for blending are endless. Children can mark

- with light chalk on dark paper, e.g., white on black for a snow scene

- with colored chalk on white paper

- with dry chalk on wet paper

- with wet chalk on dry paper

- with the tip and/or side of the chalk

- by rubbing or blending chalk dust on a cotton ball (scrape with a dull knife or Popsicle stick)

- on rough, textured paper that responds to chalk

- by dipping the chalk in liquid starch before marking

- with chalk sticks soaked in a solution of 1/3 cup sugar to 1 cup water for five to ten minutes before use. The colors will appear more brilliant and tend to resist smudging.

- on paper wet with buttermilk or a combination of canned milk and liquid starch to add sparkle

- outdoors on sidewalk and blacktop (it washes away with rain)

- with pastels, which provide a compromise between crayon and chalk. They are fairly solid and come in brilliant colors, but are slightly expensive.

Mural (N/Pre, K, Pri)

Making a mural involves many social skills and decision making. How will we share the entire mural space? Who will make what, and where? Murals can revolve around a theme, such as outer space. Young children, however, often depart from the theme. There may be three planet earths in the mural or animals floating about in space. Often, there will be a second bottom baseline at the top of the mural. This is to be expected. Murals can be the focus of a group story or dictation. Provide a long strip of paper. Place it on the floor in an out-of-the-way spot and encourage each child to make his or her unique contribution. Letters, names, numbers, and words can also be added to the art picture story.

Me Marks (N/Pre, K, Pri)

Most young children are interested in talking and learning about themselves. This can be part of social studies or a unit on "me." Some related mark-making activities include

- a self-portrait

- drawing, making marks, or making self-sketches that show being mad, happy, angry, sad, scared, hurt, lonely, or silly

- a "Me" book that shows things that make me feel one of the previous ways—for example, a separate page with "happy" on it

A wall mirror will help children notice details, including eye and hair color, clothing, and the presence or absence of freckles and front teeth. Still, even though young children can visually see, they will not necessarily represent realistically.

Object Trace-Over (N/Pre, K)

Much of the artistic junk (see Appendix A) will have a characteristic shape and outline, often geometric in nature. Lids, tops, caps, boxes, and containers can be traced over. The shapes can be creatively combined. Some can be repeated in a sequence or pattern. Some children may prefer to make something out of their traced objects. For example, a series of traced-over circular lids might suggest a caterpillar or wheels on a bulldozer.

Architect's Art (K, Pri)

You will need a ruler, pencil, protractor, and pencil compass. Older children can make a number of lines with a ruler and pencil, by tracing the arc of a protractor, or by using a pencil compass. An interesting design with lines, circles, and arcs will result. Children can add their own designs. (See Figure 18-1.)

Graph Paper Cube Design (K, Pri)

Buy graph paper with large squares. Or, make a series of 1-inch squares on a sheet of paper that you Xerox or run off on ditto. Children can be encouraged to think of an object that has a square or rectangular shape or is composed of small boxes. For example, it would be more difficult to make a round swimming pool than a rectangular skyscraper. Sketch out the exterior outline. Fill in the individual squares to complete the picture.

Figure 18-1 Architect's art

Run, Mark, Run (N/Pre)

Children will enjoy using markers on paper towels or thin fabric on which they will blend and run. Place newspaper or cardboard underneath.

Sandpaper Art (K, Pri)

Children can use crayons to make heavy marks or a design on a small 4- to 6-inch square of sandpaper. Use fine or medium grade rather than coarse. Press hard, and make solid-colored forms. When the sandpaper is fairly well covered with crayon marks, it can be heated in a warm oven at 250° for ten to fifteen seconds until the crayon melts. The crayon wax will harden and produce an interesting effect. Also, this activity can be a good tie-in to discussing the effects of heat and temperature change. What happens if we leave our crayons in the sun or on the heater? Will the same thing happen to our pencil? Who knows why?

Paper Punch Art (K, Pri)

Older children will have the muscular strength to work a hole punch with either one or both hands. They seem fascinated with the process. Variations include

- merely punching holes out of scrap paper

- making a design, outline, or picture of punched holes and pasting this paper onto another. For example, a design could be punched out of white paper and glued to a piece of red construction paper. This could be a Valentine's Day card.

Glue Design (K, Pri)

Make a design using a bottle of liquid white glue on wax paper. Make thick masses, shapes, or forms. Let dry until hard and clear. Decorate the dried glue with thin or fine-line magic markers. The dried and decorated shapes can be carefully peeled off, laced with thread, and hung overhead or worn as jewelry.

Crayon Shavings (K, Pri)

Old, broken crayons can be recycled for this activity. Carefully scrape a dull knife or Popsicle stick along the crayon and catch the shavings. Place them on a piece of wax paper and arrange them into a design. Add glitter, ribbon, tissue paper, and a piece of string if a hanging is desired. Place another piece of wax paper on top. Press with a warm iron to melt the wax and seal it. Cut the excess wax paper off or snip it into an interesting shape. Use black construction paper for the outer frame. Hang it over the window and let the light shine through.

Coffee Filter Art (K, Pri)

Crayon shavings can also be placed on a flattened paper coffee filter. Place a sheet of construction paper on top. Press with a warm iron. You will get two pieces of art. The heat will melt the crayon wax, and you will have a colored design on a round white background. You will also get a print of that design on your piece of construction paper. (See Figure 18-2.)

Iron Art (N/Pre, K)

Fold a sheet of drawing paper in half. Mark or color dark and solid on one half. Refold the paper with the colored design inside. Press with a warm iron to make a print. Open. A colored image or print will appear on the other half.

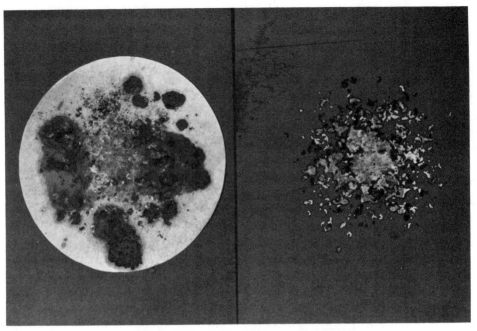

Figure 18-2 Coffee filter art and print

Fabric crayons can be used in a similar way. Mark with fabric crayons on white paper. Color heavily. Place the paper face down over fabric. Transfer the picture onto the fabric by ironing the paper with a warm iron. The wax will melt, and the heat will set the colors into the fabric.

Fabric crayons are designed to be used with fabric. Locate some material scraps—prewashed muslin, old T-shirt, or white sheet. Staple a small square of old sheet or muslin to cardboard to keep the fabric from slipping around. Use the fabric crayons to make heavy marks or a design. Place paper on top and press with a warm iron. The heat will melt the colored wax and set the design. Individual squares could be sewn together into a quilt.

Crayon Etching (K, Pri)

Probably everyone has done at least one of these in their lifetime. Older children can fill up a piece of manila paper with a crayon design. Leave no space empty. Polish with a paper towel to help the second layer of color adhere. Next, using black crayon, color darkly over the entire

surface. Polish again. Last, use a Popsicle stick to etch out a design. A fairly thick etched line will reveal a rainbow of colors beneath. This is recommended only for older children who have the patience and muscular strength to color dark over an entire sheet of paper and stay with this activity through its several steps.

Crayon Melt (N/Pre, K)

This activity needs a food-warming tray. The tray will remain warm but not dangerously hot. Still, children need to discuss the dangers and take precautions. Place a large sheet of paper on the warming tray. Children can slowly draw a picture or design. Remind them to keep their hands and arms off the warming tray. The heat from the warming tray will melt the wax, leaving a melted impression. This activity is not dangerous but needs supervision.

Rub-a-Dub-Rub (N/Pre, K, Pri)

Rubbing a marking tool over a textured surface produces an interesting rubbed effect. Some people do this over gravestones while studying family or local history. Visitors make rubbings of family and friends whose names are listed on the Vietnam Memorial. Crayons are recommended for children, although chalk could also be used. Hold a piece of paper in place while rubbing. Possible textured surfaces include

- wood grain
- tree bark
- fabric
- cement and concrete
- flocked wallpaper
- leaves and other flat nature specimens
- screens and grills
- brick
- signs with raised letters
- comb
- sandpaper

- mosaic tile
- leather
- buttons
- paper clips

Some of the author's favorite textured surfaces include

- embossed greeting cards
- keys
- license plates
- coins
- corrugated cardboard
- paper lace doilies and Valentine's Day place mats

PAINTING

Painting is a pleasurable, messy, and creative art activity. It also allows children to plan; to

Figure 18-3 The young painter at work

Figure 18-4 A trio of easel painters

make decisions about what to paint, colors, and placement; and to work on their own. Not all children will have had experience painting prior to coming to school. Painting will be a popular activity. For these reasons painting should be made available throughout the day every day. Some children panic when they see only one or two easels and fear that they will never get a turn if painting is allowed only once a day for a short period of time. (See Figure 18-3.)

Generally, painting involves the use of tempera or watercolor paints. Tempera paints are opaque and give a smooth, flat covering of intense color. They are water-soluble, and adding water will dilute them and dull their intensity. Watercolor paints are transparent and allow for a layering of colors. Children should have experience with tempera before graduating to watercolors. Still, children never outgrow their interest in tempera painting. There are many different painting arrangements, including

- standing at an easel
  This position allows for whole-arm strokes and total body involvement. It allows for the

use of long-handled brushes. Easel painting, however, does have its drawbacks. Given the slant or angle, paint tends to run and drip down. This frustrates some children who use liquid paint and expect it to defy gravity and stay put where they placed it. They expect it to act like a marker or crayon. On the positive side, easels encourage verbalization and socialization between painters, especially if the easels are placed side by side. (See Figure 18-4.)

- seated at a table
  Children can also paint on a flat surface while seated at a table. This placement keeps paint from dripping and allows layers of paint to be built up. Usually a table can accommodate a few painters at one time. Children can use short-handled brushes, as in watercoloring. Paint will be more controllable, but the amount of arm and body movement will be restricted.

- standing at a table
  This position allows for whole body movements while painting on a flat surface. Whereas four children can sit down and paint at the same time, only one can stand and paint at each end of the table. This position is highly recommended.

- on the floor
  Painting on the floor provides a flat surface, although this position also restricts whole body movement. It is hard to involve the bottom torso when one is kneeling. Children, however, enjoy sprawling on the floor and will find this position comfortable. Standing for a long period of time while painting tires and bores some young children.

- outdoors
  Use any of the above indoor arrangements to paint outdoors (See Figure 18-5).

Although painting while standing at a table or easel is highly recommended, it is wise to give children experience painting at a variety of different angles and placements.

Figure 18-5   Painting outdoors is fun.

Brushes

There are many different types of brushes recommended for painting (See Figure 18-6). Long-handled brushes with flat bristles are called "flats." They produce wide strokes. Brushes with rounded and pointed bristles are called "rounds." They produce narrow lines and strokes. Be sure to include a wide array of brushes for painting, including

- make-up or cosmetic brushes
- toothbrushes
- scrub brushes
- feather dusters
- shaving brushes
- household paintbrushes

- pastry brushes
- bath brushes
- dish cleaning brushes or pom-poms
- nail brushes
- hair brushes with plastic spikes
- shellac foam sticks
- bowl brushes
- whisk brooms

A brush is not the only tool for painting. Also, there is no reason to use only one brush at a time. Children can paint with a brush in each hand or with two tied together. Other recommended painting tools include

- fingers and hands
- eyedroppers
- Q-tips, cotton swabs, or cotton balls
- straws
- sponges
- combs
- Popsicle sticks or tongue depressors
- feathers
- toothpicks
- sticks or twigs
- string
- rags
- assorted kitchen gadgets
- powder puffs
- spatulas
- kitchen shakers
- empty plastic razors
- wads of cloth tied to thick pencils
- small paint rollers for trim

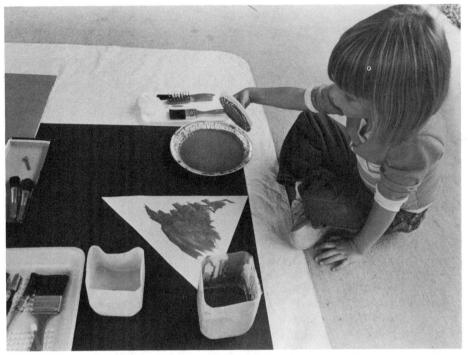

Figure 18-6 **Provide an array of brushes for painting**

- pipe cleaners twisted into unusual shapes
- shoe polish applicators

Painting Surfaces

Children do most of their painting on paper. It is important to provide paper in a variety of colors, shapes, sizes, and textures (See Figure 18-7). Children can explore painting on papers that are wet as well as dry. Painting on damp paper will provide an effect similar to that of watercolors. The colors will bleed and blend. The edges will be soft, with many unplanned creative accidents where paint ran together to form unusual shapes. Allow time before adding too many colors, which may just all run together and form a dark blot. Some other things to paint on include

- glass or windows
- Formica or table tops
- cardboard
- boxes
- wood
- wallpaper
- paper bags
- newspaper
- tin foil (over cardboard)—add liquid detergent to paint
- smooth stones
- paper plates
- Styrofoam meat trays

Painting Precautions

Remember to roll sleeves up, remove sweaters, and use a smock. Provide one brush or painting tool for each color. Do not fill paint jars full. This only adds to the dripping and mess. Instead, fill jars less than half full and add as needed. Try

Figure 18-7   The shape of Lauren's paper poses a challenge.

to use a clear container so that children can easily see the color of the paint. Glass jars are clear but also potentially dangerous. Fairly large, see-through plastic cups or containers are ideal. Or, paint a tin can the color of the paint it will hold. Encourage children to keep the paints and brushes to their left and paper to the right. This will reinforce the left-to-right progression so crucial to later reading and writing.

How many colors should be provided? Some believe that beginning painters need only one color until they have learned the basic processes involved in holding a brush, dipping for paint, wiping excess, positioning on paper, and making strokes. Others begin with two. The author recommends providing the three primary colors. Additional colors will appear on the canvas through accidental or purposeful mixing. They can also be mixed using the palette method. Containers of white and black will help children lighten or darken colors. There is no one right answer to the opening question. Those who stress the technical skills involved will recommend using only one color. Those who stress the importance of color mixing and creative expression would provide two or more. Five would be

maximum. More is not necessarily better when providing colors of paint. The same holds true for the number of crayons in a box. Children can be as creative with the basic eight as they can with an overwhelming sixty-four.

Painting is a messy activity. Remind children to scrape the side of the brush on the inside rim of the jar before they remove it from the paint. This will help eliminate the dripping of excess paint on table, floor, smock, and paper. Encourage children to replace their brush or painting tool in the one designated container. Mistakes will happen. Be sure to rinse thoroughly to avoid unwanted mixing of paints. Children should wash their hands before taking off their smocks. This will avoid unnecessary smearing of paint on skin, hair, and clothing.

Paint Palette

Children who have had some experience in color mixing can be introduced to painting with a palette. An aluminum pie plate, frozen dinner tray, or Styrofoam lid is recommended. Children take blobs of mixed paint and mix their own colors, shades, and tints on their palette. Always have the primary colors and white and black available. Children have their own brush for color mixing on their palette. They also need a cup of water for cleaning their brush between color mixings.

Some activities for painting include:

Hand Painting (N/Pre, K)

Finger painting is an activity that is not usually offered in the home. Still, most young children have had some experience spreading soap on the sides of the bathtub or food on the tray of their highchair. Finger painting is not an accurate term. The activity involves much more than merely spreading paint with the fingers. Often, adults approach hand painting by neatly dabbing their forefingers with their "pinkies" gracefully up in the air. The whole hand and arm should be involved. Some teachers allow children to paint with their feet. Hand painting is messy but developmentally appropriate. The children make direct contact with the medium. There is no brush to separate the artist from the paint. Children enjoy the cool, slimy texture. It gives young children the opportunity to get messy without fear of reprimand. It is an activity that should be provided on an ongoing basis. Some children will be reluctant. They may fear that their clothes will get dirty or that their parents will get mad at them for making a mess. They will need time and gentle reassurance. Seeing the other children and their teacher engaging in hand painting may reassure them. A child should not be forced to do hand painting against his or her wishes. (See Figure 18-8.)

When hand painting, children should be encouraged to get fully involved by using the

- front or palm of the hand—for wide strokes

- back of the hand—for wide strokes

- side of the hand—for long, thin strokes and zigzags

- fingertips and joints of the fingers—for dabbing marks

- fingers, front and back—for long marks

- thumbs—for round marks

- knuckles—for a series of marks

- fingernails—for fine lines that etch through the paint

- fists—for massive marks and round swirls

- wrists—for massive marks

- hand with fingers spread wide—for hand prints

- whole arms, toes, and feet—best involved outdoors on a warm day

Sleeves need to be rolled up and sweaters removed to encourage freedom of movement, and smocks should be worn. Hand painting while kneeling or sitting on the floor restricts movement. Hand painting while standing at a table is recommended. It allows children to use their

Figure 18-8 The teacher guides and facilitates hand painting.

large arm muscles more freely, reach all over their paper, and have a better view of what they are doing. Standing up also keeps one's smock from dangling in the wet paint.

Music sets the mood for finger painting. Slow music encourages lazy, smooth strokes. Fast music encourages rapid, swirling lines. See the section on paints in Appendix H for a variety of paints to use with hand painting.

Infants and toddlers enjoy hand painting with pudding and applesauce, although the use of food in art has already been discussed. Some would argue that there is no added expense or waste because the food will be eaten. Others fear that playing with all food is encouraged through this activity. It may be best to eliminate the use of food in art.

Shaving cream can also be used. It is thicker than most finger paints, and children enjoy the texture. Remind them that it is not whipped cream and is not edible. Squirt a glob for each child and spray water to dilute. Adding food coloring or tempera powder enhances its visual appeal but is optional.

Hand painting should be done on paper with a glossy or glazed surface. Finger paint paper is commercially available but fairly expensive. Slick cardboard, shiny shelf paper, gift boxes, magazine covers, or a nonstick baking sheet can also be used. Add liquid detergent to the paint and do hand painting directly on a Formica table top. Lay a sheet of paper over the table, rub gently, and take a print of the hand painting. This will please those children who want to save what they made. Adding some vinegar to the wash water will help clean the tables.

Begin by giving each child a piece of paper. The papers can be laid out glossy side up and sponged down with water first or occasionally squirted with a pump sprayer. Begin with the primary colors. Add one glob or teaspoon of paint. Paint that is applied too heavily will crack or chip off when dry. Or, you can pour liquid starch on each child's paper and let them take turns sprinkling powdered tempera from a kitchen shaker. It is difficult to manage hand painting with a large group at the same time. The first child may finish before you even give paint to the last child. It may be easier and less stressful to do hand painting in shifts with fewer children. This allows you to observe and interact rather than merely dispense.

Encourage children to use both hands in thoroughly spreading the paint. Squirt with water if the paint becomes dry. Add a second color. Over time the colors will become thoroughly mixed. Mixing red and blue will make purple. This may be the time to stop. You may want to add yellow or white to lighten it up if the children are still interested and want a third color. Placing the paper flat on newspaper to dry will result in a curled picture. When the picture is thoroughly dry, turn it over and press it flat with a warm iron. Or,

place the paper on a larger piece of newspaper before painting. Some paint will stick the paper to the newspaper, resulting in less curling when dry.

Etched Hand Painting (N/Pre, K) Objects such as a comb, a paper clip, a fork, a key, or a notched piece of cardboard can be pulled and swirled through the wet hand painting. This will produce an interesting etched design. Still, these are merely accessories and do not replace the active processing with both hands.

Water Painting: Where Did My Picture Go? (N/Pre)

Children need something to put on their painting tool, but not necessarily paint. Most young children enjoy painting with water. They may have done it at home in the bathtub or sink or on the pavement. It is a good introduction to using a brush and is highly recommended as an outdoor art activity. Provide old household brushes and plastic pails of water. Painting caps and old painting clothes, e.g., coveralls may help ease them into the role of painter. Children can paint cement, brick, trees, outdoor nonrusting equipment, and windows. Food coloring can be added, but it will streak the surface being washed.

Whipped Soap Painting (N/Pre, K)

See Appendix G for recipe. Whipped soap is thick and good for making snow scenes on black construction paper or white hearts on red. A few drops of food coloring or powder paint can also be added.

Roll a Line Design (N/Pre, K, Pri)

Find a lid from a box. Cut a paper to fit in. Mix paints. Find items that roll, including

- toy cars
- marbles
- small balls
- beads

Figure 18-9　Roll a line design

Carefully dip them in paint and place them in the box lid. Encourage the child to tilt, tip, and move the lid to get the items rolling in different directions. Dip them in more paint if needed. The result will be a crisscrossed linear effect.

The author prefers doing this with a pie tin or round cake pan. The round frame provides a strong contrast to the linear design. Cut a circle out of paper. Make sure that it fits into the bottom ridge. Use light paints, including white, yellow, and light blue, if working on black construction paper (see Figure 18-9).

Roll Painting (N/Pre, K)

Children can use a rolling pin or brayer to make their painting. Use a spoon to add different globs of paint on one half of a large sheet of paper that has been folded and opened. Refold. Roll over it with your rolling pin or brayer. Roll gently from center to sides. This will distribute the paint in different directions. Carefully reopen. Add additional colors. You will have a painted design on both sides, each a mirror image of the other.

Bleach Painting (K, Pri)

This activity involves the use of liquid bleach and requires direct supervision. Remind them to move the eyedropper from bleach container to paper without splashing or making contact with

their face or hands. Pour a small amount of bleach into a small container. Smocks must be used for this activity, since bleach will take the color out of clothing. Dip a cotton swab or eyedropper in bleach and draw with it. Place construction paper over several layers of newspaper. The bleach will take out the color in the construction paper. Some colors bleach out more completely than others. Bleach strokes should be fairly wide and saturated. This activity is recommended for older children.

String Painting (N/Pre, K)

Fold a sheet of paper in half. Open it and spread it flat. Place globs of paint on one half. Place a foot-long piece of string curled up on one inside half before refolding. Make sure one end of the string is sticking out. Gently pull on the string while holding the folded paper in place with the other hand.

Straw Painting: Blow a Blot (N/Pre, K)

Children enjoy blowing through a straw to spread blobs of paint. Young children will need to practice holding and blowing through a straw in preparation for this activity. Perhaps they could blow bubbles for science. Paint should be fairly thin. Place paint in the middle of the paper with a small spoon. Encourage children to hold their straw close to but not touching the paint. Blow out, not in. Move the paint from the middle to the sides of the paper. Add other colors. Blow the colors into each other. Rotate the paper if necessary. The result will be an interesting design composed of mixed colors, weblike patterns, and intersecting lines.

Special Painting with Special Painters (N/Pre, K, Pri)

Children enjoy using sponges and foam as painters. Sponges or foam of various widths can be cut into different shapes and inserted into pinch-type clothespins. A Popsicle stick can also be gently inserted and glued in place. Use a razor blade, X-acto knife, or scissors to cut the top edge into a pointed, grooved, forked, notched, or wavy pattern. This will result in a different type of stroke when painting. Encourage children to use the special painters in different ways. They can make dots and dabbing motions, twirls to make circular shapes, and long strokes, either up and down or sideways. See the recipe for special paint in Appendix G. Remember to have the painter slightly wet before using special paints.

Crayon Painting: Encaustic (K, Pri)

Children can paint with melted crayons. See the section on ways to melt crayons in Appendix H. Use one old stiff brush per color. Once they have been used with melted wax, brushes will not be good for anything else. Popsicle sticks or tongue depressors can also be used. Children can paint with melted crayon wax on cardboard. Tin foil wrapped around a cardboard base makes an interesting background.

Squeeze and Dribble Painting (N/Pre, K)

Pour paint into squeeze bottles, old liquid glue bottles, meat basters, or mustard and ketchup dispensers. Children can squeeze and dribble a design on paper. Paint can also be squeezed from a small hole in a thick plastic bag.

Shake a Painting (N/Pre, K)

Fill kitchen shakers with different colors of powder paint. Make sure the holes in the shakers are large enough for the powder to shake out easily. Wet the paper with a sponge or squirt bottle. Shake different colors onto the wet paper. Mix with a Popsicle stick or paint brush.

Drip Drop a Painting (N/Pre, K)

Children can use a medicine or eyedropper to make a painting. Provide different colors. One eyedropper can be used if the child remembers to clean it out between colors. Paint can be squeezed up into the eyedropper and slowly dropped in a design on a white paper towel, a coffee filter, or white drawing paper.

Etch a Painting (K, Pri)

Place tin foil over a piece of cardboard. Tape it on the back. Children enjoy working with tin foil. Add Ivory Flakes to your paint to help it adhere to the slick surface. Use only one color of paint to paint over the tin foil background. Let the paint dry. Use a Popsicle stick to carefully etch or scratch a picture through the dried paint. Etching too hard will tear through the tin foil. The result will be an outline of a picture in shiny silver.

Dot Painting (N/Pre, K)

Encourage children to dip the end of the paintbrush handle in paint and make a picture composed of circular dots of paint. One finger could also be used to produce the same effect.

Marbleized Painting (K, Pri)

Have children sprinkle powdered tempera on the surface of a flat tray of water. Carefully float a piece of white smooth-textured paper on top. Gently swirl the paper to get a marbleized effect. Repeat with different colors. The paper will take several hours to thoroughly dry.

PRINTING

Most young children have had experience making prints at home. Rubbing a food-stained mouth on a white bath towel or napkin will leave a print. Muddy shoes will leave a print on the kitchen floor, and touching a wall with dirty hands will leave one's fingerprints. Many children arrive in the morning with a print of mom's lipstick on their face from a kiss.

Printing is an extension of painting. Painting involves making movements with a brush or other painter across a surface. Printing involves stamping paper with an object dipped in paint. Printing involves less whole-arm activity and greater concern for placement and overall design. Discuss and show examples of patterns in wallpaper, brick wall, windows, fabric, gift wrap, flowers, and nature when introducing printing. Tempera paints should be fairly thick for the printed impression to show up. A variety of papers can be used.

Some printing activities include:

Monoprint (N/Pre, K, Pri)

A pane of glass, sheet of Plexiglas, acrylic cutting board, or any nonporous surface, such as a Formica table top, can be used. Children can paint their picture or design right on the surface. Use fairly thick paints. Place a larger piece of paper over the painted area. Rub gently with brayer or hand. Carefully lift up. As the term "monoprint" suggests, you will produce one print off the painted surface. Designs can also be etched into a solid mass of paint before the print is taken. Children will also enjoy hand painting on the surface and having a monoprint taken.

Ink-Pad Print (N/Pre, K)

Children enjoy placing their fingers on an ink pad and making a stamped impression on a piece of paper. Ink pads come in colors other than black. What does the fingerprint impression suggest? Children may want to use fine-point markers to make their basic fingerprints into something else by adding body parts, wheels, and details.

Small objects with interesting shapes and textures include

- corks
- coins
- paper clips
- buttons
- seashells
- caps and bottle tops
- nuts and bolts
- carved wooden blocks
- eraser tops on pencils
- spools
- hair rollers
- Styrofoam pieces and squiggles
- plastic tops from milk containers
- embossed guest soaps

These can also be printed as described above. Re-ink with liquid ink when the print appears dull. Several thicknesses of heavy paper towels or an old washcloth soaked with tempera paint can also serve as a stamp pad.

Sponge Printing (N/Pre, K)

Sponges can be creatively cut into an array of shapes and sizes. Encourage children to dip the shapes in paint and make a stamped print. Geometric shapes can be arranged to form a picture. Or, children can repeat a sequence or pattern of printed shapes. Provide one or more shapes per color. Wash out a sponge if it is accidentally dipped in a different color. (See Figure 18-10.)

Food Print (N/Pre, K)

Food is generally too expensive to be used for art. However, should a parent or grocer donate surplus fruits or vegetables, they can be used in a printing activity. Vegetables and fruits that can be cut and used for printing include

- orange
- potato
- lemon
- apple
- carrot
- turnip
- radish
- green pepper
- cabbage
- cauliflower
- tomato

Figure 18-10   A sponge print

- onion

- avocado

- mushroom

A Corny Print (N/Pre, K)

Painting an ear of corn and rolling it like a rolling pin on a piece of paper makes a very good print.

Roller Printing (N/Pre, K)

Printing with an ear of corn is one example of roller printing. Other examples of rollers that can be used for printing include

- a hair roller—insert a pencil to hold when rolling

- a long bottle wrapped with a yarn or string design

- a toilet paper roll with shapes cut out

- a cardboard paper towel roll with shapes cut out

- a brayer with raised shapes glued onto it

- a rolling pin with raised shapes and designs or flocked wallpaper glued onto it

- a spool with lines and designs carved or etched in—insert a pencil to hold when rolling

- a tin can with yarn or string glued to it

Roll the roller in a low dish, pan, or large Styrofoam meat tray of paint. Roll on paper.

Kitchen Gadget Printing (N/Pre, K)

There is an array of kitchen gadgets listed in the section on Paint and Painting Accessories. Others include

- plastic or nylon utensils

- slotted spoon and fork

- spatula

- pie slice lifter

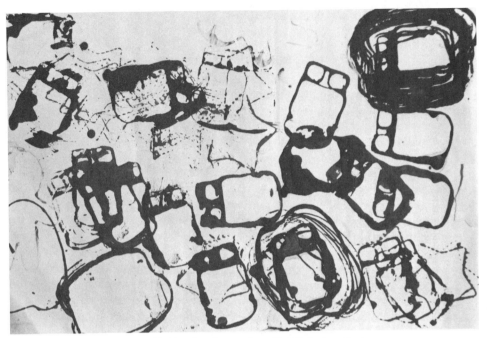

Figure 18-11 A print made with kitchen gadgets

- whip-beater
- funnel
- potato masher
- pancake flipper
- cookie cutters
- plastic forks
- pie tin (bottom)
- embossed lids and bottoms of jars
- plastic scourer and scrubber with knob handle

These can be dipped in paint and printed on paper. Encourage children to creatively combine and overlap printed shapes to form designs or pictures. (See Figure 18-11.)

Recycled Junk Print (N/Pre, K)

Actually, many of the items mentioned in the sections on printing with a stamp pad and with kitchen gadgets could fit in here. See Appendix A for a list of artistic junk. Look for objects with different textures and uneven surfaces. Some items that can be recycled into a printing activity include

- corks
- spools
- comb
- hairbrush with plastic spikes
- bottle tops and jar lids
- pill bottles and vials
- Styrofoam pieces
- corrugated cardboard
- hair rollers
- keys
- toy cars
- crumpled paper

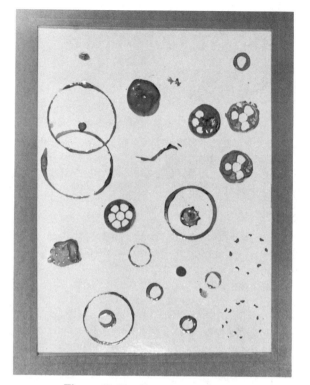

Figure 18-12   Recycled junk print

- bar of soap with raised letters or design
- license plate

Apply paint to the object and place it down on paper. Carefully remove. (See Figure 18-12.)

Styrofoam Meat Tray Print (K, Pri)

Trim the raised edges off small Styrofoam meat trays. You should have a flat piece to work with. Draw or etch a picture or design into the Styrofoam, using a Popsicle stick. Press in without breaking through. The incised line will remain white when the Styrofoam is covered with ink or paint and printed. Ideally, a brayer is dipped in ink and spread across the Styrofoam. Paint can also be brushed on. Paint over the etched surface with a single color of paint. Press the Styrofoam on a piece of paper and gently rub with your hand over the entire surface. Carefully lift the Styrofoam to see your print. A second print can be taken immediately if paint is left on the Styrofoam. Children can make a series of prints this way. Wash the Styrofoam before changing colors.

Nature Print (N/Pre, K, Pri)

Items collected from a nature walk can be inked and printed. Look for leaves, pinecones, and other nature specimens with interesting textures and surfaces.

String Printing (K, Pri)

Find small blocks of wood or small, sturdy gift boxes. Dip string in white glue and wrap it around the block or box in an interesting design. Or arrange the gluey string in a design on only one side. Let the glue dry. Dip the best side of the block in ink or paint. Place it on paper and gently push down to make an impression. Carefully remove the block to see the print. Repeat and make a continuing series or pattern. Stay with the color chosen rather than trying to wash the printer. Small wood blocks or boxes could also be stamped in an ink pad.

Pieces of dense foam in sheet or tape form can also be cut, built up into raised layers, and glued onto a printer.

Cardboard Print (K, Pri)

Secure sturdy cardboard for the background. Cut smaller pieces of cardboard or thick paper and build up a raised picture or design. Glue and let dry. Paint over it with paint. Press the cardboard on paper. Rub gently all over with your hands. Carefully lift the cardboard to reveal your print.

Corrugated cardboard is highly recommended for building up interesting line designs that go in different directions in making a print.

Ceramic Tile Print (K, Pri)

Roll a layer of ink or paint on a tile square. Etch a picture or design, using a cotton swab or your finger. Place a small piece of paper over the tile. Rub gently. Carefully remove the paper to reveal your print. A tile with raised or embossed surfaces will have a prepared surface ready for printing.

Game Piece Print (N/Pre, K)

Dominoes, checkers, game tokens, bingo markers, and magnetic letters and numbers make interesting designs when dipped in paint and used as stampers to make a print.

Bubble Print (N/Pre, K)

Fill a shallow container with water and tempera paint to which dishwashing detergent has been added. Two parts tempera paint to one part liquid dishwashing soap is recommended. Stir. Blow bubbles with a straw. Place white paper on top of the bubbles to get a print. The result will be a print made up of circular designs that can serve as a background for collage, drawing, or other art activity.

Push-Up Stick Print (K)

Ice cream bars and Popsicles often come on a push-up stick. Save the push-up stick and discard the rest. Cut a design or shape out of Styrofoam and glue it onto your push-up stick. Dip the Styrofoam in paint or on an ink pad and press it on paper.

Crayon Sandpaper Print (K, Pri)

Children can draw a picture or design with crayons on a piece of sandpaper. Encourage them to press hard and fill up the sandpaper. Place a piece of white paper over the colored sandpaper and press with a warm iron. The heat will melt the wax from the colored sandpaper and transfer the design or picture to the paper.

Glue Print (K, Pri)

Use white liquid glue to draw a design or picture on a piece of cardboard. Make sure the outline or impression is fairly thick. Let the glue dry. Spread the design with ink or paint. Gently press it on a piece of paper. The paint or ink will adhere to the raised dried glue outline. Or, glue a picture cut from a magazine to your piece of cardboard. Trace the outline with white liquid glue. Repeat the steps involved in making a glue print. This time you will get a print that resembles the picture cut out of the magazine.

STENCIL, SPATTER, AND SCREEN PRINTING

Stencil, spatter, and screen printing are fairly involved activities that require some amount of instruction and special tools. It is unlikely that young children will discover on their own how to make a stencil, spatter, or screen print.

Stencil (K, Pri)

A stencil can be cut from sturdy cardboard or thick paper, including tagboard or poster board. It can also be torn out of construction paper. When you cut a stencil, you actually get two. Recall our discussion of positive and negative space. The shape cut out occupies positive space and is called the positive stencil. The remaining frame or background occupies negative space and is called the negative stencil. Each type of stencil has its own process. Hold the stencil with one hand and use the other hand to stroke from the piece out when using the positive stencil. Hold the background or frame and stroke inward when using the negative stencil.

Stencilling can be done with crayons, paint, or chalk. The author prefers chalk dust dabbed on with cotton balls because of its ability to blend. It also does less damage to the stencil than paint does. Paint can be gently dabbed on with cotton balls, a small sponge, or a brush. Short, stiff-bristle brushes used with an upright gentle dabbing motion are recommended for the skilled stenciller. Whatever is chosen to stencil with, do not saturate it with paint. Be careful that the paint, chalk, or crayon does not get under the stencil, causing smears.

It may be difficult for very young children to cut their own stencil out of cardboard. Perhaps it could be drawn by them but cut out by an adult. Encourage them to design a very simple picture with a minimum of fine detail. An X-acto knife can be used to cut out a stencil. Remember not to cut through the frame to get to the inside. Very young children can tear out a vague abstract shape that will work very well in a stencil activity.

Stencils can also be painted with spray paint or sprayed from a sprayer, e.g., a bug sprayer filled with liquid tempera. This method is best done outdoors. Place the paper in the lid of a large box. Tape the back of the stencil in place. Let dry. Carefully remove the stencil.

Spatter Printing (N/Pre, K, Pri)

You will need a large but not too deep box, a screen or mesh wire (e.g., a window screen, kitchen grease guard, or metal strainer), and an old toothbrush. Cut or tear a stencil out of paper. Or, items with interesting shapes, such as coins, a comb, cookie cutters, keys, and nature specimens, can be used as a positive stencil and placed on a sheet of paper inside the box. Dip your toothbrush in paint and gently move it across the screen, releasing a mist of paint. Dark colors will show up best on white paper. The paint will spatter and outline your stencil or objects. The part that is covered will take on the color of your paper. The space taken up with your positive stencil or objects will remain white or the color of your background paper. Carefully move the stencil or objects and repeat with a different color. Switch stencils and work with the negative stencil.

Young children will need to use a large box covered with a fairly large spatter screen. Older children may be able to use a small, hand-held food strainer and move it around the stencil. They can carefully rub chalk across the food strainer at the same time. A small spatter screen can also be made by carefully cutting the top and bottom off a sturdy small box. Attach wire or screen to the top. Use with small stencils. Or, fasten plastic mesh or screen into an embroidery hoop.

Screen Printing (K, Pri)

An embroidery hoop, an old picture frame, or a frame cut from the lid of a shoe box can also be used for screen printing. Use an old nylon stocking or a piece of silk, organdy, dotted swiss, or cheesecloth for the silk-screen material. Cut it larger than your frame, pull it tight, and secure it with tacks, tape, or nails. Cut a stencil and place it on paper. Put the silk-screen frame over the stencil. Use a brush, tongue depressor, or cardboard strip to gently spread thick paint on the silk screen, which will cover the stencil. Carefully lift your silk-screen frame. Thoroughly rinse the silk screen after each application of paint. Add different colors if desired. Repeat the pattern while overlapping or creatively combining pieces from different stencils.

WATERCOLOR AND INK

Tempera painting is a prerequisite to painting with watercolor or ink. Using watercolor and ink requires coordination and fine motor control. These media will frustrate the very young artist. They are used with smaller brushes that are harder to manage.

Watercolor (N/Pre, K, Pri)

Watercolors tend to be wet, runny, and transparent. Often, they produce very unintended results. The wet colors may bleed when the child artist is trying to make facial features. The writer recommends that children begin using watercolors to make lines, colors, shapes, and abstract designs rather than attempting realistic, detailed art. Watercolors come in their own small sets with individual semimoist cakes. Buy a medium grade. The brushes that come with the cheapest sets will have bristles that fall out after the first washing.

Watercolors can be used on either wet or dry paper. Watercolors put on wet paper will run and bleed into very interesting patterns and designs. Papers can be wet with a sponge or from a pump spray bottle. A small sponge allows children to blot up excess water or unwanted runs. Special spots can be saturated with water dropped from an eyedropper. The author has observed one child do just that in making a bulls-eye effect or rainbow of blended colors.

Since there is only one brush for several colors, it is important that children wash their brush each time before changing colors. They will need an individual water container, which should be emptied every time it appears muddy. When they are done, excess watercolor paint in the set should be carefully blotted up. A careful rinse under the sink will remove excess paint. Be careful not to merely rinse away the unused paints. Let the set air-dry. Sets that are closed when wet tend to get gummy. Children find them unappealing.

Watercolor paper is very expensive if purchased separately by the sheet. Purchased in tablet form, it is still moderately expensive. White drawing paper is acceptable. The author finds that onionskin or good bond typing paper has a good texture for watercolor. An office with outdated letterhead stationery may have a surplus of this. You could easily trim off the letterhead.

Ink (K, Pri)

Even young children can appreciate the beauty of Chinese pen and ink drawings that capture nature with a minimum of lines. Ink comes in colors other than black and tends to be fairly expensive. One bottle of black may suffice for use with older children. Ink can be economically used on small sheets of paper with a thin brush. It is appropriate for making linear drawings and designs with a minimum of line and ink. Ink can also be used in printing and stencil activities. It is not recommended for use at the easel or for general painting.

Ink Blots (N/Pre, K) Children can drop ink on a piece of paper. Carefully fold the paper in half and open. Change colors and repeat the process. Cut around the ink blots and mount them on colored paper.

RESIST

A dried design or picture will resist a second liquid put on top. The process of resist is a fasci-nating one that intrigues children. They do one picture, put a second covering over it, and end up with a totally different effect.

Some resist activities include

Crayon Resist (N/Pre, K, Pri)

Children can make a picture or design with crayons. It is important to press hard and color fairly dark. Although much of the paper is covered, some empty space should be left. The colored picture can be covered with

- watercolor
- ink—producing a pitch black, midnight background
- hand painting
- Magic Marker
- shoe polish
- tempera paint

Whichever of these is used for the second coating, the crayon wax will resist the liquid. The liquid will fill in the remaining white negative space. It may also bead up on the colored wax to produce an interesting textured effect.

Rubber Cement, Paste, or Glue Resist (K, Pri)

The smell of rubber cement may be too tempting for very young children. Older children, however, can paint a picture or design by making thick marks or strokes in rubber cement, paste, or glue on white paper. See the recipe in Appendix G for paste resist. Or, apply adhesive to paper and fold the paper in half to get a mirror image. Quickly open up the paper. Let dry thoroughly. Later, paint over the entire paper with

- watercolor
- ink
- tempera paint

The rubber cement, paste, or glue will resist any of these liquids. The background will fill up with color, and the dried adhesive will leave a crackled white picture. Let dry thoroughly. Some children enjoy carefully rubbing off the dried rubber cement with an eraser a day or so later.

Ink Resist (K, Pri)

Children can paint a picture with tempera. Be sure to leave some space white. When the paint is dry, they can cover the entire sheet of paper with black or colored ink. The effect is striking. Black provides a good background for night scenes or Halloween. Blue ink is effective for underwater or sky scenes.

Wax Paper Resist (K, Pri)

Place a piece of wax paper over a sheet of white paper. Secure it with tape or paper clips. Use a Popsicle stick to heavily etch a thick line, design, or picture. The pressure will transfer the wax to the paper. Discard the wax paper. Paint over the entire sheet of paper with watercolor or ink. The lines drawn with the Popsicle stick will remain white. This activity takes much patience and fine motor control and is recommended for older children.

TEARING, CUTTING, PASTING, GLUING, TAPING, AND STAPLING

Very young children process with art materials long before they purposely decide to make an art product. They enjoy tearing and taping paper, smearing and spreading paste and glue, and using scissors and staples. Some very simple activities include

- tearing paper
- cutting with scissors
- pasting and gluing
- taping and sticking
- stapling

Each of these is not only enjoyable by itself but also a necessary skill for other art activities.

Tearing Paper (N/Pre)

Young children should not feel excluded from art activities just because they cannot use scissors. Very young artists can tear paper. Tearing paper is a good activity for developing the hand and finger muscles. Begin with very thin papers like newspaper, scrap tissue, or old phone directories. The individual pieces can be pasted or glued to each other or onto a piece of paper.

Torn-Paper Picture (N/Pre, K)

Torn-paper pieces can be arranged and pasted or glued onto a piece of paper to form a torn-paper picture (see Figure 18-13). Older children may enjoy using construction paper. Being able to use scissors does not mean that one has outgrown the interest in tearing paper for art activities. The author observed a classroom where kindergartners were making a Halloween mural out of torn-paper shapes. Torn shapes with rough, jagged edges were ideal for this activity. One

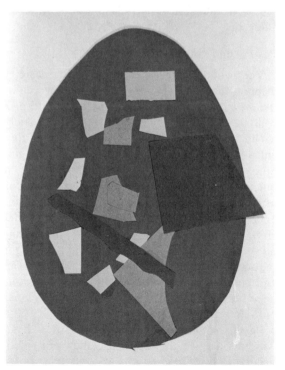

Figure 18-13 A torn-paper picture

witch's hat had a long, exaggerated point, and so did her nose!

Cutting with Scissors (N/Pre)

Refer to the previous discussion of the developmental sequence for using scissors. Successful cutting with scissors is a developmental landmark. Some children will cut for the sheer sake of cutting, with little regard for the pieces cut. Some will want to take their individually cut pieces home in a bag. Others will enjoy pasting the pieces that they have cut onto paper. You may want to tape a paper bag to the table to catch the cut paper snips as they fall rather than attempting to pick or sweep them off the floor later.

Fold and Cut (N/Pre, K)

Children can fold a thin piece of paper and use their scissors to snip out a piece. Refold the paper in a different direction and continue cutting and snipping. Open up the paper and glue it against a colored piece of construction paper for a background. This will help the cut-out design stand out.

Pasting and Gluing (N/Pre)

Very young children enjoy smearing paste or dripping glue for the sheer sake of it. They enjoy the smell, cold feel, stickiness, and texture of solid paste. It has a thick, crumbly feel that sticks to the fingers. Liquid white glue has a very different wet feel to it. Children enjoy squeezing glue onto paper. Bottles filled to the brim may be quickly emptied. You may want to add food coloring to your paste and glue to enhance its visual appeal for beginning pasters and gluers. See Hints in Appendix H. Very young children may not be interested in gluing or pasting anything in particular. Older children will combine pasting and gluing with tearing and cutting. Papers that have been cut and/or torn can be pasted or glued onto an art surface.

Paste and glue serve different purposes. Paste will hold lightweight papers together, but glue is needed to bond heavier objects, including boxes and wood. Rubber cement is meant for adhering paper.

Stapling (N/Pre, K)

Staplers and stapling fascinate young children. Stapling is more a fine motor skill than an artistic process. A hand-held stapler requires a squeezing motion with one hand, while a large stapler involves a gentle pounding, stamping, hammering, or pushing action. The miniature stapler may be too small for children to activate and control. Using a stapler is noisy, but children thoroughly enjoy it and the activity exercises their finger and hand muscles. They will staple just to get a group of staples attached to paper. Sometimes the staples will form a design or pattern on colored paper. At other times they may use a stapler in place of paste or glue for attaching small pieces of paper, fabric, or collage material to each other or a background.

Sprinkle a Picture (N/Pre, K)

Children can make a picture or design with paste or glue on paper. They can carefully sprinkle

- confetti
- paper dots (from a hole punch)
- small balls of cotton (on dark paper)
- small shells
- seeds
- pine needles
- pieces of broken jewelry
- sand (see recipe for coloring sand)
- Styrofoam chips or squiggles
- glitter

Carefully slide the excess off the paper and back into the container. Some teachers use salt, sugar, popcorn, cornmeal, or rice in shakers for this activity. The author advises against the use of food in art activities for reasons previously stated.

Taping and Sticking (N/Pre)

Very young children enjoy sticking tape. Teachers can provide tape in a variety of colors, widths, and lengths. Place cut or torn pieces of tape on a nonstick surface. Children will enjoy lifting them off and placing them on paper. Pieces of torn and/or cut paper can also be taped onto an art surface.

Lick and Stick Art (N/Pre)

Children enjoy licking and sticking the colorful labels and gummed papers available from office supply and stationery stores. Items include

- paper reinforcements
- gummed stars and labels
- stickers
- price tags
- colored dots
- book club stamps
- seals

These can also be licked and/or placed in a visual arrangement.

COLLAGE

Collage (N/Pre, K, Pri)

A collage is a picture composed of different shapes or elements. A collage can be two-dimensional and composed of flat pieces of paper, or it can be three-dimensional and made with Styrofoam chips and raised layers of fabric. Pieces of paper that are torn, cut, pasted, or taped can be creatively arranged into a collage. Although the activities are listed separately, there is no reason that materials used in one activity cannot be included in another. There is an endless variety of papers that can be used in collage. Some include

- junk mail
- postage stamps
- postcards
- greeting cards
- gift wrap
- wallpaper samples
- travel brochures
- magazines
- newspapers
- coupons
- tin foil

A collage is not limited to paper. There is an infinite supply of collage materials. The key is quality and organization. Not all junk will have artistic value or potential. Items that are dirty or damaged may hold little aesthetic appeal. A pile of unorganized junk may trigger little creative transformation. It is important to organize collage materials according to some scheme—e.g., papers in one bin; ribbon, lace, and yarn in another; magazines in a neat stack on the shelf; and so forth. Children need some basic order to help them see artistic possibilities.

Geometric Shapes Collage (N/Pre, K)

Younger children who lack scissoring skills may enjoy pasting precut geometric shapes into a design or picture. Provide an array of different colors, sizes, and shapes. Older children who have scissoring skills can draw and cut their own geometric shapes. Encourage children to place their shapes into some arrangement before gluing or pasting them. Or, a rough sketch or outline can be drawn first and later filled in with geometric shapes.

Corrugated Cardboard Collage (K, Pri)

Corrugated cardboard has an interesting texture and linear look. Older children can cut different shapes or pieces out of it and make a collage. Encourage them to note how the ridges can go in different directions. This is what gives a corrugated cardboard collage its visual appeal. Corrugated cardboard, with its raised ridges and neutral color, provides a striking contrast when it is used with flat or colorful papers or fabric.

Tissue Paper Collage (N/Pre, K, Pri)

Colored tissue paper can be torn or cut. Since it is so thin, it may frustrate the young cutter. Encourage children to note both the transparent quality of tissue paper and the possibilities for creating new colors by overlapping and building layers. Rubber cement is recommended for bonding tissue paper.

Or, form your tissue paper collage on a piece of wax paper. Lay another piece of wax paper on top. Gently press with a warm iron. The heat will melt the wax and seal the collage.

Or, use white glue to paste your tissue papers inside the plastic lid of a coffee can. This will provide a ready-made frame. Carefully punch a hole at the top, lace with yarn, and hang.

Magazine Picture Collage (N/Pre, K)

Magazines offer a wealth of letters, words, and pictures, just waiting to be torn or cut out and pasted or taped to paper.

Montage (K, Pri)

Montage refers to a collage built around a theme, such as love, friendship, family, pets, or helping. Words and pictures related to the theme can be included. A montage around the theme of vehicles might include pictures of cars, trucks, bikes, airplanes, boats, motorcycles, stop signs, and traffic lights.

Collage Mural (N/Pre, K)

A collage can also be a group project correlated with a unit or concept under study. Some examples include

- color
- shape
- size
- initial consonants
- people
- community helpers
- other classes, concepts, and categories

Children can search through magazines looking for samples or examples of the concept. A collage mural can be an extended activity; it need not be completed in a short period of time. It could be set up as a center, with children adding to it from time to time over a period of a few days.

Magazine Mix-Ups (N/Pre, K, Pri)

Children have a silly sense of humor. They might enjoy making a picture out of unrelated parts—for example, an animal with a human head or the front of a car with the tail of an airplane. One teacher introduced this activity by providing part of a picture for each child. The pieces, cut from a magazine, were different for each child. Examples included a cat's head, a person's body, the trunk of a tree, and a diving board with no steps. Children were encouraged to look through their magazine and find a part that would finish their mixed-up picture by adding a silly top, bottom, head, body, or side as needed. There was no need to correctly finish the picture.

A collage does not always have to be done on paper. Be creative. Provide

- cardboard
- paper plates
- box lids
- wood
- Styrofoam meat trays
- egg cartons
- containers

Nor does collage entail only the use of paper. Look through your artistic junk for a variety of materials that can be pasted, glued, stapled, or taped.

Nature Collage (N/Pre, K)

Nature specimens can be carefully glued onto paper or sturdy cardboard. Some examples include

- leaves
- ferns
- grass
- petals
- weeds
- flowers

Figure 18-14 Nature collage

Other examples of nature items are found in Appendix A. Some prefer to first press their nature specimens for about a week between layers of newspaper with heavy objects on top to get them flat. Or, they can be arranged on wax paper with a second sheet on top and pressed with a warm iron. (See Figure 18-14.)

Fabric, Felt, or Material Collage (N/Pre, K, Pri)

Children enjoy using materials other than paper in their collage. Provide small scraps of fabric, felt, or material for the young child to paste or glue. Older children with fairly sharp scissors and good cutting skills may be able to cut out or tear their own pieces. (See Figure 18-15.)

String or Yarn Collage (K, Pri)

A collage can be composed of string or yarn. Each can be dipped in glue and creatively arranged on an art surface. Remind the children to squeeze the excess glue out before placing the string. Obviously, string or yarn should be incorporated with other collage material.

Texture Collage (N/Pre, K, Pri)

Most of the collage activities mentioned involve textures. A collage can also specifically focus on textured papers, including

- sandpaper
- flocked wallpaper
- tissue paper
- newspaper
- magazine pages

or a variety of textured fabrics, including

- wool
- cotton
- velvet
- burlap

Figure 18-15   Fabric collage

- netting
- foam rubber

A variety of textured nature specimens, listed under Nature Collage and in Appendix A, can be included. (See Figure 18-16.)

PAPER ART

Children have many experiences with paper long before they enter school. Some papers are scrap, whereas the pages in books are not to be written on, cut, or torn. Children see their parents handle paper money and write checks. Greeting cards and mail are made out of paper. Paper serves many purposes.

Processing with Paper (N/Pre, K)

What can an artist do with paper? Many different things can be done to and with paper (see

Figure 18-16   Texture collage

Figure 18-17 Children enjoy processing with paper.

Figure 18-17). As children experiment and explore with paper, they find that it can be

- torn
- cut
- glued or pasted
- taped
- stapled
- folded
- slit
- curled
- pleated
- twisted
- braided
- fringed
- looped
- scored (made to curl by pulling it against the blade of scissors)
- chained: rings or loops made into a continuous chain
- punched with a hole punch
- pricked with a toothpick (and placed against a contrasting-color background)
- made into a cone or cylinder
- ringed: a strip made into a crown, headband, or bracelet

Cones and Cylinders (K, Pri)

Children will discover that paper can be folded into three-dimensional forms, including cubes, cones, and cylinders. Cones and cylinders are easy to make. Rolling paper into a tube shape makes a cylinder. Cylinders can be creatively combined to make people, animals, buildings, castles, towers, tunnels, spyglasses, and vehicles. A round piece of paper can be cut to its center and gently turned to form a cone. Cones suggest heads, bodies, animal beaks, hats, ice cream cones, horns, teepees, and mountains.

Monofold Creation (K, Pri)

Fold a piece of paper in half once (monofold). Keep the creased edge at the top. Children can draw an object and carefully cut through both thicknesses of paper. The object, however, must remain joined at the top. When the paper is opened, the vehicle, animal, or object will be joined at the top and able to stand up. It will be symmetrical, the same on both sides.

Stars and Snowflakes (K, Pri)

Round or square paper of thin weight, such as tissue paper or origami paper, can be used. Construction paper is too thick to fold and cut through. Coffee filters are an ideal size, shape, and thickness. Encourage children to fold their paper into quarters (in half and half again). Older children with good scissoring skills can continue folding. The more folds there are, the thicker the paper will be to cut through but the more intricate the design. Encourage children to cut out small snips or to make angular cuts into the folded paper without cutting through or cutting any off. Carefully open. Refold and continue cutting if not satisfied with the star or snowflake. Finished products can be taped over windows for the light to shine through. Or, they can be sealed between two pieces of wax paper using a warm iron.

Six-Pointed Star (K, Pri) Begin with a square of thin paper. Fold the square in half diagonally. Fold it in half again. You should have a folded triangle shape. Hold the triangular-shaped paper with the folded tip down. Fold the left side over two-thirds of the way to the right. Make sure the folded tip remains. Repeat with the right side. Cut off the shaded part. See the illustrated steps in figure 18-18. Cut designs and form a snowflake or decorate as a star.

Paper Weaving (N/Pre, K, Pri)

The teacher may need to provide most if not all of the paper for this activity. Fold a 9 × 12 sheet of construction paper in half either way. Cut slits from the folded edge out, stopping about one inch from the opposite end. The slits can be even or randomly spaced. They can be cut straight, curved, or jagged. Open your paper. Measure how long a strip of paper must be to be woven through the slits from one end to the other. Make several strips. Again, the paper strips can be cut straight, curved, or jagged. Children can weave with the paper strips, using an over-under motion. The next row will necessitate an opposite under-over motion. The ends of the woven paper strips can be secured with a dab of paste or glue. Trim paper strips that extend beyond the edge of the paper.

Cutting the paper and strips straight produces a neat, uniform checkerboard effect. Cutting strips of different widths or angles produces an optical illusion-type design. Try to provide a variety of papers to weave with. Adding strips of wallpaper provides a dramatic touch. Paper weaving is like finger painting, a basic early childhood art activity with many possibilities. Try adding ribbon, lace, yarn, and pipe cleaners along with your paper strips.

Magazine Picture Weaving (K, Pri) Children can find a large picture in a magazine that they find interesting. *National Geographic,* with its vivid animal pictures, is highly recommended. Carefully remove the page or cut the picture into a large square or rectangle. Cut the picture into strips. Use the guidelines given in the paper weaving activity to make a larger slit frame. Weave the magazine picture strips. The result will be a slightly distorted but visually pleasing rearrangement of the selected picture. Or, weave the strips in incorrect order for a visually unexpected effect. Or, interchange strips from different pictures—for example, an animal head with a child's body.

Stuffed Paper Pillow (K, Pri)

Children will need their own large grocery bag for this activity. Cut through the three joined edges until only the flat fronts and backs remain. Encourage children to draw a simple but large object that fills up most of the paper bag. Animals, vehicles, or shapes with a minimum of fine detailing are recommended. Carefully cut through all layers. Separate the layers into a top and a bottom. Children can decorate the front

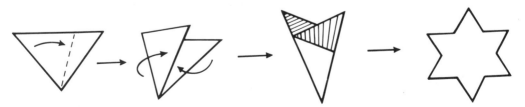

Figure 18-18 Directions for six-pointed star

and back sides with crayons, markers, or paint. Later, they can use a stapler to carefully staple the outer edge shut while slowly stuffing the bag with small pieces of wadded newspaper. Continue to staple and stuff.

I'm Stuffed (N/Pre, K)

Children will need a length of mural or butcher paper that is slightly more than twice their length. Fold the paper in half for double layers and have the child lie on top. Trace around the child with a thick pencil, crayon, or marker. Cut out the outline. Encourage children to decorate with crayons, markers, or paint. Provide a mirror for them to note the color and placement of facial features and clothing. Use a stapler to carefully staple shut the outer edge while slowly stuffing with small pieces of wadded newspaper. Continue to staple and stuff. Children will enjoy taking their "twin" home.

Paper Strip Critters (K, Pri)

Strips of paper one-half inch and wider can be formed into three-dimensional characters or animals. Three strips on top of one another form a snowman. An accordion-pleated strip of paper becomes a snake. The possibilities are endless. Try to suggest possibilities without telling children what to make. Encourage them to artfully play around with the paper and see what results.

Paper Mosaic (K, Pri)

A mosaic is a design made by placing pieces of tile, stone, glass, or other material very close together. Children can do a mosaic using paper. Begin by drawing a fairly simple large picture on a piece of drawing paper. Cut out small squares of colored paper. Here is where scrap pieces of construction paper that have been saved come in handy. Squares can range from one-half to one inch square, depending on the age of the child. A teacher may decide to use the paper cutter to cut up squares for young children. Squares can be sorted by color and placed in an egg carton for easy access. Encourage children to paste them

inside their sketched picture. Mosaic squares should be close but not touching. A paper mosaic takes much time, planning, and patience. It need not be completed in one sitting and is recommended for older children.

Paper Relief (K, Pri)

Relief refers to a raised or three-dimensional effect. One way to get this is to build up layers of paper. Begin with a cardboard base. Use additional cardboard or thick paper to cut out designs or pieces of a picture. Continue building up layers. Cut additional shapes, but make them smaller in size than the previous ones. Continue to cut and glue smaller pieces until a design or picture with different levels results. This activity takes much time and patience and is recommended for older children.

DIP AND TIE-DYE AND BATIK

The following art activities involve the use of fabric and some type of dye. The activities are involved, progress in stages, and are messy. They require direction and direct supervision, since heat, hot water, and electricity are involved. They are good outdoor activities on sunny days.

Dye Activities

Dribble Dye (N/Pre, K) Provide each child with a heavyweight, white paper towel. Encourage them to fold it into squares. Provide small bottles of food coloring. They can very carefully squeeze small dots or dabs of different colors on the corners, edges, or middle section. Use just enough to bleed through. Open up to reveal a colorful design. Let dry.

Dip and Dye (N/Pre, K) This activity is a good introduction to tie-dye. Provide a white heavyweight paper towel for each. You will also need different colors of dye. Place a few drops of food coloring in a small dish or container of water.

Adding more drops will make your color darker. Different colors can be poured into the different openings in a muffin tin. Encourage children to fold their paper towel into squares. Different folds (horizontal, vertical, diagonal, and random) will produce different effects. Carefully dip the corner or edge into one color. Gently squeeze out the excess. Dip a second small area into a different color. Colors can also be mixed. For example, dip the towel in yellow and then in red. Orange will result. Dry on layers of newspaper. These can be taped over windows for a colorful effect. They can also be carefully taped together to form a quilt, banner, or backdrop for a bulletin board.

Tie and Dye (K, Pri) You will need old sheets, muslin, or old T-shirts and Rit dyes for this activity. This activity is best done outdoors. Children will need their own piece of material. It should be clean, washed to remove all sizing (rather than new and unwashed), and at least six inches square. You will need to add Rit dye to hot water, which will dissolve the dye. Rit dye comes in either powder or liquid form. Liquid is more expensive, but it mixes easily and is worth the additional expense. It is also easy to save and store. See the section on natural dyes in **Appendix G** as an alternative to commercial dyes. Fill one small bucket about half full with hot water. Slowly add liquid dye. Follow the directions on the bottle. Constantly test the color by dipping a scrap piece of fabric. If it is too light, add more color. Repeat with at least one other color in a separate bucket. Let the water cool slightly. In the meantime the children can be preparing their material by

- folding and tying it
- tightly clamping it with clothespins
- using rubber bands to to tightly tie in coins, paper clips, marbles, pebbles, flash cubes, hair rollers, and other small objects
- gathering peaks and tying them tightly with string

- making knots
- bunching it up and tying it
- twisting and tying it
- rolling it up and tying it
- pleating it and tying it
- pinching and tying it
- gathering it randomly and tying it

Basically, any of the above, if tightly done, will produce a white outline or impression that will resist the dye.

Children will need to wear smocks and roll up their sleeves. Commercial dye will stain clothing, and it will take a few hand washings to come off. Encourage the children to place one end or section of the material into one color. Start with your lightest dye. Taking the material out quickly will produce a very light color. Leaving it in for a minute should produce a darker color. Squeeze the excess out. Place another section into a different color. Colors can also be mixed. Placing one section in yellow and then in red will produce orange. Remember, however, that adding yellow to a dark color like purple will have little or no effect other than a darkening or muddying of the original color. Rinse the material under cold water to set the colors when done. Squeeze thoroughly. Cut the string, take off the rubber bands, and remove the items. Squeeze again. Open the material and place it on several layers of newspaper to dry. Turn over in a few hours. Iron flat when damp to set the colors. Or, repeat the tying process and dip the material in a different color. One teacher sewed her samples together to make a kindergarten tie-dye patchwork quilt.

Less Mess Dye Activities

To eliminate some of the staining of hands and general mess, children can apply liquid dye directly onto the fabric by

- squeezing it from squirt bottles

- placing dots and dribbles with a medicine dropper

- painting it on with old brushes

- dabbing it on with sponges or Q-tips

The fabric should be rinsed with cold water. Rubber gloves can also be worn. It is impossible to totally eliminate the mess from a dye activity.

Batik

Batik is a method of decorating clothing using dyes and wax. Batik builds on our dye activities by adding wax to form a resist. When the cloth is dyed, the waxed areas remain white. The process is involved but recommended for older children. (See Figure 18-19.)

Batik Activities

Crayon Batik (K, Pri)   This activity is a continuation of crayon encaustic, in which we painted with the wax from melted crayons. With crayon batik, however, we will paint the melted colored wax directly on fabric, such as an old white sheet or piece of muslin, rather than cardboard. Once our picture or design is finished, the fabric is crumpled up and dipped in only one dye bath. See the procedures for tie-dying. When the fabric is dry, place layers of old newspaper on top and iron it with a warm iron. Old newspapers have dry ink. They will soak up the wax that has been melted by the heat of the iron. The colored pigment from the crayon will remain. Replace the newspaper and continue ironing. Stop when the fabric no longer feels stiff.

Color on Cloth (K, Pri)   A simplified version of crayon batik is to simply color with crayons on a piece of white sheet or muslin. Fabric crayons are preferred. You may need to staple the material to a cardboard frame to keep it from sliding around with the movement of the crayon. Encourage children to press hard with their crayons and fill the piece of fabric. The activity can stop here. Or, dip the fabric in a dye bath. Squeeze

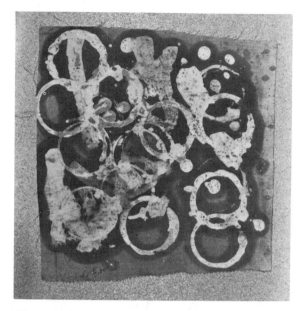

Figure 18-19   Batik

and dry. Iron with a warm iron, following the procedures for crayon batik.

Paste Batik (K, Pri)   Follow the recipe in Appendix G for Paste for Batik. Place the paste in a squeeze bottle. Staple a piece of fabric to cardboard. Encourage children to gently squeeze their bottle and form a design or picture. Squeeze the paste over the area you want to keep white and free of color. Let it dry overnight. Dip the fabric in a dye bath or directly apply dye. When the fabric is thoroughly dry, chip and rub off the dried paste. A white outline will appear. Press with a warm iron to remove wrinkles.

Wax Batik (K, Pri)   Wax can be melted the same way as crayons. Use equal amounts of paraffin and beeswax. Children can paint the melted wax onto a piece of old sheet or muslin that is stapled or taped to cardboard for support. Place it on top of several layers of newspaper. Brush the wax over the areas you want to remain white and free of color. Paint with long strokes, making sure the wax penetrates the fabric. Paint only one layer of wax. Do not use a back-and-forth motion; this will build up a thick layer without soaking through the fabric. Be prepared for unexpected splashes and dots of wax. This will enhance the creativity and one-of-a-kindness of the batik. Crumple up the fabric for a crackled or batik effect. Dip the fabric in dye. Begin with the lightest color, saving the darkest for the last dye bath. Follow procedures for color and dye. Repeat the process, adding additional colors. Hang the batik from a dowel rod, framed in a picture frame, or mounted over a piece of cardboard.

SUMMARY

This unit served as a resource of two-dimensional art media and activities. Different approaches to providing painting experiences were also discussed.

SUGGESTED ACTIVITIES

1. Implement one or more two-dimensional art activities. Use a format that your instructor provides or use the lesson plan found in Unit 13.

2. Choose any two different two-dimensional art media. Creatively combine them into a new mixed media activity. Plan, implement, and evaluate your activity.

3. Observe different arrangements for painting. Or, systematically vary the arrangements—for example, one day easel painting and the next day table painting. Observe children's reactions. Does one age prefer a certain arrangement? Does one arrangement appear to be more conducive to creative expression? Document your findings.

REVIEW

A. Discuss the importance of scribbling.

B. Critique the different media and physical positions involved in mark making.

C. Identify different painting positions.
    1.
    2.
    3.
    4.
    5.

D. Discuss provisioning for painting and related precautions.

E. List different ways to process with paper.

Unit 19

Three-Dimensional Art Activities

OBJECTIVES

After studying this unit, the student will be able to

- List major three-dimensional art media that are appropriate for use with young children
- Identify developmentally appropriate three-dimensional art activities
- Construct new activities by mixing and creatively combining three-dimensional art media

INTRODUCTION

This unit is strategically placed at the end of the book. By now you should have a working knowledge of child development, curriculum development, aesthetics, and artistic theories to serve as a framework for what you do with children. The format of this unit is significantly different. It is designed as a resource of art activities and a guide. Use it sparingly as a reference rather than teaching directly from it. Suggested age ranges are included for each activity, although age and developmental stage alone are often misleading.

THREE-DIMENSIONAL ART

Children enjoy making three-dimensional artistic creations—they are solid rather than flat, can be seen from all sides, and often can stand with their own support. Clay, construction, assemblage, and sculpture are three-dimensional art forms and media that are recommended for young children.

CLAY

Many children will have had experience at home with commercially available Play-Doh or the homemade type. They will find the look, smell, and feel very pleasurable. It may remind them of cookie dough. They will approach clay with active processing in mind: "What can I do with clay?" By manipulating and handling it they will discover that clay can be pulled, torn, cut, rolled, and so forth. Older children may have a product in mind when they approach the clay table: "What can I make out of my lump of clay?" Three seriated balls of clay on top of each other will make a snowman. Often, there is much verbalizing and socializing at the clay table. "My clay is so hard." "Keep rollin' it till it gets soft." "Can I use the roller when you're done?" Verbal exchange and social skills are demonstrated at the clay table. Children make direct physical contact with clay. There is no brush, scissors, or marker between them and the medium.

Working with clay fosters large muscle and fine motor control. Clay is fairly resistant and will need to be kneaded and worked to make it pliable. Children can stand or sit while using clay. Standing provides the advantage of a whole-body muscular reaction to the clay. Hard clay provides a solid resistance that the child must overcome. This will involve using muscles in the shoulders, arms, hands, and fingers if the child is seated. Slowly, the child gains control over the medium, making it do or become what he or she wants it to.

Children enjoy working with clay for many reasons. For one, it is a natural material and has the same appeal that water, sand, and wood hold for young children. As a preferred art form, it allows them to change or undo what they have begun. For example, a snowman can be disassembled, flattened, and transformed into a pizza. This is not always possible with crayons, markers, or paint. It also gives them control over the medium. The snowman's head will stay on top of the body if the two are joined together. The painted outline of a snowman might run or mix with other colors. If the clay head falls off, it can always be put back on. It is more difficult to correct a painting, especially if it has dried.

Clay is a multisensory experience. It has a distinct texture, temperature, color, and smell. Involving children in making homemade play dough provides a learning opportunity to read a recipe, measure, and mix ingredients. Children enjoy the primitive, almost taboo feel of clay. It allows them to get dirty and messy. It might remind them of infantile pleasures attained during earlier toilet training days. Because of this, some children will find clay appealing, while others may find it repulsive. Playing with clay should be an option. Over time and with subtle encouragement, the reluctant child may become an active participant at the clay table. Seeing that clay will wash off hands and from under fingernails may also add reassurance.

Using real mud provides an earthy experience in which children are brought in close touch with nature. Working with clay provides an opportunity to release feelings in a socially acceptable way. A child may not display aggression against a peer but is free to pound on a clay person. Clay has a therapeutic effect. It allows the working through of emotions and creating of model situations. A child who is upset by a recent divorce may be unable to verbally express how he or she feels. Clay, however, provides this child with the opportunity to work through his or her feelings by talking to and dramatizing with a family made out of clay.

Children need lots and lots of clay. A grapefruit-sized ball for each sculptor is recommended. Play dough and clay, in particular, will require a lot of kneading to get pliable. Clay must be kept in a sealed container, such as a plastic tub with a snap-on lid. Over time, certain types of clay (earth) washed from hands will clog up the sink. Some teachers prefer that children rinse their hands in a bucket and flush this down the toilet.

Types of Clay

Different types of clay let children process in different ways. Some major types include:

Real Clay Different parts of the country have their own characteristic clays. Many types can be used in the classroom. Soak the clay in a bucket and pour it through a screen to remove sticks and stones. This will help make it more pliable. Real clay is dug up from the earth and can be purchased in art supply stores. Water-based or potters clay allows products to be fired and preserved. It is the type of clay that adult sculptors work with. Make sure the brand is non-toxic. It can be bought in a ready-to-mix powder or premixed form. Premixed is more expensive. However, extra time will be needed if you are using a ready-to-mix powder that also needs to set. Real clay is less expensive, messier, but more pliable than plasticene. Its dull gray or brown color may not be visually appealing, but its cool feel and inviting texture will attract participation. Since it is water-based, it will dry out when exposed to air.

Provide a small pan of water and encourage children to wet their fingers and moisten real clay to keep it pliable. This clay will also dry unfired or can be reused by forming it into four-inch balls and putting it back in the storage container wrapped in a wet paper towel. Poke a hole in each clay ball and fill it with water to further preserve pliability. Check your clay from time to time. If it is too wet, it will get moldy and smell. If it is too dry, it will become hard. Add or remove moisture as needed. Real clay is messy and is best suited for outdoor use. Simply hose down the area when you are finished. Products made from real clay can be glazed and fired in a kiln for the beautiful shiny finish that you see on ceramic pieces. Most centers and schools for young children will not have access to a kiln. This is no problem. Finished pieces can also be left to dry on their own; this will take several days. Of course, most young sculptors will be happy returning their mass of clay to its original ball shape for the next clay session.

Plasticene Plasticene is a type of clay with an oil base. It is fairly inexpensive, does not stick to surfaces, and will not dry out if kept covered when not in use. It is fairly solid and requires a good deal of kneading and heat from the hands to get it pliable. It is reusable and cannot be fired or painted. It may frustrate the toddler or young preschooler who lacks muscular strength in the fingers and hand. Not all children like the smell of plasticene.

Play Dough Play-Doh is commercially available. It comes in bright colors and is fairly inexpensive. It is also very fragrant and may tempt the young sculptor into tasting it. Its major disadvantage is that it tends to crumble and flake, with tiny pieces spreading all over the table and floor. Even in its lidded can, Play-Doh will dry up, harden, or mold over time. Try placing the Play-Doh in a sandwich bag sealed with a twist tie before storing it in the container to make it last longer.

Play dough can also be homemade. Children enjoy making and using play dough because it is soft and pliable. It also combines cooking with art. One major ingredient is flour, making this type of clay fairly inexpensive and able to be baked and preserved. Place it in a covered container and store it in the refrigerator. See Appendix G for a series of recipes for play dough. Different recipes provide different textures. Be sure to vary the color and scent added.

Very young children will find play dough more appealing and easier to work with than plasticene. Inhibited children may prefer play dough or plasticene to real clay. Still, young children should be exposed to a wide variety of clays and play doughs.

Processing with Clay

Young children can discover that there are many, many different ways to work with clay (see Figure 19-1). Processing with clay need not result in a finished clay product. Some ways to process with clay, and examples, include

- fingering and squeezing clay

- rolling clay into round balls, eggs, eyeballs, marbles, peas, or meatballs

- coiling, stretching, and lengthening clay into long snakes, worms, rope, hot dogs, spaghetti, noodles, or sausage; smaller coils often become a ring, bracelet, or necklace

Figure 19-1 These children discover what they can do to and with clay.

- patting, flattening, hammering, squashing, or pounding clay into a pancake, pie, hamburger, cookie, pizza, or face

- pinching off pieces of clay to make facial features, bugs, or bits of candy

- cutting clay with blunt scissors to make french fries

- poking holes or openings into clay to make a donut or facial features in a face or head

- tearing or pulling apart as well as joining pieces of clay

- stamping or imprinting clay with cookie cutters, bottle caps, buttons, pinecones, seashells, and so forth

- twisting or braiding lengths of clay

- forming or molding clay into nests, bowls, or birthday cakes

- squeezing or sculpting clay into a solid three-dimensional, self-standing form, such as a snowman, animal, or human figure

- incising or cutting into clay with a plastic knife, fork, Popsicle stick, toothpick, fingernails, and so forth

- processing with clay and a variety of clay tools and accessories

- folding or bending clay into a taco, flower, or boat

Stages of Clay

More has been written about stages of children's drawing and painting than about clay. The author has synthesized the research on the child's developmental progression in the use of clay (Brittain, 1979; Golumb, 1974; and Hartley, Frank, and Goldenson, 1952) in proposing the following stages:

Stage 1 What Is Clay? In this first stage, two-year-olds experiment with and explore the properties of clay. They use their senses to visually explore, touch, smell (and often stick up their nose), lick and taste, and listen to clay being worked with their hands. They will drop it, step on it, throw or try to bounce it, and stick it to their skin. They are not interested in making something out of clay. Their talk will be limited to words related to their sensory experiences with clay, for example, "yucky," "gooey," "mushy," or "mmmmmm."

Stage 2 What All Can I Do with Clay? The first stage quickly builds into the second. Three-year-olds are more systematic in their attempts at processing with the clay. As scientists, they put clay to a series of tests by rolling, pinching, tearing, pulling, and poking it. By physically acting on clay they discover its properties. Clay can roll, but it cannot bounce or pour. The child does not deliberately set out to make something at this stage. By chance and through active manipulation, simple forms such as small balls, patted cakes, or snakes may result. These actions will be repeated, with the child making several products.

Stage 3 Look What I Made! Four-year-olds will creatively combine clay forms and actions performed on them. One clay ball is put on top of another. Flattening and rolling a piece of clay produces a new shape. Openings will be pushed into the mass of clay, and pieces will be pulled out. There is more labeling and talking about what they are making. For example, while a stage 2 child might simply poke a hole through a thin sheet of clay, the older stage 3 sculptor might make a total of three pokes and call it a face. The finished product may be crude and simple. Balls of clay can be added to a coiled snake, with the child saying, "My snake can see you." Children in this stage often dramatize with their clay products. The clay snake slithers around the table, hissing and biting the children. Clay products are becoming more complex at this stage. Still, many clay creations are more the accidental result of processing than the result of systematic planning in advance or intention. Clay creations are idiosyncratic and personal, and others may not recognize the finished product.

Stage 4 I Know What I'm Going to Make out of My Clay! Five-year-olds approach the clay table knowing what they want to make out of clay and announce this in advance. They have an idea, a name, and a finished product in mind. They need to find a process or technique that is suitable. There is more discussion while processing and about the finished clay product. Products evidence fairly realistic representation and can be recognized by others. Children in this stage know that their clay food or snake is only a symbol or model and not the actual object itself. They will not try to eat the food as a younger child in stage 3 might. Five-year-olds enjoy adding details using clay tools and accessories, as well as artistic junk such as buttons and toothpicks.

The stages of clay appear to parallel stages of the child's artistic development in painting or mark making. Scribbles come to be named just as children give names to their clay creations. Still, clay is a three-dimensional art form, whereas painting and mark making are two-dimensional. Since children live in a three-dimensional world, it may be easier for them to use clay to represent their world. Putting the three-dimensional world on a flat two-dimensional surface with paint, crayons, or markers involves abstraction and may be more difficult. Does this mean that children should be given clay before other art media? Brittain (1979) conducted a study to determine whether clay would facilitate a more advanced type of representation than drawing. In carefully examining the artwork of seventeen preschoolers, he found no superiority of clay over drawing when judging the accuracy of representation. A child who is having difficulty drawing a person would have similar difficulties making one out of clay. Young children need experience with a wide variety of artistic media, and no strict order of presentation is supported by the research. Still, our working knowledge of children and their development tells us that batik is inappropriate for most two- and three-year-olds, whereas play dough is recommended.

Clay Techniques

Above and beyond processing with clay, there are specific techniques for making clay products that the older child might enjoy learning. Often, they are discovered. Some of these techniques or methods include:

Pinch Using the pinch method will result in a clay bowl or pot. Begin with a clay ball. Stick both thumbs into the center of the clay ball with the fingers holding the outside. Gently press the thumbs against the sides while pinching and rotating the clay ball. Continue pinching and pulling the sides upward and out into a pot or bowl.

Coil The coil method builds on the child's experiences with rolling long clay snakes. A pot or bowl can also be formed with this method. American Indians made pottery using the coil method over a pinch pot. Begin by wrapping coils of clay over the basic pinch pot or into any shape or form desired.

Slab Begin with a slab of clay. Roll it flat with a rolling pin until it is about one-half inch thick.

Use a plastic knife or other clay tool to cut out the outline of your desired object. Smooth out the cut edges.

Adding Clay Start with a ball or lump of clay and slowly add parts and details. For example, one child made a horse from a solid mass of clay. A head, legs, and a tail were carefully added. Clay pieces made this way tend to be fragile, and the added parts do not always stay attached. The child was very frustrated because her horse's legs kept breaking under the weight of its heavy body.

Pulling Out Clay This method will avoid the problems associated with adding clay. Start with a fairly large mass of clay. Think of the total object as a solid piece rather than as made up of connected parts. Slowly pull out the parts you need. For example, by molding and carefully pulling out legs, arms, and a head, one child made a person out of clay. It was fairly sturdy and stable, since it was an intact mass without added-on parts and pieces.

Taking Clay Away Start with a fairly large mass of clay. Take away or remove the excess or unwanted pieces of clay, using fingers or clay tools and accessories. For example, one child used a plastic knife to carve her irregularly shaped clay ball into a round jack-o-lantern. Facial features were cut out.

Outlining with Clay Some children use strips of flattened clay as if they were strokes of paint or lines drawn with pencil, crayons, or markers. They approach clay as if it were a two-dimensional medium and overlook its three-dimensional possibilities. This is to be expected, and for most it will be a temporary stage. Objects can be outlined in clay rather than represented with a solid mass of clay. Since the object is outlined flat and stationary on the clay board, there is no need to worry about it moving, falling over, or coming apart. This technique allows children to add small details.

Some recommended clay activities include:

Clay Creations (N/Pre, K, Pri)

Children may enjoy decorating their clay creations with recycled junk materials. Some items that go together with clay include

- toothpicks
- pipe cleaners
- nuts and bolts
- screws and nails
- keys
- buttons
- straws
- Popsicle sticks
- paper clips
- acorns
- seashells
- small sticks and twigs
- golf tees
- short pencils

Baked Ornaments (N/Pre, K, Pri) Check the recipe section in Appendix G for play dough recipes that allow you to paint, bake, and preserve the finished product. Remember to poke a hole in the product before baking if you want it to hang.

Plasticene Print (N/Pre, K, Pri)

Children can use clay tools and accessories, such as a plastic knife, to carve designs into a thin slab of plasticene. Carefully dip the carved piece of plasticene in paint or press it on a stamp pad. Press on a piece of paper. Repeat the impression to make a pattern.

Clay Numbers and Letters (N/Pre, K)

Young children who are interested in the world of letters and numbers may enjoy using magnetic letters and numbers to make clay impressions. Remove the small magnet piece from each. Children can also use plastic knives, Popsicle sticks, or toothpicks to carve their name, their initials, the alphabet, words, their address, or their phone number out of clay. These could also be formed by combining small coils of clay.

Clay Overs (N/Pre, K, Pri)

Children may enjoy sculpting clay pieces or parts and attaching them to a larger base. For example, a small juice can or box can be decorated with coils and balls of clay.

CONSTRUCTION, ASSEMBLAGE, AND SCULPTURE

Assemblage refers to a three-dimensional collage in which children creatively assemble an array of objects. Construction and sculpture are similar terms referring to three-dimensional art that may or may not resemble anything. Technically, children can also sculpt with clay; this was discussed in the previous section. Our present discussion of sculpture will address forms other than clay. Even young children are aware that objects are composed of parts and pieces. A table needs a top supported by legs. People have a trunk that supports their head and rests on limbs. Cars have a body supported by a frame on wheels. "How can I make my own three-dimensional model of the things that are important to me?" asks the young sculptor.

Some construction, assemblage, and sculpture activities recommended for young children include:

Stringing (N/Pre, K)

Stringing objects is not only a good activity for improving eye-hand coordination but is also a construction or assemblage art activity. Use a shoelace or sturdy yarn with a plastic needle. Knot the far end of the yarn or shoelace to keep the objects from merely sliding off. Children will enjoy stringing

- spools
- paper reinforcements
- hole-punched paper
- tin foil
- egg carton cups
- sections of paper straws
- pieces of colored paper
- sections of tissue rolls
- Styrofoam pieces

Some people use macaroni, but the author advises against the use of food in art activities. Items that have been strung can be tied into a necklace, bracelet, or belt and proudly worn.

Container Creations (N/Pre, K, Pri)

The shapes of containers suggest the shapes of people, animals, vehicles, buildings, machines, and objects. Children enjoy using tape, glue, and staples to hold together an array of boxes, bottles, and cartons. Encourage children to think of something—an animal, a vehicle, or an object— that the containers suggest. For example, square boxes stacked together might suggest a robot. A row or strip of egg cups from an egg carton might suggest a caterpillar, snake, or train. A plastic milk container might suggest a head if yarn is added for hair. Look for boxes, bottles, and cartons that have an unusual shape. As always, container creations need not resemble anything at all. Some recommended containers include

- oatmeal boxes
- salt boxes
- small gift boxes
- cereal boxes
- pill bottles
- milk cartons, cardboard and plastic
- coffee tins

Figure 19-2A Working on a container construction

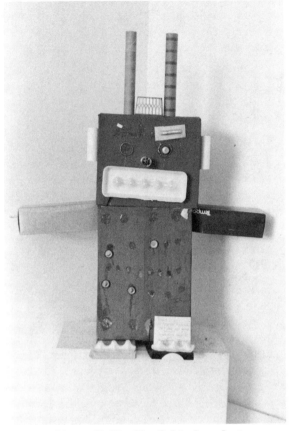

Figure 19-2B The finished product

- detergent bottles
- toilet tissue rolls and cardboard tubes
- egg cartons, Styrofoam or cardboard
- berry baskets
- cigar boxes
- round pizza plates

Containers can be glued or taped together. Decorate them with bottle caps, lids, ribbon, paper cups, paper scraps, straws, and other small pieces. Creations can be painted, with detergent added to paint to help it adhere. (See Figures 19-2A and 19-2B.)

Egg Carton Art (N/Pre, K)

Individual egg cups from egg cartons or groups of cups can be creatively combined on a piece of cardboard. Children will enjoy varying the color, placement, shapes, and sizes. The raised, patterned three-dimensional effect is visually pleasing.

Wooden Wonders (N/Pre, K, Pri)

Children can use liquid white glue to assemble small wooden scraps together. A hammer and nails can also be used. The resulting construction may represent something or merely be an assemblage of wood pieces. Check with local lumberyards, carpenters, or high school shop teachers for small wood scraps. Request wood scraps with interesting shapes and angles. Creations can also be decorated with trim or nature specimens, and painted if the child decides it is necessary. One teacher suggested that children think up their very own machine and then try to make it out of wood scraps. Some children decided to make candy, toy, and fun machines. Pieces of string (for fan belts), wire, nuts and bolts, and small machinery parts were added for decoration. Others decided to merely glue together their wooden scraps. All products were accepted and valued.

Tin Foil Treasures (K, Pri)

Children can glue an array of small objects onto a piece of sturdy cardboard. Small three-dimensional items, including

- golf tees
- rubber bands
- paper clips
- buttons
- nuts, bolts, washers, and screws
- small nature specimens
- beads
- Q-tips
- pieces of yarn or string

are recommended. Use an old brush to paint white liquid glue over the entire surface. Carefully place a larger sheet of tin foil over the raised surface. Very carefully, press, wrinkle, and mold the tin foil around the raised objects to reveal their characteristic shape. Be careful that the embedded objects do not tear through the tin foil. Fold the excess tin foil under the cardboard and secure it with tape or glue. The result will be an interesting raised effect or relief done in silver.

Thoroughly wash the glue out of the paintbrush before it gets a chance to harden.

Tin Foil Sculpture (K, Pri)

Children will enjoy working with tin foil as the base for their sculpture. For example, tin foil can be rolled to form an elephant's trunk and wadded to form its head. Individual parts can be taped together or stuck together with straight pins. Or, children can form their sculpture out of one piece of tin foil. For example, in making the elephant, the legs can be carefully pulled, pinched, molded, and rolled out from the body. Remember to start with a fairly large piece of tin foil—about 12 × 16. Remind children that since they are starting with a large, flat sheet, they can expect their finished three-dimensional product to be much smaller.

Styrofoam and Toothpick Sculpture (N/Pre, K)

Children enjoy sticking toothpicks into Styrofoam. An upside-down meat tray or thicker solid piece can form the base. Smaller pieces of Styrofoam—chips, squiggles, or egg carton sections—can be stuck on toothpicks and inserted into the base. Individual Styrofoam pieces can also be connected with toothpicks to add height and a three-dimensional effect. The sculpture can also be decorated with paper, ribbon, lace, and other scraps. These sculptures will be very fragile and may not make it home intact. They can be proudly displayed in the classroom art gallery.

Hanger Heads (N/Pre, K, Pri)

You will need old stockings or pantyhose and coat hangers for this activity. Stretch your hanger out into a fairly round face shape. Cover it with pantyhose or a stocking and tie to secure. This will form the head. Encourage children to complete the face by adding yarn, felt, fabric scraps, or paper. Leaving the hook on top will allow it to hang. Keeping the hook on the bottom allows it to be held and used as a mask.

Spool Sculpture (N/Pre, K, Pri)

Wooden spools are getting harder to find. Children love to stack them and glue them together. Spools can be added to a basic wood construction. Spool shapes may suggest people, animals, or vehicle forms.

Paper Sculpture (K, Pri)

As previously discussed in the section on Paper Art, paper can be rolled, folded, coiled, and made into three-dimensional cones, cubes, and tubes. These might suggest legs or body forms and the base for further paper sculpting.

Paper Strip Sculpture (N/Pre, K)

Strips of construction paper are ideal for making sculpture. Start with a Styrofoam tray for a base. Children can secure one end of a paper strip to the base. The balance of the strip can be pleated, folded, or connected to other strips. Continue processing with paper in sculpting a three-dimensional form. Remind children that the result can be an interesting intersection of paper strips and need not look like anything.

Stuffed Newspaper Sculpture (K, Pri)

This activity is identical to I'm Stuffed, which appears in the section on Paper Art. The present activity, however, extends the activity beyond a self-portrait. Each child will need four large sheets of newspaper. Older children may want to draw their outline first and then cut it out. For example, a large dinosaur can be sketched. Avoid adding fine details and small parts. Carefully cut out the outline through all four layers of newspaper. Two layers will form the front and two the back. Slowly, stuff with small wads of crumpled newspaper while stapling shut. Use paint, crayons, or markers to decorate.

Totem Pole Sculpture (N/Pre, K, Pri)

Ice cream parlors might save round commercial ice cream cartons for you. The shape and size is ideal for making masks. Individual cartons can be decorated and stacked on top of each other like a totem pole. Secure with tape between cartons.

Soap Sculpture (K, Pri)

Older children who know how to use a knife properly can be trusted to do this activity with supervision. They will need their own bar of soap and a small but fairly sharp knife for carving. Encourage them to draw the outline of an object on their bar of soap and to use their knife to sculpt. Advise them to select a fairly simple shape, without intricate parts or details. Rough edges or cut sides can be smoothed by rubbing with a wet finger.

Wire Wonders (N/Pre, K, Pri)

Use a fairly sturdy but flexible grade of wire for sculpting. Thin copper, florist's, aluminum, bailing, insulated telephone (in a rainbow of colors), or no. 19 stovepipe wire are recommended. Children will enjoy twisting and turning the wire into unusual shapes. They may also try to represent something. The wire sculpture can be glued or nailed to a small piece of wood for a sturdy, supportive base.

Scene in a Box (K, Pri)

Children will need their own shoe box for this activity, which is also called a diorama. This activity takes much time, planning, and patience in positioning smaller items and is recommended for older children. The shoe box becomes the overall three-dimensional frame or stage. Children can choose a theme—for example, family or a favorite story. The inside of the box can be decorated like one's house, with family members added. Remember, the internal space is deep, allowing for three-dimensional placement. Objects can be placed in several rows to suggest depth. Items such as fish could be suspended from the inside top with string for an underwater scene. One young girl did just that, basing her Scene in a

Box on the book *Swimmy* by Leo Lionni. See Appendix F for a list of art-related books.

Salt Sculpture (K, Pri)

Children will need their own clear glass bottle or jar with a lid. You will need several different colors of salt. Salt can be colored by rubbing it with colored chalk. Place one color in each section of a muffin tin or in a paper cup. Gently pour one color into the bottle or jar. Use a small spoon or paper cup, or let it slide in from the fold of a creased paper. Make the layer any height. Add a second color by carefully directing the flow and position as you pour. There is no need to shake or tip the bottle or jar. Each layer will form its own uneven shape. Use a pencil to carefully poke along the sides and through layers for an interesting effect. Add different colored layers until the jar is full. Let it sit overnight to settle. You may need to add an additional color the next day to get it completely full. Cover the jar tightly with the lid. This makes an excellent gift, especially if the children did most of the work by themselves. Very young children may need to use a fairly small container with a wide top.

Shrink-Ups (N/Pre, K)

You will need an oven for this activity. Children enjoy using crayons or markers to decorate pieces cut from a Styrofoam meat tray. When heated, the Styrofoam pieces curl and twist into interesting shapes. Follow the directions under the recipe section in Appendix H for this activity.

Glue Overs (N/Pre, K)

Each child will need a piece of Styrofoam cut from a meat tray. Encourage them to use markers to make a picture or design. Use a wide variety of colors, and leave little empty space. Let dry. Use an old paintbrush to paint liquid white glue over the entire surface. Let dry thoroughly. This will produce a sealed, slick surface that enhances the colors underneath. These make at-tractive ornaments or items to hang from a mobile.

Papier-Mâché (K, Pri)

Papier-mâché means chewed paper in French and refers to the process of building up layers of paper that has been torn, wadded, and molded (although not chewed) to make a three-dimensional form. The paper is dipped in an adhesive mixture. There are many ways to do papier-mâche. Some of the ways appropriate for young children include:

Paper Strip Method Strips of newspaper or paper towels, about one-half to one inch in width, are dipped in a mixture of white glue and water or other papier-mâché medium. See recipe section in Appendix G. Strips cut from paper bags are also recommended because of their thickness and texture. Carefully squeeze out the excess liquid between your fingers. Layers that are too thick with glue or paste will mold when drying. Begin to form your object. The strips should be smooth and overlapping. The layers should go in different directions to provide strength. Remove wrinkles or bubbles by smoothing with the hand. Apply only two or three layers at a time. Let dry. Details can be added to transform the basic shape. Or, add additional layers. For example, a wadded ball of newspaper can be added to the top of a jar or bottle to form a head. Secure with masking tape. Let dry thoroughly before adding additional layers. Add a final layer of paper toweling to give a clean top surface for painting or final decorating. Set on wax paper to dry thoroughly before painting. Seal tempera paint by spraying with a fixative or cheap hair spray. This activity should be conducted over a series of days. It may prove frustrating for the very young child who wants the project completed in one short session.

It is recommended that young children do their papier-mâché over some solid base or form including a

- blown-up balloon: carefully cut in half to get two bowls or two face masks

- bottle or jar

- gift box

- tissue roll

- container

- crushed or rolled newspaper

- plastic milk or detergent bottle

- light bulb: to make a sound shaker or music maker similar to a maraca. When it is decorated and dry, gently hit it on the floor to break the inside bulb without damaging the exterior papier-mâché shell. Patch if necessary.

Hanger Objects (K, Pri) The Hanger Head activity can also be used with papier-mâché. Stretch a coat hanger into a desired shape or form. Add long strips of newspaper dipped in papier-mâché mixture to form a solid base. Decorate as a face or whatever the shape suggests. For a self-portrait, add yarn for hair and buttons for eyes.

Stuffed Bag (K, Pri) A paper bag can be filled with wads of newspaper and shaped into a general form. This can be the base. Strips of newspaper dipped into a papier-mâché mixture can be wrapped around the base and used to form details, such as arms, legs, head, tail, and so forth.

Papier-Mâché Relief (Pri) The older child who is experienced in papier-mâché might like this variation. A piece of cardboard is needed for the base. A simple picture or design should be sketched in pencil. The picture or design will be continued in relief by building it up with strips or small pieces of paper that have been dipped in a papier-mâché mixture. The paper can be twisted, rolled, coiled, or formed into the needed shape. For example, a round, flat mass could be used for the sun and thin rolled paper snakes could be the

rays. Keep building up additional layers to give the three-dimensional or relief effect.

Piñata (K, Pri) A blown-up balloon can be used as the base for a Mexican piñata. Wrap papier-mâché over the balloon. Follow the directions for papier-mâché. Poke the balloon with a needle when you are finished. Cut open a small hole and fill the piñata with stickers, candy, tokens, or small treats. Cover the hole with additional strips of papier-mâché. Hang it overhead or from a tree limb outdoors. Blindfolded children will enjoy swinging a stick at the piñata. Breaking the piñata will result in a shower of goodies and shrieks of excitement.

Casting Capers (N/Pre, K, Pri)

See the recipe section in Appendix G for making plaster. You will also need some damp sand to form the mold for casting with plaster. Line a box, grocery bag, or old dishpan with a plastic trash bag or tin foil and fill it with four inches of sand. Make an impression by carefully scooping out the sand. Wiggle your fingers for an interesting effect. Do not scoop down to the bottom of your container. Add nature specimens and small pieces of artistic junk. This will form the front of your cast sculpture and will become your mold. Remember, your casting will be the opposite of the impression you make. For example, holes dug into the sand will be cast as bumps protruding out of your sculpture.

Always add water to powder and mix plaster to a milkshake consistency. Carefully pour plaster into your mold. Add food coloring or tempera if coloring is desired. Gently shake or tap the container to help settle the mixture. Insert a hairpin, paper clip, or bent wire at the surface (which will really be the back side) if you want the sculpture to hang. Or, simply insert both hands to cast a hand print. The top will now be your front side. Let the plaster dry overnight. When it is thoroughly dry, gently brush away the sand. Do not pour excess plaster down the sink. Casting is a time-consuming activity that only one child can do at a time, given this setup. It may be easier to do this outside in the sandbox or ideally at the beach!

Squeeze a Sculpture (N/Pre, K, Pri) For this activity, simply pour your plaster into a small, sturdy plastic bag. Fill it three inches full, squeeze out excess air, and tie securely with string. Feel free to add nature specimens, artistic junk, or coloring. Wait several minutes for the plaster to thicken. Encourage children to squeeze and manipulate the filled bag into an interesting shape. Hold it in place for a few minutes until it begins to harden. Let the plaster dry overnight. Tear away the plastic bag and paint or decorate the sculpture with markers. The result will be a piece of sculpture with an interesting shape that would also make a good paperweight or gift for parents.

PUPPETS AND MASKS

Puppets and masks serve many developmental ends. They are psychological props. They give young children something to hold and hide behind when speaking. After all, if a child makes a mistake or speaks incorrectly, it is the puppet or mask rather than the child who is to blame. Puppets and masks allow children to hide their identity and become someone or something else for a period of time. Children also have a way of telling us emotionally important events through their play with puppets and masks, often things they would never say or do without the props.

Young children enjoy making puppets and masks as much as they enjoy dramatizing and verbalizing with them. They also provide the opportunity for problem solving. Puppets can help children decide how disagreements can be resolved. A teacher can use a puppet to play the part of an imaginary young child who refuses to share. Children can use other puppets to discuss and act out this scenario and possible solutions.

There are an infinite number of ways to make puppets and masks. Some that are recommended for use with young children include:

Puppets from Paper

Papier-Mâché Puppet (K, Pri) A puppet head can be slowly built up by draping gluey paper over a crushed ball of newspaper and a tissue paper roll. Refer back to the section on papier-mâché. Begin winding paper around the roll to form a neck and continue to build up a head over the crushed newspaper ball. Paint with tempera when thoroughly dry. Attach a piece of fabric for a body.

Or, the papier-mâché can be made over a clay base. Children can use clay to make their puppet head. Next, wind strips of papier-mâché over the form. Make the layers go in different directions for strength. Let dry thoroughly. Carefully cut the head in half with a sharp knife and remove the clay. Use additional papier-mâché to seal the two halves together. Reinforce the neck with additional strips. Carefully smooth rough spots with sandpaper. Paint and/or decorate with trims. Seal with cheap hair spray if it is painted with tempera. Add a puppet body following the directions given here.

Puppet Body A very simple puppet body or clothing can be made from a twelve-inch-square piece of scrap fabric. Fold it in half and cut three small openings along the center fold. The middle opening will be for the index finger, which also supports the puppet head. The two side openings are for the thumb and middle fingers, which serve as hands. Measure the children's hand span before cutting to ensure that the openings are neither too close nor too far apart.

Paper Bag Puppet (N/Pre, K, Pri) Provide each child with a sandwich-size paper bag, neither too big nor too small for their hand to fit in and grasp. Paper bags are recommended because their construction provides a built-in movable mouth. Children will enjoy using paint, crayons, markers, and trims to decorate their puppet. Clear, undecorated sandwich bags provide a small, snug-fitting, see-through puppet that can be used as a last resort.

Stuffed Paper Bag Puppet (N/Pre, K, Pri) Stuff a large paper bag with crumpled newspaper. Insert a stick, ruler, or dowel. Make sure the end of the handle is sticking out for a handle. Continue stuffing. Gather the bag and tie it securely at the handle with string to form a neck. Decorate the stuffed paper bag head with paint, crayons, or markers. Add paper scraps, yarn, and trims.

Paper Plate Puppet (N/Pre, K, Pri) An easy puppet can be made by decorating a paper plate and attaching it to a handle, such as a stick or ruler. Or, paper plates can be folded to make a talking puppet. Each child will need two paper plates. Fold one in half. Cut the other in half. Staple one half to the top and the other half to the under side of the folded paper plate. This will allow four fingers to be inserted into the top jaw and the thumb in the lower jaw. This will help the child move his or her fingers and get the puppet to talk. Although a frog readily comes to mind, a folded paper plate puppet can be used to make a variety of animals, people, and objects. Decorate with crayons, markers, paper scraps, and trims. A cloth sleeve can be placed on the child's arm for an added effect. For example, one child wore a sleeve made out of green printed fabric, which worked well with his dragon puppet made from a paper plate.

Cardboard Tissue Roll or Tube Puppet (N/Pre, K) Children will enjoy using paint, crayons, or markers to decorate their cylindrical puppet. A roll or tube is an ideal size for small hands. Nothing else is needed. A smaller section can also be used as the head with a puppet body made from fabric. Place the puppet's cloth body over the fingers and insert the puppet head over the index and middle fingers.

Puppets from Wood

Wooden Stick Puppet (N/Pre, K) Tongue depressors and Popsicle sticks can be used and decorated as the puppet itself. They can also be used as the base or handle to which a paper plate, magazine picture, cardboard, poster board, or other type of puppet is attached. Dowel rods or straws can also be used as handles for puppets.

Wooden Block Puppet (N/Pre, K) A small rectangular piece of scrap wood that can be held in a young child's hand can be fashioned into a puppet. Features can be added with paints, crayons, markers, small wood scraps, or trims. Make sure the edges are sanded smooth and free of splinters.

Wooden Spoon Puppet (N/Pre, K) An old, large wooden cooking spoon can be turned into a puppet. Decorate with fine markers. A piece of scrap material can be tied at the neck of the spoon to add the element of clothing and conceal the stick handle. Add yarn for hair. Children can hold onto the stick handle while working their puppet.

Puppets from Fabric

Sock Puppet (K, Pri) Find an old sock. Cut a slit across the toe, halfway to the heel, for the puppet's mouth. Cut a piece of felt or material to fit inside the mouth. Fold it in half, position it in place, and sew it on. See figure 19-3. Four fingers will fit into the upper jaw. Glue a piece of cardboard under the lower jaw. This will help the thumb. Add trims: buttons and beads for eyes, yarn for hair, and so forth.

Glove Puppet (N/Pre, K) Old garden, work, utility, driving, or dress gloves can be made into puppets. Encourage the child to put on the glove and think of decorative possibilities. Small trims—buttons, yarn, and so forth—can be sewn or glued on. Or, single fingers can be cut off to make one puppet, which will nicely fit on one or two child-sized fingers.

Fabric Puppet (N/Pre, K) See the pattern (figure 19-4) for making a basic animal puppet. Changing the ears will change the type of animal, as will altering the nose and eyes and adding a tail.

cut   sew   reinforce
with
cardboard

Figure 19-3   Sock puppet

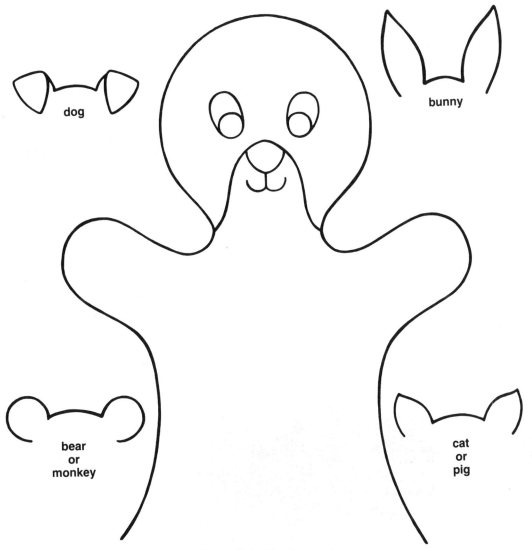

dog

bunny

bear
or
monkey

cat
or
pig

Figure 19-4   Hand puppet

Puppets from Containers

Styrofoam Cup Puppet (N/Pre, K) Cut one hole into a Styrofoam cup. Encourage the child to put one finger through. Does it remind you of anything? It could be an elephant with the finger for a trunk. Or could it be a head, tail, leg, or tongue? Try cutting two holes at opposite sides. Encourage children to put one finger into each hole. What does it remind you of? Could these be arms or legs? Do four holes allow fingers to represent arms and legs or wheels on a vehicle? Or, the cup could be decorated with markers without cutting holes and snugly positioned on a toddler's clenched fist or raised fingers.

Tin Can Puppet (N/Pre, K) A juice can that is tall and slim can be transformed into a puppet. Discard any with rough or sharp inner rims and edges. Cans can be covered with paper and decorated. Add yarn, pipe cleaners, buttons, and other trims.

Container Puppet (N/Pre, K, Pri) Plastic and cardboard containers for holding milk, detergent, shampoo, toothpaste, or bleach have their own characteristic shapes and will suggest vehicle, person, or animal puppets to make. Skinny necks on containers make good handles to hold when using the puppet. Other containers come with built-in handles. Decorate the containers with paper and other trims.

Box Puppet (N/Pre, K, Pri) Boxes with interesting shapes, including toothpaste and fast-food boxes, may suggest puppet possibilities. Decorate them with paper and other trims. Add dishwashing detergent to tempera paint to make it stick if the surface is slick. A small milk carton is an ideal size for a fist puppet.

Coat Hanger Puppet (K, Pri) Bend a coat hanger into a geometric or abstract shape of a puppet. Keep the hook at the bottom for a handle. Place a nylon stocking or pantyhose over the coat hanger and fasten it with string or a rubber band. Decorate the puppet with fabric scraps, yarn, ribbon, trims, and paper.

Puppet Stage

There is no need to spend a lot of money on a commercially made puppet stage. Children will enjoy making, painting, and decorating their own. Find a very large appliance box, such as a refrigerator carton. Carefully remove the back side and cut a window opening in the front panel for the puppets. The opening or window should be placed such that when the children are sitting or kneeling behind the screen it is above their heads but within arm's length. Children might enjoy a window in their puppet stage that opens and closes by folding the cardboard back. Curtains can also be hung. To provide a backdrop, hang scenery that the children create from a dowel rod, curtain rod, or broomstick. Make sure that the pole fits across the top. Make a small notch in each side panel of the carton in which the scenery hanger can securely rest. Allow ample room for the puppets to move about freely in front of the scenery. One foot from the front is recommended. The puppet stage can be painted and decorated as the children see fit. It should be a group project inviting group participation and planning. The result may not be as pretty as a commercially available puppet stage, but the children will be proud of their accomplishment and will most likely use it as a result.

Masks

Making masks is an ancient art form that is presently practiced in many cultures. Often, the masks also have utilitarian value in religious and cultural celebrations. Presently, masks are used in the celebration of Halloween. Many children are frightened by masks. Some will refuse to put something over their head or against their face. They may fear suffocation or loss of identity. Their wishes should be respected. Others enjoy losing their identity, at least for the time being, by putting on a mask and becoming someone or something else.

There are many different ways to make a

mask. Basically, there are two ways to wear a mask: by putting it over the head or by attaching it to the face. Some examples that are appropriate for use with young children include:

Over-the-Head Masks

Grocery Bag Mask (K, Pri) Find a grocery bag that will easily slip over the child's head. Place it over the child's head and use pencil to indicate where the eyes should be placed. Cut out eye holes for the child. Cutting additional openings for the nose and mouth may help the child to breathe. Slit the four sides so that the bag easily slips over the child's shoulders and stays in place. Encourage the child to use paint, crayons, or markers as well as trims to decorate the mask.

Cardboard Box Mask (K, Pri) Find a cardboard box that will fit easily over a child's head. Place it over the child's head and use pencil to indicate where the eyes should be placed. Cut out eye holes for the child. Add openings for the nose and mouth if needed. Encourage the child to use paint, crayons, or markers as well as trims to decorate the mask.

Ice Cream Carton Mask (K, Pri) Ask ice cream parlors to save the drum-shaped commercial ice cream tubs for you. They are good for making a stacked totem pole as well as individual masks. Place the tub over the child's head and use pencil to indicate where the eyes should be placed. Cut out eye holes for the child. Encourage the child to use paint, crayons, or markers as well as trims to decorate the mask.

Face Masks

Paper Plate Mask (K, Pri) Hold a paper plate over the child's face and indicate where the eyes should be placed. Cut out eye holes for the child. Encourage the child to use paint, crayons, or markers as well as trims to decorate the mask. When the mask is completed, attach a string to each side and tie in back. (See Figure 19-5.)

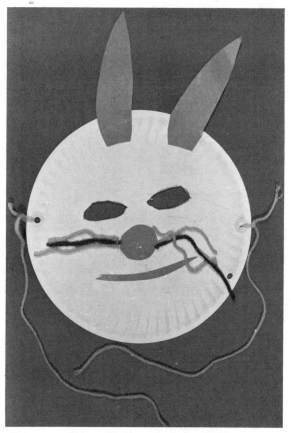

Figure 19-5   Paper plate mask

Pie Plate Mask (K, Pri) Hold a pie plate over the child's face and indicate where the eyes should be placed. Cut out eye holes for the child. Make sure the cut metal leaves no sharp edges. The mask can be painted with paint to which dishwashing detergent has been added. Trims can also be glued on. When the mask is completed, attach a string to each side and tie in back. Children like the slick, shiny metal surface, which often suggests robots or superheroes.

MOBILES AND STABILES

Mobile

A mobile is a hanging sculpture that moves. Generally, it has pieces that are suspended and are free to move about (see Figure 19-6). Wind or movement will activate a mobile. Wind chimes and hanging infant toys suspended over the crib are good examples of mobiles. Mobiles contain at least one level from which items are suspended. A mobile can be suspended from a ceiling or doorway using string and a thumbtack. Advanced mobile makers are faced with the problem of balance when they work with more than one level. To start, one must find a sturdy overhead base from which the items will be suspended, using string, rope, yarn, thread, or fishing tackle line. Some recommended bases from which heavy items can be suspended include

- driftwood
- dowel rod
- broom handle
- thick tree branch
- pencil
- stick
- yardstick
- coat hanger
- three coat hangers wired together at their hooks
- wood ruler

Smaller versions from which light objects can be suspended include

- straws
- tongue depressors
- Popsicle sticks

These smaller supports can be creatively combined with the items previously listed. Some mobile activities recommended for use with young children include:

Group Nature Mobile (N/Pre, K) You will need a fairly sturdy tree branch. Look for one that has an interesting branched-out shape. This will provide a number of different levels from which items can be suspended. Rest or prop up the branch as it will later be hung, but closer to the children's level. They need to be able to reach the branches to attach nature items. Nature items can be collected on a nature walk or brought from home. Encourage children to look for nature specimens that have fallen to the ground. Not all items will be able to be tied or secured. Seashells, feathers, acorns, mushrooms, twigs, leaves, and pinecones are well suited. Attach them with string or yarn and suspend them from a branch. Nature specimens should be suspended at different lengths rather than in a neat row. Lengths of string can have more than one item suspended from them. When the mobile is completed, place it near a window or doorway where a breeze will activate it. This is a good multisession activity. Items on the mobile can be continually added to or changed.

There is no reason why group mobile projects need to be restricted to the use of nature items. Include any of the recycled junk items listed in Appendix A as well as

- paper scraps, cut and torn pieces
- pictures from magazines
- tissue paper shapes sealed in wax paper
- plastic tops and caps
- anything interesting that can be suspended; be creative!

Remember to decorate the front and back, since both sides will be visible. Mobiles can be made around the above-mentioned nature theme or

- main characters in a favorite story, book, or song
- weather and seasons
- holidays
- animals

- community helpers

- traffic signs and safety

- food groups

- transportation

Yarn Shapes Mobile (N/Pre, K) Begin with a papier-mâché mixture. See recipes in Appendix G. Children will need their own piece of wax paper to work on. Take lengths of rug yarn and dip them into the papier-mâché mixture. Squeeze out the excess between your fingers. Arrange the yarn lengths into a shape or object. Be sure to crisscross and overlap your yarn. Let dry thoroughly. Carefully peel off the wax paper. Hang the yarn shape from a mobile.

Multilevel Mobile (K, Pri) Advanced mobile makers can make a mobile that has more than one level. For example, begin with a dowel rod and suspend pencils attached to string of different lengths. Do not worry if the mobile does not balance at this point. Start to suspend items and glue string or yarn in place. Slowly work toward balance. One object on a very short line may balance a much lighter object suspended from a long line. More than one object can be placed on any one line, which will also influence balance. Older children may enjoy the challenge presented by this activity.

Baked Clay Mobile (N/Pre, K) Check Appendix G for a clay recipe that involves baking the finished product. This will provide a nice tinkling sound when the items rustle in the wind. Children can use cookie cutters or clay tools when making their items. Remember to make a hole through each item to allow for hanging.

Picture Parts Mobile (N/Pre, K, Pri) Discuss with children how objects can be cut up into parts. For example, a person could be divided into the head section, body, and legs. Each could be connected separately on a line, with a small space left in between. This would provide a com-

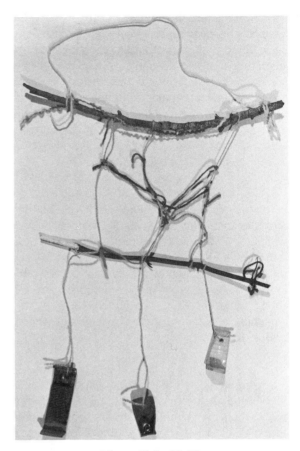

Figure 19-6   Mobile

ical effect when the wind moved the cut-up parts about. This same process can be done with animals, vehicles, or whatever. Magazine pictures are a good source, or children may want to draw their own pictures. A clown, a rocket ship blasting off, and a Christmas tree are just a few that the author has observed.

Stabile

A stabile is nothing more than a self-standing, stationary mobile. Whereas a mobile is suspended, a stabile with one or more arched wire arms rests on a fixed base. Although it is fairly similar to a mobile, a stabile is more difficult to make. You will need at least one length of fairly sturdy wire attached to a wood base. The base must be large and heavy enough to support the wires and suspended items without tipping over. Basically, any of the activities recommended for the mobile apply to the stabile. Suspended items that are too big or heavy will pull down the wire. Also, it will be much more difficult to get several layers hanging from a wire that is bent close toward its base than from a mobile hanging overhead.

SEWING AND WEAVING

Sewing, stitchery, appliqué, and weaving are activities that allow both creative expression and practice in eye-hand coordination and fine motor control. They are recommended for both boys and girls. Unfortunately, they are often overlooked when developing an art program for young children. Some simplified ways of approaching these activities are provided in the following activities.

Sewing

Sewing involves little more than painting with needle and thread or yarn. Young children can invent their own simple in-and-out or over-and-under way to sew and need not learn fancy stitches like the French knot. Some simple sewing activities include:

Yarn Picture (N/Pre, K) This is a presewing activity that is recommended for young children who are not able to use a needle and yarn. You will need a piece of wood. Sandpaper the edges to remove sharp edges or splinters. Hammer in nails randomly. One-inch round-head brass brads are recommended. Nail them halfway in. Encourage children to take a length of yarn and wrap it around the nails to make a picture or design. Rug yarn is recommended because it is heavy and sturdy, and will not tear easily if pulled too tight. It is also possible to make an outline of a specific object, such as a house, with nails, but that would severely restrict the range of artistic possibilities.

Simple Sewing (N/Pre, K) We can reduce some of the steps and frustration involved in sewing by providing a sewing surface that is already perforated with holes. Such a surface is similar to the commercially available sewing cards, although we need not provide a specific outline to complete. Carefully poke or punch out smooth holes. All the child needs to do is guide a needle and yarn in and out of the holes. Select a fairly sturdy surface. Some recommended sewing surfaces include

- Styrofoam meat tray
- cardboard
- berry basket
- poster board
- mesh hardware cloth (quarter inch), cut into squares with tin snips
- plastic screen

Flimsy sewing surfaces, such as burlap and other open-weave fabrics or the mesh bags that onions or grapefruit come in, should be secured in an embroidery hoop. Beginning sewers have a tendency to sew over the hoop. This poses no problem, since the stitches can later be cut to provide a fringed effect. Provide a large, blunt plastic needle and yarn. Or, used a bobby pin as a needle. Enclose the yarn and wrap the open ends shut with tape. There is no need to even use a needle. Merely dip the sewing end of the yarn into white glue. Form the yarn into a point and let it dry. The end can also be wrapped with clear tape and shaped into a point. Tie a knot at the opposite end. The older child with experience in sewing can move on to using a smaller needle with embroidery or sewing thread.

Paper Stitchery (K, Pri) The older child with experience in sewing might enjoy making stitches in heavy paper. This will be a good preparation for sewing on fabric. Paper has the advantage of being easier to come by and providing a sturdy surface. A large plastic needle with yarn will tear the paper. Provide a large metal needle and embroidery or sewing thread. A picture can also be drawn in advance. This same activity could also be done on a Styrofoam meat tray.

Mixed Media   Why not encourage children to creatively combine art media that usually do not go together? For example, they could stitch a frame around their drawing. Or, they could use needle and thread to highlight lines in their painting. Or, they might enjoying stitching fabric to a paper collage. What are some other creative ways to combine art media?

Fabric Stitchery (K, Pri)   The older child with experience in sewing would enjoy using cloth as the background for his or her stitchery. Any loosely woven fabric will do. A piece of old sheet can be secured in an embroidery hoop as a preparation for fabric stitchery.

Appliqué (K, Pri)   Appliqué involves sewing pieces of fabric onto one another. The result might be a stitched fabric collage. Burlap, with its open weave, makes an excellent background. Try to find material scraps with interesting colors, patterns, sizes, shapes, and textures. Some recommended ones include

- gold lamé
- silver brocade
- velvet
- felt
- fur

Items other than fabric scraps to appliqué include

- lace
- buttons
- ribbon
- rick-rack

- beads
- shells
- small straw sections
- jingle bells

Encourage children to glue their fabric scraps in place first before sewing. This will help them sew without the scraps moving around.

Stuffed Pillow (K, Pri)   Children will need to draw the outline of an object, e.g., an animal, on a piece of folded fabric, e.g., an old white sheet. Carefully cut through both pieces of material. Begin to sew the two together while stuffing with

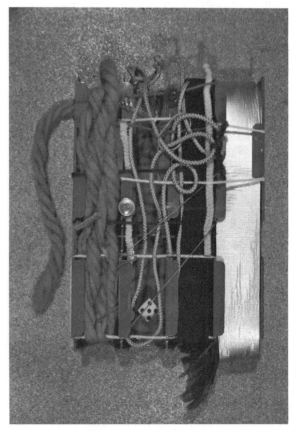

Figure 19-7   Items are creatively combined in this weaving.

small pieces of crushed newspaper, cotton, or stuffing. Continue to sew and stuff. Decorate the pillow with fabric markers when it is completed. Children enjoy making stuffed people pillows by adding yarn for hair and buttons for eyes after their sewing and stuffing are completed.

Weaving

Weaving is another art activity that is often overlooked in early childhood programs. This may be because weaving is a detailed activity, involving much patience, eye-hand coordination, and fine motor control. The paper weaving activities discussed in the Paper Art section provide a good introduction. Once children have mastered the alternating over-under and under-over movement with paper, they may want to continue by weaving with yarn. Weavers use their own terminology. (See Figure 19-7.)

- The loom is the thing you weave on.
- The warp is the lengthwise yarn or string that is strung on your loom.
- The weft is the yarn that is woven over-under and under-over the warp.

Some simplified weaving activities recommended for use with young children include:

Twig Weaving (K, Pri) Provide each child with a Y-shaped or forked twig for a loom. Try to find one that has fallen to the ground or been carefully removed from a dead tree. Wrap the twig with parallel rows of yarn stretching between the two branches. This will form the warp. Do not pull too tight or the branches will snap. Weave lengths of yarn (weft) with an alternating over-under, under-over movement, starting from the notch and moving to the top of the Y shape. Encourage children to push their rows fairly close together. Alternate colors. Since no two twigs will be exactly the same, the finished products will be unique. Older children who are experienced weavers may enjoy weaving on a larger twig with three or more forked branches.

God's Eye Weaving (K, Pri) *Ojo de Dios* means "eye of God" in Spanish. Mexican Indians made these for good luck. They are visually attractive and culturally meaningful. You will need two crossed sticks for the base. Some recommended sticks include a pair of

- pencils
- dowel rods
- plastic straws
- Popsicle sticks
- Q-tips
- sticks
- plastic stirrers
- chopsticks
- pickup sticks
- Tinker Toys

Form a cross with your two sticks and tie yarn in a knot around the sticks where they cross. Add a dab of glue to secure. Encourage the children to use their over-under and under-over motions. With a length of yarn, weave over one stick and under the next, back over and under again to where you started. Continue this pattern without crossing over previous rows. Each successive layer will build the diamond-shaped pattern, or God's eye. Change colors of yarn often if you want a multicolored effect. Also, vary the thickness of the yarn. Lengths of yarn can also be twisted before wrapping to provide a different visual effect.

Burlap Weaving (K, Pri) Burlap, with its loose, open weave, is recommended for sewing and weaving projects. Cut small individual square or rectangular pieces. Pull out ten to twenty threads every few inches to allow open space for objects to be woven into the burlap. Objects to weave in include

- feathers
- yarn
- lace
- ribbon
- old jewelry
- paper strips
- tin foil
- leaves, stems, twigs, and other nature specimens
- fabric strips
- plastic straws
- rick-rack
- sewing tape
- bias tape

Nature specimens are especially attractive when woven into a natural fabric like tan-colored burlap.

Mixed Media Sewing and weaving go well together. Experienced weavers may enjoy sewing or stitching onto their weaving. Individual lengths or widths of burlap can be gathered and tied with thread, ribbons, or lace to break the monotonous solid appearance.

Loom Weaving (K, Pri) Professionals use a large commercial loom to do their weaving. Child-sized looms are commercially available but costly. It is very easy to provide a child-sized substitute. Objects that make good improvised looms include

- wooden picture frame
  Place the picture frame flat and hammer a row of evenly spaced nails across the top and bottom. Wrap string or yarn from the top nail to the matching bottom nail. Continue until the warp is completed. Children can weave from right to left and left to right

Figure 19-8 Weaving with a berry basket.

using their alternating over-under, under-over motion. Weave with yarn, but feel free to add lace, ribbon, nature specimens, fabric, paper, and other recycled junk.

- berry basket
  Small plastic berry baskets come with the warp completed. Children will enjoy weaving yarn, fabric, or paper strips in and out of the openings. This is a good starting point for the young, inexperienced weaver. (See Figure 19-8.)

- Styrofoam meat tray, flat cardboard, or cardboard box
  Carefully cut ¼-inch slits into the top and bottom edges. Wind string or yarn from top to bottom. Your warp will cover the front and back. Children can weave with yarn with an over-and-under alternating motion. The raised edges of the meat tray and cardboard box will allow room for the child's hand when weaving under.

- coat hanger

  Carefully spread the wire hanger into a round, square, or diamond-shaped loom. Wrap string around one end and pull it to the other side. Continue until the open section is filled with parallel lines. The warp is then completed. Encourage children to use lengths of yarn to weave in and out of their loom.

- Two hanging sticks

  You will need two sticks for this loom. Lay them out on a table, about one foot apart; one will be the top, and the second will be the bottom. Begin to fashion a warp by wrapping yarn around the top stick, down to the bottom, around the bottom, and then back up to the top. Continue this process until the warp is completed. Tie the yarn to the top stick and hang it on the wall where children can weave with yarn and other nature specimens. This loom is flimsy and is recommended for the more experienced weaver.

- paper plate or round cardboard or poster board

  Cut an uneven number of slits, such as seven, on the outer edge. Make each slit one-quarter inch deep. Cut a one-inch circle out of the center. Your loom is ready. To prepare the warp, wrap yarn or string from the center hole over the notch, around the back, through the center hole, and up to the next notch. Continue until all spokes and notches are filled. Start at the center and weave in and out or over and under the spokes with a length of yarn. Tie a different color to the end and continue weaving. The back side can also be woven. When finished, cut through the yarn covering the notches. The result will be a colorful, round, woven, fringed hot plate or decorative piece.

  Or, cut an uneven number of slits from the outer edge in. Stop about one inch from the center. Weave lengths of yarn over and under the wedges, starting from the center and working out. Change colors of yarn often.

- soda straws

  You will need four or five plastic straws to make this loom. The straws become the warp and are held in place with the hand. Tape the ends together. You may want to start this weaving for the child. Hold the straws in a spread fan position. Begin with the ends that are held close together in your hand and slowly wrap them with yarn in an over-under motion. When they are fairly secure, let the child take over. Continue weaving to the top of the straws.

SUMMARY

This unit served as a resource of three-dimensional art media and activities. Extensive coverage was given to clay. Types of clay, ways to provide experiences with clay, and stages of clay use were also discussed.

SUGGESTED ACTIVITIES

1. Implement one or more three-dimensional art activities. Use a format that your instructor provides, or use the lesson plan found in Unit 13.

2. Choose any two different three-dimensional art media. Creatively combine them into a new mixed media activity. Plan, implement, and evaluate your activity.

3. Observe how a young child works with clay and answer the following:
   - Which stage of clay is your child in? Document what your child says and does while working with clay.
   - Which clay technique(s) or processing does your child use?
   - Compare and contrast your child's clay work with that of a peer. Did you note any similarities or differences in what they said and did with clay? Explain. Do age or sex differences enter in?

REVIEW

A. Name the author's stages of development in the child's use of clay.
   Stage 1:
   Stage 2:
   Stage 3:
   Stage 4:

B. Compare and contrast the different types of clay.

C. Identify the type of clay you would provide for
   1. older infants and toddlers:
   2. three- and four-year-olds:
   3. older four- and five-year-olds:
   4. six-, seven-, and eight-year-olds:
   5. exceptional children with limited muscular strength and poor fine motor control:

Appendix A

Artistic Junk

Dear Parents,

We need your help! In our daily art program we use all kinds of creative junk. Our slogan is, "Don't throw it away! Recycle it by sending it along with your child."

If you have any of the following objects, please send them along with your child. We also encourage donations of creative junk from your office, business, workplace, or other sources in the community.

Thank you!

A apple divider
  appliances (small, broken—good for parts)
  artificial flowers

B bakeware
  baking cups
  baskets (plastic)
  bath brush
  beads
  berry baskets
  blocks (wooden)
  bolts
  bottle caps and tops
  bottles: plastic pump-type, squeeze, and
    roll-on deodorant

  bowl brush (new)
  bowls (plastic mixing)
  boxes (gift)
  braiding
  brayer
  burlap
  butter tubs
  buttons

C cancelled stamps
  candles
  carbon paper
  cardboard fabric bolts
  cardboard sheets and tubes
  cards (old greeting)
  catalogues
  cellophane (colored)
  checkers
  cheese slicer
  cigar boxes
  clock parts
  cloth
  clothespins
  coat hangers
  coffee filters
  combs (cleaned)
  computer paper
  confetti

contact paper
cookie baking tray
cookie cutters
cord
corks
corrugated cardboard
cosmetic brushes, sponges, and applicators
costume jewelry
costumes
cotton balls and puffs
crayons (old, broken)
cupcake liners
cupcake tins
curtain rings
cutting board

D deodorant bottle (roll-on)
detergent bottles (squeeze-type with lids)
dice
dominoes
dowels

E egg cartons: cardboard and plastic
egg slicer
electronic parts
embroidery hoops and thread
envelopes
excelsior
eyedropper

F fabric scraps
feather duster
feathers
felt
film spools
flannel
floor-length mirror
florist's foil, foam, and Styrofoam
foam
foil
food grater
food savers (Rubbermaid, Tupperware)
fruit trays
funnels
fur

G game pieces
gift boxes
gift wrap
glass beads
glass pane (small)
glitter
grater (metal, food)
greeting cards
grocery bags
gummed labels
gummed paper and stickers

H hair rollers (cleaned)
hairbrushes (cleaned)
hangers
hat boxes
hats (old)
holiday decorations
hot plate
housewares

I ice cream cartons (large, commercial)
ice cube trays
iron (electric, in working order)

J jar tops
jars
jewelry
junk (any and all!)
junk mail

K keys
kitchen gadgets and utensils
kitchen shakers and containers

L lace
leather
lids
linoleum

M machine parts (small)
magazines
magnets
maps
marbles
margarine tubs
material remnants
measuring cups and spoons

meat trays (cleaned)
meatballer
melon baller/scoop
mesh: potato, onion, grapefruit bags
milk carton plastic tops
mirror (hand-held, full-length)
mosaic tile
muffin tins
muslin

N nail brush
nails
necklaces
needles and thread
netting
newspaper
newsprint rolls
nuts
nylons and pantyhose (old)

P packing material
pails (plastic)
paint charts
pans (old)
pantyhose (old, clean)
pantyhose plastic egg containers
paper bags
paper doilies
paper plates
paper reinforcements
paper scraps and tubes
pastry blender/brush
pastry tube
picture frames
pie slice lifter
pie tins
pill bottles and vials
pipe cleaners
pizza cardboards
place mats
plastic containers
plastic fruit baskets
plastic pieces and parts
plastic spiked hairbrush (cleaned)
poker chips
polyfiberfill

pom-pom dish mop
Popsicle sticks
pot scrubber with knobbed handle
pots
puzzle pieces

Q Q-tips
quilts, quilt scraps

R razors (empty, plastic)
rhinestones, rhinestone jewelry
ribbon
ribbon rolls
rick-rack
rolling pin

S sandpaper
scraper spatula
screening: plastic and wire
seals (holiday)
sequins
sheets (old white)
shoe boxes
shoelaces
shoe polish applicator
shopping bags
sieves
socks
spice bottles (empty)
splatter screen (for catching cooking
  grease)
sponges (household)
spools
spray paint can lids
sprayers
springs
squeeze bottles
stamps (cancelled domestic and foreign)
stationery
stationery boxes
stickers
stockings (old)
straws
string
Styrofoam balls, bits, meat trays, packing,
  and pieces

T telephone wire
thread
tiles
tin foil
tongue depressors
toothbrushes (old)
toothpicks
towels (old)
tracing paper
travel brochures and posters
trays
trinkets
tubes: toilet paper, paper napkin, mailing
tubs (margarine with lids)
twine

U upholstery fabric and stuffing
utensils (old, cooking)

V vegetables
velvet
vitamin bottles

W wallpaper sample books and scraps
wax paper
weaving loom
wire (thin)
wire mesh
wire screen
wire whisk/whip (kitchen)
wood scraps
wooden beads
wooden blocks
wrapping paper

Y yarn

NATURE SPECIMENS
acorns
bark
corn husks
cornstalks
dried flowers and plants
driftwood
feathers
fossils
gems
gourds
hives
leaves
minerals
moss
natural clay
nests
nuts
pebbles
pinecones
pods
pressed flowers
reeds
sand
sawdust
seed pods
seeds
shells
smooth stones
straw
twigs
wood shavings

Appendix B

Where to Go in Your Local Community for Artistic Junk

The following list is by no means complete. The number and variety of possible sources will vary depending on the size and location of your community. Feel free to add, delete, and personalize depending on where you live and work. Please request more than is listed below. Individual sources may have a vast supply of colorful parts and pieces just waiting to be claimed. Most sources will be very willing to save so long as you provide a prompt pickup. Specifically stating your purpose and suggesting some sample activities may help them identify artistic junk that is not contained on the list. Happy hunting!

Architectural firm
  blueprint paper
  outdated tools
  surplus paper
Art supply store
  damaged supplies
  surplus stock
  used goods

Attic sale
  anything and everything reasonably priced!
Builder's supply
  carpeting
  Formica
  linoleum
  tile
  wallpaper samples
  wood scraps, trim, and molding
Building site
  discarded hardware
  Styrofoam packing
  wood scraps, trim, and molding
Carpentry and woodworking shop
  sawdust
  wood scraps, shavings, molding, and trim
Church sale
  anything and everything reasonably priced!
Computerized office
  outdated forms
  scrap computer papers and forms
Craft and hobby shop
  damaged goods

packing
small boxes
Dentist's office
see Hospital/medical
Department store
hosiery boxes
outdated forms
small boxes
store displays
Styrofoam packing
Doctor's office
see Hospital/medical
Dressmaking and alteration shop
bobbins
buttons
fabric
spools
thread
trims
Drugstore and pharmacy
pill bottles
plastic containers
store displays
vials
Electric power company
packing materials
wire
Electronics firm
pieces
plastic parts
wire
Estate sale
anything and everything reasonably priced!
Etc., Etc., Etc.
Flea market or swap meet
anything and everything reasonably priced!
Florist shop
dried flowers
ribbon
scrap Styrofoam
surplus nature items
Furniture showroom
cartons
packing materials

Garage sale
anything and everything reasonably priced!
Garment manufacturer
buttons
empty spools
fabric scraps
trim
General office and small business
envelopes
general supplies
old rubber stamps
outdated business forms
surplus or outdated business machines
surplus paper
Gift shop
boxes
ribbon
spools
Styrofoam packing
tissue paper
Gift wrap service
cardboard rolls
damaged gift boxes
ribbon
scrap wrapping paper
tissue paper
Hardware store
linoleum
spare parts and pieces
tile
Hospital/medical
boxes
containers
pill bottles
plastic parts and pieces
trays
vials
x-rays
Ice cream shop
cardboard packing
commercial drum-shaped ice cream cartons
Interior design studio
boxes
displays

fabric
packing
sample books
Lumberyard
dowels
molding
sandpaper
sawdust
wood scraps and shavings
Machine shop or small plant
small specialized pieces and parts
Moving and storage company
cardboard
cartons
wrapping paper
Nature and outdoors
nature specimens
Newspaper plant
newsprint
paper roll ends
scrap papers
Office supply
cardboard
damaged goods
packing
small boxes
Paint store
linoleum
paint charts
surplus water-based paint
tile
Photography shop
containers
scrap papers
Plastic company
parts
plastic pieces
Plexiglas
tubing
wire
Plumbing supply
plastic pipes and pieces
Print shop
cardboard pieces and tubes

heavyweight papers
paper "seconds" and scraps
tickets
Rug store
rug scraps
samples
Rummage sale
anything and everything reasonably priced!
Stationery store
"as is" papers
paper scraps
small boxes
Supermarket and grocery store
baskets
cardboard lining and packing
old price stampers
small boxes
store displays
Styrofoam
thin tissue paper
Tag sale
anything and everything reasonably priced!
Telephone company
large spools
thin colored wire
Textile and fabric shop
cardboard bolts
fabric scraps
material remnants
spools
yarn cones
Thrift shop
anything and everything reasonably priced!
Tile and ceramic shop
linoleum
tile
Travel agency
displays
old posters
outdated forms
surplus brochures
tickets
Upholstery shop
buttons

fabric
  spools
  trims
Wallpaper store
  drapery samples
  wallpaper books and scraps
White Elephant sale
  anything and everything reasonably
  priced!

Wine and liquor store
  cartons
  displays
  fancy boxes
  gift paper
  ribbons
  wooden boxes
Yard sale
  anything and everything reasonably priced!

Appendix C

Artistic Styles

PREHISTORIC OR PRIMITIVE ART

Era: 25,000 years ago during the Paleolithic or Old Stone Age.

10–15,000 years later during the Neolithic or New Stone Age.

Artists:

Unknown cave artists

People have been doing art for many years, way back to the days of dinosaurs. Just as we have artists' pictures hanging on our walls today, people decorated the walls of their caves with pictures. Cave artists mixed their own paints out of plants, berries, and other foods as well as earth, mud, and clay, most likely mixed with animal blood. They used sharpened sticks to draw and etch pictures. Cave artists liked to draw simple stick-figure people and animals, including leaping bison and deer, using only a few lines. Outlines were bold, and pictures were decorated with geometric patterns and designs. Proportion was correct. Cave people drew what they knew: themselves, others, and wild animals. That is what their life was about: survival, hunting, food, and safety from wild animals. Primitive people viewed art as magic. To symbolize something meant to somehow capture or control it.

An activity based on this style could be to have children paint a person or animal of their choice on a fairly large, smooth stone.

NATURALISTIC OR REALISTIC ART

Era: 1700–1800s

Artists:

Honoré Daumier
Francisco Goya
Rembrandt

Era: 19th century on (United States)

Artists:

John James Audubon
Winslow Homer
Edward Hopper
Norman Rockwell
James Whistler
Grant Wood
Andrew Wyeth

Although naturalism and realism are somewhat different terms, we will use them interchangeably. Both terms emphasize the artist's attempt to make art objective and like the actual object. During the 1700s and 1800s painters attempted to portray life exactly as it was. This was a reaction against a neoclassic and romantic view of the ideal life. Naturalists chose to depict life as it was, often sordid and evil, and people as they were, overweight, ill, and less than beautiful. For example, a still life with flowers and fruit might include bugs and decaying food.

Naturalism and realism also became popular in the United States in the nineteenth century. Landscapes, birds, farms, the wilderness, and people represented the struggle and simplicity of early American life. Children can examine naturalistic or realistic art and appreciate all the time, effort, skills, and talent needed to make a photographic likeness.

An activity for older children could be to set up a very simple arrangement, for example, a stuffed animal and a doll. Encourage the children to try to draw or paint the two toys just as they are. They will need to examine them repeatedly for color, detail, and shape. This activity may prove frustrating, so it should be offered as an option.

AMERICAN FOLK ART

Era: 1700–1800s and currently

Artist:

Grandma Moses

American folk artists do art with little or no formal training. They are proof that anyone and everyone is capable of making an artistic statement. As an artistic movement American folk artists lived in New England, New York, and Pennsylvania in the late 1700s to mid 1800s. Folk artists continue to work at their art form or craft today. Folk art can be identified by its bold, simple designs, vivid colors, and simplistic handling of light, proportion, and perspective. Generally, folk art makes a social, political, or religious statement. Often common objects and events, including flowers, baking bread, going to market, or getting married, are depicted. It is this primitive, homey quality that appeals to the public.

Folk artists are versatile and work in a variety of media and crafts.

An activity could be to let children make a person out of a wooden clothespin (nonclip type). Details could be added with fine markers. Yarn could be available for hair, material scraps for clothing.

IMPRESSIONISM

Era: late 1800s to early 1900s

Artists:

Mary Cassatt
Paul Cézanne
Edgar Degas
Eugène Delacroix
Raoul Dufy
Paul Gauguin
Édouard Manet
Claude Monet
Camille Pissarro
P. A. Renoir
Henri de Toulouse-Lautrec
Vincent van Gogh

Impressionists were fascinated with color, sunshine, contrasts, light, reflection, and shadow. They were concerned with making only a quick sketch of an object to capture its essence. Later they rapidly filled in their crude outline with intense patches of pigment. They used color and light to represent the artist's impression. Impressionists painted what they saw rather than what they knew to be there. They preferred painting outdoors with natural light. Landscapes were popular subject matter. When viewed from up close, Impressionist paintings depict a vibrating brilliance of colors, pure and unmixed. When viewed from a distance, however, the eyes fuse these neighboring color patches, constructing form and perceiving movement.

An activity could be to make an outdoor painting by dabbing paint with an index finger. Encourage children to place separate dabs rather than mixing them. Or, children could use bright fluorescent crayons in making their strokes.

POINTILISM

Era: late 1800s to early 1900s

Artist:

Georges Seurat

Pointilism, an offshoot of Impressionism, involved a concern for color and an innovative technique for representing it. Pointilists worked on large canvases, spending as much as a year or more on one canvas. Small dots or points of pure color were used instead of Impressionist dashes or strokes. Pointilists were concerned with the complementary relationship between colors. They did not mix colors, but instead required that the observer fuse neighboring colors. For example, Pointilists would represent water as composed of neighboring dots or points of green and yellow. When viewed from up close, the observer would see only green and yellow dots. From a distance, however, the eyes would blend the yellow and green and perceive blue water.

An activity could be to use crayons or markers to make a picture composed entirely of different colored dots. Encourage children to use dots rather than lines at all times. Or, children can make a picture by dipping the eraser end of a pencil into red, blue, and yellow paint and making a print in the shape of dots. This activity is recommended after children have had an opportunity to do color mixing. For example, if they want to make a purple car, they can use the Pointilist technique of alternating red and blue dots in printing. Dots are placed close together with white space between. Younger children who do not have a command of color mixing should be encouraged to merely make a picture or design with colored dots.

EXPRESSIONISM

Era: late 1800s to 1900s

Artists:

Paul Gauguin
Wassily Kandinsky
Piet Mondrian
Edvard Munch
Emil Nolde
Georgia O'Keeffe
Diego Rivera

Expressionists, reacting against Impressionism, searched for emotional expression in their artistic statements. Expressionists purposely altered space, form, line, and color to make an emotional statement that was expressionistic rather than realistic, naturalistic, or impressionistic. The actual subject matter was often lost in the colorful and even violent play of color, line, shape, contrast, and movement. Expressionists distorted reality to express their own view and mood. Since this movement was popular at the time of World War I, it is easy to see how the art reflected contemporary culture. Much of the art work at this time was violent, depressing, and highly emotional.

An activity could be to let children finger paint to mood music. Music that conveys sorrow, joy, and anger could be played. Encourage children to paint how they feel.

ABSTRACT EXPRESSIONISM

Era: 1940s

Artists:

Willem de Kooning
Hans Hofmann
Jackson Pollock
Mark Rothko

Abstract expressionists were intrigued with color and the physical qualities of paint: "What can I do with paint on canvas?" Abstract expressionism began after World War II. Jackson Pollock is a good example of an abstract expressionist who practiced action or gesture painting by dripping, dribbling, spraying, pouring, throwing, and splashing paint. Design was often left to chance or accident. These painters worked on very large canvases with no concern for capturing reality or shape, or telling a story through pictures.

An activity could be to put globs of paint on paper and let children use a soda straw to blow the paint around. The straws should be held close to the paint but not make contact with it. Remind children to exhale or blow out and not inhale or suck in. Children may also like to work outdoors on a group mural. Children can take turns dripping paint, using squeeze bottles or carefully trickling paint from a paper cup.

FAUVISM

Era: 1910s

Artists:

André Derain
Raoul Dufy
Paul Gauguin
Henri Matisse
Amedeo Modigliani
Georges Rouault

Fauvism is an offshoot of Expressionism. Fauvists experimented with pure, bright colors in daring and innovative ways to represent positive emotions, including joy, pleasure, comfort, love, and happiness. Often there was little concern for the naturalistic or realistic use of color. Fauvists might not be concerned with mixing the proper color for skin. Human skin could be painted pink, green, or whatever, depending on the artist's mood. In this way, Fauvists believed that they could use color to make an emotional statement. Objects were characterized with bold outlines and abstract lines. An emotional use of color was of primary concern.

An activity could be to make a picture depicting a positive emotion or feeling, such as joy, love, hope, happiness, or caring. Encourage children to select and use the crayons that they believe best capture their feeling, with little or no concern for the naturalistic or realistic use of color. What does "happy" mean to you? Let's find a "happy" colored crayon to make our happy picture. "No, Sara, your happy picture doesn't have to look like anything!"

CUBISM

Era: 1900s

Artists:

Georges Braque
Paul Cézanne
Marcel Duchamps
Juan Gris
Fernand Léger
Piet Mondrian
Pablo Picasso
Georges Rouault

Cubism is the source of all twentieth-century abstract art. It seeks an intellectual conception of form and shape. Cubists attempt to break everything down into its component geometric and/or architectural shapes. How can three-dimensional form, including the back side and bottom, be represented on a two-dimensional flat canvas? To do this, Cubists abandoned traditional treatment of space and form, and instead focused on the use of the cylinder, sphere, and cube. For example, a Cubist might represent a tree by simultaneously depicting its top, sides, back, insides, and bottom. Intellectually, we are shown the entire tree. There is little concern for color, depth, or proper perspective. Objects appear flat, with little concern for background or foreground. They may be repeated in an overlapping sequence to suggest motion and movement. Cubists introduced the art form of collage.

An activity could be to make a collage using only geometric paper shapes, either cut or torn. Since a collage often has letters embedded in it, children could search through magazines and add letters to their own collage.

KINETIC ART

Era: 1920s

Artists:

Alexander Calder
Marcel Duchamps

Why must art be flat and motionless? Kinetic art attempts to incorporate physical movement by using levers, gears, and movable parts. Kinetic art invites participation. People interacting with kinetic sculpture cause it to move or change. Wind also causes the hanging objects on a mobile to move.

An activity could be to have children make a mobile. Or, older children could attempt a moving junk sculpture or assemblage. For example, a robot could be constructed using fasteners, yarn, string, wire, nuts and bolts, and rubber bands, which would facilitate movement.

SURREALISM

Era: Twentieth century

Artists:

Marc Chagall
Salvador Dali
Jean Dubuffet
Max Ernst
Raoul Hausmann
Paul Klee
René Magritte
Joan Miró
Georgia O'Keeffe
Man Ray
Henri Rousseau
Ben Shahn

Surrealism means superrealism. It attempts to create a magical, dreamlike world that is more beautiful than reality. Dreams, images, fantasies, and the subconscious are chosen as subject matter and portrayed either realistically or abstractly. Objects, space, symbols, size, perspective, time, and shape may be distorted, transformed, or superimposed. For example, a fish with a human head may fly through a rock-laden sky. The viewer may appear shocked and ask, what is it? What is it supposed to be? What does it mean? The artist has been successful in causing the viewer to stop, observe, and emotionally respond.

An activity could be to encourage children to represent their dreams, wishes, fantasies, nightmares, and innermost thoughts and feelings. Encourage children to make a personal statement that may not always be pleasant, pretty, or intelligible.

POP ART

Era: 1950s

Artists:

Jasper Johns
Roy Lichtenstein
Andy Warhol

Pop or Popular art makes a social statement or critique of contemporary American culture. Pop artists chose subject matter that was familiar to everyday life—soup cans, soft drink containers, movie stars, cartoons, and other examples of advertising art. The common, taken-for-granted product becomes art. Although obvious in subject matter, these objects were represented, often in repeated fashion, with painstaking, realistic detail. Again, photographic realism was attempted and attained. There was no intent to make an emotional statement beyond the satire of the commercialism of contemporary culture.

An activity could be to have older children design their own package or wrapper for a candy bar, cereal, or soft drink. Or, children could attempt to draw their own or a group cartoon strip with fine-point markers. Four or five frames may be sufficient.

OP ART

Era: 1960s

Artists:

Frank Stella
Victor Vasarely

Op or Optical art was an artistic style that developed in the psychedelic 1960s. Op artists were intrigued with the effects of black and white, color, figure-ground relations, and depth. They used the principles of optics and perception to create optical illusions with shapes, lines, and patterns. Wiggly and concentric lines and patterns suggested movement and form in the eye of the beholder.

Op art may be a style that demands much in the way of technical proficiency and does not easily translate into an early childhood art activity.

Appendix D

Art Resources

The following is an incomplete list of art resources: postcards, prints, reproductions, slides, posters, books, films, and videotapes related to art. If possible, use school letterhead stationery in requesting catalogues. Remember to also check local bookstores, museums, and art galleries.

American Federation of Arts
41 East 65th Street
New York, New York 10021

Art Education, Inc.
28 E. Erie Street
Blauvelt, New York 10913

Art Extension Press
Box 389
Westport, Connecticut 06881

Art Institute of Chicago
The Museum Store
Michigan Avenue at Adams
Street
Chicago, Illinois 60603

Guggenheim Museum
Mail Order Department
1071 Fifth Avenue
New York, New York 10128

Metropolitan Museum of Art
Fifth Avenue at 82nd Street
New York, New York 10028

NASCO West Inc.
P.O. Box 3837
Modesto, California 95352

National Gallery of Art
Department of Extension
Programs
Washington, D.C. 20565

New York Graphics Society
P.O. Box 1469
Greenwich, Connecticut
06836

Print Finders
15 Roosevelt Place
Scarsdale, New York 10583

Shorewood Fine Arts
Reproductions, Inc.
27 Glen Road
Sandy Hook, Connecticut
06482

Smithsonian Institution
Information and Reception
Center
Washington, D.C. 20560

University Prints
21 East Street
P.O. Box 485
Winchester, Mass. 01890

Appendix E

Catalogues

The following is an incomplete list of companies that carry art-related toys and basic art supplies. Generally they will send catalogues upon request. If possible, use school letterhead stationery. Shop around and compare prices, handling and shipping charges, discounts, and return policy.

A+ Discount Distributors, Inc.
300 Airport Executive Park
Spring Valley, New York 10977
1-800-443-7900

ABC School Supply Inc.
6500 Peachtree Industrial Blvd.
P.O. Box 4750
Norcross, Georgia 30091
(404) 447-5000

Arthur Brown & Bro., Inc.
2 West 46th Street
New York, New York 10036

Beckley-Cardy
7111 Perimeter Park Drive
Houston, Texas 77041
1-800-231-4620
1-800-392-2813 (Texas)

Chaselle, Inc.
9645 Gerwig Lane
Columbia, Maryland 21046
1-800-CHASELLE

Child Guidance Toys
Questor Education Products Co.
200 Fifth Avenue
New York, New York 10010

Childcraft Education Corp.
20 Kilmore Road
Edison, New Jersey 08817
1-800-631-5657

Community Playthings
Rifton, New York, 12471

Constructive Playthings
Main Business Office
1227 East 119th St.
Grandview, Missouri 64030
(816) 761-5900 (Missouri)
1-800-255-6124

Crayola Educational Products
Binney & Smith
P.O. Box 431
1100 Church Lane
Easton, Pennsylvania 18042
(215) 253-6271

Creative Education Supply
House, Inc.
4416 York Street
Metairie, Louisiana 70001
(504) 885-6700

Creative Playthings
Princeton, New Jersey 08540

DIDAX Inc.
6 Doulton Place
Peabody, MA 01960
(617) 535-4757/4758

DLM Teaching Resources
P.O. Box 4000
One DLM Park
Allen, Texas 75002
1-800-527-4747
1-800-442-4711 (Texas)

Economy Handicrafts
50–21 69th Street
Woodside, New York 11377

Educational Teaching Aids
159 West Kinzie Street
Chicago, Illinois 60610
(312) 559-1400

Fisher-Price Toys
East Aurora, New York 14052

Galt Toys
1-800-448-GALT

Hammett
Box 545
Dept. DM
Braintree, MA 02184
1-800-225-5467

Kaplan
P.O. Box 25408
Winston-Salem, North Carolina
27114-5408
1-800-334-2014
1-800-642-0610 (North Carolina)

Lakeshore Curriculum
Materials Co.
2695 E. Dominguez St.
P.O. Box 6261
Carson, California 90749
1-800-262-1777 (California)
1-800-421-5354 (outside California)

Nasco Arts & Crafts
901 Janesville Ave.
Fort Atkinson, Wisconsin 53538
1-800-558-9595

Nasco West
1524 Princeton Ave.
Modesto, California 95352
1-800-558-9595

Playskool, Inc.
4501 West Augusta Blvd.
Chicago, Illinois 60651

S & S Arts and Crafts
Colchester, CT 06415
(203) 537-3451

Appendix F

Art-Related Books

The following list contains books that focus on the artistic elements, including color, shape, and line, and the five senses, artists, and art in general.

Adams, A. *Easter Egg Artists*. New York: Charles Scribner's Sons, 1976.
  A family of bunnies design and paint beautiful Easter eggs as well as their surroundings.
Bang, M. *Tye May and the Magic Brush*. New York: Greenwillow Books, 1981.
  Tye May is a poor orphan who is mysteriously given a magical paint brush. Whatever she paints comes alive. She gives what she paints as gifts to the poor. The greedy emperor discovers this and makes her paint only for him. Tye May, however, wins in the end when she sends him off sailing in the ocean on a painted ship.
Baylor, B. *When Clay Sings*. New York: Charles Scribner's Sons, 1972.
  A book for older children on the use of clay in prehistoric and primitive art. The book relies on a long narrative and explores symbols on Indian pottery. Highly recommended for multicultural education.
Brandenberg, A. *My Five Senses*. New York: Thomas Y. Crowell Company, 1962.
  This book overviews the five senses. The choice of colors is limited and restricted to black, white, green, and blue.
Brandenburg, F. *What Can You Make of It?* New York: Greenwillow Books, 1977.
  Fieldmouse family moves to a new home. They collect all sorts of junk, including milk cartons, toilet paper tubes, yarn, spools, egg cartons, and old magazines. In their new home they find wonderful uses for all this valuable junk.
Brenner, B. *Faces*. New York: E. P. Dutton & Co., Inc., 1970.
  This book tells how we learn about the world through our senses. Four of the standard five senses are covered, with touch left out. The book is illustrated with black-and-white photographs.
Carle, E. *I See a Song*. New York: Thomas Y. Crowell Company, 1973.
  The book is a collage of colors and shapes without words. A violin player plays

colorful music that forms designs and suggests realistic objects. The book will help children visualize, imagine, and come up with creative possibilities.

Chase, A. E. *Famous Paintings—An Introduction to Art*. New York: Platt & Monk, 1962.

The author presents approximately two hundred large pictures of famous artworks. The pictures are organized around themes, for example, children and their pets, playing games, and mother and child.

Cohen, M. *No Good in Art*. New York: Greenwillow Books, 1980.

Jim's art teacher in kindergarten did not approve of his work. Jim did not feel very creative during that year. Now, in first grade, he has a teacher that helps him see how creative and artistic he can be. Recommended for children who do not see themselves as skilled or creative in art.

Crews, D. *Carousel*. New York: Greenwillow Books, 1982.

Children climb atop a carousel animal. The music begins and the animals circle round and round, faster and faster. What results is a blur of color. The music stops and the horses slow down. The original colors return. Illustrated with full-color collages and special photographic techniques.

———. *Freight Train*. New York: Greenwillow Books, 1978.

This is the story of the journey of a colorful train as it goes through tunnels, by cities, and over trestles. The book is very well illustrated. The bright, colorful cars of the train bear their color name. The colors of the cars blend to suggest speed and movement and also depict color mixing.

Cumming, R. *Just Look . . . A Book About Paintings*. New York: Charles Scribner's Sons, 1979.

This book contains over fifty full-color reproductions of famous paintings. It discusses how artists have used the artistic elements, including line, shape, and color, in their work. The book contains some difficult vocabulary and may be more appropriate at the kindergarten or primary level.

Emberley, E. *Green Says Go*. Boston: Little, Brown and Company, 1968.

A story about colors and color mixing. The author suggests that colors remind us of many different things, like holidays. Unfortunately, he stereotypically equates pink with girls and blue with boys.

———. *Wing on a Flea: A Book About Shapes*. Boston: Little, Brown and Company, 1961.

The author uses rhymes and lively drawings to help children recognize rectangles, circles, and triangles in everyday objects.

Fisher, L. E. *Boxes! Boxes!* New York: The Viking Press, 1984.

As the name implies, the book shows many possible uses for a box. The book has beautiful color illustrations. The words in the simplified text are set to rhyme. The book focuses on squares and rectangles.

Freeman, D. *Chalk Box Story*. New York: Lippincott, 1976.

When the lid of a chalk box opens, each colored stick helps tell the story of a little boy stranded on a deserted island and the little turtle who comes to his rescue.

Friskey, M. *What Is the Color of the Wide, Wide World?* Chicago: Children's Press, 1973.

Different animals each claim that the world is their color. Each appears on a separate page telling about things that are their color. A beautiful white bird corrects them by saying that colors change with light and seasons. The world is full of many beautiful colors. A good book for older children.

Hawkinson, J. *Pat, Swish, Twist and the Story of Patty Swish.* Chicago: Albert Whitman & Co., 1978.

The book has beautiful watercolor illustrations and is divided into two major parts. First, there is a wordless picture story of Patty Swish, a horselike animal. Second, there is a discussion of tools and techniques for watercolor.

Hoban, Tana. *A, B, See!* New York: Greenwillow Books, 1982.

This is one of many highly recommended books by this author. Hoban is a talented photographer. In this book, black-and-white photograms of familiar objects from A to Z are portrayed. Photograms reveal the form or shape in white against a black background. This book shows how there is beauty and design all around us.

———. *I Read Symbols.* New York: Greenwillow Books, 1983.

Colorful photographs are used to introduce the child to signs and symbols frequently seen along streets and highways.

———. *Is It Red? Is It Yellow? Is It Blue?* New York: Greenwillow Books, 1978.

There is no text, but the book is illustrated with beautiful photographs in vibrant colors. The author focuses on colors and concepts of shape, quantity, and direction. The author has creatively chosen what to include for the colors. For example, rather than apple for red, the author chooses a girl with a red raincoat and red umbrella. Each page is coded with color bubbles representing the colors stressed.

———. *Is It Rough? Is It Smooth? Is It Shiny?* New York: Greenwillow Books, 1984.

There is no text, but the book is illustrated with beautiful photographs in vibrant colors. The author focuses on textures and surfaces. The author has creatively chosen items such as a squashed soft drink can, caramel apples, and bales of hay. The author's photographs confirm the aesthetic belief that beauty is all around us.

———. *Look Again.* New York: The Macmillan Company, 1971.

Excellent black-and-white photography. The sequence begins with a square cutout of a page with a photograph underneath. Guess what it is? Turn the window and see if you were right. Look again for a different view of the same object by turning the page, which brings you to the next sequence.

———. *Round and Round and Round.* New York: Greenwillow Books, 1983.

There is no text, but the book is illustrated with beautiful photographs in vibrant colors. The author's choice of examples is creative and unusual. For example, round holes in a Swiss cheese sandwich on a round bun and round ripples in water are but two of her clever examples.

———. *Shapes and Things.* New York: Macmillan, 1970.

There are no words, but beautiful photograph-type white impressions of common objects appear against a black background. This book will help children see the beauty in shape, outline, and form.

Hughes, S. *Noisy.* New York: Lothrop, Lee & Shepard Books, 1985.

This book is part of a series on concepts. It is the story of a little girl who describes the many noises that can be heard inside and outside her house. The illustrations are charming and depict family members as real people. Children will be able to relate to these characters. The parents appear frazzled, and baby sibling always seems to have food spilled on the floor.

Hutchins, P. *Changes, Changes*. New York: The Macmillan Company, 1971.
There is no text, and illustrations tell the creative adventures of two wooden toys and their building blocks. The blocks catch on fire, convert into a fire truck, and float in the water. Children will enjoy guessing what is going to happen next. What else could they do with blocks?

Johnson, C. *A Picture for Harold's Room*. New York: Harper & Row, Publishers, 1960.
One of a series on the adventures of Harold and his purple crayon. This one has been made into an I Can Read Book with simple words for the beginning reader. Harold thinks his room needs a picture and decides to draw one with his purple crayon. Before finishing his picture, however, Harold takes you on a journey with his purple crayon. This particular adventure includes attention to perspective when Harold draws railroad tracks that recede into the background.

————. *Harold and the Purple Crayon*. New York: Harper & Row, Publishers, 1955.
The story of Harold and his adventures with a purple crayon. Harold goes out for a walk and sketches some adventures. The book is small, compact, and made for small hands. The illustrations are simple, and the purple line is bold. The story resolves itself with Harold falling asleep and dropping his purple crayon.

Kampmann, L. *The Children's Book of Painting*. New York: Van Nostrand Reinhold Company, 1971.
This story was originally written in German, and the story line gets a little wordy at times. It is the story of the painting adventures of two puppets, Alexander and Katinka. They experiment with watercolor, crayons, and markers. Beautiful samples of real children's art are included.

Keats, E. J. *The Trip*. New York: Greenwillow Books, 1978.
The story of a boy, Louie, who is having trouble adjusting to his new move. Louie's new neighborhood is portrayed with vibrant-colored collage, paint, and pastels. Homesick, Louie makes a shoe box diorama and imagines that he flies back to see his old friends, who are dressed for Halloween. A quick fantasy flight and Louie returns to his new home just in time to go trick-or-treating with his new neighbors. A good ethnic mix of characters.

Kellogg, S. *Mystery of the Stolen Blue Paint*. New York: Dial, 1982.
Belinda plans to paint a special blue picture but is interrupted by her cousin and his friends. She gives up and decides to pack away her art supplies. Where is the blue paint? The others do not have it. The mystery is solved when Belinda's dog Homer gives everyone a blue kiss.

Kessler, E., and L. Kessler. *Are You Square?* Garden City, New York: Doubleday & Company, Inc., 1966.
Square and round are emphasized, with other shapes introduced. The illustrations are fair, and the book relies on a strong story line.

Krauss, R. *I Want to Paint My Bathroom Blue*. New York: Harper & Row, Publishers, 1956.

A boy's fantasy adventure with painting people and things different colors. Illustrated by Sendak, one of his earliest.

Kunhardt, D. *Pat the Bunny*. New York: Golden Book, 1962.
This book is a multisensory experience for very young children. Look at the pictures, listen to the words, pat the bunny, and smell the scented illustration.

Lamorisse, A. *The Red Balloon*. Garden City, N.Y.: Doubleday & Company, Inc., 1956.
A classic that still appears on television. It is the tale of a young boy, Pascal, who lives in Paris and his encounters with his magical red balloon. There are many black-and-white photographs, with only a few color ones emphasizing red.

Lionni, L. *Colors to Talk About*. New York: Pantheon, 1985.
This is a small, sturdy book with cardboard pages and rounded edges. It is highly recommended for older infants, toddlers, and young preschoolers. There are no words. The book relies on attractive illustrations to show the antics of colorful mice.

———. *Little Blue and Little Yellow*. New York: Ivan Obolensky, Inc., 1979.
This book depicts the adventures of torn colored paper shapes: Mama, Papa, and Child Blue. The book shows color mixing. Little Blue hugged a friend named Little Yellow and they became as one—green. The story may be a bit contrived, but it is a good introduction to color mixing and will encourage readers to use their imagination and creativity.

———. *Swimmy*. New York: Pantheon Books, 1968.
Young children love Swimmy, a small, black orphan fish who comes to save the day. Equally important are the beautiful watercolor illustrations of sea creatures and seascapes. The words have been carefully chosen and are equally beautiful.

Lobel, A. *On Market Street*. New York: Greenwillow Books, 1981.
An A to Z picture book of old-fashioned sellers at market. Each seller is composed of the wares that he or she sells. For example, L is made up solely of lollipops. The book is colorful and a creative way to discuss shapes and composition, as well as the alphabet.

Loss, J. *What Is It? A Book of Photographic Puzzles*. Garden City, N.Y.: Doubleday & Company, Inc., 1974.
A series of puzzles. Each one starts with a photographic close-up. Can you guess what it is? Turn the page and see it as it usually appears at normal range. Clear black-and-white photography. Challenging for both young and older children.

Lund, D. H. *The Paint-Box Sea*. New York: McGraw-Hill Book Company, 1973.
The story of a brother and sister who explore the seashore to discover the real color of the ocean. Beautiful illustrations. Older children may be better able to relate to the older characters. Words are set in rhyme.

MacAgy, D., and E. MacAgy. *Going for a Walk with a Line—A Step into the World of Modern Art*. Garden City, N.Y.: Doubleday & Company, Inc., 1959.
Samples of the artwork of different artists are included to show different ways that the line has been used in art.

Martin, B., Jr., *Brown Bear, Brown Bear, What Do You See?* New York: Holt, Rinehart and Winston, 1967.

Children see a variety of animals, each one a different color, looking at them. Big, bold, colorful illustrations. Children will enjoy the repetitive, catchy rhyme.

O'Neill, M. *Hailstones and Halibut Bones*. Garden City, N.Y.: Doubleday & Company, Inc. 1961.

A very highly recommended book of poetry for all the different colors. Excellent and very appropriate for young children. This book is a must for any early childhood book collection.

Raboff, E. *Art for Children Series,* 1969.

The books on Picasso and Chagall provide beautiful color reproductions combined with simple text.

Reiss, J. J. *Colors*. Scarsdale, N.Y.: Bradbury Press Inc., 1969.

Different pages focus on different colors. The pictures are large, glossy, colorful, and done with a concern for good design. Young children will enjoy the colorful shapes.

————. *Shapes*. Scarsdale, N.Y.: Bradbury Press Inc., 1974.

The book focuses on geometric shapes in the environment. It is very well illustrated. Shapes are creatively combined with one another to make different ones. Shapes are all around us.

Samton, S. W. *The World from My Window*. New York: Crown Publishers, Inc., 1985.

This book can serve many purposes. It focuses on numbers, colors, and poetry. The book is beautifully illustrated in vibrant colors. The numbers one through ten and corresponding objects appear as seen from one window. The story line is set in rhyme.

Sazer, N. *What Do You Think I Saw? A Nonsense Number Book*. New York: Pantheon Books, 1976.

This book introduces the numbers one to ten while describing in rhyme the unusual things a young rhino sees on the way to the train. The book is illustrated with animals done in watercolors.

Shapur, F. *Round and Round and Square*. London: Abelard-Schuman, 1972.

The book is illustrated with basic shapes in bright colors. It shows how common objects like sailboats and kites are composed of simple shapes. Identifying shapes in the night and city scenes will be more difficult, since they tend to be busy.

Shaw, C. G. *It Looked Like Spilt Milk*. New York: Harper & Row, Publishers, 1947.

A classic. The story of a white blob that is searching for an identity. What can it be? The book shows how it can be many things, including spilt milk. Hopefully, children will see that their own drawn or painted shapes can also be many things. Still, the author ends on a closed-ended note by stating that it was a cloud rather than spilt milk. Why couldn't it be all or none of the above?

Slobodkina, E. *Caps for Sale*. Reading, Mass.: Addison-Wesley Publishing Company, Inc., 1968.

A classic tale of a peddler, some monkeys, and their monkey business. Children love the suspense and antics. They also learn their colors from the peddler's checkered, gray, brown, blue, and red stacked caps.

Tudor, T. *Five Senses*. New York: Platt & Munk, Publishers, 1978.

This book tells the adventures of a little girl who uses all her senses on a farm. It is set in the recent past. The illustrations are quite pretty, and the story may hold more appeal for girls than for boys.

Ventura, P. *Great Painters*. New York: G. P. Putnam's Sons, 1984.
This book is a resource book rather than a storybook. There is no story, but rather an explanation of artistic styles. Children may enjoy looking through this book. Not all the pictures are large enough to show to the whole class during story time.

Weisgard, L. *Treasures to See*. New York: Harcourt, Brace & World, Inc., 1956.
The book depicts a trip through an art museum. The pictures are illustrations rather than photographs. The book is dated, and the children appear as they did in the 1950s. Still, for the child who has never been to an art museum, it is a good start.

Wildsmith, B. *Fishes*. London: Oxford University Press, 1984.
A close-up look at a variety of fish illustrated in a rainbow of bright colors and set against an equally colorful background. You can see the artist's initial sketches and how the paint is washed over.

Wolff, R. J. *Feeling Blue*. New York: Charles Scribner's Sons, 1968.
A focus on the color blue. How do we make blue? How does blue make us feel? Where do we see blue in our world? What are the shades and tints of blue? The book is a good introduction to one primary color. The author has also written *Hello Yellow* and *Seeing Red* with an identical format.

Appendix G

Art Recipes

These are some basic art recipes. Try to see which recipe gives the best results for you. Altitude and geographic location have been known to affect the length of cooking time and results, especially with play dough.

BOILED PAPER

wrapping or shelf paper
fabric dye (light color)
water

Dissolve dye in hot water. Crumple up paper and place it in dye bath. Boil for 5 minutes. Rinse paper in cold water. Carefully squeeze out water. Spread paper out to dry. Boiled paper will end up looking like leather.

BREAD-DOUGH CLAY

4 slices bread
3 tablespoons white glue
2 drops lemon juice
plastic bag

Remove crusts from bread. Tear bread into small pieces. Mix pieces of bread with glue and lemon juice. Knead. Do not eat. Sculpt. Allow to dry for a couple of days before decorating. Place unused bread-dough clay in a plastic bag and store in the refrigerator.

CANDY CLAY

1/3 cup margarine
1/3 cup light corn syrup
1/4 teaspoon salt
1 teaspoon vanilla or peppermint extract
1 pound box powdered sugar
food coloring

Mix all other ingredients, then add powdered sugar. Knead until smooth. Add more powdered sugar if necessary to make nonstick, pliable clay. Sculpt and eat.

EDIBLE DOUGH CLAY

1 package of dry yeast
1½ cups very warm water
1 egg
1/4 cup honey
1/4 cup shortening
1 teaspoon salt
5 cups flour

Mix yeast with water. Add egg, honey, shortening, and salt. Slowly add flour until a ball of dough forms. Add more flour if too sticky. Knead dough. Sculpt. Make only flat figures, since dough will rise. Cover the sculptures with a towel. Let rise in a warm place for about a half hour. Let it rise longer if you want it fatter. Bake at 350° for 20 minutes or until golden brown. Sculptures can be eaten or painted and coated with shellac to preserve.

CLAY AND PLAY DOUGH
Decorating Dough

4 cups self-rising flour
1 cup salt
1½ cups water
food coloring or powder tempera (optional)

Mix flour and salt in large bowl. Slowly add water. Mix thoroughly. Add food coloring. Knead for 5 to 10 minutes. Add more water if dough is too stiff, more flour if too sticky. Food coloring is optional. Sculpt or cut with cookie cutters. Sprinkle board with flour to keep from sticking. Press in hairpin holder if hanging is desired. Dry at room temperature for several days, or bake at 300° for 1½ hours. Refrigerated dough will last for 5 days.

GOOP

2 cups salt
water
1 cup cornstarch

Mix salt and ⅔ cup water. Heat in pot for 3 to 4 minutes. Remove from heat and quickly add a mixture of the following:

1 cup cornstarch
½ cup cold water

Stir quickly. Return to the heat if too "goopy."

HOMEMADE PLAY DOUGH

2 cups flour
1 cup salt

2 cups water
2 tablespoons cooking oil
4 teaspoons cream of tartar
food coloring (optional)

Mix the flour, salt, and cream of tartar together. Add the water, oil, and food coloring (if desired). Cook the mixture over low to medium heat for 3 to 5 minutes. Keep stirring until the mixture forms a solid ball. Cool. Items made can be baked at low heat for 20 to 25 minutes, depending on their thickness.

PLAY DOUGH

2½ cups flour
½ cup salt
1 tablespoon alum
3 tablespoons cooking oil
1½ cups hot water
food coloring

Combine oil, water, and food coloring. Combine dry ingredients. Pour liquid into dry ingredients. Mix thoroughly. Knead.

SOAP AND SAWDUST CLAY

1½ cups soap flakes
1½ cups sawdust
water

Slowly add water to soap flakes. Make a thick, creamy mixture. Whip soap until it is stiff and fluffy. Slowly mix in sawdust. Sculpt. Let figures dry for several days.

SODA AND CORNSTARCH CLAY

1 cup cornstarch
2 cups baking soda
1¼ cups water
food coloring

Combine cornstarch, baking soda, and water in pan. Cook over medium heat. Stir constantly. Stop when mixture thickens like dough. Knead and add food coloring when cool.

COLORED SALT OR SAND

salt or sand
powdered tempera paint or food coloring

Mix powdered tempera or food coloring with salt or sand. If using food coloring, spread mixture in large pan to dry. Pour into shakers. Shake over lines or designs made with white glue.

FINGER PAINTS

Cornstarch Finger Paint

½ cup cornstarch
4 cups boiling water
cold water
food coloring or tempera powder

Dissolve cornstarch in small amount of cold water. Gradually add boiling water. Stir constantly. Cook until mixture is clear. Continue stirring. Glycerine can be added to remove stickiness and provide a smooth texture. Add food coloring or tempera powder. Scents can also be added. Cool.

Detergent Finger Paint

liquid dishwashing detergent
water
food coloring or tempera

Add water slowly to detergent until you get a pasty mixture. Add coloring. Easy to clean up.

Flour and Water (Paste) Finger Paint

½ cup flour
½ cup cold water
1½ cups boiling water
2 teaspoons alum
food coloring or tempera powder
extract, e.g., peppermint, lemon, or perfume
   (optional)

Mix flour and cold water. Stir in boiling water and bring mixture to a boil. Stir constantly. Remove from heat. Add alum and coloring. Add extract if children are able to enjoy the smell without tasting. Finger paintings done with this recipe tend to dry flat.

Liquid Starch Finger Paint

1 cup liquid starch
1 teaspoon tempera powder

Slowly add tempera to liquid starch until you reach the color desired.

Paste Finger Paint

flour
water
food coloring

Mixing flour and water provides a very economical paste. Add food coloring to it and use it as finger paint. Add water to flour until you get a paste consistency, easy to spread around but not too thin or runny. Paint on table top or cookie tray for easy clean-up.

Starch Finger Paint

2 cups instant laundry starch
1 quart water
3 cups Ivory flakes
¾ cup talcum powder
1 teaspoon oil of cloves
food coloring

Dissolve starch in water and mix. Slowly add soap flakes. Add talcum and then oil of cloves. Continue mixing until thick and forms peaks. Add food coloring to water before mixing.

Wheat Paste or Wallpaper Paste Finger Paint

wheat paste or wallpaper paste
lukewarm or cold water
food coloring or tempera powder
wintergreen (available at drugstore)

Slowly add water to paste to get a creamy texture. Stir until smooth. Add coloring. A drop or two of wintergreen will disguise the odor if children find it unpleasant. Check to make sure paste ingredients are nontoxic.

MUD DOUGH

2 cups mud
2 cups sand
½ cup salt
water

Slowly add water until pliable. Children enjoy
the texture.

NATURAL DYES

Natural dyes can be used to color fabric. Examples include:

yellow: from saffron, crocuses, daffodils, yellow
onionskins
green: from grass, broccoli, spinach
blue: from blueberries
red: from beets
brown: from coffee, tea, walnut shells

Place in enamel pot and cover with water. Boil
for 5 minutes, or longer if darker shade is desired. Strain through colander. Let cool.

PAPIER-MÂCHÉ

Paste (cooked)
Paste (cooked)
3 cups water
1½ cups flour
oil of peppermint

Stir flour into cold water. Cook over low heat
until mixture thickens and resembles creamy
paste. Add more water if too thick. Cool. Add a
few drops of peppermint oil. Use this paste to
coat strips of paper.

Paste (uncooked)

8 cups wallpaper paste mix
10 cups water

Slowly add water to wallpaper mix. Mix thoroughly.

Watered-Down Glue

white liquid glue
water

Slowly add water to glue. Stir thoroughly. Add
more water if too thick. Use this to coat strips of
paper.

PASTE

Paste (for paper, cooked)

1 cup sugar
1 cup flour
1 teaspoon alum
4 cups water
oil of cloves

Mix the sugar, flour, and alum. Add water. Cook
until thick. Stir constantly. Let cool. Add several
drops of oil of cloves. Store in covered jar.

Paste (cooked)

1 cup flour
1 teaspoon salt
2 cups water

Slowly add water to salt and flour mixture. Simmer about 5 minutes. Stir constantly.

PASTE I (uncooked)

½ cup flour
½ cup water

Slowly add water to flour. Mix thoroughly. Add
more water if too lumpy, more flour if too runny.

PASTE II (uncooked)

cornstarch
water

Slowly add water to about 1 cup of cornstarch.
Mix thoroughly. Add more water if too lumpy,
more cornstarch if too runny.

WHEAT PASTE

Wheat paste is available from hardware stores.
Add wheat paste to water. Mix thoroughly until
smooth.

PASTE FOR BATIK

1 cup flour
1 cup cold water
4 teaspoons alum

Mix thoroughly until all lumps are gone. Place in squirt bottles or squeeze containers.

PASTE RESIST

3 tablespoons flour
1 cup cold water

Mix thoroughly. Heat until mixture is transparent. Let cool. Place in squirt bottles or squeeze containers.

PEANUT BUTTER CLAY (edible)

4 tablespoons peanut butter
1 tablespoon honey
1 tablespoon wheat germ
2½ tablespoons powdered milk

Mix. Sculpt. Eat!

PEANUT BUTTER PLAY DOUGH (edible)

1 cup peanut butter
1 cup honey
1 cup powdered milk
1 cup oatmeal
food coloring (optional)

Mix thoroughly. Adding food coloring is optional. Sculpt as if it were clay. Eat!

PLASTER (for molds)

8 cups patch plaster
5 cups water

Mix thoroughly. Recipe will make enough for four molds. This recipe can be used in place of plaster of paris, which dries very fast. Patch plaster is inexpensive and takes at least 30 minutes to dry.

PRETZEL CLAY I (edible)

1 package dry yeast, dissolved in cold water
3 cups flour
1 teaspoon sugar
1 teaspoon salt
water

Mix yeast mixture and flour. Slowly add about 1 more cup of flour until the mixture can be kneaded. Let children take turns kneading it on a floured counter top. Sculpt as clay. Sprinkle with kosher salt. Bake at 350° for about 20 minutes. Makes approximately 20 small pretzels.

PRETZEL CLAY II (edible)

1 cup warm water
1 package yeast
1 tablespoon salt
2½ cups whole wheat pastry flour

Mix water and yeast. Let sit for a few minutes. Add salt and flour. Mix and knead. Roll into shapes. Place on lightly greased cookie sheet. Bake in preheated oven at 425° for 12 minutes or until brown. Beat an egg and brush on your creations if you want a glazed look.

SALT PAINT

½ cup liquid starch
2 cups salt
1 cup water
tempera powder or food coloring

Thoroughly mix liquid starch, salt, and water. Slowly add food coloring or tempera powder. Use as paint. Pictures will sparkle when the salt paint dries.

SHRIVEL ART

clear plastic lid, as from a margarine tub
permanent Magic Markers

Cut out shapes from clear plastic lid. Decorate with markers. Place on cookie sheet and put in oven at 350° for a few minutes. Check. The heat will make the shapes curl up and shrink into interesting designs.

SILK-SCREEN PAINT

paint: liquid or powder
soap flakes (not detergent)
warm water

An inexpensive silk-screen paint can be made by mixing the above three ingredients. Start with a cup of warm water and slowly add soap flakes. Beat until mixture is stiff. Add paint.

SILLY PUTTY

white liquid glue
liquid starch
food coloring

Mix equal parts of white liquid glue and liquid starch. Stir immediately. Add a few drops of food coloring. Knead until silly putty is soft and smooth. Store in container with lid.

SOAP CRAYONS

mild powdered laundry soap
food coloring
water

Add 1 cup of laundry soap to bowl. Add many drops of food coloring. Slowly add water by the teaspoon until the soap is liquid. Stir well. Pour into ice cube trays. Set in sunny, dry spot for a few days. Allow crayons to harden. Great for writing on sinks or bathtubs.

SOAPSUDS PAINT

soap flakes
warm water
food coloring (optional)

Pour soap flakes into a bowl. Slowly add water. 1 cup soap flakes to ½ cup water is a good ratio. Beat with rotary eggbeater until frothy but not stiff. Use as paint on black construction paper. Good for making winter snow scenes. It has a thick, heavy texture that adds a three-dimensional effect. Or, add food coloring and use on white or with other colors of paper.

SPECIAL PAINT

1 part glycerin (available at drugstore)
1 part water
1 part white glue
tempera paint (powder or liquid)

Mix to the consistency of cake icing. Add tempera slowly. Stir well. Cover with lid and let set for a few days. Use with foam-head paintbrush. See section on special painting using special painters.

WAX (for batik)

1 part beeswax
1 part paraffin

Place in double boiler. Or, place broken chunks in tin cans sitting in a skillet filled with water. Bring water to a boil, which will melt the wax. Do not melt wax directly over heat.

Appendix H

Art Basics

The following would comprise the basics required to set up and stock an early childhood art center.

ADHESIVES: GLUE, PASTE, TAPE, AND ACCESSORIES

cloth tape—for color coding

colored tape—for taping and sticking

E-Z up clips—held with wax to the wall; claims to stick to any surface; holds artwork; reusable

glue sticks—no drips or mess

masking tape—for taping and sticking

paste—individual containers with applicators for bonding paper

paste brush—rather than using fingers

paste cups—with lids; small margarine tubs are ideal

paste refill—pint, quart, or gallon

plasti-tak—reusable, no-mar adhesive for displaying art on walls

Popsicle sticks—make good paste spreaders

roll-on glue—same as glue stick, no drips or mess

rubber cement—individual bottles with applicators. Limited to gluing papers together; won't work with wood. Rubber cement doesn't make the papers wrinkle. Be careful of strong fumes with the very young.

Scotch or clear tape—for taping and sticking

wall clips—same as E-Z up clips; for displaying artwork on wall

white liquid glue—good all-purpose adhesive; buy individual small bottles and large refill. Good for paper, wood, Styrofoam, nature specimens, and most junk.

HINT Some young children enjoy eating paste, given its smell and touch. Provide a damp sponge or paper towel and encourage periodic wiping of fingers before the big gob of paste gets too tempting.

HINT Since paste dries out very fast, it is important to replace the lids. Children will forget. Try gluing a small piece of wet sponge to the inside lid to keep the paste moist. Use baby food jars with lids, margarine tubs, or other small, covered containers.

HINT Small bottles of white glue are easy to hold and use. Also, some children feel obligated to use up a whole bottle. A smaller bottle may discourage this need to empty the container.

HINT Some teachers prefer to pour small amounts of white glue into a small plastic bowl or lid. This bypasses the use of individual bottles, which dry out very quickly because children often forget to twist the tops shut.

HINT Some children enjoy spreading the liquid glue with their fingers. Small sponges can also be used to dab the glue and apply it. A special glue stick is easy to make. Wrap a piece of netting twice around a Popsicle stick and secure it with a rubber band at one end. The weave in the netting holds the glue until the child is ready to apply it.

HINT Mix water, white glue, and food coloring for the very young paster. Toddlers would also enjoy placing pieces of precut or pretorn papers onto a piece of construction paper with glue. Glue can be mixed with water to both extend it and eliminate its crusty appearance when dry. Mix water and white glue in equal parts, for example, ½ cup white glue to ½ cup water.

BRUSHES

bath brush—for easel painting
bowl brush—new, not used, for easel painting
detergent dispensers—fill with paint and use as brush
dish pom-pom—for a novel paintbrush
easel—long-handled for painting while standing at the easel
feather duster—for interesting effects while easel painting
foam-head brush—for innovative painting

household brushes—an array of inexpensive household and paintbrushes found at discount stores is also recommended
make-up brushes—provide nice variety for the older artist
paste brush—for spreading paste
pastry brush—for painting while seated
scrub brush—for large, vigorous, sweeping strokes
shaving brush—stubby handle is easy to grip
short-handled brush—for painting while seated or close up at easel
silverware sorter or tray—to sort and store brushes
spoon rest—for holding wet brush while painting
stencil brush—short-handled with stiff bristles for dabbing and small strokes when making a stencil
toothbrush—for general painting, stencil, and spatter printing
varnish brush—wide, inexpensive, found at discount stores
vegetable brush—for general painting
watercolor brush—short and thin, with pointed bristles

HINT Brushes come in a variety of sizes, shapes, qualities, and expense. It is best to get a variety. Some have round, pointed, oval bristles and are called rounds. Flat brushes with wide bristles are called flats. Long-handled brushes are good for easel painting, where a child stands a short distance from the paper. Short-handled brushes are often used for painting while seated at a table, where the distance between artist and paper is minimal. Buying flats, rounds, and both short- and long-handled brushes will encourage a variety of paint strokes. Brush tips are made of red sable, camel hair, bristle, natural, or synthetic materials. A moderately expensive brush with stiff bristles is a good investment. The bristles will hold up to thick paint and not fall out with the first washing. Never use a brush to mix paint. Instead, use a stick or spoon.

HINT Brushes need to be washed soon after each use, preferably before the paint has become dried and crusty. Rinse out excess paint. Add a small drop of liquid detergent and gently wash the bristles. Rinse thoroughly with warm but never hot water. Hot water will melt the glue that holds the bristles in place. Squeeze out excess water. Reshape bristles to their natural shape (e.g., twirl a watercolor brush into a pointed shape). Let air dry. Always store brushes with their handles down and bristles up. Tall, thin potato chip cans are ideal.

HINT Brushes can be homemade. Clamp a small sponge with a pinch-type clothespin and use as a brush. A wad of cloth tied to a pencil makes a good paintbrush. Q-tips can be tied with string or yarn and used for dabbing paint.

HINT Bristles on brushes will split and spread over time. Carefully use a razor blade to trim jagged edges or stray bristles.

HINT Insert a small paintbrush into a hair roller or ball of clay. This will provide a larger, graspable surface for the child with limited fine motor coordination and control.

CHALK

white—for marking on chalkboard and on black and colored construction paper
colored—for marking on chalkboard and on black, white, and colored construction paper
chalkboard—good for marking with long, sweeping strokes
pastels—leave a soft, smooth, velvety line; not recommended for beginners. Use to draw on cloth or paper but not chalkboard. Pastels provide the best of chalk and crayons. They are powdery but do not rub off like chalk. They are not as hard as crayons but are just as colorful and brilliant.

HINT Chalk can be used wet or dry. Chalk is messy, and older children will enjoy blending colors made with chalk. Chalk needs a fixative. Brushing liquid starch or buttermilk on the paper first will help the chalk adhere. Chalk can also be dipped into either of these fixatives and then applied. Children tend to dislike the smell of buttermilk. Spraying with hair spray will help the chalk adhere. Use outdoors and sparingly.

HINT Chalkboard paint is available at hardware stores. You can paint on your own chalkboard surface.

HINT Like crayons, chalk will quickly break, especially if loosely thrown into a box. A piece of foam rubber can make a chalk holder. Use a scissors point to carefully bore small holes or openings into the foam rubber. Insert one piece of chalk per hole. Make sure that the chalk fits tightly in an upright position.

CLAY AND ACCESSORIES

alphabet clay cutters—commercial set makes miniature ABCs
apple divider—for slicing clay
cake decorator—for making decorations out of clay
cheese slicer—for slicing clay
clay board—with no-stick surface
clay cutters—plastic knives and spoons
clay hammers—for pounding and flattening clay
cookie cutters—for making shapes out of clay
dough press—for making decorations out of clay

dowel rods—for rolling, poking, and designing clay

egg slicer—for slicing clay balls

Formica—for clay boards

funnels—for making circular impressions in clay

linoleum—for clay boards

meat baller—for scooping and making clay balls

meat tenderizer mallet—for flattening and making impressions in clay

melon baller—for scooping and making clay balls

modeling clay

natural or real clay

pastry blender—for kneading and working clay

pastry tube—for making decorations out of clay

pie crimper—for incising clay

pizza cutter—for cutting through clay

plasticene

Play-Doh

play dough

potato masher—for mashing clay

rolling pins—for rolling clay

scoop—for scooping and making clay balls

self-hardening clay

storage container—with tight lid to keep clay from drying out

HINT Remember that clay tools are mere accessories and are not intended to replace manipulative processing with the fingers and hands. Do not begin with the tools, but slowly add them as a variation to working clay with the hands.

HINT Floor tiles, Formica, and linoleum make good individual clay boards. Some have interesting colors, lines, and designs. Cut into one-foot squares if they come in a large sheet or roll.

HINT Add a few drops of perfume, bath oil, or peppermint oil to homemade play dough to keep it sweet-smelling and prevent spoiling.

HINT Add a few tablespoons of vegetable oil to play dough to make it easier to sculpt.

HINT Add a tablespoon of powdered alum when making homemade dough to keep it from getting moldy.

CLEAN-UP SUPPLIES

bar soap

brooms: child-sized and whisk

dustpan with rubber edge and small broom

liquid dishwashing soap

mop

paper towels

plastic pail, bucket, dishpan; utility organizer with compartments and handle for clean-up supplies

rags

scrub brush

shower curtain—to protect floor or carpeting

smocks

sponges

table covering, e.g., newspaper, oilcloth, vinyl, plastic

throw rug—old, washable, to put under easel

wastebasket

CRAYONS AND ACCESSORIES

Chunk-o-Crayon—a small, square stick of heavily pigmented color; comes in primary colors, black, and a rainbow of colored specks; good for wide strokes and rubbings

Cray Away—washable crayons, water-soluble. Or, dip in water for watercolor effects.

crayon melter—commercially available

crayon sharpener—save the colored shavings!

Easy-Grip or Chubbi Stump—look like small ice cream cones and fit tiny hands

Easy-Off—can be removed from washable surfaces, e.g., walls; good for use at home

fabric—for marking directly on cloth, or use on paper and then transfer to fabric with a hot iron

fluorescent—bright, vibrant colors

food warming tray—for special melted crayon activities

grater—for shaving crayons

hexagonal—six-sided crayons; they will not roll and are a good size for little hands

jumbo or extra large—may be too big and heavy for youngest

nonroll—for children working on slanted surfaces or who find the major use of crayons is for rolling

So Big—first crayons for older infants and toddlers

standard size—thin and prone to break with pressure

thick or large—sturdier than standard

triangular—long, three-sided, good for wide, sweeping strokes

HINT Young children do not need large boxes of crayons with every color under the sun. Colors, shades, and tints can be made by using the basic set. Children or parents assume that more and bigger is necessarily better. This is not the case with crayons.

HINT Some children enjoy keeping their own basic set of eight crayons in a cigar-box-type container in their cubby. However, some teachers feel that it is important to provide a mass of crayons and encourage children to share. Add exotic and metallic colors like silver, gold, copper, and bronze.

HINT Never throw away a broken crayon. They can be melted down and made into new ones. Place several small, peeled, broken crayon pieces into a nonstick muffin tin resting in a skillet of boiling water. Or, line metal muffin tin openings with tin foil to eliminate sticking. The skillet rests on a hot plate. Colors can be kept separate or creatively combined in the muffin tins. Remember the principles of color mixing.

Mixing purple and brown will yield a dark color. Let cool. Carefully remove and use as a fat crayon. Remember, never melt crayons directly over heat; they are highly flammable. Or, place the muffin tin in the oven at 250° until the crayons have melted. Turn off the oven when crayons are completely melted. Remove the muffin tin when the oven is cold. Remove crayon cookies by pushing on the bottom of the muffin tin. Remind children that these tempting cookie-type creations are made of wax and not to be eaten. Or, layers of different melted colors can be poured into a film container or pill bottle. Carefully pour from a muffin tin or use an old pot, making sure to wipe it clean between color meltings. Let harden between layers of color. Put it in the refrigerator to hasten hardening. Gently tap the bottom to remove, or quickly dip in hot water to loosen. The result will be a lipstick-shaped crayon that produces stripes and rainbow colors when used on its side. Or, broken crayons can be slowly melted together in a plastic egg carton placed on a cookie sheet in the hot sun. Or, pour melted crayon wax into a sturdy paper cone. Wrap several layers of sturdy paper into an ice cream cone shape. Tape securely. Pour in layers of colored wax. Carefully unwrap the paper when the colored cone is hard. Small colored cones will fit nicely into small hands. Remind children that these are special crayons and not food.

HINT Children will inevitably break crayons to hear the pleasurable popping noise and peel the paper off. It is a way for them to exhibit their power over objects. They can break a crayon in two with their own bare hands! Thicker crayons are harder to break, but are also more difficult to manage. Removing the paper allows children to use the sides in wide, sweeping strokes. There are many parts of a crayon other than the pointed tip that can be used. Children may also quickly discard the box, since fitting the crayons back in once they have been removed is difficult and frustrating.

HINT There is no one best way to store crayons. Montessori might advocate grouping a mass of crayons by color and sorting each in its own container—for example, all the reds together. She would most likely provide only the primary colors and encourage children to mix these basic three to get all others.

EASEL AND ART SURFACES

art storage and easel—a long, double-sided easel with room for four children and shelves for storage. Commercially available, but fairly expensive.

chalkboard—for use with chalk

double- or triple-sided easel: self-standing with paint rack

easel clips—two clips to hold the upper corners; large paper clips or clothespins will do. Make sure children can work them.

messy tray—a plastic self-contained area for one finger painter. A large cookie sheet will also do.

see-through easel—acrylic plastic or Plexiglas, transparent, see-through, wipe-off surface

wall easel—a board attached to the wall that swings out when in use and stores flat against the wall the rest of the time. A real space saver and a good project for a volunteer parent/ grandparent/carpenter.

HINT Easels are expensive but a good investment. Standing easels allow for whole arm sweeping strokes. Make sure the easel is at the child's height. Paper should be placed in front of the child's chest and within easy reach, neither too high nor too low. Saw off the legs of the easel if necessary. Actually, a minimum of two easels should be provided for a large group of children. Having too few easels makes children anxious and concerned that they will never get a turn.

It is also possible to construct a homemade tabletop easel out of a sturdy cardboard carton. Actually, two pyramid-shape tabletop easels can be made by cutting the carton diagonally. Cut two slits at the top for inserting clothespins or clips to hold the paper. Two identical hardwood panels can be hinged together to make a more durable tabletop easel. Add a small chain between the panels to keep the easel stationary when it is open.

HINT There is another way to make a homemade tabletop easel. Find a large wallpaper sample book. Remove the pages and save the cover. One book makes a double-sided easel. Find a shallow carton lid that the book can rest on. Select your angle and cut notches on the book covers. Insert the carton into the notches. Use clothespins or clips at the top to hold paper.

HINT Remember to use easel clips or clothespins that the children can work by themselves. Some teachers prefer to place several pieces of paper at each easel in the morning. This eliminates the continual taking down of the completed painting and hanging up of the clean sheet. Also, remember to place some form of covering under the easel. Newspaper is easy to come by and disposable. An old washable throw rug, however, will not only protect the floor but also be more attractive and comfortable to stand on.

FABRIC

burlap
cloth
material scraps
muslin

sheets—old, white
trims

FASTENERS

clothespins—pinch-type
metal fasteners
paper clips
paper fasteners
pipe cleaners
rubber bands
stapler—small with staples, but not miniature
string
twist ties
wire
yarn

FRAMES

construction paper—for mats and frames
old picture frames
precut mat frames in a variety of sizes and
  shapes are commercially available, or you can
  make them

INGREDIENTS

alum
buttermilk
cooking oil
cornstarch
dishwashing detergent—liquid
flour
food coloring
glass wax—for hand painting
laundry starch
plaster
salt
sand
shaving cream
water

MARKERS

Crayola decorating markers—fancy points for
  fancy strokes

fine-point or thin-line—for details
permanent—for fabric
stencil—no-run, nonstain tempera markers
tempera markers—tempera paint in a no-drip,
  nonspill thick marker
watercolor—pretty colors
wide-point, thick-line, or jumbo—for broad,
  heavy strokes

HINT Encourage children to replace the caps on
markers as soon as they are through using
them. Markers dry up quickly. Dip the
tips of dried-up markers in water to get
them flowing.

HINT Buy only markers that have water-based,
washable, nonpermanent, nontoxic ink.
Children like to smell markers, and some
will put them in their mouth. Since children have been known to adorn their skin
with markers, a water-based ink will wash
off easily and not leave a stain. Parents
will appreciate it.

HINT Avoid markers with fruit or exotic scents.
Markers are for marking, not for smelling
or sucking. The scents may be toxic or
cause an allergic or hyperactive reaction
in some children who put them in their
mouth or suck on them.

HINT Permanent markers can be used to mark
on fabric. The color does not need to be
set with an iron. The color will not wash
out of children's clothing.

HINT Roll-on deodorant bottles can be filled
with tempera paint and used as large
markers. Pry off the ball roller and clean
the ball and bottle thoroughly. Fill the
bottle with tempera paint and snap the
roller ball back on.

HINT Colored markers show up best on a variety of white or light papers. They do not
show up on dark-colored construction
paper.

PAINTS AND PAINTING ACCESSORIES

brushes—see appropriate section

condiment bottles—squeeze ketchup and mustard bottles with pointed tips make good paint dispensers

dispensers—ketchup or mustard bottles for squeezing paint

drying rack or line—to let pictures dry undisturbed

extender—a bulking powder that extends your paint without losing its brilliance

finger paint—good for hand painting, given its thick, chunky texture

fluorescent, water, or tempera colors—for the advanced child artist

food coloring—added to water makes a fast paint

funnels—to avoid waste when pouring powder paint and for printing

glass—pane of glass or sheet of Plexiglas for monoprinting

ice cube trays—for color mixing

ink—one bottle of black is standard

kitchen gadgets—for printing with paint

kitchen shakers—for sprinkling powder tempera

liquid laundry starch—add to tempera to make finger paint

magic brush set—paint, water, and brush are combined into one magic brush tube. A cross between a marker and a paint brush. The set is commercially available.

media mix—add to tempera to make finger paint; it claims to intensify colors

messless sign caddy paint system—a complete rainbow assortment of nontoxic water-soluble paints in squeeze bottles, used with special felt brushes. Spillproof containers available. Pretty colors and expensive.

muffin tin—for paint palette

no-spill paint cups—hold paint and resist tipping

paint pots—with lids; fit snugly in a tray

paint stirrers—Popsicle sticks, tongue depressors, or coffee stirrers will do

paint tumblers—with snap-on lids to keep paint from drying out

plastic dryer—a hanging dryer with pinch clips for holding wet pictures. Available in housewares at discount stores.

plastic spoons—for mixing paint

poster paint—brighter and more expensive than tempera. Good for making signs, posters, or banners on poster board.

pumps—fit gallon paint containers; one pump yields one ounce

Q-tips—for dabbing paint

spatula—to mix paints in bulk

splatter screen—for spatter printing

sponges—for printing

spoon rest—to hold brush with paint

squeeze bottles—good for dispensing tempera paint. Some companies offer liquid tempera in squeeze bottles.

sweater dryer—wire screen or net for spatter printing

syrup dispensers—good for storing mixed paint and for use with art palette method of painting

tempera cakes or color paint cakes—concentrated tempera; use like watercolor, comes in tray, refills available, no spilling or mixing involved, more expensive

tempera liquid—more expensive than powder but saves on measuring and mixing. Colors more brilliant than powder.

tempera powder—more economical but requires mixing

watercolor—individual sets of eight are recommended

HINT Remember to buy and use only lead-free, nontoxic paint.

HINT Buy red, blue, yellow, black, and white in bulk. These can be mixed to produce other colors, shades, and tints.

HINT Add liquid dishwashing detergent to tempera paint. It will make it bubbly and easier to wash off hands and out of clothes. It will also help paint adhere to slick or glossy surfaces, such as glass, plastic, metal, tin foil, and waxed cartons.

HINT Add a drop or two of oil of cloves or oil of wintergreen to prevent spoilage if you mix paint days in advance.

HINT Add evaporated milk to give paint a creamier consistency and glossy look.

HINT Add coffee grounds, salt, or sand along with white glue to paint to give it a rough, coarse, gritty texture. Adding sugar will give it a sparkling appearance when dry. Adding sawdust will give it a thick, lumpy texture. Adding white glue to paint thickens it.

HINT Finger paint can be made by
- adding liquid laundry starch to tempera or food coloring.
- using mud—messy, but children love it.
- mixing wheat paste (wallpaper paste), water, and tempera paint until smooth.
- mixing liquid starch, soap flakes, and tempera paint.
- adding small pieces of finely ground colored chalk to paste. Add a few drops of water if too stiff.
- using glass wax.

HINT To mix powder paints
Pour powder through a funnel into your paint container. Mix with enough water to form a thick, creamy liquid. Aim for the consistency of yogurt. Test on paper. It should not run. Add more water if too thick, more powder if too thin and runny. 2 parts tempera powder to 1 part water is a recommended ratio. Add a few squirts of liquid dishwashing detergent to aid clean-up. Shake or mix well until smooth and creamy.
Or, use tempera powder directly from the can without mixing it with water. Dip a wet brush or cotton ball directly into tempera powder and paint. You can also wet your paper, sprinkle tempera powder directly on the paper, and use a brush to paint.

HINT To mix liquid paints
Place a spoonful in a container. Slowly add water. Test on paper. Add more water if still too thick, more liquid paint if too thin and runny.

HINT To simulate oil painting
Place different colors of tempera powder in separate containers. Do not add water. Place liquid starch in a separate container. Encourage children to dip their brush in starch and then in the tempera powder. The result is a thick brush stroke and a different effect.

HINT Individual jars or bottles of paint can be stored in a plastic tub to keep them from tipping over. You can also make a paint holder out of a Styrofoam egg carton. Use only the top section and discard the individual egg holders. Trace three circles using the jars, milk cartons, or juice cans that will later hold the paint. Carefully cut out the three holes. Insert the containers and fill each with paint and one brush. A shoe box could also be used because it is deep and sturdy.

HINT Glass baby food jars are slowly becoming obsolete. Since they are glass, they are potentially dangerous, but they have the advantage of letting the child quickly see the color of the paint inside. Tall plastic cups or see-through containers are recommended. Juice cans or small milk cartons are an ideal size but do not allow the child to see the color within. Painting the outside of the container the same color as the paint it will hold will solve the problem.

PAPERS

adding machine tape—for paper sculpture and paper chains

blotter—for soaking up excess water with watercolors

boxes—for painting and marking on

brown wrapping paper—for murals, puppets, papier-mâché, paper sculpture, and paper art activities requiring sturdy paper

butcher paper—a long roll for making murals; good for finger painting

carbon paper—for transferring designs

cardboard—flat, corrugated, tubes for a variety of art activities

catalogues—for paper tearing, cutting, pasting, and collage

cellophane—for color paddles, collage, and paper art activities

coffee filters—for use with mark making, melted crayons, or dip and dye with food coloring

computer paper scraps—use the clean side for paper art activities

construction—good for crayons, chalk, and paint but not watercolor; difficult to fold in different directions; will fade over time; buy large sheets in assorted colors and cut down

contact paper—solicit scraps for paper art activities

crepe paper—optional; buy other basic art papers first

doilies—for collage and other paper activities

egg cartons: cardboard and Styrofoam

envelopes—good for mark making and artistically addressing

fadeless art paper—easier to fold and cut than construction paper but more expensive; only one side is colored and will not fade

finger paint—glazed surface; buy the largest size!

gift wrap or wrapping paper—for collage and other paper activities

graph—large squares; you can easily make your own

greeting cards—recycled, for cutting, pasting, mobiles, and collage

grocery bags—all sizes and colors, heavy weight for painting and paper work activities

gummed stars, stickers, and labels—for licking and sticking on paper

kraft paper—three feet wide to make murals, trace over children, and use for bulletin boards

magazines—for collage and montage

manila—a better grade than newsprint: rough surface, cream color, heavier weight; more expensive than newsprint but less expensive than white drawing paper. Manila paper is good for collage, gluing, coloring, painting, and pasting activities. Buy big and cut down.

manila file folders—old, used, sturdy

matboard—for making mats in picture frames; expensive

metallic paper—too expensive to put out on a daily basis

newspaper—for painting, stuffing, and clean-up

newsprint—your least expensive paper for marking, scribbling, drawing, and coloring. Thick or heavy paint will bleed and soak through. Easy to fold, but tears with pressure. Comes in a variety of sizes. Buy big and cut down.

oak tag board—comparable to manila paper in use and cost

oatmeal paper—textured paper for crayons, chalk, and prints

onionskin paper—nice texture for watercolor

origami—special paper for Japanese art form of paper folding

paper bags—in all sizes, for puppets, masks, and so forth

paper plates—plain white for masks and a round art surface

paper reinforcements—for stringing and making eyes, O's, and buttons

paper scrap saver—empty box or container

paper towels—for painting, dyeing, papier-mâché, and clean-up

picture story—to draw a picture and dictate a story

place mats—a good background for paper and other art activities

poster board—cheaper than mat board for making mats and frames

rice paper—fairly expensive; good surface for ink and watercolor

sandpaper—for resist, collage, and melted crayon wax

shelf paper—for making murals; good for hand painting if surface is glazed

shopping bags—cut open and lay flat for painting

tin foil—for sculpture and special paper activities

tissue—comes in a variety of colors. Buy big and cut down.

typing paper—good for ink and watercolor

velour paper—nice velvety texture but expensive; use sparingly

wallpaper scraps, samples, and books—for matting, framing, collage. Also, most wallpaper will hold up to painting.

watercolor paper—expensive if bought by the sheet; also comes in tablet form

wax paper—for sealing paper shapes, resist

white drawing—a very good grade, heavy and fairly expensive. Good for all art projects, including painting. It looks clean and stands up to erasing. 60-pound weight is recommended. Buy big and cut down.

wrappers—from gum and candy, for pasting and collage

HINT The larger the paper size, the more expensive it will be. Still, large sheets can be used sparingly in their entirety and creatively cut down into smaller sizes and shapes. This will avoid boredom and needless waste and be more economical in the long run.

HINT Try butchers, carpet stores, print shops, and newspaper plants for newsprint, end rolls of paper, and brown wrap. These are good for making murals.

HINT Use different types of paper, and be sure to include newspaper, grocery bags, and cardboard. The want ads make a good backdrop for a painting or collage. The colored comics section makes a good background for linear designs in black. Different surfaces pose a new problem and challenge for the painter. A torn-paper collage would work on the colored advertisement section. Grocery bags are heavy and can stand up to the repeated strokes of heavy paint from the very young painter.

HINT Provide papers that pose a challenge. For example, cut papers into flag, diamond, rhombus, or amorphic shapes. Cut circles, squares, rectangles, and triangles from the inside of papers. This will force the artist to modify or adapt his or her processing to fit the paper. For example, one cannot merely sweep paint, crayons, or markers across a figure-eight-shaped paper. The curves will suggest a different swirling or circular type of arm movement and stroke.

HINT A cookie sheet or tray makes a good separate space for one finger painter. The area is marked off and self-contained. Clean up by rinsing under a sink or with a damp sponge.

PENCILS

colored—for advanced mark makers

drawing—#2 for making marks

erasers—to be used sparingly, not in striving for perfection

grips—three-sided pencil holders, more important for printing than for artistic mark making

lead—#2 for making marks

primary—thick; may be too heavy for smallest hands

SCISSORS AND CUTTERS

blade cutter—for cutting mats

blunt—steel scissors; blunt is fine so long as they still cut

comfy or cushie grip—with rubber-coated finger holes

lefty—designed specifically for left-handed children

paper cutter—for cutting paper into a variety of shapes and sizes as well as paper strips

pinking shears—jagged edge on paper and fabric adds variety

safety—lightweight plastic for right- and left-handed cutters

scissors rack—metal or wood for safely and neatly storing scissors

sharp—steel, in right- and left-hand models, for experienced and older four-year-olds and five-year-olds

snip loop or easy grip scissors—recommended for beginning cutters or for children with limited motor control

teacher's straight shears—very sharp; for teacher's use only!

training—double-handled with four rubber-coated finger holes; teacher and child cut together

X-acto knife—for cutting mats

HINT Regardless of the type selected, scissors must cut. There is nothing more frustrating to a young cutter than a pair of scissors that snag, tear, or clog up with paper but do not cut it.

STORAGE AND CONTAINERS

art carryall—plastic divided carrier with handle. Good for storing art supplies. Available at discount stores in housewares. Recommended for artist at home.

art cart—a two- and three-tiered cart on wheels. Lets you take your art program around the room and outdoors.

baby food jars—allow child to see color of paint; breakable

bakeware

baskets—for storing ribbons, lace, trims, crayons

beverage carriers—cardboard with individual compartments to hold jars of paint

bleach bottles—for holding water or paint

bookcase—with deep shelves for storage

boxes—to organize art supplies

bureau—old, for storing art supplies

cabinet—with doors removed and shelves for storage

caddy carryall—plastic carrier with handle

cake pans

cardboard cartons

cardboard soft drink carriers—make good paint caddies

chest—old, for storing art supplies

cigar boxes—for crayons, markers, lace, ribbon, and trims

classroom materials organizer—good for cubbies or for organizing different types of paper

coffee cans—with lids to store clay

commercial ice cream containers—fasten together and stack pyramid-style with open end visible; use for storage or art cubbies

corrugated cardboard cartons—sturdy, for storage

crates—stackable, for storage

cutlery tray—plastic, with compartments for organizing art supplies that go together, such as brushes

desk organizer—with compartments for small art supplies

dishpans—to hold papers, paste, glue, jars of paint, and brushes

dresser—old, for storing art supplies

easel and art storage—expensive but ideal! A large easel allows two painters at each side. Below are shelves for ample storage. Commercially available.

egg cartons—cardboard or Styrofoam for storing small art supplies, such as buttons and beads file cabinet—metal or cardboard; can hold art supplies. The problem is that the contents are not visible.

food keepers—see-through, good for storage

frozen food tray—with dividers, for holding small items

fruit basket—plastic, for holding ribbon, lace, spools, and so forth

hardware organizer—small plastic drawers for holding nails; good for organizing very small art items like buttons and jewelry pieces

ice cream tubs—commercial, to hold paper and fabric scraps

juice cans—large, for storing paint, pencils, rulers, brushes, and other tall items

lazy susan—good for organizing small items; rotate to bring close the items you need

loaf pans

margarine tubs—for storing paint, clay, and small art supplies

mini bins—stackable; good for storing art supplies

muffin tins—for melting crayons and sorting small art supplies like buttons and beads for collage

pie tins—to hold paint when making prints

pizza pan

plastic dishpans or bins—good for holding small jars of paint

plastic: pail, tubs, containers, squeeze bottles, pump sprayers, lidded food savers, cups, housewares

shoe boxes—several the same size could be uniformly stacked and labeled with the word and picture of contents

shoe file—cardboard organizer with individual compartments, good for cubbies; available at discount stores

shelving—sturdy, wood planks stacked on cinder blocks

shoe organizers—with pockets to hang on wall; can hold rolled paper and other art supplies

storage bins—stackable in different sizes and colors

storage boxes—large plastic boxes with lids.

Select clear so that you can see at a glance what is inside.

storage crates or cubes—plastic milk-type crates to stack; great for storing; found at discount stores; some can bolt together for stability

storage pails or buckets—with lid and handle; good for clay

storage unit—with shelves

Styrofoam: produce, meat, and fruit trays

sweater boxes—plastic with lids for storage

tin boxes—for holding crayons, chalk, and markers

trays—to define individual art space, hold paper, and so forth

Tupperware

utility pan

utility cart—plastic pullout drawers in stand with wheels. Carts with solid frames are more durable and stand up to constant pushing and pulling. Available in housewares at discount stores.

HINT Shelving can be made using sturdy lumber, thick and wide, stacked on cement blocks. Boards should be sanded free of splinters or covered with fabric or contact paper. Position the blocks in a safe way so that young walkers will not bump into or trip over them.

HINT A pegboard with hooks by the art center is very useful. Smocks can be hung up on hooks. A sign system to indicate the number of people allowed at the art center at any one time can be displayed—for example, four palettes, one per hook, in the top row. Some art accessories can be hung from the hooks. For example, clear plastic or vinyl bags containing ribbon, fabric, and trims can be hung.

HINT Regardless of the storage facility, make sure all containers are clearly labeled in print as well as with a picture. For example, a cigar box filled with markers would have the word "markers" and a sketch or picture of markers on the side facing front.

HINT Display paper on flat shelves. Put paint and brushes on a plastic-lined shelf. This will stand up to water and drops of wet paint.

TOOLS/ACCESSORIES/ MISCELLANEOUS

brayer—for painting and making prints
cutting board—acrylic, undecorated for monoprints and clay
cookie sheets—as an art surface
eggbeater, rotary—for art recipes
Formica—as an art surface
hangers—for making mobiles, weaving, puppets, and so forth
hot plate—for melting crayons and wax for batik, heating water for tie-dye
kitchen tools—for mixing ingredients, painting, and printing
linoleum—as an art surface
measuring cups and spoons—for recipes
mixing bowls—for mixing ingredients in recipes
paper punch—for making marks
pencil compass—for mark making
protractor—for mark making
rolling pin—for clay, painting, and printing
rubber stamps—for printing
ruler—for making marks with a pencil
screen—for spatter screen prints
spatula—for mixing paint and ingredients, work with clay, and printing
sponges—for painting and printing
spray bottle—for adding water to paint, as during hand painting and for wet watercolor

stamp pad—for printing
trays—for art surfaces
wax—for resist and batik
wire—florist's, telephone, electronics for construction, assemblage, weaving, sculpture, mobile, and stabile

HINT Formica and linoleum make good art surfaces for painting with brushes, hand painting, sculpting with clay, or monoprinting. They define the individual artist's space, are easy to come by, and are easy to clean. Old trays or cookie sheets are also recommended.

SEWING AND WEAVING ACCESSORIES

easy weaver loom—commercially available and suited for young weavers
plastic screen—for sewing, weaving
standard-weight yarn—double-weight rug yarn is too thick
string—for a variety of art activities
thin crochet yarn—for sewing, stitchery, weaving, and appliqué
thread—colored, for sewing, stitchery, weaving, and appliqué
yarn needles—large, plastic, blunt, with big eye for threading

HINT Yarn cones can be purchased in special containers that keep the yarns from tangling or getting unwound. You could stand each yarn cone in a box slightly larger than the cone itself, e.g., an oatmeal box. Cut a small hole at the top, pull the yarn through, and use the box as a yarn dispenser.

References

Alkema, C. J. *Alkema's Scrap Magic*. New York: Sterling Publishing Company, Inc., 1976.

———. *Art for the Exceptional*. Boulder, Colo.: Pruett Publishing Company, 1971.

———. *The Complete Crayon Book*. New York: Sterling Publishing Company, Inc., 1974.

Anderson, R.; Manoogian, S. T.; and Reznick, J. S. "The Undermining and Enhancing of Intrinsic Motivation in Preschool Children." *Journal of Personality and Social Psychology* 34 (1976): 915–922.

Arnheim, R. "Child Art and Visual Thinking." In *Child Art: The Beginnings of Self-Affirmation,* edited by H. P. Lewis. Berkeley, Calif.: Diablo Press, Inc., 1973.

Bland, J. C. *Art of the Young Child*. New York: Museum of Modern Art, 1968.

Bos, B. *Don't Move the Muffin Tins: A Hands-off Guide to Art for the Young Child*. Roseville, Calif.: Turn the Page Press, 1978.

Brittain, W. L. *Creativity, Art, and the Young Child*. New York: Macmillan, 1979.

———. "Some Exploratory Studies of the Art of Preschool Children." *Studies in Art Education,* 10 (1969): 14–24.

Buton, L., and Kuroda, K. *Artsplay*. Reading, Mass.: Addison-Wesley, 1981.

Chapman, L. H. *Approaches to Art in Education*. New York: Harcourt Brace Jovanovich, Inc., 1978.

Chenfeld, M. B. *Creative Activities for Young Children*. New York: Harcourt Brace Jovanovich, Inc., 1983.

Chernoff, G. T. *Clay-Dough Play-Dough*. New York: Scholastic Book Services, 1974.

Cherry, C. *Creative Art for the Developing Child*. Belmont, Calif.: Pitman Learning, Inc., 1972.

Cook, R. E., and Armbruster, V. B. *Adapting Early Childhood Curriculum*. St. Louis: Mosby, 1983.

Debelak, M.; Herr, J.; and Jacobson, M. *Creating Innovative Classroom Materials for Teaching Young Children*. New York: Harcourt Brace Jovanovich, Inc., 1981.

DeBono, E. *Lateral Thinking: A Textbook of Creativity*. London: Ward Lock Educational, 1970.

Dennis, W. *Group Values through Children's Drawings*. New York: John Wiley and Sons, Inc., 1966.

Dewey, J. *Art as Experience*. New York: Capricorn Books, 1958.

DiLeo, J. H. *Children's Drawings as Diagnostic Aids*. New York: Brunner/Mazel, 1973.

————. *Young Children and Their Drawings*. New York: Brunner/Mazel, 1970.

Dimondstein, G. *Exploring the Arts of Children*. New York: Macmillan, 1974.

Eberle, R. F. *Scamper: Games for Imagination Development*. Buffalo, N.Y.: D.O.K. Publishers, 1971.

Eisner, E. W. *Cognition and Curriculum—A Basis for Deciding What to Teach*. New York: Longman, 1982.

————. "What We Know about Children's Art—And What We Need to Know." In *The Arts, Human Development, and Education,* edited by E. W. Eisner, pp. 5–18. Berkeley, Calif.: McCutchan, 1976.

Erikson, E. H. *Childhood and Society*. New York: Norton, 1963.

Fiarotta, P., and Fiarotta, N. *Sticks and Stones and Ice Cream Cones*. New York: Workman Publishing Company, 1974.

Fisher, E. F. *Aesthetic Awareness and the Child*. Itasca, Ill.: F. E. Peacock, 1978.

Fowler, V. *Paperworks*. Englewood Cliffs, N.J.: Prentice-Hall, 1982.

Frank, M. *I Can Make a Rainbow*. Nashville, Tenn.: Incentive Publications Inc., 1976.

Furrer, P. J. *Art Therapy Activities and Lesson Plans for Individuals and Groups*. Springfield, Ill.: Charles C Thomas, 1982.

Galin, D. "Educating Both Halves of the Brain." *Childhood Education* 53 (1976): 17–20.

Gardner, H. *Artful Scribbles: The Significance of Children's Drawings*. New York: Basic Books, 1980.

————. *The Arts and Human Development*. New York: Wiley, 1973.

————. "Children's Sensitivity to Painting Styles." *Child Development* 41 (1970): 813–821.

Getzels, J., and Jackson, P. *Creativity and Intelligence*. New York: John Wiley and Sons, 1962.

Golomb, C. *Young Children's Sculpture and Drawing—A Study in Representative Development*. Cambridge, Mass.: Harvard University Press, 1974.

Goodenough F. L. *Measurement of Intelligence by Drawings*. New York: Arno Press, 1975.

Goodnow, J. *Children Drawing*. Cambridge, Mass.: Harvard University Press, 1977.

Guilford, J. P. *Way Beyond the IQ*. Buffalo, N.Y.: The Creative Education Foundation, Inc., 1977.

Hardiman, G. W., and Zernich, T. *Art Activities for Children*. Englewood Cliffs, N.J.: Prentice-Hall, 1981.

Harris, D. B. *Children's Drawings as Measures of Intellectual Maturity*. New York: Harcourt, Brace and World, Inc., 1963.

Haskell, L. L. *Art in the Early Childhood Years*. Columbus, Ohio: Charles E. Merrill, 1979.

Herberholz, B. *Early Childhood Art*. Dubuque, Iowa: William C. Brown, 1974.

Hoover, F. L. *Art Activities for the Very Young*. Worcester, Mass.: Davis Publishing Company, 1961.

Indenbaum, V., and Shapiro, M. *The Everything Book for Teachers of Young Children*. Livonia, Mich.: Partner Press, 1983.

Jameson, K. *Art and the Young Child*. New York: Viking Press, 1970.

Janson, H. W., and Janson, D. J. *Janson's Story of Painting*. New York: Harrison House/Harry N. Abrams, 1984.

Jones, S. *Learning for Little Kids*. Boston, Mass.: Houghton Mifflin, 1979.

Kamii, C., and DeVries, R. *Physical Knowledge in Preschool Education: Implications of Piaget's Theory*. Englewood Cliffs, N.J.: Prentice-Hall, 1978.

Kellogg, R. *Analyzing Children's Art*. Palo Alto, Calif.: Mayfield Publishing Company, 1969.

———. *Children's Drawings/Children's Minds*. New York: Avon Books, 1979.

———. "Stages of Development in Preschool Art." In *Child Art: The Beginnings of Self-Affirmation,* edited by H. P. Lewis. Berkeley, Calif.: Diablo Press, Inc., 1973.

Kellogg, R., and O'Dell, S. *The Psychology of Children's Art*. San Diego: CRM-Random House, 1967.

Kohl, M. A. *Scribble Cookies and Other Independent Creative Art Experiences for Children*. Bellingham, Wash.: Bright Ring Publishing, 1985.

Kramer, E. *Art as Therapy with Children*. New York: Schocken Books, 1974.

Lansing, K. M. *Art, Artists, and Art Education*. New York: McGraw-Hill, 1969.

Lasky, L., and Mukerji, R. *Art: Basic for Young Children*. Washington, D.C.: National Association for the Education of Young Children, 1980.

Lepper, M. R., and Greene, D. "Turning Play into Work: Effects of Adult Surveillance and Extrinsic Rewards on Children's Intrinsic Motivation. *Journal of Personality and Social Psychology* 31 (1975): 479–486.

Lewis, H. P., ed. *Child Art—The Beginnings of Self-Affirmation*. Berkeley, Calif.: Diablo Press, 1973.

Linder, T. W. *Early Childhood Special Education*. Baltimore, Md.: Paul H. Brooks, 1983.

Linderman, E. W., and Heberholz, D. S. *Developing Artistic and Perceptual Awareness*. Dubuque, Iowa: Wm. C. Brown, 1974.

Linderman, E. W., and Linderman, M. *Arts and Crafts for the Classroom*. New York: Macmillan, 1984.

Lowenfeld, V., and Brittain, W. L. *Creative and Mental Growth*. New York: Macmillan, 1987.

Lowenfeld, V. "On the Importance of Early Art Expression." In *Viktor Lowenfeld Speaks on Art and Creativity,* edited by W. L. Brittain, pp. 20–27. Washington, D.C.: National Art Education Association, 1968.

MacKinnon, D. W. "The Nature and Nurture of Creative Talent." *American Psychologist* 17 (1962): 484–495.

Marzolla, J. *Supertot—Creative Learning Activities for Children from One to Three and Sympathetic Advice for Their Parents*. New York: Harper & Row, 1977.

Mattil, E. L., and Marzan, B. *Meaning in Children's Art*. Englewood Cliffs, N.J.: Prentice-Hall, 1981.

McFee, J. K. *Preparation for Art.* Belmont, Calif.: Wadsworth, 1970.

Moll, P. B. *Children and Scissors—A Developmental Approach.* Tampa, Fl.: Hampton Mae Institute, 1985.

Montessori, M. *The Absorbent Mind.* New York: Holt, Rinehart and Winston, 1967.

Naumberg, M. *An Introduction to Art Therapy.* New York: Teachers College Press, 1973.

Parnes, S. J. *Creative Behavior Guidebook.* New York: Charles Scribner's Sons, 1967.

Piaget, J., and Inhelder, B. *The Child's Conception of Space.* London: Routledge and Kegan Paul, 1956.

Piaget, J. "Art Education and Child Psychology." In *Education and Art,* edited by E. Ziegfeld. Switzerland: UNESCO, 1953.

———. *Play, Dreams, and Imitation in Childhood.* New York: W. W. Norton, 1962.

———. *Mental Imagery in the Child.* New York: Basic Books, 1971.

———. *The Psychology of the Child.* Translated by H. Weaver. New York: Basic Books, 1969.

Pile, N. F. *Art Experiences for Young Children.* New York: Macmillan, 1973.

Rubin, J. A. *Child Art Therapy.* New York: Van Nostrand Reinhold Company, 1978.

Russell, I., and Waugaman, B. "A Study of the Effect of Workbook Copy Experiences on the Creative Concepts of Children." Cited in Lowenfeld, V. and Brittain, W. L. *Creative and Mental Growth.*

Saracho, O. N., and Spodek, B., eds. *Understanding the Multicultural Experience in Early Childhood Education.* Washington, D.C.: National Association for the Education of Young Children, 1983.

Schirrmacher, R. "Child Art." In *Toward a Theory of Psychological Development,* edited by S. Modgil and C. Modgil, pp. 733–762. Windsor, England: National Foundation for Educational Research, 1980.

———. "Talking with Young Children about Their Art." *Young Children* 41 (1986): 3–7.

Scott, L. B.; May, M. E.; and Shaw, M. S. *Puppets for All Grades.* New York: The Instructor Publications, Inc., 1972.

Shallcross, D. J. *Teaching Creative Behavior.* Englewood Cliffs, N.J.: Prentice-Hall, 1981.

Silberstein-Storfer, M., and Jones, M. *Doing Art Together.* New York: Simon and Schuster, 1982.

Smith, N. R. *Experience and Art: Teaching Children to Paint.* New York: Teachers College Press, 1983.

———. "The Visual Arts in Early Childhood Education: Development and the Creation of Meaning." In *Handbook of Research in Early Childhood Education,* edited by B. Spodek, pp. 295–317. New York: The Free Press, 1982.

Spodek, B.; Saracho, O. N.; and Lee, R. C. *Mainstreaming Young Children.* Belmont, Calif.: Wadsworth, 1984.

Striker, S. *Please Touch—How to Stimulate Your Child's Creative Development.* New York: Simon and Schuster, 1986.

Taunton, M., and Colbert, C. "Artistic and Aesthetic Development: Considerations for Early Childhood Educators." *Childhood Education* 61 (1984): 55–63.

Taunton, M. "Reflective Dialogue in the Art Classroom: Focusing on the Art Process." *Art Education* 37 (1984): 15–16.

Topal, C. W. *Children, Clay and Sculpture*. Worcester, Mass.: Davis Publications, 1983.

Torrance, E. P., and Myers, R. E. *Creative Learning and Teaching*. New York: Harper and Row, 1970.

Torrance, E. P. *Creativity*. Washington, D.C.: National Education Association, 1963.

———. *Guiding Creative Talent*. Englewood Cliffs, N.J.: Prentice-Hall, 1962.

———. *Minnesota Tests of Creative Thinking*. Minneapolis, Minn.: University of Minnesota Bureau of Educational Research, 1963.

———. *Rewarding Creative Behavior: Experiments in Classroom Creativity*. Englewood Cliffs, N.J.: Prentice-Hall, 1965.

———. *The Search for Satori and Creativity*. Buffalo, N.Y.: The Creative Education Foundation, Inc., 1979.

———. *Torrance Tests of Creative Thinking: Technical-Norms Manual*. Lexington, Mass.: Personnel Press, 1966.

Uhlin, D. *Art for Exceptional Children*. Dubuque, Iowa: Wm. C. Brown, 1979.

Wachowiak, F. *Emphasis Art*. New York: Harper and Row, 1985.

Wallach, M. A., and Kogan, N. *Modes of Thinking in Young Children*. New York: Holt, Rinehart and Winston, 1965.

Wankelmen, W. F.; Wigg, P. R.; and Wigg, M. K. *A Handbook of Arts and Crafts*. Dubuque, Iowa: Wm. C. Brown, 1974.

Weikart, D. L.; Rogers, C.; Adcock, C.; and McClelland, D. *The Cognitively Oriented Curriculum: A Framework for Preschool Teachers*. Washington, D.C.: National Association for the Education of Young Children, 1971.

Wolf, A. D. *Mommy, It's a Renoir! Art Postcards for Art Appreciation*. Altoona, Pa.: Parent Child Press, 1984.

Index

DATE DUE